Patterns of Action

Patterns of Action

Religion and Ethics in a Comparative Perspective

DAVID CHIDESTER

WADSWORTH PUBLISHING COMPANY
Belmont, California
A Division of Wadsworth, Inc.

Religion Editor:	Sheryl Fullerton
Production Editor:	Leland Moss
Managing Designer:	Andrew H. Ogus
Designer:	John Osborne
Print Buyer:	Barbara Britton
Copy Editor:	Jennifer Gordon
Editorial Assistant:	Cindy Haus
Compositor:	G&S Typesetters
Cover:	John Osborne

Printed in the United States of America   49

1 2 3 4 5 6 7 8 9 10—91 90 89 88 87

ISBN 0-534-07416-2

Library of Congress Cataloging-in-Publication Data
Chidester, David.
    Patterns of action.

    Bibliography: p.
    Includes index.
    1. Religious ethics.   I. Title.
BJ1188.C47   1987   291.5   86-18893
ISBN 0-534-07416-2

CONTENTS

PREFACE

This book is a brief introductory tour through the world of religious ethics from the vantage point of the comparative history of religions. It is designed as a basic tour guide, an interpretive map to the territory of religious action. Indeed, I wrote this book while on a kind of world tour: Conceived in New York, the book was discussed in Dallas, tested in Santa Barbara, contemplated in China, written in Israel, revised in Africa, and finished back in California. The fact that this book has literally been around the world, however, does not account for its global perspective. I would have felt the need for a global approach to religious ethics even if I had never left home. But through these travels I was convinced of how small the human world can be—a mere speck in the vast expanse of cosmic space, a brief moment in the measureless eons of time. And yet within that small space and time human beings have generated tremendously diverse ways of being human. The study of comparative religious ethics provides one avenue of access into that diversity. This book is committed to providing a basic interpretive framework for understanding the diverse religious norms that inform ordinary human behavior in the history of religions.

Such a global perspective on religious ethics is necessary because the overriding religious fact of our age is religious pluralism. We are confronted, confounded, and confused, as perhaps never before in human history, with the irreducible variety of religious experience. Modern human beings confront the dramatic differences among religious worldviews, the conflict among different religious traditions claiming absolute authority, and the great difficulties involved in appreciating and understanding the religions of others. Throughout this tour of religious ethics I have kept in mind this fact of religious pluralism, as it defines our current religious environment.

But there is a problem inherent in the nature of the tour itself. The modern avocation of tourism has been described as a tendency to "museumize the pre-modern." We take objects, tools, and artworks out of their original living context and display them within a single collection. A statue of Apollo, a Chinese bracelet, a suit of armor, a Roman coin, a painting of Saint Barbara, a spinning wheel, an Egyptian mummy, a printing press, and so on are not only taken out of the context in which they were once used, worshiped, or enjoyed, but they are also placed together within the same cognitive architecture of the museum. A certain inevitable displacement occurs in this "museumization." If we are not seeing the object in its intended context, within the frame of reference in which it originally made sense, then perhaps we are not really seeing the object.

A similar kind of displacement occurs when we take norms, rules, and values out of their living traditions, out of the context in which they made sense for the people who lived with them, and display them in a general survey such as this book attempts to be. Something is surely lost in the process. But while this book attempts to record, catalog, and describe as accurately as possible actual ethical norms for human action, drawn from a wide range of cultural traditions, the real cultural situation it addresses is that of religious ethics in the modern world. Every discussion of ethical experience, ethical rules, and ethical values will return to this situation. Modern challenges in personal and social ethics is the primary concern of this book; hence the displacement of materials from different traditions—all appearing under the same roof, so to speak—does make a certain kind of sense in the context of the general displacement that seems to pervade the modern world when it confronts traditional patterns of life, action, and social relations.

One symptom of that displacement is the assumption that religious ethics must be subject to the demands of reason: The sacred authority invested in traditional patterns of ethical action must be evaluated by independent rational criteria of ethics. Recently, important work has been done in the field of comparative religious ethics, but I feel that much of this work has been tied too closely to the categories of philosophical ethics. Major recent contributions to the comparative study of religious ethics—such as *Religious Reason* (1978) by Ronald Green and *Comparative Religious Ethics* (1978) by David Little and Sumner Twiss—have provided rigorous examinations of the demands of reason, rational argumentation, and rational justification in religious ethics. The clarity, precision, and quality of thought that have gone into these projects is admirable, but I have opted for a more eclectic and interdisciplinary approach to the interpretation of religious ethics. I think the approach is consistent with the interpretive categories and interests

that have emerged in the discipline of religious studies.

My primary aim is descriptive—to describe materials for an imaginative engagement with the variety of ethical options that have been generated within religious worldviews. But the critical issue is one of interpretation. How do we interpret this variety? Each of the three major parts of this book explores a different interpretive perspective in the study of comparative religious ethics. An interpretive study of religious ethics can be organized around three basic perspectives: the concern with ethical experience, the concern with ethical rules governing the human life cycle, and the concern with ethical values embodied in social relations.

Ethical experience can best be appreciated, interpreted, and perhaps understood within the phenomenology and history of religions. Ethical experience can be located within the multidimensional texture of religion. The human experience of confronting the obligations of sacred authority can best be understood, not through scientific explanation or philosophical reduction, but by interpreting the conditions of possibility for ethical action within religious worldviews. Patterns of ethical action are woven into the fabric of religious symbol, myth, and ritual that comprise any religion. The experiential encounter with authoritative norms for ordinary human behavior is an integral part of religion. That experience is intimately connected to all the other dimensions of belief, action, and experience that make up a religion. The interpretive categories of the history of religions, therefore, provide the best framework for locating religious ethics within human experience.

Ethical rules can best be interpreted as responses to the basic dilemmas, challenges, and crises of the human life cycle. Van Gennep, Malinowski, Turner, and many others have observed that religious rituals mediate life-cycle transitions of birth, adolescence, marriage, and death. Erik Erikson has outlined the psychological challenges that arise at different stages of the life cycle. Ethical challenges also arise—abortion, infanticide, adulthood, gender roles, sexuality, euthanasia, and suicide—as human dilemmas that relate directly to the liminal crises of life-cycle transitions. Ethical rules pattern human behavior in response to the challenges of these transitions. They suggest basic patterns of action in the personal ethics of religious communities and traditions.

Ethical values can best be interpreted as they are embodied in social relations. Networks of human social relations define values, produce values, exchange values, and preserve values. That which is considered ethically valuable, desirable, or good in human experience is embodied and reinforced within a network of social relations. Ethical rules also govern social relations, but these rules are practical reinforcements of the underlying values that are embodied in institutions, technology, economic exchange, and strategies for collective survival. These shared values give concrete and tangible form to the religious worldview that is acted out in the ordinary interactions of any social group. Such ethical values support basic patterns of action in the social ethics of communities and traditions.

These three perspectives on religious ethics in the history of religions define the outline of this book. Part One is concerned with *ethical experience* in relation to the obligatory norms of sacred authority; Part Two explores *ethical rules* governing human behavior in response to the challenges of life-cycle transitions; and Part Three examines *ethical values* that are supported by a religious worldview and embodied in social relations. In each section, a separate important aspect of religious ethics is explored.

In Part One the patterns and processes of ethical experience are isolated in relation to religious norms for ordinary behavior. The section provides a phenomenology of ethical experience

in the history of religions, a typology of ethical responses to obligation, and an analysis of the tensions of dissonance and the strategies for achieving harmony in ethical experience. This most explicitly theoretical, and most broadly comparative, section of the book does not, however, develop a theory of comparative religious ethics that is then imposed on the issues raised in the other two sections. It is an analysis of ethical experience that can stand on its own. However, the analysis of dissonance as an integral experience in religious ethics (see Chapter 3) links this section to the rest of the book. The dissonance experienced in guilt, shame, and any sense that things are not as they ought to be is necessarily connected with the ethical dilemmas of the human life cycle and social relations that the other two major sections examine. But religious ethics is not simply issue-oriented: It involves patterns of action that negotiate an experience of ethical and ritual harmony in relation to the demands of sacred obligation governing everyday, ordinary behavior. Part One, therefore, presents a diagram of the basic pattern of ethical experience in the history of religions.

The other two sections are issue-oriented explorations of the most significant ethical dilemmas, challenges, and conflicts of the human life cycle and social relations. The ethical issues considered in Parts Two and Three are those that have arisen primarily in modern, western, industrialized societies. The resources of the history of religions, and the categories of cross-cultural and interdisciplinary analysis, provide opportunities for exploring in new ways those dilemmas that have appeared most acutely in the modern world. For individuals living in modern, western, industrialized societies, these sections provide an occasion for re-imagining crucial dilemmas of the life cycle and social relations by referring these issues to traditional norms, rules, values, and patterns of action in the history of religions. No attempt is made to provide a complete inventory of religious beliefs and practices regarding these issues; this is not an encyclopedic collection of religious beliefs and practices in personal and social ethics. Rather, my intention is an interpretive engagement with specific issues of personal and social ethics in the modern world from the perspective of the history of religions. The emphasis is on the interpretation of basic patterns and processes in personal and social ethics. Contemporary ethical issues in personal ethics (such as abortion, sexuality, and suicide) and in social ethics (such as technology, economic exchange, and war) may appear in a new light from this perspective. Parts Two and Three, therefore, explore some of the available resources in the comparative study of religions for understanding crucial, contemporary ethical issues.

The Introduction places these explorations of religious ethics within the comparative study of religion and religions. Although a survey of the world's religions is not intended, this section provides an overview of the phenomenon of religion, classifying religions into primal, archaic, traditional, and modern, and exploring the comparative possibilities in the study of religion as a prelude to the study of comparative religious ethics. No prior knowledge of the history of religions is assumed, and suggestions for supplemental reading in religion and ethics are provided in the notes to the Introduction. The most important section of the Introduction for this interpretive study of comparative religious ethics is the discussion of ethical experience,

rules, and values, which will be developed in detail in the three parts of the book. Patterns of ethical experience, rules, and values within traditional and modern religious life form the subject matter of this book. It is possible that an encounter with the variety of these patterns may help to expand our ability to imagine ethical patterns of action.

I would like to acknowledge my gratitude to teachers, colleagues, and members of the Board of Directors who have provided support, encouragement, and inspiration over the years: Walter Capps, W. Richard Comstock, John Cumpsty, Crerar Douglas, Deborah Sills Gunn, Richard D. Hecht, Roger Hinkins, Abba Nathan J. Hoffman, Edward Tabor Linenthal, Molly Lowe, James McNamara, Robert Michaelsen, and Ninian Smart. I would particularly like to thank Professor Smart for reviewing earlier drafts and supporting this project. When we met on a tennis court, almost ten years ago, I had no idea that I would write a book on ethics, live outside the United States, or give up the game of tennis. He has been largely responsible for these three things. Thanks also to the following reviewers of the manuscript: Professors Bruce Lawrence, Stephen Sapp, Stephen Snyder, and Lee Yearley. Special thanks go to Sheryl Fullerton of Wadsworth Publishing Company for her editorial skills and support in making this project possible. It is probably not necessary to say that these people are absolved of any and all ethical responsibility for the sins of commission and omission in this book on comparative religious ethics.

INTRODUCTION

RELIGION, ETHICS, AND THE COMPARATIVE PERSPECTIVE

Religion is a vital dimension of human experience that can be identified, analyzed, described, and interpreted in a variety of ways. The approach taken in this book attempts to be simultaneously detached and empathic. A detached approach views religious phenomena in as objective a manner as possible. The investigator's own value judgments are temporarily suspended in order to permit the values, meaning, and power inherent in different religious worldviews to appear in their own integrity. An empathic approach respects that integrity, allowing the irreducible variety of religions to be appreciated as different experiments in being human. Detachment and empathy are both implied in the disciplined study of religion.

The study of the history of religions requires techniques for interpreting the religious dimension of human experience. First, religion itself must be identified. Perhaps the simplest definition would locate religion in the human engagement with sacred norms that inform belief, action, and experience. Second, this involvement with sacred norms can be analyzed in three dimensions:

1. a theoretical dimension of religious belief, myth, and doctrine

2. a practical dimension of religious action (rituals, laws, customs, and rules for behavior)

3. an experiential dimension of religion that includes individual experience and social forms of association, organization, and community

Third, religious beliefs, practices, and experiences can be described in different cultural contexts; the history of religions presumes a cross-cultural frame of reference. Finally, the central task of the history of religions is the interpretation of the sense and significance of religious phenomena. The interpretive strategies of the study of religion explore the basic patterns and processes of religious belief, action, and experience in order to deepen and expand our understanding of this important dimension of human life.

Religious ethics, which includes all the sacred norms that inform ordinary behavior, is one important aspect of religion. When we explore patterns of ethical action in the history of religions we find that ethical norms—standards, guidelines, rules, regulations, laws, values, and so on—for conducting human behavior in daily life are interwoven with all other aspects of belief, action, and experience that make up a religion. Patterns of ethical action form an integral part of religion. If we were to study patterns of ethical action in order to decide what are the proper standards for human conduct, then we would be involved in normative religious ethics. This is an important ongoing activity within any living ethical system. But if we simply wanted to survey the actual ethical beliefs and practices of a number of different traditions, and to make an inventory of the history of religious ethics, then we would be engaged in descriptive religious ethics. The first step in the approach to religious ethics suggested by the history of religions is to set aside our own normative judgments in order to enter into the work of description. A second step, however, involves the work of classification, analysis, and interpretation. The study of basic patterns and processes in ethical action within the history of religions may be called interpretive religious ethics.

We will be examining three basic interpretive perspectives on religious ethics in the history of religions. First, we will be concerned with the nature of ethical experience. Any ethical system contains certain powerful images of ethical behavior, and any individual may experience degrees of conflict or harmony in relation to those controlling images of action. We need to be sensitive to the experiential dynamics in the human engagement with ethical norms in the history of religions. Second, we will examine ethical rules. An ethical system will develop an explicit code of rules for behavior. As we survey different ethical codes, we may find that although particular rules differ, they respond to very similar challenges in the human life cycle and social relations. Third, we will try to uncover the nature of ethical values. Values may be simply whatever people feel they need, want, or desire; on a deeper level, however, values reveal fundamental ethical judgments about what is considered good in human life. Such values may be deeply embedded in the quality of social relations supported by an ethical system. The study of ethical experience, rules, and values forms the primary classification of the field of religious ethics in interpretive religious ethics.

Finally, ethical experience, rules, and values will be explored in a cross-cultural context. The comparative method will form the basis for our interpretations of religious ethics in the history of religions. Comparisons are not made for the purpose of judging whether particular ethical systems are right or wrong, better or worse, superior or inferior; such an approach would be an exercise in normative religious ethics. Rather, a comparative interpretation of religious ethics clarifies the cultural variety of ethical experiments in being human. The global scope of comparative religious ethics suggests an almost endless variety of ethical possibilities. We will be concerned with identifying the sheer diversity in that play of possibilities. But at the same time we will find that similar underlying structures in human life provide the basic conditions of possibility for ethical action. In a variety of ways ethical systems respond to the same challenges: the challenge of forming personal identity and the challenge of cooperation among persons in a network of social relations. The human life cycle and social relations provide fairly constant underlying structures that generate a range of different ethical patterns of action.

Exploring comparative religious ethics in this way calls for an imaginative engagement with different possibilities of being human. Through the interpretation of otherness, strange, foreign, or different ethical beliefs and practices may become more familiar. Imaginative involvement may make the strange familiar, but it also has the potential for producing the corresponding effect of making the familiar strange. Many patterns of action that we take for granted may suddenly seem unusual, curious, and perhaps even foreign. The comparative study of religious ethics may open up new possibilities for ethical action. Ultimately, the value of this interpretive approach to comparative religious ethics lies in the possibility of returning from these encounters with otherness to look at ourselves with new eyes. As the poet T. S. Eliot put it, "The end of all our exploring will be to arrive where we started and know the place for the first time."[1]

Religion and Religions

The term *religion* designates a general class of human beliefs, practices, and experiences; religion*s* are particular subspecies of that class. Religions, or religious traditions, are identified as particular illustrations of the general class of religion, just as apples, oranges, pears, and bananas might be subspecies of the general class, fruit. Since most cultures do not have terms for religion or religions, these designations are problematic in the comparative study of religion. Their precise definitions are stipulated by the study of religion itself. The historian of religion Jonathan Z. Smith makes this point with regard to the concept of religion:

> If we have understood the archaeological and textual record correctly, man has had his entire history in which to imagine deities and modes of interaction with them. But man, more precisely western man, has had only the last few centuries in which to imagine religion . . . . That is to say, while there is a staggering amount of data, of phenomena, of human experiences and expressions that might be characterized in one culture or another, by one criterion or another as religious—there is no data for religion. *Religion is solely the creation of the scholar's study. It is created for the scholar's analytic purposes by his imaginative acts of comparison and generalization.*[2]

If the class of *religion* is constructed out of our imaginative encounter with historical records, the same is the case with our concept of *religions*. The historian of religion Wilfred Cantwell Smith has observed that all that exists for our study are accounts of personal faith and the cumulative traditions within which that faith is expressed. The notion of discrete religions—Hinduism, Buddhism, Confucianism, and so on—is also the result of academic classifications.[3]

But if we are going to use these terms, we should at least be clear about what we mean by them. Outlining some basic working definitions will provide a preliminary orientation for our exploration of comparative religious ethics. Some sense of what it means to identify and analyze religion (and to classify different religions) will provide a useful map to the territory we will be exploring.

Identifying Religion

We have suggested that a simple definition of religion would identify it as that dimension of human experience engaged with sacred norms. But how should we understand the term *sacred?* In one sense, a descriptive approach to the study of religion requires a circular definition of sacred: Whatever someone holds to be sacred is sacred. Our task is to describe and interpret the sacred norms that are actually held by individuals, communities, and historical traditions. We can carry this analysis a step further, however, by recognizing that what people hold to be sacred tends to have two important characteristics: ultimate meaning and transcendent power.

Religion has been defined as a vital concern with the ultimate meaning of human existence. The theologian Paul Tillich suggested that the religious dimension in experience is awakened at those points in which human beings are grasped by an ultimate concern.[4] Some have interpreted Tillich's proposal to mean that whatever is held as a supreme or pre-eminent human concern qualifies as religion; in this sense the worship of gods, nation, or wealth could be considered as a religious concern if it provides the ultimate frame of meaning for human life. But the word *ultimate,* from the Latin *ultima,* indicates something that is last, final, or the end of a series. An ultimate concern, therefore, must come up against the absolute limits of human life. In the face of the ultimate human limit situations of birth, change, and death, religion appears as a creative response that generates a sense of meaning. In the face of the apparent limitations of human consciousness and will, religion generates a context of sacred ultimate meaning.

Sacred norms are also characterized by transcendent power. Some scholars have located the essence of religion in the human relationship with super-human powers. E. B. Tylor defined religion as simply "the belief in spiritual beings."[5] And more recently the anthropologist Melford Spiro has clarified the culturally specific context in which religion emerges by suggesting that religion is "an institution consisting of culturally patterned interactions with culturally postulated superhuman beings."[6] Both definitions recognize that religion involves an engagement with powers that rise above or go beyond ordinary human experience. Religion is not simply a concern with the meaning of human life, but also an engagement with the transcendent powers, forces, and processes that human beings have perceived to impinge on their lives. Rudolf Otto tried to describe this sense of sacred power as the *sensus numinous*—the felt sense of an awesome, terrifying, yet at the same time mysteriously attractive power beyond ordinary human capacities.[7] But religion is not simply a feeling; human beings act in observable ways in relation to the transcendent power that is invested in sacred norms. The engagement with transcendent power may be observed in a wide range of religious behavior: rituals of worship, techniques of meditation, and the whole range of ethical action. These forms of behavior are religious because they are involved with sacred norms that provide a living context of ultimate meaning and transcendent power.

Analyzing Religion

In analyzing the concept of religion it is possible to distinguish three basic dimensions: belief, action, and experience. Each dimension can be divided into two aspects, producing a basic schematic outline, and clarifying the terminology that will be used in our description and interpretation of religious phenomena.[8]

Religious Belief

Religious belief, the first dimension, takes two forms: myth and doctrine. By *myth* we mean a story or set of stories referring to sacred beings, sacred objects, and sacred events. Myths often tell of events such as the creative acts of gods and goddesses, the deeds of culture heroes, and the origins of natural processes and human institutions. These events all tend to take place in a time outside of ordinary time. Sacred narratives are much like histories in that they tell stories about the deeds of divine beings, ancestors, and communities; they are not, however, subject to the same criteria of truth that holds for historical narratives. It is more important to ask if a myth is alive or dead than to ask if it is true or false. If a myth is alive, then it creates a context in which the living reality of a religious tradition emerges. Human beings, to the extent that they are religious, live in a world of myth, a world that is meaningfully structured by the sacred stories preserved and handed down in a tradition. These stories provide a living model for the identity of both the community and individuals within the community. They set a pattern of images, ideals, and values that carry sacred authority over human behavior. Myth represents a fundamental orientation to the world. To be a human being is not simply to live in a world, but to live in a meaningful world; myth is one important way in which human beings invest their world with meaning.[9]

By *doctrine* we mean statements of religious belief. Where myth takes the form of stories, doctrine takes the form of propositions of belief that are affirmed within a given religious community. For example, the story of creation in seven days takes the form of a myth; the statement that there is one God who created heaven and earth is a doctrine. The story of the birth, death, and resurrection of Jesus functions as a myth; the statement that Jesus is one person with two natures, human and divine, is a doctrine. The stories of Muhammad's flight from Mecca to Medina and his miraculous ascent into the heavens are myths;

the statement that there is one God and Muhammad is his prophet is a doctrine.[10] Doctrine can be worked out more or less systematically within a religious tradition. But, in most cases, subscribing to a religious doctrine serves as a sign of membership within a religious community that holds that particular doctrine. So although doctrine represents one aspect of religious belief, it is not simply a conceptual exercise. Doctrine may perform an important social function by serving as a sign that a believer belongs within the world-view of a particular religious group.

Religious Action

Religion is not simply a matter of belief. Belief may, in fact, be the least important dimension of religion. What people do and what they experience are far more important within a religious tradition. So the second dimension of religion is action. Here again religious action may be divided into two aspects: ritual and ethics. *Ritual* is symbolic action with reference to what is held to be sacred. Rituals are performed in extra-ordinary times and places. They respond to life-cycle transitions, marking out the passage of birth, the initiation from childhood to adulthood, the ceremonies of marriage, and the funerary rituals of death. Rituals also mark transitions in the sacred calendar of a community. Specified practices are performed for the new year, harvest festivals, and other holy days. And rituals occur as creative responses to the afflictions of human existence, such as illness, drought, famine, and uncertainty. Ritual takes the various forms of religious worship, prayer, sacrifice, techniques of meditation, festival, celebration, and pilgrimage—all of which provide structured and formalized ways of participating in the power of the sacred through meaningful, symbolic action. The living ritual practices of a religious tradition are not empty, mechanical routines, but a vital, active means of access to sacred power.[11]

Ethics is also an aspect of religious action.

But whereas ritual is performed in extra-ordinary circumstances (or special times and places set apart from everyday life), ethics represents standards for conducting ordinary human behavior. The ethical aspect of religious action governs behavior in everyday life. It provides a sense of obligation, not in the ways of worship, but in the appropriate ways of behaving as an individual and as a member of a human community. We will have more to say about religious ethics later. Here it is important to note that religious ethics does not simply consist of sets of instructions for what to do and what not to do; it is not simply a code of injunctions and prohibitions. Religious ethics involves a more dynamic pattern of behavior in relation to the sacred norms—in the forms of religious images, rules, and values—than might be suggested at first glance. It consists of not only standards for everyday, ordinary, human behavior, but also the variety of human responses to those standards.[12]

Religious Experience

Religion is not only defined by what people believe and do, but also by the quality of their experience. Religious experience can be divided into two aspects, psychological and social experience. *Psychological experience* represents the inner dimension of religion; it refers to whatever may be going on in the inner life of the individual. The inner aspect of religious experience includes the sense of numinous awe before the power, majesty, and authority of the sacred. And it also includes a sense of mystical union, an intimate sense of connection, with the sacred. We are interested in the variety of religious experiences. Feelings of piety as well as sacrilege, attraction as well as repulsion, conviction as well as doubt, love as well as hate, are all interwoven in the complex and ambiguous textures of religious emotion.[13]

Social experience refers to the collective religious experience of social groups. First, the social aspect of religion includes the relation between a religious group and its social context. Is a particular religious group at the center of the social network in which it exists, adapting and accommodating to the pressures of its social environment? Or is it on the margin of its society, a force of resistance or opposition in tension with its social world, and providing a social alternative? In this sense religion can be engaged both to validate and to resist certain social practices.

Second, the social aspect of religion includes the institutional forms of religion, which may be as simple as the kinds of religious architecture that embody the social authority of a religious group or may involve intricate questions of religious authority. How is the religious group organized? What is the structure of authority? How do you get in? How do you get out?

Finally, the social aspect of religion includes the relation between religious groups. Different religious groups may be in conflict or in cooperation, as the interaction of different worldviews, involving different beliefs, practices, and forms of association, has social consequences. Often different ethical standards will translate into social conflict. A particular religious group may try to impose its ethical standards on other groups that come within the orbit of its power, and such a situation may even give rise to alternative ethical standards as a sign of social resistance to the dominant group. All of these issues are part of the social experience in which religion is necessarily involved.[14]

These six aspects—myth and doctrine, ritual and ethics, psychological and social experience—suggest that religion is a multidimensional phenomenon. In analyzing religion it is important to clarify this vocabulary, but it is also essential to recognize that all of these aspects are interrelated in the life of a religious tradition. Particular religions are historical constellations of these six aspects.

Classifying Religions

Our primary source of data in the cross-cultural study of religions is texts, whether written or oral, that relate religious beliefs and describe religious practices and experiences. This material tends to be organized in terms of religious traditions. *Tradition* literally means "that which is handed down." It marks the historical lineage of religious beliefs, practices, and experiences, but it also signifies that particular religions are grounded in history. Traditions take their distinctive shapes within particular historical situations and circumstances. A classification of religions may be useful if it reveals something of this historicity. We will use a preliminary outline for classifying religions into four types: primal religions, archaic religions, traditional religions, and modern religions.

Primal Religions   Primal religions used to be referred to as "primitive." The religious beliefs and practices of small-scale, local, or tribal societies seemed to be at an earlier stage of human development and appeared to be residual remnants of human prehistory. The prejudice against the local community religions of Africa, Australia, Polynesia, Melanesia, and the Americas, reflected in the term *primitive,* was part of a western ethnocentric ideology of progress. In the western imagination, primal religions represented a stage in human development that had been left behind by the advance of civilization.

These local religions, however, have survived (often displaced and disrupted by the incursions of western missionaries and colonizers) to reveal a great diversity and complexity of religious worldviews. They share a number of similar characteristics: relatively simple subsistence-level economies, basic survival technologies, oral rather than written traditions, and a strongly integrated sense of community. But from these relatively simple social foundations, primal religions generate complex religious worldviews. The primary source materials through which we are able to reconstruct these worldviews are ethnographic reports of travelers, missionaries, and anthropologists. These accounts provide a wealth of material on the religious beliefs, practices, and experiences of these relatively small-scale, local social groups.

Primal religions tend to reveal a very high degree of integration among the various aspects of religion. Patterns of ethical action are interwoven with the shared sacred narratives of myth, and these patterns are reinforced through the ritual practices of the community. The anthropologist Bronislaw Malinowski devoted his fieldwork to the study of the Trobriand Islanders in Melanesia. He emphasized the importance of myth and ritual in providing an essential basis for ethics in primal religions. Malinowski observed:

> *Myth, ritual, and ethics are definitely but three facets of the same essential fact. . . . Take away from the natives the belief in the reality of their sacred lore, destroy their sense of the spirit world as it exists and acts upon them, and you will undermine their whole moral outlook.*[15]

The way of the gods and the way of the ancestors embody the sacred norms for ethical action. Myth and ritual provide access to a sacred world of meaning and power in which the patterns of everyday behavior take shape.

The study of primal religions has revealed that ethical standards for human conduct are by no means dependent upon social complexity. The anthropologist Ruth Benedict pointed out that clearly defined codes of ethical conduct, supported by shared religious beliefs and practices, are an integral element in primal religions. It is not the case, Benedict noted, that

> *all the cultures that use religion as a sanction for ethical conduct [are] found upon the plane of complex civilization. The Manus people of the Bismarck Archipelago have an ethical religion, and it would be hard to imagine a culture that more consistently used all their supernatural concepts to back a puritanical code of morals.*[16]

Although the ethical codes generated within primal religion may differ from one another, they all appear to rely on myth as a social charter for ethical action and ritual as a system of shared practices that reinforce the ethical relations among individuals in the community.

Archaic Religions

The religions of ancient civilizations—Egypt, Mesopotamia, Persia, India, Greece, and Rome—may be referred to as archaic religions. These ancient religions, spanning over 2000 years before the common era, were based upon powerful sacred images of order. The historian Cornelius Loew observed that transcendent principles of cosmic order in these ancient religions unified all aspects of human life. Loew noted that these were religions based on "the conviction that the meaning of life is rooted in an encompassing cosmic order in which man, society and the gods all participate."[17] First, that cosmic order was seen to permeate every level of existence. In ancient Egypt that universal symbol of sacred order was *Ma'at;* in ancient India it was *Rita;* in the religion of ancient Persia it was *Asha.* In each case this was a symbol of sacred order, truth, and righteousness infusing the cosmos, and it provided the ultimate sacred standard against which individual actions could be measured.

Second, this cosmic order was upheld by the gods. Archaic religions developed complex pantheons of divine beings. In Egyptian religion the royal god Osiris ruled in the halls of Ma'at and supervised the judgment of the dead; in ancient India the celestial sky-god Varuna sustained the cosmic order represented by Rita; and in ancient Persia Ahura Mazda and his attendants were the guardians of Asha. These divine beings were responsible for maintaining the cosmic order. Often archaic religious pantheons also featured powerful warrior gods, who battled against the forces of chaos. In the creation myth of ancient Mesopotamia, the divine warrior Marduk defeated the sea monster Tiamat, and out of the sacrificed body of Tiamat chaos was ordered into the pattern of creation. The gods in archaic religion represented those divine forces that sustained the cosmic order.

Third, the central ethical challenge of archaic religions was to attune the human order to the cosmic order. Two interrelated institutions were responsible for bringing human life into harmony with sacred order: divine kingship and the royal priesthood. The king was invested with the sacred authority of the gods. In Egypt the pharoah was a son of the solar deity Ra and at death would assume his place in the divine pantheon of the gods. In ancient Mesopotamia the king was the earthly representative of the gods and derived his authority from Shamash, the solar god of cosmic order. The king provided the central focus for both religious and political authority. Royal power was supported by elaborate professional priesthoods, temple complexes, and a sacred calendar of sacrificial rituals and religious festivals. The royal priesthood created an interlocking ritual network that served to re-create the sacred cosmic order on earth.

The sources for recreating these archaic religious worldviews lie in a variety of sacred texts. Documents such as *The Egyptian Book of the Dead,* the Babylonian *Enuma Elish* and *Gilgamesh Epic,* and the *Vedas* of India are magnificent compendiums of sacred myths, ritual instructions, and ethical standards for behavior. These works only suggest the wealth of sacred literature that was generated within archaic religions, and they hint at the tremendous religious creativity in the ancient world. The images of cosmic order embodied in these texts provide the ultimate standards for ethical action within each of these ancient traditions. They represent patterns of sacred order within which individuals were able to place themselves. Knowing one's place in the cosmic order and acting accordingly was the supreme ethical accomplishment in archaic religions.

Traditional Religions

The living world religions are accumulations of historical traditions that have persisted over many centuries, while at the same time adapting to changing circumstances. They each represent fairly unified cultural traditions, with distinctive constellations of religious beliefs, practices, and forms of association. For convenience of classification, traditional religions are somewhat arbitrarily divided into eastern and western religions, which is curious because the eastern religions originated in what might be called the Far East—India, China, Southeast Asia, and Japan—while what we call western religions originated in the Near East. Rather than providing exhaustive descriptions of each traditional religion, we will simply identify the primary textual sources that will be used to locate the ethical norms in each tradition.

Eastern Traditions. Classical Hinduism developed in India around two basic religious themes: moksha and dharma. *Moksha* means liberation from the mechanical cycle of reincarnation within which each person is bound. Various techniques were developed to achieve this liberation from the cycle of rebirth: the path of knowledge (*jñana-marga*), which cultivated techniques of meditation in order to realize that the self was one with the divine; the path of de-

votion (*bhakti-marga*), which provided access to divine power through the worship of personal deities; and the path of works (*karma-marga*), which encouraged a detached attitude toward the world of action. These paths of liberation were outlined in a vast body of sacred literature, beginning with the mythic narratives and ritual instructions of the *Vedas,* the philosophical treatises of the *Upaniṣads,* the devotional poetry of the *Bhagavad Gītā,* and the popular mythology of the *Puranas.* At the same time, the quest for moksha was integrated into a vast network of personal and social ethics designated by dharma. *Dharma* represents ethical duty; it is practically synonymous with Hindu religion. The major text detailing the ethical requirements of dharma is the *Laws of Manu,* which explains the demands of ethical duty in each stage of the human life cycle and in each station within the network of social relations.[18]

Buddhism and Jainism are two other traditional religions that originated in India and developed techniques for liberation from the world of action and rebirth. The Buddha proposed a radical critique of action. Since all action leads to suffering, the only appropriate goal is a supreme detachment from the desires, cravings, and graspings that animate action. *Nirvana* is this ultimate detachment from the world of action, from the cycle of death and rebirth. It is achieved through specific techniques of meditation; but it is also supported through a discipline of ethics. Ethical action (*sila*) provides a preliminary preparation for meditation. The *Dhammapada,* as well as numerous other Buddhist texts and commentaries, outlines the necessary pattern of ethical action on the way to enlightenment.[19] Although it also encouraged a radical spiritual detachment, the central concern of Jainism was a strict ethical purity. The *Jaina Sutras* exhort monks to achieve a perfect harmlessness (*ahimsa*) in the world. Only through such perfectly detached harmlessness can the necessary ethical purity be achieved to prepare for ultimate spiritual liberation.[20]

The traditional religions of China have all assumed that the cosmic order of the heavens (*T'ien-tai*) overarches all human endeavors on earth. Confucianism, as a tradition of ethical reflection and training, outlined the basic patterns of human action that would serve to uphold the cosmic harmony. The *Analects of Confucius* detail the requirements of righteous action (*li*) in the cultivation of specific virtues of humaneness, reciprocity, and the proper relations between persons in a well-ordered society.[21] The Chinese tradition of Taoism, embodied in the *Tao-te ching* of Lao-tzu and the writings of the Taoist mystic Chuang-tzu, suggests the potential for participating in the way and power of nature. As an ethical program, these classic Taoist texts propose a natural, effortless style of behavior in harmony with the Way (*Tao*) of the universe.[22] The traditional religions of China developed attitudes and dispositions toward action that are very different from the religions of India; and yet one Indian religion—Buddhism—was successfully adapted to become one of the major religious traditions in both China and Japan.

Western Traditions. Judaism is based on the central concept of a *covenant*, or a unique contractual bond, between God and the people of Israel. The God of Israel, Yahweh, revealed the conditions of that covenant to Moses on Mount Sinai. The details of the ritual and ethical laws implicit in the covenant, along with the narrative history of the Israelites, are contained in the first five books of the Hebrew Bible. These five books, the Torah, represent the revealed sacred norms for both ritual practice and ethical behavior in the religion of ancient Israel. The rest of the Bible is traditionally divided into the prophetic writings of the *Neviim* (Prophets) and the poetic, proverbial, and wisdom literature of the *Ketuviim* (Writings). This library of sacred texts provides the scriptural basis for the Jewish tradition. Like the other western traditions, Judaism is an ethical monotheism: It holds to one God who requires conformity to specific ethical standards

of behavior. The Ten Commandments and the 613 specific laws in the Torah provide the outline for those ethical standards. In order to apply those standards to various life situations, it was necessary for the tradition to engage in the ongoing work of interpretation. The results of centuries of interpretation are contained in the Talmud; and the sections of the Talmud that deal directly with matters of Jewish ethical law are referred to as Halakha.[23]

Christianity emerged as a messianic movement within Judaism and, therefore, adapted the Hebrew Bible as its Old Testament. But its new gospel, or "good news," was that a unique salvation was available through Jesus as a universal savior. Although the grace offered through Jesus promised to fulfill all the traditional requirements of ethical law, a body of ethical teachings can be distilled from the sayings of Jesus, the letters of Paul, and other texts collected in the sacred canon of the New Testament. The work of distilling, organizing, and interpreting these precepts was carried out by the leaders of the early church—theologians such as Justin Martyr, Tertullian, Origen, and Augustine—who are referred to as the Church Fathers. Systematic formulations of Christian doctrine and ethics were worked out in councils; a body of ethical injunctions and prohibitions took shape in *canon law,* which was the authoritative ethical code during the Catholic middle ages. By the sixteenth century Christianity was separated into three major divisions: Eastern Orthodox, Roman Catholic, and Protestant. But even from its inception the tradition has generated a wide variety of approaches to Christian ethics.[24]

Islam is based upon the revelations of Allah to the prophet Muhammad, which were collected in the sacred text of all Muslims, the Qur'an. The Qur'an sets out the requirements for ethical behavior, and promises Allah's final judgment, which will reward the righteous and punish the wicked. Underlying all ethical conduct, however, is a prayerful disposition of surrender to the will of Allah. The word *Islam* in Arabic literally means surrender. The ethical ideal of Islam is a willing submission to the supreme will of Allah in all matters of human conduct. In Islamic ethics, the authority of the Qur'an is supplemented by reports of Muhammad's teachings, instructions, and accounts of his exemplary conduct collected in the Hadith. The Hadith is a compendium of religious teachings traditionally derived from the eyewitness accounts of Muhammad's companions. That portion of the Hadith that deals directly with ethical questions is called the Sunnah. The Sunnah, along with the Qur'an, forms the authoritative foundation of Islamic law.[25]

Modern Religions

Although traditional religions have survived in the modern world (and have periodically experienced dramatic resurgences in reaction to the modernization process), they have been displaced, to a certain degree, by the trend toward secularization in modern, industrial, western societies. A secular society is simply one in which traditional religious beliefs, practices, and forms of association have lost their pervasive and unifying power to hold a given society together. In the modern world, religion tends to be displaced from the social center of gravity, and it becomes one competing source of authority within a complex network of institutions that demand the attention, allegiance, and commitment of modern individuals. This displacement of religion has assumed three basic forms.

First, religion has been isolated as one particular social institution. Traditional religions in modern, secular societies become separate institutions, with little or no direct social authority over legal, economic, or political institutions. Religions have undergone a process of differentiation in the modern world, and the appearance of modern religions as separate institutions is one effect of the complex differentiation of social roles in modern societies. Religion has become one specialized institution among many.

Second, traditional religious functions have been diffused through a range of other social institutions: science, the arts, and political structures. Scientific beliefs may take on the character of sacred knowledge; sports and entertainments may assume the devotional quality of religious ritual; and political allegiances may take the form of a civil religion. A range of secular ideologies in the modern world—such as democratic liberalism, romantic nationalism, and radical socialism—may function in the ethical lives of individuals as if they were religions. Nationalism has been a particularly powerful focal point for religious collective representations in the modern world.

Third, religious commitments have become increasingly privatized. Religion may appear as the way individual human beings work out a system of meaning and value in their own lives; individuals become something of consumers of religious beliefs and practices, picking and choosing to serve their own interests, deriving elements of religion from different sources. Individuals may make basic life choices regarding personal identity, life style, and ethical action from a variety of religious resources available in the environment. Such an orientation represents an eclectic approach to religion in line with the free-market orientations of modern, western societies and the increasing availability of different religious values from which to choose. The authority of traditional religions, which grounded religious ethics in myth and ritual, has been markedly diminished. A range of new ethical values has emerged: the rationalization of behavior, economic productivity, and technological efficiency. This tension between traditional and modern values defines the situation of religious ethics in modern, industrial, western societies.

Religious Ethics

Religious ethics is that aspect of religion concerned with normative patterns of action in the ordinary situations and circumstances of the human life cycle and social relations. It is a pattern of obligation that sets the standards for *fitting* action; it is a pattern of rules that sets the standards for *right* action; and it is a pattern of values that sets the standards for *good* action. First, the ethical process involves striving to conform behavior to images of perfect action embodied in myth and reinforced in ritual. The central challenge in ethical experience in the history of religions is to behave in ways that fit within sacred patterns of action. Second, the ethical process involves attempting to observe specific rules for behavior, and ethical rules create a context in which some actions are right and other actions are wrong. Ethics is rule-governed behavior. Finally, the ethical process cultivates certain virtues, dispositions, and attitudes in behavior in the interest of religious patterns of good behavior. The values embodied in a system of religious ethics represent basic value judgments regarding the qualitative difference between good and bad actions. These three aspects of religious ethics—ethical experience in relation to images of fitting action, ethical rules for right action, and ethical values that define good action—will be explored in this interpretive study of religious ethics.

Ethical Experience

Religious ethics does not simply establish standards for ethical action; it includes a dynamic range of human responses to those standards. The experience embodied in the ethical process involves basic tensions in relation to the sacred norms that inform everyday behavior. We can gain some insight on the experiential dynamics of religious ethics by dividing the ethical process into four stages: (1) the sense of *obligation,* in which certain kinds of behavior "ought" to be done and certain specific behaviors "ought not" to be done; (2) the variety in human *response* to what is held to be obligatory in ordinary behavior; (3) the condition of *dissonance,* in which an individual is in a state of conflict, tension, or distress as a result of not doing or not wanting to do what is obligatory; and (4) mechanisms for achieving *harmony,* usually through ritual techniques of purification, atonement, expiation, and so on, which restore a sense of alignment between individuals and their sense of ethical obligation. These four stages provide the underlying structures of human experience in the ethical process as it actually appears in the history of religions.

Ethical obligation defines the range of norms, duties, and imperatives to which the ordinary patterns of personal and social action must conform. Obligation has the binding force of necessity, and any system of religious ethics suggests that there are simply certain ways in which a person *must* act in order to conform to the demands of obligation. The dominant images of obligation within a religious tradition are given in sacred texts, the exhortations of prophets, the examples of ancestors, and codes of religious law. These symbols of obligation are invested with the authoritative power of cumulative tradition; ultimately they represent the sacred pattern of order that impinges on every aspect of ordinary human behavior. To the extent that individuals stand within a religious tradition they stand before certain powerful images of ethical obligation.

A number of different responses, however, are available in relation to the images of obligation within a tradition; ethical responsibility represents the quality of personal involvement with obligation. First, responsibility means that a person takes a given obligation seriously. Obligation is experienced as personally binding, and individuals assume the responsibility for making sense out of that obligation and determining its significance within their particular situation. Second, responsibility may also suggest that a person has the ability to respond in different ways to the demands of obligation. The experiential quality of that response is very important. It may be very different to observe an obligation because you want to than because you feel you have to. The dynamics of personal desire in relation to ethical obligation reveal different qualities of response in ethical responsibility. Finally, responsibility may mean taking responsibility for the direct experience of ethical values. Values are not objects to be obtained but experiences to be cultivated through the development of specific virtues, abilities, and capacities for action. Recognizing this means taking responsibility for the experience of values.

Perhaps the central ethical experience in the history of religions is dissonance. A condition of dissonance arises when a person is in conflict with obligation: when ethical obligations are not fulfilled, when ethical rules are not observed, and when ethical values are not experienced. People are in states of dissonance when their behavior is not in harmony with the normative images of fitting, right, or good action embodied in the tradition. The two basic forms assumed by ethical dissonance in the history of religions are shame and guilt. A sense of shame results from transgressing shared ethical norms within a community; it represents a public embarrassment, defilement, or impurity before the demands of obligation. With guilt a person stands accused, convicted, and condemned before the judgment of obligation. Both are powerful experiences of

tension, turmoil, and distress before ethical obligation, but they may also reflect the extent to which individuals internalize the requirements of obligation in the internal self-perception of their own behavior. For this reason many ethical traditions will cultivate a sense of shame or guilt as a prerequisite for ethical action. Dissonance may indicate a level of personal investment with the ethical norms that are embodied in a religious tradition.

Finally, the process of religious ethics involves strategies for dealing with dissonance. The system of religious ethics within a religious tradition will also include methods for achieving harmony. Ritual techniques designed to relieve shame and absolve guilt are important ingredients in the ethical process in the history of religions. Ethical harmony could certainly be achieved by changes of behavior to bring action into alignment with the demands of obligation. But religious traditions have developed powerful ritual resources for easing the tensions of ethical dissonance. Techniques are employed for resolving the dissonance produced by contrary actions and the dissonance that is generated by contrary attitudes, dispositions, and desires. The culmination of the ethical process is a prevailing sense of harmony with the normative patterns of action embodied in the religious tradition. Both ritual practices and ethical behavior are designed to support this ultimate harmony.

Ethical Rules

Systems of ethical rules take the form of explicit codes of conduct in religious traditions. Rules may be positive injunctions for what people should do, and they may be negative prohibitions specifying what people should not do. In either case they represent specific normative guides for action. Human behavior within religious traditions is rule-governed behavior. In addition to defining the guidelines by which ordinary action ought to be conducted, explicit ethical rules also suggest the normative standards by which that action should be judged. Rules provide the norms for right action, but there are important qualitative differences among three types of rules that operate in religious traditions: law, custom, and morality.

Legal rules are always backed up by force or the threat of force. Law is a coercive system of rules. A community that operates with a certain legal system is compelled to observe the rules of that system or suffer the consequences of legal sanctions. Laws are invested with the threat of punishment for disobedience, and the nature of those punishments may also be specified as essential corollaries of the laws themselves. Legal authority not only imposes certain coercive obligations on the members of a community, but it also assumes responsibility for exacting retribution on those members who violate its rules. The power of punishment implies a certain degree of violence inherent in any legal system. When the legal system of a community is synonymous with the traditional system of religious authority, religious ethics will assume some measure of coercion. Behavior within religious traditions is often reinforced with threats of punishment in this life or the next. To the extent that such punishments are made explicit, the ethical rules of that tradition take on the character of law.

Other rules within a tradition, however, govern life styles, manners, and customs that often seem quite arbitrary. Custom acts out rules that are not imposed by coercive force; rather, they seem to be enacted out of a certain cultural capriciousness. Customs may be the result of collective cultural habits. The term *ethos* refers to such distinctive cultural styles of behavior; it includes the particular character, quality, and temperament of a shared life style. Custom also comes under the purview of religious ethics. A

religious tradition may cultivate particular styles, rhythms, and patterns of behavior that are quite important to its sense of ethical obligation. But often the rules behind such customary behavior are only implicit, and they may be simply taken for granted as the way things are to be done. Standards of dress, etiquette, and table manners may appear as customary rules in traditional systems of religious ethics.

Moral rules are a subspecies of ethical obligation that guide human behavior through a more or less free exercise of choice. Although a legal rule might be observed by coercion and a customary rule might be followed through unconscious habit, a moral rule requires the individual's free assent. Morality implies a certain kind of behavior based on both intellectual and emotional assent. By definition, morality cannot be legislated, coerced, or forced. Intellectual agreement and emotional commitment are needed to bring the individual into a moral harmony with the sense of obligation that animates ethical rules. Most religious traditions find ways of facilitating moral choices by enveloping sacred norms in symbolic forms that make them both obligatory and desirable. These traditions awaken moral choices by making ethical rules convincing and, at the same time, attractive. Moral experience, based on choice, assent, and desire, is very different from the disciplinary obedience of rules through coercion. The rules may be literally the same, but the human experience in observing these rules is qualitatively different.

Ethical rules are relative. Many rules—such as the prohibitions of murder, theft, and incest—are common to almost all religious communities. But other rules may vary between cultures; their significance is relative to the cultural context in which they appear. One tradition may forbid, for example, abortion, or divorce, or mercy killing, or suicide, while another tradition may permit these acts. Part of the task of interpretive religious ethics is simply to outline the cultural diversity of ethical rules. But ethical rules are culturally relative for a more subtle reason. The same rule may have a different character, weight and significance within different religious traditions. Many traditions seem to have the equivalent of the Golden Rule, but the meaning of this rule—to do to others what you would want them to do to you—may vary considerably depending on what different people may in fact want done to them.[26] And the significance of this rule may vary according to the particular sacred norms for action in the different traditions in which it appears. The rule of reciprocity in human behavior meant something very different for Confucius, who saw it as a way to maintain the harmonious pattern of cosmic order on earth, than it meant for Jesus, who seemed to understand it as a demonstration of neighborly love. The cultural relativism of ethical rules is an important descriptive observation in comparative religious ethics.

Simply because ethical rules may differ among communities, cultures, and traditions, however, does not mean that the rules generated within religions do not respond to similar ethical challenges. Ethical rules address basic ethical dilemmas of the human life cycle and social relations. Cultures are similar in that they have systems of ethical classification, however different may be the elements within each classification system. The most basic ethical classifications devise rules for dealing with the challenges of personal development and social cooperation. We will be particularly concerned with the ethical rules that govern personal development in the transitions of the human life cycle. Ethical challenges of birth, childhood, adulthood, sexuality, and death provide a fairly constant substructure upon which systems of ethical rules are constructed. It will be possible to interpret, in a systematic way, the variety of ethical rules that define the normative character of behavior at each stage of the human life cycle.

Ethical Values

Values are needs, wants, and desires. The essential human needs for food, shelter, and clothing are grounded in what may be more basic, though perhaps less tangible, needs for love, communication, and a sense of community. A description of human nature may start with an inventory of such basic needs: eating, breathing, sleeping, procreation, elimination, bodily comfort, safety, movement, growth, and health. In working out his *Scientific Theory of Culture,* the anthropologist Bronislaw Malinowski wanted "to show how economics, knowledge, religion and mechanisms of law, educational training and artistic creativeness are directly or indirectly related to the basic . . . physiological needs."[27] These various human institutions represent values because their primary function is to address the basic needs of the human body, to sustain its biological survival, and to support the extension of its physical energy through creative action. But it is also true that these basic survival needs are inseparable from a larger network of social, cultural, and spiritual values.

Human values are structured by valuation, which is the process by which human beings attribute a positive or negative charge, or *valence,* to particular objects, actions, and experiences. Human beings put a positive charge on what they value; what they need, want, or desire is positively charged. They put a negative charge on what they do not want. The philosopher Stephen Pepper, in his *Source of Values,* suggested that values are based on attraction and aversion.[28] Humans are constantly evaluating their environment, evaluating food, art, tools, and even other humans, in terms of the charged process of valuation inherent in attraction or avoidance. Positive or negative charges may have different degrees of intensity, and some things may register close to neutral on the valuation scale. But in all cases valuation implies basic ethical judgments regarding the world of action.

In addition to this dynamic evaluative process of attraction and repulsion, values are conditioned by the power in human thought exercised by binary classification. The most basic ethical coding of our environment consists of separating things into two opposing classes; and, as the sociologist Emile Durkheim observed, "the mind irresistibly refuses to allow the two corresponding things to be confused, or even to be merely in contact with each other." [29] In his *Elementary Forms of the Religious Life,* Durkheim suggested that the separation of everything into two classes—sacred and profane—was the most basic form of binary classification. One of his students, Robert Hertz, pursued this line of analysis by exploring the relationship between binary classification and ethical polarities. He started with the observation that most cultures put a positive value on the right hand and a negative value on the left. The right hand is associated with the sacred; the left with the profane. The right hand symbolizes brightness, physical strength,

justice, beauty, and moral integrity; the left hand represents the opposite of all these positive values. This opposition is reflected in language— such as the Latin terms for right (*dexter*) and left (*sinister*)—reflecting a binary valuation built into the human body. Binary classification is the basic structure of ethical reason, which not only distinguishes between right and left, but also charges them with ethical value. It is the creative human impulse, as Hertz observed, "to spiritualize the body by marking upon it the opposition of values and the violent contrasts of the world of morality." [30]

Values, then, are positively charged physical needs, wants, and desires that are immediately embodied in personal identity and social relations. The interpretive work of comparative religious ethics provides access to the shared values that are supported by structured social relations. Forms of social organization represent a certain orientation toward values, and they also represent cultural experiments in producing values, exchanging values, and preserving values. In Part Three we will be particularly concerned with interpreting the role of religious and ethical values within the network of human social relations.

The Comparative Perspective

The study of religious ethics in the history of religions requires a comparative perspective. We must be aware of both the potential and the limitations of this kind of comparative work. Comparison involves a consideration of the play of similarities and differences. In this sense, comparison is a basic function of any exercise of reason and imagination. The systematic study of different cultures has required a disciplined comparative method. Social and cultural anthro-

pologists have sought to make their strategies of comparison explicit. The anthropologist A. R. Radcliffe-Brown felt the purpose of comparative study was to arrive at valid generalizations about human behavior "by the systematic study of resemblances and differences." [31] Perhaps the real work of such comparisons, however, is to identify and interpret differences. E. E. Evans-Pritchard insisted on this point when he observed that the purpose of any comparative method is "to explain differences rather than similarities."[32] He saw social anthropology as "a comparative discipline of differences."[33] Yet, in this observable play of cultural divergence, we can discern underlying structures, patterns, or typologies that will allow for the interpretation of the vast array of differences. After identifying the differences, the next step in the comparative method is the interpretation of whatever underlying patterns may emerge. The anthropologist Raymond Firth suggested this possibility when he noted that comparisons are made "with the object of establishing types and seeking variants from them."[34] The comparative method holds the potential for studying cultural differences as variations on underlying types of human behavior.

There are four basic kinds of comparison that may be involved in the cross-cultural study of human behavior.

1. Ethnographic comparisons are documentary descriptions of the customs of other people.

2. Encyclopedic comparisons are systematic collections of ethnographic reports that are gathered, organized, and catalogued.

3. Morphological comparisons are inventories of basic patterns, forms, and structures of behavior that seem to underly the customs of more than one culture.

4. Temporal comparisons are interpretations of the relations between customs in one historical period and those customs that appear at other points in the historical record.[35]

Each of these four types of comparison plays an important role in comparative religious ethics.

Ethnographic Comparison

The earliest ethnographic comparisons of which we have any record were undertaken by the ancient Greek traveler, historian, and anthropologist Herodotus. His ethnographic reports of the beliefs, practices, and customs of other cultures were basically attempts at description; but these descriptions of other people necessarily involved elements of comparison in order to make these accounts intelligible back home in Greece. The historian of anthropology Margaret Hodgen observed that "the most significant bequest made by Herodotus to subsequent thought was his use of comparison, and his recognition even in the fifth century B.C., of some of the problems which have emerged whenever the comparison of cultures has revealed either similarities or differences."[36] In describing the culture of the Egyptians, for example, Herodotus was particularly impressed by striking differences. Egypt appears as an entirely unique culture: "Not only is the climate different from that of the rest of the world, and the rivers unlike any other rivers, but the people also, in most of their manners and customs, exactly reverse the common practice of mankind."[37]

The discipline of anthropology has inherited a concern for preserving the unique character of each particular cultural complex of beliefs, practices, and social organization. The ethnographic reports that form much of the data for our understanding of primal religions are detailed studies in a single culture; comparisons with other cultures tend to be avoided. Edmund Leach, for example, has attacked the comparison of cultures that are "socially incommensurate."[38] Even temporal comparisons that are necessary for a sense of history are eschewed for the ethnographic present. Many historians of religion are also averse to comparisons. They will insist that a particular religion can only be understood within its specific cultural context.

Comparative religious ethics has also been challenged for taking accounts of ethical behavior, rules, and values out of context. Critics such as Jeffrey Stout and Donald Swearer have insisted that any system of religious ethics can only be interpreted within the context of the religious tradition in which it has arisen. Any comparison between traditions tends to be misleading and inappropriate, like comparing the proverbial apples and oranges.[39] In response to this criticism two points need to be raised. First, it is important to recognize that apples and oranges may be different, but they are nevertheless both varieties of fruit. There may be underlying properties to be analyzed that link them in the same system of classification. In this regard, comparison is necessary in order to clarify our classification of the variety of religious ethics. Second, some form of comparison in the study of religion is unavoidable. Without comparison, even in the activity of translation, definition, and description, the sheer otherness of other religious worldviews would be unintelligible. Even knowing one other system of religious ethics already involves us in the work of comparison. As the father of comparative religions F. Max Müller declared, "He who knows one, knows none."[40] The understanding of religion—and religious ethics—can only begin with a comparative frame of reference.

Encyclopedic Comparison

An encyclopedia is simply a collection of information that is organized according to an arbitrary principle of classification. Modern encyclopedias tend to organize their information according to the principle of alphabetical order; but ancient encyclopedists, such as Callimachus, Pliny, or Isidore of Seville, employed various principles of organization. The poet Borges suggests how unsettling different systems of encyclopedic classification can be by outlining the organization of an imaginary Chinese encyclopedia.

> *This passage quotes a "certain Chinese encyclopaedia" in which it is written that "animals are divided into: (a) belonging to the Emperor, (b) embalmed, (c) tame, (d) sucking pigs, (e) sirens, (f) fabulous, (g) stray dogs, (h) included in the present classification, (i) frenzied, (j) innumerable, (k) drawn with a very fine camelhair brush, (l) et cetera, (m) having just broken the water pitcher, (n) that from a long way off look like flies."[41]*

What is revealed in this fable of the Chinese encyclopedia is the idiosyncratic nature of all encyclopedic collections. Comparisons tend to be drawn from the most arbitrary systems of classification.

The earliest work in comparative religious ethics, at the beginning of this century, was of this encyclopedic variety. Edward Westermarck and L. T. Hobhouse were both appointed in 1907 to Martin White Professorships in Sociology at the London School of Economics, and they both proceeded to produce monumental compendiums of ethical beliefs and customs from all over the world. Westermarck's *Origin and Development of the Moral Ideas* and Hobhouse's *Morals in Evolution* are vast collections of strange beliefs, curious customs, and bizarre behavior.[42] For all their scope and meticulous detail, these volumes resemble the academic equivalent of *National Geographic* or Ripley's "Believe It Or Not." Serious objections to the encyclopedic approach to comparative religious ethics were raised by anthropologists. Edmund Leach has called the encyclopedic method "butterfly collecting."[43] And Malinowski has complained about such encyclopedic surveys as collections of "customs, beliefs and rules of conduct floating in the air."[44] But for all the objections raised by these "contextualists," the work of Westermarck and Hobhouse can be admired for its perhaps impossible, yet nevertheless fascinating global sweep of the almost endless variety of religious ethics. The value of encyclopedic comparison may lie simply in its capacity to document that diversity.

Morphological Comparison

To interpret and perhaps understand the diversity of religious ethics we need to uncover the patterns beneath the appearances. This is the work of morphological comparisons. It is similar to comparative anatomy: A human being and a pig may very well be different, but they have analogous underlying skeletal structures. Although systems of religious ethics are certainly different, there may be characteristic types, patterns, and processes of ethical action that can be compared by analogy. The most important work in morphological analysis in the history of religions has been done by Mircea Eliade. His *Patterns in Comparative Religion,* for example, provides an inventory of symbolic patterns, or what he calls *archetypes,* that appear in a wide range of different religious traditions.[45] This recognition of patterns, however, does not imply that such archetypes actually exist; it simply suggests that human beings organize their religious experience within certain recurring symbolic forms. A morphological approach to the study of religious ethics is sensitive to the characteristic patterns and processes that organize ethical experience.

These patterns, which represent the basic conditions of possibility for ethical action in the history of religions, appear on two levels. First, there is the pattern of basic generative challenges inherent in human life: the challenges posed by the different stages of the human life cycle and the challenges posed by human social relations. The challenges of personal development and interpersonal relations are interwoven in any given society, but these challenges are the fundamental conditions within which systems of personal and social ethics are generated within religious traditions. Second, there are the observable patterns of ethical response to these challenges. A comparative anatomy of ethical traditions might reveal that although there is great diversity, there is a limited range of possibilities for responding to the challenges of the life cycle and social relations. The identification of recurring patterns of ethical action may serve as a first step in the interpretation of the conditions of possibility for religious ethics.

Temporal Comparison

Temporal comparison is used to make sense out of the historical record; it documents both continuity and change in human history. The problem with temporal comparison in the history of religions, including the work of Westermarck and Hobhouse on religious ethics, is that it has often been used to support a theory of cultural evolution. Many early historians of religion at the turn of the century were influenced by the Darwinian model of evolution. They argued that religion was a primitive stage in the development of the human species and that it would dissolve as human beings evolved into the new world opened up by modern science. This view, of course, is a heavily biased approach to temporal comparisons. It reflects strong ideological commitments to modern values of science and technological progress. It would be hard to argue, however, that a modern age that has produced global conflicts, the horrors of the holocaust, and the prospect of nuclear annihilation is necessarily more highly evolved in matters of religion and ethics. Such evolutionary theories of religion distort the historical record through temporal comparisons.

Nevertheless, there is an important role for temporal comparison, as long as it is recognized that the changes that can be observed are not necessarily better and are not necessarily inevitable. Many of the observable changes in religious ethics in the modern world are the result of major developments in institutional arrangements, technology, and modes of economic production and exchange. Modern developments in medical practice in particular have created new ethical dilemmas involving artificial insemination, life-support systems, genetic engineering, and so on that were simply not present in other historical periods. Traditional religions do continue to serve as resources for ethical guidance, but they are in competition with a new set of values generated by the conditions of the modern world. One of the persistent themes in comparative religious ethics must necessarily be this tension between traditional and modern ethical values. The use of temporal comparison exposes the tension between traditional and modern patterns of ethical action in different stages of the life cycle and in the network of social relations.

Summary: Religion and Ethics in a Comparative Perspective

The comparative perspective of interpretive religious ethics is consistent with the cross-cultural frame of reference of the general history of religions. This perspective locates the basic patterns and processes of ethical action within the multidimensional phenomenon of religion. In order to do this, it must draw upon the widest possible range of historical materials, and it must organize that material in terms of recurrent patterns of action. The patterns that emerge reveal the diverse ways in which religious traditions inform ordinary human behavior in response to the challenges posed by life-cycle transitions and the challenges of collective cooperation in human societies.

From the vantage point of the history of religions, ethics and ritual are integrally connected. Both are normative patterns for action; they define the practical dimension of religion. Ritual functions in sacred times and places, ethics in ordinary situations and circumstances. Traditional systems of religious ethics are grounded in ritual. But traditional religious rituals have lost much of their compelling power, force, and authority over behavior in the modern world. Patterns of ethical action depend to a greater extent on the rationalization of behavior, technological efficiency, and economic ends. Interpretive religious ethics provides an opportunity for observing both the continuity and the change in patterns of ethical action within the history of religions.

PART

ONE

ETHICAL EXPERIENCE IN THE HISTORY OF RELIGIONS

*R*eligious experience has been analyzed in considerable detail by historians, philosophers, and psychologists of religion. Most often the concerns of such analyses focus on the extraordinary manifestations of religious experience: numinous feelings in relation to a transcendent, unapproachable, yet mysteriously attractive deity; mystical experiences of intimate union with the sacred; ascents into higher realms of reality; emotional plunges into the depths of ardent devotion; dramatic conversion experiences; ecstatic states, trance states, and altered states of consciousness. These have all been included within the domain of religious experience. Although such experiences represent an extraordinary, yet characteristic, involvement in the phenomenon of religion, an exclusive concern with these unusual experiences neglects the quality of experience, and the range of experiences, invested in the everyday, ordinary, and even mundane patterns of action supported by systems of religious ethics. Part One presents a schematic outline for analyzing, in all its variety, the experience of being involved in a system of religious ethics.

In Chapter 1 we consider the nature of ethical obligation. First, this chapter suggests that it is necessary to appreciate the role of ritual in traditional systems of religious ethics as a model of perfect, controlled action, which spills over into everyday life and sets up expectations that ordinary human action, in the ordinary situations and circumstances of daily life, could also be brought into a pattern of ritualized perfection. Ritual practices of worship, sacrifice, prayer, and meditation not only establish models for obligatory action in religious ethics, but they may also cultivate the attitudes required to empower human beings to fulfill the demands of ethical obligation. As the practical dimension of religion, ritual and ethics weave a coordinated pattern of obligation in action. Second, this chapter suggests that religious ethics is more like aesthetics than logic. Obligation takes the form of images, patterns, styles, and rhythms of action with which behavior must fit, match, or conform. This sense of aesthetic fittingness is central to the pattern and process of ethical obligation in the history of religions. This first chapter is called *Obligation*.

Chapter 2 examines the range of possible human responses to the demands of obligation. A typology of responses can be suggested: moral, disciplinary, antinomian, and improvisational responses. Each response involves a qualitatively different experience in relation to the sacred norms embodied in a sense of ethical obligation. Each is a different disposition of human desire with regard to obligation. One variation of the improvisational response is found in the tradition of western philosophical ethics. Here the independent, improvised criteria of reason, proposed in different schools of philosophical ethics, have been applied to judge, evaluate, and call into question the authority of traditional sacred norms in religious ethics. But comparative religious ethics suggests that ethical responsibility in the history of religions is not confined to exercises of moral reason or rational justifications for standards of behavior. Rather, ethical responsibility is the ability to respond, in a variety of ways, to the patterns of sacred meaning and power invested in ethical obligation within religious communities and traditions. This second chapter is called *Response*.

Chapter 3 explores the dynamics of feelings of disturbance, distress, and anxiety, which may arise when a person is in conflict with obligation.

These experiences of ethical conflict fall under the term *dissonance*. Ethical dissonance in the history of religions is manifested as shame and guilt. Dissonant experiences are found within complex patterns of defilement and purification, sin and judgment, and the symbolism of evil. Ethical dissonance may be, in fact, the single most important experience within many systems of religious ethics because it signifies a direct, intense involvement with the demands of obligation, even when actions do not conform to its requirements. When behavior is out of alignment with expectations that are supported by a sense of ethical obligation, the inevitable result is some degree of dissonance. This third chapter is called *Dissonance*.

Chapter 4 surveys representative mechanisms for easing, resolving, or eliminating dissonance, and for achieving a certain degree of ethical harmony, that have been devised within religious traditions. There are two kinds of strategies of harmony: (1) ritual actions of catharsis, purification, exchange, confession, absolution, penance, and so on, which resolve the dissonance produced by specific actions that are contrary to the pattern of obligation; and (2) the cultivation of internal dispositions, virtues, or qualities of character that resolve the dissonance produced by desires that are in discord with the pattern of obligation. The aesthetic tension between dissonance and harmony is at the heart of ethical experience in the history of religions. These patterns of ritual and ethical action are employed to resolve the dissonance that prevents an experience of ethical harmony in action. This final chapter of Part One is called *Harmony*.

CHAPTER

ONE

OBLIGATION

A ny system of religious ethics weaves together a fabric of duties, responsibilities, and imperatives that produces a powerful sense of obligation. Where do human beings derive the sense that they "ought" to do certain things, to behave in certain ways, to cultivate certain virtues and values? Where does this sense of obligation come from? Obligation is at the heart of religion. Some indication of the central importance of obligation for religion may be suggested by the etymology of the Latin word *religio,* which comes either from *religare,* meaning "to bind oneself," or from *relegere,* meaning "scrupulous observance."[1] Religion may therefore consist primarily in binding obligation and/or scrupulous observance of specific norms that govern behavior. The power of ethical obligation in religious traditions is derived from myth and ritual. These powerful symbolic forms of belief and action define the normative context within which a sense of ethical obligation takes shape.

Myths relate stories of a higher, more enduring reality that determines the present human condition. The sacred stories that narrate the primordial acts of gods, ancestors, and heroes provide a symbolic charter for human behavior in both ritual and ethics. The sacred knowledge acquired through myth, as the anthropologist Bronislaw Malinowski has observed, "supplies man with the motive for ritual and moral actions, as well as indications as to how to perform them."[2] Myth is invoked within religious traditions when ritual and ethics require authoritative justification, the warrant of antiquity, and a sense of sanctity in action.

But it is not enough simply to know what to do. Human beings must also feel empowered to fulfill the demands of obligation. Ritual provides a sense of contact with sacred powers. Set apart from ordinary times and places, ritual actions create a highly structured and controlled context within which human beings gain access to a sense of sacred power. Ritual creates a kind of communications network to mediate sacred power, and this reservoir of power, generated in sacred times and places, is felt to spill over into the ordinary challenges of daily life. "The believer who has communicated with his god," the sociologist Emile Durkheim observed, "is not merely a man who sees new truths of which the unbeliever is ignorant; he is a man who is *stronger*. He feels within himself a force, either to endure the trials of existence or to conquer them."[3] This sense of power provides important resources within religious traditions for meeting the demands of obligation.

Ethical standards in the history of religions presuppose a context of worship, communication, and interaction with sacred powers that is acted out in ritual. The norms that govern ethical behavior are predicated upon a certain relation between human beings and what they hold to be sacred. As the sociologist of religion Max Weber noted, religious traditions tend "to treat legal prescriptions in exactly the same manner that they treat ceremonial and ritual norms. All law is

sacred law."[4] The sense of obligation in religious ethics can best be interpreted by examining the norms, rules, and values embodied in ritual action.

Finally, obligation requires that individuals conform their behavior to authoritative patterns of action; there must be a certain fit between behavior and obligatory norms. The demand for fitting action in religious ethics suggests an aesthetic dimension to ethical experience. Obligation operates as an artistic design, pattern, or picture that people try to imitate through their actions. This imitative, or mimetic, quality of religious ethics is an aesthetic process. Ethical obligation functions as an artistic design to be produced on the painter's canvas, as a musical score to be performed through the musician's instrument, as a dramatic script to be enacted on the stage. These artistic processes require an aesthetic fit between an ideal pattern and an actual performance. The creative struggle to produce aesthetically fitting actions is at the heart of the ethical experience of obligation.

Ritual in the History of Religions

Ritual actions are patterns of sacred obligation. Characteristic types of ritual action include rituals of sacrifice, methods of worship, festivals of celebration, formulas for prayer, and techniques of meditation. These practices are perceived as necessary, essential, and even binding obligations within the traditions in which they are developed. It will be important to consider the dynamic power inherent in ritual patterns of action, as well as the ways in which ritual is related to religious ethics.

A certain perspective on ritual has emerged in the cross-cultural study of religions. Patterns of ritual action have basic characteristics that can be

identified in a five part definition of ritual. Ritual is (1) symbolic action (2) that focuses a certain kind of power (3) through the use of natural symbols; (4) this power transforms the participant's experience of time and space (5) in the face of human limit situations. These five aspects provide a descriptive definition of ritual as it appears in religious traditions. They are common features of ritual action, whether it appears in primal, archaic, traditional, or modern religions. Each aspect of the definition needs to be explored in more detail. The ritual practices within the Christian tradition can be used to illustrate each part of the definition.

Symbolic Action

Rituals are essentially symbolic actions. The ritual sacraments of baptism and eucharist within the Christian tradition are meaningful actions because they have significance within a larger context of religious symbolism. The actions of washing in baptism, and the actions of eating bread and drinking wine in the communal meal of the Lord's Supper, are meaningful actions because they are part of a larger religious system of signification. The reservoir of symbolic reference for these performative significant actions is myth. The historian of religions Mircea Eliade emphasized the importance of the mythic charter that supports Christian rituals. Baptism and eucharist symbolically re-enact events in the authoritative scriptural narrative of the life of Jesus that "begins with the nativity at Bethlehem and ends, provisionally, with the Ascension."[5] These rituals are obvious symbolic re-enactments of mythic prototypes in the life of the founder of the tradition. The ritual participation with water, bread, and wine derives its symbolic significance from acting out certain elements in the normative myth of the tradition.

Sacred Power

These symbolic actions are experienced as vehicles of sacred power. The historian of religions Joachim Wach defined ritual as "an instrument of divine power."[6] In Christian ritual, according to Wach, Christ is perceived as the single sacred power that is manifested through various sacramental actions. Regardless of how many different Christian rituals might be catalogued (the medieval theologian Hugh of St. Victor listed as many as 30 sacraments), they are all regarded as trans-

missions of one power. Eliade felt that the notion of power in religious ritual is clarified by the radical distinction between the sacred and the profane. The unique power that is focused through ritual is in antithetical opposition to profane, ordinary, or mundane existence. The power generated in ritual, therefore, is understood to be categorically different from the kinds of power exercised in ordinary life.

Natural Symbols

Ritual utilizes natural symbols in order to focus sacred power. The paradox in the antithesis between sacred and profane lies in the fact that ritual necessarily involves the use of natural objects. Ritual symbols are drawn from the objects, artifacts, and activities of everyday life, but these ordinary things are used in extraordinary ways; they become symbolic instruments of sacred power. The employment of natural symbols in religious rituals involves, according to Eliade, "the consecration of human life itself, the sacrality with which man's vital functions (food, sex, work, and so on) can be charged."[7] It may well be the case that nothing is sacred in itself unless ritualization sanctifies it.

The ritual of water baptism represents, as Eliade observed, the "religious valorization of the waters."[8] As such, baptism can be interpreted with reference to cross-cultural examples of water symbolism in the history of religions. Water displays a fairly consistent range of symbolic associations. The natural symbolism of water seems to be essentially two-fold: It represents the dissolution of old forms and the source for new potential. Water's dual symbolism tends to be present in any ritual of immersion, where the form of the old individual dissolves and a new individual emerges. This process takes place in religious rituals of purification, lustration, and baptism. "What is immersed in it," Eliade suggests, "'dies' and, rising again from the water, is like a child without any sin or any past, able to receive a new revelation and begin a new and a real life."[9]

Interpretations of the ritual of baptism from within the Christian tradition seem to bear out this understanding of the natural symbolism of water. First, ritualization transforms water into a natural instrument of sacred power. The second century North African Church Father Tertullian described this process in his *De Baptismo:*

> *All waters, in virtue of the pristine privilege of their origin, do, after invocation of God, attain the sacramental power of sanctification; for the Spirit immediately supervenes from the heavens, and rests over the waters, sanctifying them from Himself; and being thus sanctified, they imbibe at the same time the power of sanctifying.*[10]

Tertullian understood the sanctification of the water used in baptism as a re-enactment of the movement of the spirit across the face of the primordial waters described in the creation account of *Genesis.* Second, the ritualization of water in baptism involves the natural associations of aquatic symbols: dissolving the old form and giving birth to new potential. The Eastern Orthodox Church Father John Chrysostom suggests the importance of these elements in his understanding of baptism by declaring that "when we plunge our heads into the water as into a sepulcher, the old man is immersed, buried wholly; when we come out of the water, the new man appears at the same time."[11]

The eucharistic ritual of communion, the sacrament of bread and wine, participates in what might be called the natural symbolic structure of eating. Just as the natural symbolism of water consistently tends to involve certain necessary associations, the archetypal symbolism of eating also involves certain characteristic layers of religious meaning. According to Eliade, "Eat-

ing signifies assimilating a part of the cosmos, or more precisely, the mystical essence of the cosmos." The natural symbols of swallowing, digesting, and assimilating food and drink reveal "the importance of eating for the moral and spiritual development of man."[12] The ritualization of these activities invests them with a unique sacred power. In the eucharist, the participant is understood to assimilate that sacred power through the natural symbolism of eating.

Time and Space

Rituals are performed in special arenas of human action marked out by sacred time and sacred space. Natural symbols are sanctified because they appear within the extraordinary context of sacred occasions and places. But more fundamentally, the participant's ordinary experience of time and space may be disrupted, altered, and transformed by ritual events. The alteration in the sense of time does not simply occur because rituals occur at special times to mark life-cycle transitions, holy days in the sacred calendar, or periods of social crisis. In ritual the participant is symbolically removed from the flow of ordinary time and enters the sacred time of myth. The ritual liturgy of the Christian tradition, which is a commemoration of the life and passion of Christ, abolishes the separations of historical time and makes the participants contemporaries with Christ. In the words of Eliade, these rituals are "in fact a reactualization of those days."[13] As such, participants transcend the sequential flow of ordinary time in a ritual return to sacred time.

Rituals also transform the participant's experience of space. This is not simply because the sites for ritual action tend to be set apart from ordinary places. Ritual does occur within special sacred enclosures, but there is also a sense of overcoming the kinds of spatial separations that affect ordinary experience. In Christian rituals, for example, the participant is able to enter into a sanctified space that is continuous with the space in which Christ resides. Ritual provides opportunities for the symbolic transcendence of the limits of ordinary space.

Limit Situations

The ritual transformation of human experience in time and space occurs in the face of human limit situations. A limit situation—from the Latin *limen*—represents a threshold, a crossing, or a transition in human life. We tend to think of limits as walls; but in ritual they are doors to pass through. Rituals respond to limit situations: the passage through different life-cycle transitions, the passage from one social group to another, and ultimately the passage through death. Ritual responses to the human awareness of death, as the final limit situation, are important ways in which religions act out whatever they may hold to be the ultimate meaning of life. Joachim Wach noted that "the life of one who lives in the knowledge of death, in the awareness of what death really is and how it functions in existence, will be lived differently from the life of one whose knowledge and understanding of himself does not include the awareness of such a life-death relationship."[14] Religious rituals provide ways of acting out this awareness of the necessary relationship between life and death.

In Christian ritual the sacred power of baptism and eucharist is partly derived from their capacity for creating a symbolic situation in which death comes within the sphere of human control. In baptism's symbolic death and rebirth, and the eucharist's ritual enactment of the death of Christ, perfect environments are created in which human beings achieve a certain power over death. The ritual mediation of the life-death relationship is found in Christian rituals in which the individual symbolically participates in the liminal crisis of death by participating in the death and rebirth of Christ. In baptism the participant is "buried into the death of Christ . . . so that as Christ was raised from the dead by the glory of the Father, we too might walk in newness of life" (Rom 6:3–4). And in the eucharist, "as often as you eat this bread and drink this cup, you proclaim the Lord's death until he comes" (I Cor 10:16; 11:26). These rituals illustrate the way in which religious ritualization can respond to the ultimate challenges of life and death.

Religious rituals are symbolic actions that focus sacred power through natural symbols, which are used in special times and places. They tend to arise in the limit situations of human life and death. Although these symbolic actions are an essential part of the practical dimension of any religion, there may be great diversity in the actual ritual practices within different traditions. Obligation is defined by specific ritual practices. It will be important, at this point, to consider a brief survey of the relation between ritual and ethical obligation in the history of religions.

Ritual and Ethics in Primal Religions

The central ritual act in primal religious traditions is sacrifice. The sacrificial killing of animals, the offering of the fruits of the field, and the ceremonious presentation of various potions, libations, and sacred objects may all appear at different times and occasions within the ritual practice of primal religions. The significance of such sacrifices may be difficult to interpret. The sacrificial act draws its meaning from the context in which it is performed: Sacrifice might be an act of thanksgiving offered to the gods, ancestors, or spirits that support human life; it might be a celebration of communion in which human and divine beings share in the common feast from the sacrificial animal; or it might be a special offering to restore the harmony of the community and the cosmos, which may have been disrupted by some sin, impurity, or defilement. These interpretations may all come into play at one time or another in the self-understanding of those who participate in ritual sacrifice.[15]

To appreciate the significance of any particular sacrificial ritual it is necessary to consider how it operates in the context of the community that practices it. The bear sacrifice practiced by many hunting communities in the circumpolar regions of Siberia provides an illuminating illustration of the significance of animal sacrifice as an important ritual act in one form of primal religion. And it suggests the importance of that ritual for the ethical life of the community.

Bear Sacrifice

The archaeological record of human prehistory indicates that small-scale subsistence-level communities, based on the arts of hunting and gathering, formed the basis for human societies for countless millennia before recorded history. On the human time line, a vast expanse is occupied exclusively by hunters and gatherers. For societies that are based on some form of settled agriculture, hunting is an activity that may supplement their economy. But for hunting societies it is the very heart of the support and survival of the community. The European colonizers of North America in the seventeenth century had a difficult

time understanding the hunting and gathering societies they encountered. European civilization was based on settled agriculture and animals raised for slaughter; hunting was the nobility's leisure pastime in private game reserves. For this reason, the Europeans believed that the Native Americans they encountered in the new world did not work. But the hunting, tracking, and killing of animals is the basic form of work for the Native Americans, as well as for other hunting societies. Hunting also forms the basis for a network of religious beliefs and ritual practices.

One religious ritual that is fairly common among Siberian hunting societies is the ceremony of bear sacrifice.[16] In this periodic festival, a special bear is ritually killed. The bear is taken into the village, displayed in a cage, and treated with great honor, respect, and courtesy. The villagers raise this bear with all the care and concern that would be shown to a member of a human family. After several years this tamed, domesticated bear becomes the central focus of the religious festival. The bear is escorted through the village and made to dance, play, and walk on its hind legs in the celebration. With great ceremony the bear is then tied down and addressed with ritual poetry. The villagers ask the bear to return to the spirit world of its ancestors and to testify to how well it has been treated by human beings. Finally, the bear is killed according to special rules, and the meat is divided among the community according to each person's rank and position in that hunting society. This feast concludes the bear ceremony.

Hunting Ethics

The bear sacrifice ritual dramatizes the community's sense of ethical obligation toward the animals upon which it depends for survival. Within this formal and highly structured ritual process, the care and respect for animal life is demonstrated. The ritual is closely linked with the ethics of the hunt; these hunters are able to describe precisely how the hunting of bears ought to be conducted. Ethnographers have collected reports of the ethical norms, rules, and regulations for bear hunting provided by the hunters themselves. These rules specify that a bear may be killed only if it is facing the hunter. In some accounts, the bear may be killed only if it is standing on its hind legs and moving toward the hunter. The bear may never be killed when it is sleeping in its den, unable to defend itself, or running away from the hunter.

The central obligation in bear hunting ethics is that a hunter should never kill a bear that is not offering itself to be killed. For this reason, the hunter is to meet and kill the bear face to face; according to some reports, the hunter is required to talk to the bear, address it with poetry, and even sing love songs to it. One ethnographer describes some of these obligations:

> *The Yakuts say that if one kills a bear in his hibernation den, without taking care to awake or warn him, other bears will attack the hunter while he sleeps. A Nanay hunter, upon encountering a bear in the open does not kill him at once, but begins by addressing dithyrambic praise poems to him and then prays that the bear will not claw him. Finally he addresses the bear: "You have come to me, Lord Bear, you wish me to kill you . . . . Come here, come. Your death is at hand, but I will not chase after you."* [17]

These descriptions of hunting ethics reveal a pattern of norms, rules, and regulations that defines a basic sense of ethical obligation in the ordinary activities of a bear hunting society.

A problem arises, however, when it becomes apparent that this is not in fact how they actually hunt bears. Actual descriptions of bear hunting point out a striking difference between ethical obligation and ordinary practice. The Koryak and Chukchi hunters, while hunting bears in winter, will trap the bear by rolling a log in front of the den's opening; the hunters then cave in the roof and stab the helpless bear to death. In other months, when they encounter a bear out in the open, hunters will first set packs of dogs on it to wear it down. The hunting practices of the Nivkhi illustrate the discrepancy between ethical obligation and actual behavior. Their hunting rules require that they fight the bear fairly, face to face, and with all the obligatory signs of honor and respect. But the way they actually kill bears is quite different. One account of their bear hunting practices reveals that "a spear, the head of which is covered with spikes, is laid on the ground, a cord is attached to it and, as the bear approaches [the ambush] the hunter [by pulling up on the cord] raises the weapon and the animal becomes impaled on it." [18] This account suggests that there is a dissonance between the norms, rules, and principles of obligation and the actual behavior involved in the hunt.

Ritual provides a means of overcoming the dissonance between the pattern of obligation and the actual practices of the hunt. The bear ceremonial allows the basic obligations of the hunt to be meticulously observed; the ritual offers a controlled environment in which action can conform to an ideal image of order. By constructing a unique, sacred pattern of action, the ritual process is able to control all the various circumstances, accidents, and uncontrollable occurences that may disrupt the sense of living in an ordered human world. Jonathan Z. Smith has recently analyzed ritual along these lines:

> *Among other things, ritual represents the creation of a controlled environment where the variables (i.e., the accidents) of ordinary life may be displaced precisely because they are felt to be so overwhelmingly present and powerful. Ritual is a means of performing the way things ought to be in conscious*

tension with the way things are in such a way that their ritualized perfection is recollected in the ordinary, uncontrolled, course of things.[19]

The ritualized perfection of the bear sacrifice enacts all the necessary hunting obligations held by the community. The pattern of this perfect hunt, symbolized in ritual, may be recalled in the ordinary situations and circumstances of hunting, where things do not always happen as they ought to happen. The bear sacrifice in these circumpolar hunting societies illustrates the close relation between ritual and ethical obligation. It suggests that ritual provides important resources for harmonizing the dissonance that occurs when behavior in ordinary, daily life does not conform to the demands of ethical obligation.

Ritual and Ethics in Archaic Religions

Ancient civilizations were based on the centralized power and authority of divine kings and royal priesthoods. The authority of these ancient institutions was localized in the sacred space marked out by a city, and this authority emanated from the city to include often vast areas under its domain. The historian Paul Wheatley observed that the formation of cities in the ancient world provided a distinctive ethical ordering of the human world. The city was the political center of royal power, but it also supported elaborate temple complexes, sacred architectures, and powerful priesthoods. As Wheatley noted, these "instruments in the creation of political, social, economic and sacred space, at the same time, were symbols of cosmic, social and moral order."[20] These sacred institutions of political and religious power reinforced the divine pattern of cosmic order as it was recreated in the human world. The ritual power of divine kings and royal priesthoods sustained this order, and their power was closely linked to the patterns of ethical obligation. The necessary connection between ritual and ethics can be briefly illustrated by considering the ethical standards in the religions of ancient Egypt and Mesopotamia.

Ancient Egypt

In ancient Egypt ethical standards emerged out of the ritual procedures, established by the priesthood, for preparing a person for the passage through death. In the earliest *Pyramid Texts* those rituals were exclusively reserved for the king, or pharoah; but in the later *Coffin Texts* and *The Egyptian Book of the Dead* the texts suggest that these rituals were performed for persons of wealth and prestige. These rituals included embalming and mummifying the body, chanting prayers and magical formulas, and teaching the person precisely what should be done and said in order to pass successfully into the land of the dead. *The Egyptian Book of the Dead* is a tour guide to the world of the dead. In addition to detailed ritual instructions, it provides a visionary journey through the other world. There the deceased enters the judgment hall of Osiris to be judged according to the supreme ethical standard of *Ma'at*. The deceased's heart will be weighed against this cosmic standard of truth and order.

At this point the text makes a list of ethical laws that must not have been transgressed in order to move successfully through the judgment of the dead. This list of ethical obligations has been called the Negative Confessions because it consists of a catalogue of ethical violations that the deceased has not committed. The dead is instructed to declare: "I have not defrauded the humble man of his property. I have not done what the gods abominate. I have not vilified a slave to his master. I have not inflicted pain. I have not caused anyone to go hungry. I have not made any man weep. I have not committed murder." These declarations of ethical innocence culminate with the exclamation, "I am pure. I am pure. I am pure."[21] This ethical purity is grounded in ritual; the deceased would not have been able to declare his innocence if the necessary rituals had not first been performed. The demands of religious obligation require both ritual and ethical purity in order for the deceased to be permitted into the halls of Osiris and to achieve eternal life.

Ancient Mesopotamia

Ethical obligation in the religious worldview of ancient Mesopotamia was clearly based on the ritual authority of divine kingships. The gods maintained the luminous order of the universe; the king maintained that order on earth. The scholar of Mesopotamian religion Leo Oppenheim has emphasized the importance of the symbolism of light in the understanding of both gods and kings in ancient Mesopotamia.

> *The deity in Mesopotamia is experienced as an awesome and fear inspiring phenomenon endowed with a unique, unearthly, and terrifying luminosity. Luminosity is considered a divine attribute and is shared in varying degrees of intensity by all things*

considered divine and holy, hence also by the king himself.[22]

The divine king, as representative of the luminous gods on earth, held absolute authority to govern the ethical behavior of all his subject people.

Babylonian King Hammurabi's code of laws, which is one of the most comprehensive ethical codes in the ancient world, is based upon this ritual format of divine kingship. The Code of Hammurabi is preserved on a stone monument currently housed in the Louvre. A carved relief shows Hammurabi receiving his authority to write his code of laws directly from Shamash, the sun god. The sun god has supreme authority over human behavior as it is mediated through the ethical code of the divine king. The detailed legislation regarding property rights, business transactions, prohibition of murder, and so on, as well as the authority to punish any transgressions, is grounded in the ritual relations established by the institution of divine kingship.[23]

The central ethical obligation incumbent upon ordinary individuals is to know and to keep their place in the larger pattern of cosmic order. The Babylonian legends collected in the *Gilgamesh Epic* suggest that the place reserved for human beings in the overarching cosmic order is defined by their mortality. Gilgamesh, the hero of the epic, is exhorted to accept the fact that "when the gods created man, they let death be his share, and life withheld in their own hands."[24] The quest for an immortality that would elevate human beings to the level of the gods is ultimately futile. The most that can be expected is to find pleasure in work, home, and family. The primary ethical obligations require that human beings cultivate that place in the cosmic order that they have been allotted. Ritual actions that support the gods, and ethical actions that maintain human beings in their given place, both serve to sustain the distinctive order of the cosmos.

Ritual and Ethics in Traditional Religions

Traditional systems of religious ethics may combine the obligation for human beings to know and keep their place in the cosmic order with exhortations to go beyond, rise above, or transcend that place through prescribed sets of religious practices. Although there are patterns of action that serve to reinforce that sense of place, there are other patterns of action that serve to direct human beings on a trajectory out of this world and into a higher, better, and more enduring reality. In all cases, ritual practices support the specific patterns of ethical obligation that emerge in each tradition. This necessary relation between ritual and ethics can be suggested by a brief survey of eastern and western traditional religions.

Eastern Traditions

Ethical obligation's dependence on ritual can be illustrated in the religious traditions of India and China. The Hindu renunciate, the Buddhist monk, the Confucian sage, and the Taoist mystic all cultivate certain patterns of action that, to one degree or another, transcend the ordinary world. These patterns of transcendence are grounded in specific ritual and ethical practices. The ethical norms, rules, and values that shape action in ordinary, everyday life emerge in a context of action defined by ritual.

Hinduism   The basic ethical code within the Hindu tradition of India presupposes a ritual context of sacrifice (*yajna*) and worship (*puja*). Ritual forms of sacrifice, worship, and the disci-

plined study of sacred texts are intricately interwoven into the pattern of ethical life that is outlined in the *Laws of Manu*. As a collection of ethical rules in the Hindu tradition, the *Laws of Manu* is an important resource for understanding how Hindu ethics responds to the challenges of the life cycle and social relations. At this point it is simply necessary to recognize how that sense of ethical obligation is related to ritual.

The central concept of ethical obligation is *dharma*. A specific *dharma*—set of ethical rules, duties, and responsibilities—applies to individuals at each level of the social structure and in each stage of the life cycle. Each social class within the hierarchy of traditional Hindu society had its own dharma to perform. Different ethical obligations were incumbent upon the different social classes: priests, warriors, agriculturalists, and servants. Dharma, however, was not simply an ethical concept of duty; it was perceived as a principle of social order that was derived from the very nature of the cosmos.

The *Rig Veda,* part of the most ancient Hindu scriptures, relates a myth that explains the origin of the four social classes as the result of an original sacrifice offered by the gods. The primordial cosmic man Purusha was sacrificed by the gods, and his body became the four social classes that comprised traditional Hindu social life. The *Rig Veda* declares: "His mouth became the Brahmin; his arms were made into the Warrior; his thighs the People, and from his feet the Servants were born." Each class had its unique ethical duty to fulfill, its own dharma. The primary ethical obligation that was binding on each class was to know and perform the dharma that was appropriate to its place in the social and cosmic order. This entire ethical design was produced by a primordial ritual act, and the pattern of obligation that was produced was specified in terms of ritual laws. The passage from the *Rig Veda* concludes: "With the sacrifice the gods sacrificed to the sacrifice. These were the first ritual laws."[25] Each class was obligated to maintain the ritual and ethical laws appropriate to its position in the social hierarchy.

The ethical principle that accounted for an individual's placement in a particular social class was *karma*. *Karma* literally means action. The term was used for the ritual actions prescribed by the Vedas; *karman* referred to the spiritual power derived from performing the sacrifices. Karma acquired special ethical significance in Hindu thought. It represented the idea that all actions have built-in ethical consequences. An individual's actions will produce corresponding consequences in this life and in future lives. Karma is a mechanical cycle of cause and effect: As you sow, you reap. The consequences of actions extend over a series of lifetimes. An individual's placement in a particular social class was felt to be a natural consequence of the relative ethical character of the past karma. Status in future lives will be the karmic result of the individual's response to the present demands of obligation.

For the three higher classes, the *Laws of Manu* suggests, there are different obligations at each stage of the life cycle. The pattern of life-cycle stages—*asramas*—implies that life is a progression of changing obligations: First, the student must be devoted to the study of sacred texts; second, the householder must work to support a family; third, the forest dweller must leave family to follow the disciplines of yoga in an ascetic community; and fourth, the renunciate must withdraw from all worldly action and direct every energy toward liberation from the karmic cycle of action. This final stage in the life cycle is a culmination of an ethical life devoted to dharma, but it signifies a supreme transcendence of place. The ritual and ethical obligations of dharma prepare the individual for a radical liberation from the world of action at the end of the life cycle.

At each stage of the life cycle, individuals have different responsibilities for maintaining the ritual practice of the tradition. Even the householder must conform his daily life to the demands of ritual. The landowner, agriculturalist, or trader, involved in the daily management of wealth and property, must offer the sacrifice of the *Agnihotra,* or fire sacrifice, prescribed in the ancient Vedas. He must perform the rituals appropriate to those days in the sacred calendar when the sun and moon are in certain positions in the heavens. In the midst of the gaining of wealth, the practice of farming, and the conduct of business, the *Laws of Manu* exhorts: "Let him untired perform daily the rites prescribed for him in the Vedas." The ongoing study of sacred texts, begun during his student days, must continue to provide a ritual framework for fulfilling all other obligations. His work must be in harmony with the devotion to the sacred texts of the tradition. The *Laws of Manu* continues: "Let him avoid all [means of acquiring] wealth which impede the study of the Vedas; [let him maintain himself] anyhow, because that [devotion to the Veda-study secures] the realization of his aims."[26] The rituals of sacrifice, worship, and study are intricately interwoven into the pattern of daily ethical life outlined in the *Laws of Manu*.

Buddhism

Traditional Buddhist thought assumes the principle of karma in its basic understanding of practical action, but it tends to place a more concentrated emphasis on achieving liberation from the karmic world of action. That radical liberation is referred to as *nirvana;* it literally means extinguishing the flame of desire that binds a person to the world of action. At the center of Buddhist thought is a radical critique of the desiring, clinging, and grasping after experience in the world that inevitably produces human suffering. The goal of Buddhist practice is to eliminate the causes and conditions of suffering through radical detachment; the central ritual techniques involve forms of meditation.

The *Majjhima-nikāya* is a traditional Buddhist text that outlines the Eightfold Path that leads to the liberation from suffering. It is a therapeutic program designed to cultivate detachment. The culmination of this program is meditative practice—specific ritual techniques of detachment—that effectively removes the practitioner from the cycle of action and from the experience of suffering that is inherent in action. The Eightfold Path outlines the proper attitudes, behaviors, and meditation techniques that allow for a radical detachment from the world of desire. The elements of the path are outlined as follows:

1. *Right View* aware of suffering in human life, the knowledge of its cause, and a sense of the possibility of its extinction

2. *Right Aspiration* dedicates the Buddhist to the goals of detachment, renunciation, and harmlessness in the world

3. *Right Speech* not false, slanderous, or harsh

4. *Right Behavior* abstains from killing, theft, or sensory pleasures

5. *Right Mode of Livelihood* preferably as a monk removed from the world

6. *Right Endeavor* directs every effort toward the liberation from suffering

7. *Right Mindfulness* becomes conscious of the nature of physical, emotional, and mental states in order to control them

8. *Right Meditation* aloof from the world in a state of joyful liberation[27]

Buddhist ethics may be viewed as a preparation for nirvana; the ethical obligations that govern ordinary behavior provide a foundation from which the work of mindfulness and meditation can begin. Ethics (*sila*) teaches the proper attitudes and behavior that will allow the Buddhist to effectively practice the liberating ritual techniques of meditation. However, the very character of these ethical obligations depends upon the kind of dispositions that are nurtured through meditation techniques. The ethical values of detachment, harmlessness, and equanimity, which are embodied in specific Buddhist rules governing conduct, are cultivated through the ritual disciplines of meditation. Traditional Buddhism involves this reciprocal relationship between ritual and ethical obligations: Ethics provides the necessary training, but meditation rituals cultivate the necessary inner dispositions that enable the Buddhist to fulfill the requirements of obligation.

Confucianism

The religion of ancient China was based on the perception of a pervasive cosmic harmony. As in many other archaic religions, that harmony was displayed in the heavens and focused on earth through the authority of the royal emperor. The divine heavens (*Ti'en*) represented both a cosmic and ethical order in the universe; the ancient Chinese Book of Rites declared: "The courses of the heavenly [bodies] supply the most perfect lessons."[28] The pattern of cosmic order revealed by the heavens was referred to as the *Tao*. This term signified the supreme order, balance, and harmony that was evident in the Way of the universe. The emperor and the priesthood were responsible for maintaining that harmony through regular rituals of sacrifice. Through ritual action, or *li,* it was felt that the harmony of the cosmos was sustained and the unity of the people was strengthened.

The Chinese sage Confucius (Kung Fu-tse), emerging from this religious context, extended the principle of li over both ceremonial and ethical behavior. Li represented the harmonious order of both ritual and ethical action. The ultimate Confucian values of humaneness and righteousness (*jen* and *i*) were the product of careful education, training, and discipline in proper ritual practice and good conduct. According to traditional Confucian computations, there were 300 major ritual rules and 3000 minor observances that must be mastered. The obligations of ritual not only extended over the sacrifices, but also proper garments, body postures, gestures, music, and so on, which all contributed to harmonious ritual practice. Li represented a highly refined aesthetic of ritual conduct.

In ethics this graceful sense of ritual beauty, harmony, and proportion represented an ideal of balance in daily conduct. When asked what the essence of right conduct in life might be, Confucius responded, "It is the word *shu*—reciprocity: Do not do to others what you do not want them to do to you." [29] The harmony of the universe, which is maintained through ritual action, is also achieved by means of reciprocal, balanced, and harmonious human interactions in everyday life. To be in a state of ethical harmony is to conform every aspect of conduct to the harmony of the Tao. By imitating the harmonious balance of the Way of the universe, the Confucian sage demonstrates ethical virtue.

So important was this ideal of harmony, as it was cultivated by the ritual and ethical practices of li, that it was felt to attune all of the individual's inner dispositions to the harmonious order of heaven and earth. In a passage from the *Doctrine of the Mean,* Confucius expresses this ideal of ethical harmony.

> *Before the feelings of pleasure, anger, sorrow, and joy are established, there is equilibrium. The establishment of these feelings in proper measure of each and proper rhythm is called harmony. This equilibrium is the great source of the world; this harmony is the world's universal Way (Tao). With the full attainment of equilibrium and harmony comes the proper ordering of heaven and earth and the nourishment of all things.* [30]

Ritual and ethical obligations within the Confucian tradition were synchronized in the interest of achieving this harmony. Confucian ethics draws its most basic resources from the potential

for harmonizing behavior that lies in ritual. The central ethical obligation is the harmonious ritualization of every aspect of human conduct.

Taoism

The Taoist tradition in China is based on the enigmatic poetry of the *Tao-te ching* of the sage Lao-tzu. This book's 81 chapters describe the nature of the Tao and its power and virtue as a fundamental harmony that permeates the universe. The ethical virtues that flow from being in harmony with the Tao are not the ritualized practices of li. In fact, Lao-tzu suggests, the ethical disciplines of li only appear when true ethical values have declined. The virtues that emanate from a natural state of harmony are spontaneous, effortless, and genuine expressions of an inner attunement with the Tao. "The best man," according to Lao-tzu, "is like water." [31] And like water the Taoist flows effortlessly along the natural channels of life carved out by the Tao. For this reason, the *Tao-te ching* recommends that human beings should "act without action." [32] Ethical action flows from an inner harmony, not from struggling to achieve certain ends. A natural ethical life is one in which people "manifest plainness, embrace simplicity, reduce selfishness, have few desires." [33] Ultimately, "by acting without action, all things will be in order." [34]

The natural order and harmony of the Tao is also realized in the Taoist tradition through specific ritual practices. Taoism is not simply a philosophical attitude toward the world; it is also a religious path of meditation techniques and even magical rituals of transformation. Taoist yoga involves meditation techniques in which a spiritual light is imagined to circulate throughout the body. The circulation of light is felt to harmonize and balance the internal energy flow (*chi*) through the body and allow the meditator to cultivate an inner sense of balance. [35] As in Hindu yoga and Buddhist meditation, the traditional Taoist spiritual exercises nurtured the inner dispositions needed for a person to fulfill the ethical obligations of detachment, desirelessnes, and equanimity. Popular Taoism developed an elaborate array of religious and magical rituals in order to activate the energy of the Tao.[36] Even the natural ethical virtues of harmony could be sustained by ritual participation in the Way and its power.

Western Traditions

Judaism, Christianity, and Islam are ethical monotheisms: They require exclusive belief in one god, and they hold that the one divine being judges human behavior based on specific ethical standards for conduct. They are also textual traditions with sacred scriptures containing outlines of revealed laws for ethical behavior. The Torah, the New Testament, and the Qur'an contain authoritative ethical rules and values for each community. Ethical reflection primarily involves the interpretation and application of these revealed ethical standards as guidelines for behavior in all the situations and circumstances of ordinary life. In each tradition there are normative ritual processes that inform, condition, and empower ethical behavior in response to an overarching sense of obligation.

Judaism   In the Jewish tradition ritual and ethical obligations are interwoven to form a comprehensive normative pattern of action. The rabbis discerned a total of 613 specific laws in the Torah: 248 positive injunctions and 365 negative prohibitions. The majority of these laws are ritual instructions relating to the performance of sacrifices, observances of priests, and requirements of ritual purity. This emphasis suggests that the demands of ethical obligation are grounded in worship and that a truly ethical life is one that is lived in the sacred context that is defined by the ritual covenant with God.

The revelation of the Ten Commandments to Moses on Mount Sinai, related in the mythic narrative of the people of ancient Israel, stands at the heart of that covenant. The ethical code in these commandments clearly depends on proper ritual practice. The first four commandments do not concern the conduct of human behavior in ordinary life, but refer to the proper form of worship. These laws are essentially ritual instructions that define the appropriate manner of worship that should be directed to Yahweh, the God of Israel.

1.   "You shall have no other gods before me" instructs the Israelites not to worship and, more specifically, not to offer sacrifices to other gods.

2.   "You shall not make for yourself a graven image" insists on a style of ritual worship appropriate to a god who is invisible.

3.   "You shall not take the name of the Lord in vain" implies that the invocation of the name of God should only occur in the proper ritual context.

4.   "Remember the sabbath day" sets aside a sacred time in which specific ritual observances are to be performed and the work of ordinary, everyday life is to be suspended. This ritual observation of sacred time was regarded to be so important that later rabbis determined that to observe the sabbath is to fulfill all the ethical laws.

Only with the fifth commandment does the decalogue enter the realm of religious ethics. Ethical standards governing ordinary human conduct are given in the remainder of the Ten Commandments:

5.   "Honor your father and mother"

6.   "You shall not kill"

7. "You shall not commit adultery"

8. "You shall not steal"

9. "You shall not bear false witness against your neighbor"

10. "You shall not covet your neighbor's wife, or his manservant, or his maidservant, or his ox, or his ass, or anything that is your neighbor's"[37]

These last six commands govern the ethical relations between human beings in daily life, but they certainly presuppose the first four ritual commandments that govern the proper relations between human beings and God. In this sense, the ethics of the Hebrew Bible is grounded in ritual.

The Hebrew Bible contains ritual instructions that not only apply to sacrifice, but to the ritualization of everyday life. Perhaps the most basic ritual framework for daily life is provided by the dietary laws of *kashrut*. This is a basic system of ritual classification applied to food. It identifies unclean animals that may not be eaten, prescribes the proper manner of preparing permitted animals, and separates the eating of milk and meat products. Distinctions that have been made by God in the creation of the cosmos apply to the selection and preparation of foods consumed by human beings. Kashrut submits the whole of life, beginning with its most fundamental sustenance, to ritual standards of holiness. The ritual distinction between clean and unclean, which has nothing to do with modern medical notions of hygiene, becomes an ethical obligation that governs the ordinary behavior of eating for Orthodox Jews.[38]

The Hebrew prophets exhorted the people of Israel to a heightened sense of ethical obligation. They often spoke against what they perceived as an exclusive concern for ritual at the expense of ethics. The prophet Amos, for ex-ample, was representative of this attack on ritual. He claimed to speak for the God of Israel:

> *I hate, I spurn your feasts, and I take no pleasures in your festal gatherings . . . And the thank-offerings of your fatted beasts I will not look upon. Take away from me the noise of your songs, and to the melody of your lyres I will not listen. But let justice roll down like waters, and righteousness like a perennial stream. (Amos 5:21–24)*

The prophets, however, did not reject ritual; they only dismissed the value of ritual worship that was not also accompanied by a commitment to personal and social ethics. The prophets emphasized the need to link ritual purity with ethical forms of social action. If ritual is divorced from ethics, then worship is empty.[39]

With the destruction of the Temple in Jerusalem and the displacement of the Jews from Israel in the first century of the common era, the connection between ethics and the rituals of sacrifice was broken. In this context of cultural upheaval, rabbis worked to record the ethical laws that had been preserved in oral tradition. A definitive edition of *Halakha* was produced under the direction of Judah the Prince in the second century. This is called the *Mishna*. The study, interpretation, and application of this text to everyday life became a new kind of ritual activity that informed Jewish ethics. Study itself became a major ritual practice. The ritualized study of Talmud, which is the body of commentaries that surround the text of the Mishna, forms the major resource that defines Jewish ethical obligation and nourishes Jewish ethical life.

Christianity

The documents of the Christian New Testament reveal tensions between a radical faith, which declares that traditional Jewish law is no longer binding in the messianic age ushered in by Jesus, and the need to formulate ethical standards for the early Christian communities. The radical faith in Jesus as Messiah (particularly in the formulations worked out by Paul) was perceived as a transformative inner experience that fulfilled all the traditional demands of the ritual and ethical law. The establishment of a new covenant signified that the revealed law of the Torah, and all of its specific requirements governing circumcision, dietary regulations, sabbath observance, and so on, was not strictly binding for Christians. Freedom from sin was not achieved through observance of the law but by means of redemption through a radical faith in Jesus. The ethical obligations that emerged within early Christianity were based on an inner experience, rather than specific ritual actions. However, there were specific ritual practices that informed and nurtured the cultivation of that inner experience of faith.

The Sermon on the Mount in the Gospel of Matthew records an unconditional ethical standard based on love of God and love of neighbor. It begins with a list of blessings that will be bestowed on those who are poor, sorrowful, gentle, righteous, merciful, pure of heart, and those who are peacemakers, and martyrs. All receive the kingdom. As the tradition developed, even in the first century, this kingdom was defined by those who participate in the two most important rituals of Christianity: baptism and eucharist. Baptism signifies initiation into the community, and eucharist represents an ongoing participation in the body of Christ. Baptism and eucharist provide the ritual context of the present kingdom, as well as the hope of resurrection, which represents the mythic image of the future kingdom. These rituals became the concrete signs and symbols of the kingdom promised by radical faith.

The Sermon on the Mount itself also directly concerns ritual. It instructs Christians in proper sacrifice, which must be performed while at peace with others; proper fasting, which should be done in private and without ostentation, and, most importantly, proper prayer. Prayer is a ritual practice that cultivates the interior faith that is necessary to fulfill Christian ethical obligation. The Lord's Prayer is a ritual formula that invokes the kingdom—"Thy kingdom come"—and submits the individual to the demands of the divine will in both heaven and earth. This prayer is not as concerned with behavior in this world as much as it is with the possibility of forgiveness for actions and attitudes that might alienate the individual from the other-worldly kingdom.

The ritual practice of prayer, however, cultivates the necessary intentions, commitments, and capacities that are required for the fulfillment of ethical obligation. Christian ethics cannot be separated from this ritual practice. As the theologian John A. T. Robinson said, "Prayer and ethics are simply the inside and the outside of the same thing."[40] The primary ethical obligation in the Christian tradition is to act in ways that are consistent with the quality of worship cultivated in the ritual of prayer. This ethical ideal, of course, has not always been realized in practice. The challenges posed by Christianity's institutionalization, expansion, and political power required more detailed codes of ethical law than the simple requirements of faith. The faith nurtured by the ritual of prayer, however, remained a standard against which those ethical codes could be measured.

Islam

Prayer also provides a powerful ritual context for generating the necessary inner dispositions required to fulfill ethical obligation in Islam. Daily life is structured around a pattern of regular prayer. Five times a day the Muslim leaves the concerns of ordinary life for ritualized exercises of formal prayer. Facing the sacred city of Mecca, kneeling in a sacred space marked out by a prayer mat, and lowering the head to the ground, the Muslim ritually communicates with Allah. This ritual cycle of daily prayer cultivates at least two inner dispositions that are felt to be essential to the fulfillment of ethical obligation.

First, the ritual of prayer symbolizes submission to the will of God. *Islam* literally means surrender. Submission to the will of God that is demonstrated by the ritualized posture of prayer is central to the Islamic sense of ethical obligation in daily conduct. The specific ethical requirements of Allah are revealed in the detailed ethical instructions of the Qur'an, the oral instructions and living example of Muhammad as reported in the Hadith, and the clarification of Islamic law that forms the *Shari'ah*. But the attitude that must animate the human response to these ethical obligations is cultivated in the humility, submission, and surrender to Allah, which is demonstrated in regular ritual prayer.

Second, the ritual cycle of prayer five times a day creates a sense of being in the constant presence of God. This awareness of the omnipresence of Allah is essential for the proper response to ethical obligation. A passage in the Hadith reports that according to Muhammad "ethics consists in serving God as if you see Him, for even if you do not see Him, He sees you."[41] The ritual sense of being in the presence of God carries over to ethical behavior: All human conduct stands before the judgment of God; it will be recorded in a divine book and reckoned on the day of resurrection. This sense of acting in the constant presence of Allah is necessarily reinforced through the regular cycle of ritual prayer. Ritual cultivates the inner response to ethical obligation, and it conditions the Muslim to always behave as if in the presence of God.

Ritual and Ethics Summary

The practical dimension of religion produces an interlocking network of ritual and ethical obligations that generates a range of behavioral responses in each religious tradition. To appreciate the power of obligation in religious ethics, it is necessary to first consider patterns of ritual action. In ritual the uncontrollable variables of ordinary human life are eliminated and a perfect image of action is created. This ritualized perfection may then spill over into the ordinary situations and circumstances of daily life, and it may be drawn upon as a source of inspiration, power, and energy that will enable individuals to respond to the challenges of the life cycle and social relations.

The attempt to fit ordinary behavior to the ritualized perfection embodied in sacrifice, worship, meditation, and prayer is essentially an aesthetic process at the heart of religious ethics. We will briefly consider some of the aesthetic qualities inherent in a sense of ethical obligation within the history of religions.

Ethics and Aesthetics

Religious ethics is more aesthetics than logic. Although the ethical process involves considerable thought—we may think about what we do, reason about the best course of action, and rationalize our behavior—religious ethics engages a more fundamental process. We are already acting before we even pause to think about it, and that action flows from more vital sources of energy, desire, and interests than rational reflection. Only rarely do people submit to a discipline of logical reasoning to determine their behavior. We tend to catch ourselves, if we reflect on our behavior at all, midstream in the course of action, acting on images and impulses that precede rational analysis.

The philosopher Ludwig Wittgenstein observed that "Ethics and Aesthetics are one and the same."[42] A religious tradition embodies a certain picture of reality. The forms of life that are generated within that tradition are attempts to fit, match, or conform behavior to that picture. Religious ethics involves aesthetic experiments in harmonizing behavior with normative images of the sacred. This does not mean that ethics and aesthetics are both simply matters of taste; but they are both constituted by aesthetic qualities of order, image, metaphor, symbol, style, structure, pattern, and rhythm. These qualities represent the fundamental aesthetic impulses in religious ethics.

Religious ethics is essentially a creative enterprise striving for harmony between images and actions. It begins with images of who we are and who we could be. These images, symbols, and metaphors are given within religious traditions. Systems of religious ethics create the conditions within which there might be an aesthetic fittingness between a person's sense of identity—the self-image that is shaped through religious symbols, myths, and rituals—and behavior that visibly manifests that self through action. People try to act in ways that fit their self-image. Religious ethics is a living drama: It provides a stage upon which human beings create a dynamic sense of self through the medium of action.

Aesthetic Order

If everyday actions do not seem chaotic, random, or disconnected, it is because some aesthetic order is perceived to provide their design. Systems of religious ethics provide ideal images of order. They give the sense that human beings are acting in an ordered universe. To develop a sense of identity people need to have a sense of order. Aesthetic qualities of order—perspective, proportion, and orientation—generate a meaningful context within which a sense of self-identity can emerge. The sociologist Hans Mol observed: "Maximization of order and continuity in the interpretation of reality are prerequisites for identity. Moral rules in turn are the almost visible outlines and concretizations of that order."[43] One of the most important aesthetic qualities inherent in ethical rules lies in the simple fact that people can, in fact, conform to rules. Human beings can order their behavior and thereby demonstrate through action an underlying order in reality. This aesthetic sense of order, as Hans Mol noted, is required for a stable sense of personal identity to emerge.

Religious traditions may generate very different senses of aesthetic order through systems of religious ethics. Most systems strive to define the outlines of ethical order in the service of the aesthetic values of clarity and simplicity. "The moral valuation of the geometrically simple," observed the anthropologist Edmund Leach, "is a markedly human characteristic."[44] But often the aesthetic simplicity of the ethical order will be elaborated in complex patterns of obligation governing different stages in the life cycle, different roles in human society, and perhaps even different levels of reality. All of these systems produce a fundamental sense of aesthetic order in ethical action.

Aesthetic Images

The appropriation of images is at the center of the ordering process within which a sense of self is formed. Cultural images in the form of sacred myths, powerful symbols, exemplary models for personal behavior and social arrangements are appropriated, imitated, and internalized in the creation of a sense of self. The self is not a thing; it is a changing, fluctuating, and unstable process by which people take images from their environment and make them their own. In essence, the self is really a self-process. Every cultural tradition has a reservoir of images that may be used, rejected, or variously combined and recombined in order to create a sense of self-identity. The use of these images may vary in different stages of the life cycle and in different circumstances of social life. The self-image may be in a process of constant change as result of changing strategies of response to cultural images in these different situations.[45]

One of the more stable sources of images within a cultural tradition are those symbols or metaphors for the sacred in religious traditions. These metaphoric images provide the ultimate context within which action derives its ethical significance. These may be metaphors for a divine being who is a king, or a father, or a redeemer, or a clockmaker; or they may be metaphors of cosmic emptiness or fullness; or they may even be quasiscientific metaphors of big bangs, atomic particles, or nuclear destruction. Within a religious tradition, behavior in the world of action only assumes a meaningful ethical pattern if it can come to terms with the tradition's dominant metaphors for the sacred.

Aesthetic Structure

Structure refers to the way in which a system of religious ethics organizes the various demands that are placed on human behavior. It involves a certain sense of proportion. Not all ethical norms carry the same weight in a religious tradition. Some norms are more normative than others. We might say that some obligations serve as a center of gravity within a particular religious worldview. The Ten Commandments, for example, are sometimes described within Judaism as a genus of ethical guidelines; the other 613 laws of the Torah can be arranged as subspecies within that genus. The aesthetic structure of an ethical system apportions the relative weight of ethical norms and arranges them in a coherent pattern.

Often the aesthetic structure of an ethical system has as its center of gravity a sacred role model who becomes a living pattern for ethical behavior. Sacred role models, such as Confucius, the Buddha, and Muhammad, are extolled in extensive bodies of popular literature within their respective traditions. The imitation of Christ as an ethical imperative in many forms of Christianity exemplifies this pattern. The model of Jesus's behavior serves as the center of gravity that supports the entire ethical structure. But the many images of Jesus in the New Testament and in the tradition create some ambivalence regarding exactly which Christ a Christian should imitate: the innocence of the babe in Bethlehem, the righteous anger of the cleansing of the temple, or the unconditional surrender to divine will in the passion. Here the many diverse images must be structured through the work of interpretation. Some measure of emphasis, nuance, and proportion is necessary to work these images into a coherent structure of ethical obligation.

Aesthetic Style

Style refers to the way in which a particular tradition of religious ethics cultivates certain tones, moods, or qualities of behavior. A tradition establishes a certain style of action. Obligation also extends over life styles, in this fundamental sense, as a distinctive way of being in the world. The sociologist Robert Redfield noted that "the phrase 'style of life' has come into this discussion to meet the need for a term that will suggest what is most fundamental and enduring about the ways of a group persisting in history."[46] An enduring sense of ethical obligation will be communicated as much through a general style of action as it will through explicit rules, laws, and customs that govern behavior.

Ethical style may be referred to as *ethos*. The anthropologist Clifford Geertz has explained that "a people's ethos is the tone, character, and quality of their life, its moral and aesthetic style and mood; its underlying attitude toward themselves and their world that life reflects."[47] Religious ethics, as a way of being in the world, cultivates distinctive styles of acting as a human and interacting with other humans. Aesthetic style reveals something important about the unique ethical character of a community. Geertz has characterized the style that governs both ethics and aesthetics in the lives of people he studied in Java. "Javanese ethics (and aesthetics) are," according to Geertz, "correspondingly, affect-centered without being hedonistic: emotional equanimity, a certain flatness of affect, a strange inner stillness, is the prized psychological state, the mark of a truly noble character."[48] This aesthetic, emotional, or affective quality reflects the dominant style of Javanese ethical obligation. Hence, aesthetic style is an important constituent ingredient in any tradition of religious ethics.

Aesthetic Rhythm

Traditions of religious ethics cultivate distinctive rhythms of behavior. Following an ethical path may be something like walking down life's highway with a particular kind of rhythm. The anthropologist Michael Gilsenan, in his book *Recognizing Islam,* captured the distinctive behavioral rhythm of the Islamic communities he lived with precisely by their manner of walking. He contrasts their rhythm with his own purposeful, determined strides,

> *looking direct when he should be glancing sideways, cutting a straight line when everything—tact, manners, self-interest, knowledge—demands that he move in the slow, meandering stroll of his friends with frequent stops at almond trees, shoulders loose, hands arcing expansively through the air, knees almost disjointed with relaxation, having some interchange with everyone they saw, apparently going nowhere, sitting, and then, only then, approaching on an apparently momentary wish, the house of such a one.[49]*

The gestures, movements, and postures, are coordinated in a distinctive rhythm that pervades a whole pattern of behavior.

Some ethical rhythms are quiet, slow, and passive; others may be more active and aggressive. One may try to act in harmony with the perceived rhythms of the natural environment, while another may try to make those natural rhythms conform to some human or divine ideal. The urban rhythms of modern, western, industrial societies put new pressures on the older rhythms that permeate traditional ethical life styles. An aesthetic sense of ethical rhythm forms part of the subtle pattern of ethical obligation. It contributes to the creation of a fundamentally aesthetic perception of harmony in action that is the highest demand of any system of religious ethics.

Patterns of Obligation

Obligation forms the basis of religious ethics. Ethical experience begins with the sense that certain things ought to be done and certain things ought not to be done. A sense of obligation is integral to religion in the original sense of the word, *religio:* the scrupulous observance of binding obligations that govern action, conduct, and behavior. Religion, therefore, is more than simply a set of beliefs: It is a binding power and authority that informs human action. The theoretical dimension of religious beliefs, myths, and doctrines may support certain types of behavior, but within religious traditions, what people do is usually regarded as ultimately more important than what they believe. Religious identity, in this sense, is acted out through patterns of action, and those patterns of religious action begin with obligation.

1.   *Obligation is based on sacred authority.* The sacred authority that governs action in any religious tradition is embodied in norms, rules, and values that are experienced as obligatory. These practical norms are felt to be invested with sacred power. Myth provides a sacred charter for practical action; it generates powerful images of what human beings are, what they could be, and what they ought to be. There is a certain givenness about myth; just as no one seems to invent jokes, no one invents myths. They are part of a shared cultural heritage that is handed down, preserved, and acted out in a religious tradition. Myth establishes powerful and authoritative im-ages of personal and social identity. In religious ethics, human beings strive to adapt their behavior to these images of identity. They feel obligated to act in ways that fit, match, or correspond to the self-images that are generated through myth.

2.   *Sacred authority governs ritual practice.* The first aspect of religious action is ritual. Ritual is formalized, symbolic action that refers to what is held to be sacred. Rituals are performed in extraordinary, set apart, sacred times and places. As patterns of action, they serve as vehicles for sacred power in religious worship, life-cycle transitions, celebrations of a sacred calendar, and times of personal or social crisis. The primary obligation of ritual is to act in harmony with the sacred. Ritual provides the very notion of perfection in human action. It establishes a model of ritualized perfection in which human beings can conform their behavior to the requirements of sacred obligation.

3.   *Ritualized perfection sets the pattern for ethical obligation.* The second aspect of religious action is ethics. Ethics governs behavior in the ordinary situations and circumstances of human life. In this regard, ethics is different than ritual. But ethics begins and ends in ritual. First, ritual provides the possibility that human behavior can be organized in an ideal, perfect, or normative pattern. Ritual actions establish a perfect environment that eliminates all the uncontrollable forces

that impinge upon ordinary action in the world. Ritual provides the model of a perfect pattern of action that spills over into ordinary experience in the aspiration to conform everyday behavior to a perfect pattern of ethical obligation. Second, ritual provides a means of resolving the tension between this expectation and actual behavior. When the Siberian bear hunters, for example, experience their ethical dilemma (in the awareness that actual bear hunting does not conform to the perfect pattern demanded by their bear hunting ethics), they are able to act out a perfect hunt in ritual. The bear ceremonies create a controlled environment within which behavior and experience may conform to the obligations that govern the hunt. Ritual, therefore, provides a notion of ritualized perfection in action, and a way of resolving the experiential conflict that occurs when action, conduct, and behavior do not match the pattern of perfection.

————

4.   *Ethical obligation is grounded in ritual.* Rituals of worship, prayer, meditation, and sacrifice give shape to ethical obligation. Religious ethics is grounded in a context of worship that is acted out in ritual; it is not simply a set of rules, laws, and customs that a religious tradition requires. Religious ethics involves the cultivation of certain attitudes, dispositions, and desires that are nurtured by ritual practices. African tribal religions, for example, may perform sacrifices to the ancestors as an integral part of their religious practice, but these rituals also serve to reinforce a network of ethical relations between persons in ordinary life. In ritual, a person offers the same quality of service to a deceased relative that is expected to be offered to a living relative in the ethical relations of everyday life. Similarly, Buddhist ethics is grounded in rituals of meditation; Christian ethics is grounded in rituals of prayer. It is not enough simply to know what one ought to do; it is also necessary to have the desire, power, and strength to do it. Ritual provides resources, in the cultivation of these inner dispositions, for the fulfillment of ethical obligation.

————

5.   *The fulfillment of obligation is an aesthetic fit between normative patterns and human actions.* The aesthetic quality of religious ethics is revealed through the order, images, structures, styles, and rhythms of action that are supported within a given tradition of religious ethics. Moreover, the aesthetic process of obligation requires human beings to fit, match, or conform their behavior to normative patterns of action. Fitting action fulfills a sense of harmony between expectations and behavior, between images of identity and conduct, between pattern and action. When this aesthetic sense of fittingness is achieved, a sense of ethical harmony may be experienced in religious ethics. This aesthetic sense of harmony marks the fulfillment of obligation within an ethical pattern of action.

CHAPTER

TWO

RESPONSE

Religious ethics is based on a sense of obligation. The ideal images of human behavior that religious traditions present, however, call for a response; obligation creates a sense of responsibility. In one sense, responsibility means taking a set of obligations seriously, feeling personally responsible for fulfilling the demands of obligation. The sacred norms for behavior within a system of religious ethics become a person's own responsibility. In another sense, however, responsibility means the ability to respond creatively to the ethical challenges of ordinary behavior in the human life cycle and social relations. It is not sufficient to simply outline, describe, and analyze the variety of ethical norms that have been proposed in the history of religions. We must also be sensitive to the various ways people respond to these norms. The variety of human responses to obligation reveals a dynamic human engagement with the dilemmas of ethical responsibility.

Religious ethics brings a sense of obligation—in the form of norms, images, structures, styles, and rhythms of behavior—to bear upon human desires and interests. Ethical action is animated by a dynamic range of intentions, and these intentions determine the quality of ethical experience that is generated in the encounter with obligation. People may observe obligations because they *want* to, or they may observe obligations because they feel they *have* to. One response is based on choice; the other is based on a sense of compulsion. People can also respond to obligation by rejecting, subverting, or ignoring it, or by otherwise modifying its demands to adapt to specific circumstances. These responses involve different qualities of ethical experience, and they suggest the variety of ways people may be able to respond to ethical obligation.

One response, which has dominated the history of ethics in western thought, is to reduce the field of ethical obligation to the demands of reason. Tension has existed in western thought between sacred authority and independent philosophical reason: If reason alone can produce normative standards for human behavior, then there is no need for the sacred authority represented by the commands of divine beings, the norms of sacred texts, or the examples of prophets. Reason can even produce independent ethical criteria by which these sacred authorities themselves may be evaluated. A good illustration of the evaluation of sacred authority by the demands of reason is found in the edition of the Christian New Testament produced by Thomas Jefferson. Jefferson carefully went through the Gospels with scissors to extract the sayings of Jesus that he felt conformed to the requirements of reason. He explained that "by cutting verse by verse out of the printed book and arranging the matter which is evidently his and which is easily distinguished as diamonds in a dunghill," he was able to extract "the most sublime and benevolent code of morals which has ever been offered to man."[1] This ethical code passed the test of rational assent and practical application, but only after it had been removed from the "dunghill" of

sacred authority in which it had been embedded.

We will consider such rational improvisations in religious ethics as part of an ongoing tradition of philosophical reflection on ethics in western thought. The tradition of philosophical ethics has proposed a number of different rational criteria for determining exactly what is good behavior, and we will briefly survey some of the major proposals. Rational criteria developed in philosophical ethics have also been used in the study of comparative religious ethics. We will look at some of the recent projects in analyzing the improvisations of practical reason within different religious traditions. Philosophical reflection on ethics, through the formulation of rational criteria and rational justifications for behavior, is certainly an important dimension of religious ethics. But the variety of responses to obligation suggests a more dynamic range of experience in religious ethics than might be suggested by an exclusive concern with the requirements of reason. We can begin by reviewing the possible responses to a sense of ethical obligation.

Varieties of Ethical Response

An individual within a religious tradition may respond to the call of obligation in a variety of ways. The response may be one of obedience, resignation, rebellion, or some kind of creative improvisation. Many different intentions may animate the response to obligation. The normative images of obligation may be in conflict with actual behavior, desires, and interests. Religious ethics is not simply a matter of knowing what is right or wrong: It is a complex, ambiguous, and

often contradictory process of negotiating personal identity in relation to a sense of obligation.

We can outline the different kinds of response to ethical obligation. These options represent the basic conditions of possibility for responding to obligation in any system of religious ethics.

1. *Morality:* to do what you *ought* to do because you feel you *want* to do it.

2. *Discipline:* to do what you *ought* to do because you feel you *have* to do it.

3. *Antinomianism:* to do what you *want* to do because you do not *have* to observe ethical laws.

4. *Improvisation:* to do what you *want* to do because you are *able* to *respond* creatively to ethical situations.

Each option represents a different response to the demands of ethical obligation. They are different varieties of ethical responsibility. And each option creates a qualitatively different set of experiences within the ethical process.

Morality

Morality, as we will use the term here, suggests a certain alignment between personal desire and the sense of obligation; it implies harmony between what the person wants to do and the normative obligations of the tradition. The moral response is based on choice. It involves a different quality of experience, therefore, than the coercion of law or the habitual responses of custom. The harmony with ethical obligation achieved through moral choices is a result of a personal investment of desire, enthusiasm, and interest in the sacred norms of the tradition. The moral response can be illustrated by two examples—one from the Confucian tradition and the other from the Buddhist tradition—but these examples define a process common to all ethical systems. The moral response is felt to harmonize desire with the demands of obligation.

Confucius described his own life in his *Analects* as a journey through different stages of engagement with ethical obligation. At the beginning of that journey he learned the requirements of li; at the end his desires were attuned to the pattern of ritual and ethical obligation that li represents. Confucius said: "At fifteen my mind was fixed on learning. By thirty my character had been formed. At forty I had no more confusions. At fifty I understood the Mandate of Heaven. At sixty it was easy for me to hear the truth. At seventy I could follow my desires without transgressing what was right."[2] This final stage in his ethical training in li, the arts of ritual and ethical propriety, would seem to describe the desired objective of all systems of religious ethics. The individual's personal desires are in a state of harmony with the image of right conduct. There is no tension, conflict, or imbalance between what the individual wants to do and the sense of obligation. This inner sense of harmony is the supreme moral virtue in Confucianism.

This moral situation is also described in Buddhist ethics. Buddhaghosa's commentary in the *Papancasudani* describes the basic pattern of Buddhist ethical obligation. The commentary outlines the five ethical precepts of Buddhism. On a deeper level, Buddhaghosa analyzes stages in the individual's response to those precepts, culminating in a moral harmony between desire and obligation.

The ethical precepts are rather straightforward commitments to abstain from certain actions. These five rules are common to most Buddhist systems of religious ethics. The Buddhist is instructed to declare: "I undertake to observe the rule to abstain from taking life; to abstain from taking what is not given; to abstain from sensuous misconduct; to abstain from false speech; to abstain from intoxicants as tending to cloud the mind."[3] Buddhaghosa's commentary, however, proceeds through a more subtle psychological analysis of precisely what is involved in following these ethical norms. He explains exactly what it means to abstain from killing, stealing, lying, sensuous misconduct, and intoxicants.

Buddhaghosa identifies three stages that move toward a fully moral response to these precepts: First, one feels obliged to abstain; second, one formally undertakes to do so; and third, one has lost all temptation not to do so. The first stage is the sense of ethical obligation. With regard to killing, for example, a powerful image is established suggesting that one of the conditions of being a Buddhist is to abstain from killing anything that lives. In order to be a Buddhist, a person must first accept the compelling authority of this obligation. The second stage is the individual's personal response; the Buddhist undertakes to fulfill the obligation. But that response might be animated by various motives. Characteristically at this stage, the Buddhist may refrain from killing simply in order to submit to the discipline of the Buddhist tradition.

The final stage in the ethical process is described as the truly moral response: doing what is obligatory because you desire it and have no desire not to do it. Buddhaghosa elevates this final stage to a special status. "This last kind of abstention," he declares, "is association with the holy Path. It does not even occur to the Holy Persons to kill any living being."[4] At this stage there is harmony between the person's desires and the sense of obligation. This is the moral response. It represents a complete commitment of energy, enthusiasm, and desire to the ethical objective. Buddhaghosa suggests that the harmony with obligation is so complete at this stage that it would not even occur to a Buddhist to do anything that does not conform to the ethical precepts of the tradition.

The moral response involves more than simply following ethical precepts. It involves cultivating moral virtues through the inner attunement of attitudes, dispositions, and desires to the demands of obligation. In this inner attunement, people may feel empowered to respond to the ethical challenges of ordinary life. The power of the moral response flows from an internal sense of harmony with the normative sense of obligation.

Discipline

A response to obligation based on discipline is very different from the power of the moral response. Disciplined individuals do what is obligatory whether they like it or not. Often there is a sense of compulsion or coercion in discipline, where the power is not generated from the individual's own desires, interest, and enthusiasm, but is directed from some external authority to which the individual's behavior must be adapted. The disciplinary response usually reinforces behavior with threats of sanctions. Discipline may be achieved under coercion, with threats of punishment in this life or the next. The demands of obligation may be fulfilled, but an entirely different experiential character animates those actions. Some traditions have rejected any recourse to the disciplinary response, while others have adapted disciplinary strategies into a larger program of ethical obligation.

The classical Taoism of the *Tao-te ching* provides an example of one tradition that rejected discipline as a valid response to ethical obligation. Lao-tzu suggested that discipline and the disciplinary management of human behavior only occur when true morality is absent. Disciplinary control of behavior—even though it may be called virtue, humanity, and justice—only emerges when the natural, unforced, and spontaneous way of the Tao declines.[5] This indicates that a genuine morality, in which the individual is in harmony with the pattern of ethical obligation inscribed in the cosmos, can never be disciplined. By controlling the individual's natural freedom through discipline, Lao-tzu implied that true morality becomes impossible.

Certainly, within these terms morality cannot be legislated. And yet many systems of religious ethics call for precisely such a disciplined response to obligation. In religious codes of ethical law, discipline may not simply be a preparatory stage on a path toward moral harmony; rather, discipline becomes an ongoing method of managing, regulating, and controlling human behavior. Since law by its very nature is always backed up by force, or the threat of force, the disciplinary response required by legal obligations necessarily involves coercion. Most of the ethical rules governing human behavior at different stages of the life cycle and in social relations have been legalized at one time or another by the major religious traditions. Legalizing a rule does not mean simply placing it within a systematic code of rules; it means backing up that rule with the threat of punishment. The ethical laws embodied in the *Laws of Manu,* the Torah, the Qur'an, and the Christian codes of canon law all include certain threats of punishment for violating the laws. The severity of prescribed punishments for particular violations may reflect the weight, or seriousness, of each law. But the very presence of such sanctions indicates that these ethical laws call for a disciplinary response.

Where the moral response tends to empower people to act in harmony with obligation, discipline forces people to conform to the demands of obligation through the power of sanctions, punishments, and reprisals. In this sense, discipline robs individuals of the ability to act with all the energy, enthusiasm, and power available in human action. Of course, a person can *choose* to follow an ethical law, but that would represent an experiential shift from discipline to moral choice. The contrast between discipline and morality emerges in the different quality of experience that is involved in these basic ethical responses to obligation. The behavior may be the same, but the intentions, feelings, and desires are qualitatively different.

Antinomianism

Antinomianism is the belief that people can be free from any obligation to ethical norms, rules, or laws. Antinomians are beyond obligation, or at least they assume that traditional ethical obligations are not binding on their own behavior. The term *antinomian* usually refers to individuals or groups who have developed ethical strategies for subverting the pattern of ethical action that operates for most people. This elitist ethical response maintains that the obligations that apply to the behavior of the masses do not hold for a select group of initiates, chosen ones, or free spirits. Antinomianism is a creative response to ethical obligation that is found in many different religious traditions.

Passages in the New Testament letters of Paul suggest that traditional Jewish law is no longer binding on Christians. The law has been fulfilled by the grace of Christ. This theological position within Christianity has sometimes been described as antinomian. Antinomianism is an important element in Buddhist ethics. In Buddhist thought, karma determines the character of future births: The quality of ethical actions in this life determines the situations and circumstances of future rebirths. Good deeds that conform to the ethical precepts of the tradition lead to a superior rebirth. But the Buddhist's goal is to be free of the cycle of rebirth altogether. One who has achieved enlightenment, an *arahat,* will not be reborn. For this reason we find antinomian statements in Buddhist ethics that reflect a spiritual ideal beyond action. "He who would be an arahat," reads one cryptic pronouncement, "should not do good deeds."[6] Simply following the ethical norms of the tradition will not produce enlightenment, which is a condition that is beyond ethical law.

More radical forms of the antinomian response to ethical obligation appear in religious communities that initiate their members into what they consider a higher spiritual reality beyond the restraints of ethical obligation. In Tantric Buddhism, for example, individuals practice secret techniques of yoga, meditation, and spiritual exercises, and those who have been initiated into the mysteries of *tantra* are no longer subject to the same pattern of ethical obligations that governs most people. One Tantric text states, "By the same acts that cause some men to burn in hell for a thousand years, the yogin gains his eternal salvation."[7] The master of tantric techniques is above the ordinary demands of ethical obligation.

Another example of initiatory antinomianism is found in the medieval religious sect of the Bretheren of the Free Spirit. This movement arose in a very different religious tradition, yet it expressed a similar kind of freedom from ethical obligation. In fourteenth century Europe, the Bretheren were labeled heretics by the Catholic church for maintaining the antinomian position that "one can be so united with God that whatever one may do one cannot sin."[8] The Bretheren apparently felt that their unique spiritual union with God made their every action holy, even if their behavior conflicted with the traditional ethical norms of Christianity. Their ethics liberated them from the ordinary ethical rules that applied to people who had not achieved their special spiritual status. Their behavior was so radically spiritualized by being united with God that they considered themselves beyond ethical obligation.

Occasionally the antinomian response does not simply reject or ignore the ethical pattern of obligation within a tradition; instead, it systematically inverts it. The English Ranters, a radical Puritan group in the seventeenth century, represented such an example of symbolic inversion in their ethical response to obligation. They declared, "Devil is God, Hell is Heaven, Sin Holiness, Damnation Salvation."[9] The entire pattern of sacred norms was turned upside down to demonstrate freedom from traditional ethical obligations.

Sometimes, the antinomian response aims to destroy the entire pattern of ethical obligation. Jacob Frank and his Jewish messianic movement in eighteenth century Poland exemplifies the antinomian attack on ethical norms. "I have come to redeem [the world]," Jacob Frank declared, "from all the laws and customs that have ever existed. It is my task to annihilate all this so that the Good God can reveal Himself."[10] Jacob Frank claimed to be the messianic representative of this Good God, and he led his followers under the slogan "Holiness through sin." Such movements represent radical antinomian responses to the standards of ethical obligation within their respective religious traditions.

Antinomianism is a legitimate, although highly unorthodox, response to ethical obligation. It is clearly a response to the normative pattern of ethical behavior that is handed down in a tradition. But it is a dramatic, radical revision of those inherited ethical values. The antinomian response, like the other options, is a way of negotiating personal identity in relation to ethical norms; but antinomianism ultimately places personal identity beyond the reach of obligation.

Improvisation

The final option for responding to obligation we will call improvisation. Like antinomianism, it represents a certain freedom to experiment with the images, structures, styles, and rhythms of ethical behavior. An improvisational response, however, strives for a more independent status; it is often eclectic, putting together various elements, models, and qualities of behavior as desires and interests inspire it. The poet Charles Bukowski suggested this kind of response to ethical obligation when he observed:

> *it could be that*
> *what we think is*
> *right*
> *is often*
> *not very interesting.*[11]

Human interests may account for basic modifications in ethical obligation. Creative improvisations in response to ethical obligation may make a system of religious ethics more interesting by adapting it to the human needs, wants, and desires that arise within certain situations.

Systems of religious ethics usually allow for improvising when special situations and circumstances call for it. On these occasions the letter of the law may be modified in order to preserve what may be perceived as its spirit. In Jewish law, for example, sabbath observances may be suspended for the purpose of saving a life. In the Confucian tradition, the sage Mencius once noted that the ethical rule against a brother touching the hand of his sister might be temporarily waived if she was drowning. In these cases certain ethical improvisations may be necessary to preserve basic human values that are supported by the tradition.

Some improvised responses, however, may look like creative ways for avoiding responsibility. Interesting examples of improvisation are often found in creative responses to religious dietary regulations. Different strategies for avoiding responsibility may appear in dietary ethics. An important study of the ethical practices in a Buddhist community in Thailand has shown how one group has been able to improvise on the dietary regulations of the tradition. Vegetarianism is an ethical obligation within the Buddhist

tradition. It is an extension of the ethical precept that prohibits the taking of any life. The Buddhist vegetarian diet even prohibits eating eggs. Thai Buddhists have found ways to improvise around this restriction. One way of eating eggs, while still conforming to the prohibition against taking life, is to eat only unfertilized eggs. But a second strategy for eating eggs involves a more creative improvisation. If the master of the household orders the servants to prepare fertilized eggs, he feels that the servants are responsible. They will accrue the bad karma. But the servants respond by transferring the responsibility right back to the master. The result is that fertilized eggs are eaten, but no one appears to be responsible.

A final compromise was worked out that allowed for eating fertilized eggs that had already been broken. If the eaters did not personally break the eggs, then they could not be held ethically responsible for violating the prohibition against killing. Observers of these Thai Buddhist communities have described a brisk business in broken eggs. A large percentage of these eggs, it has been suggested, are intentionally broken behind the counters of clever Muslim shopkeepers.[12] These improvisations with Buddhist dietary ethics illustrate the potential to produce elaborate strategies for adapting obligation to human interests within ethical traditions. They represent some of the creative potential in ethical improvisation.

The tendency toward improvisation in religious ethics has accelerated in the modern world. Rigid adherence to conventional, traditional ethical patterns has in many cases become more difficult and less desirable. Some ethical obligations governing diet, marriage, divorce, family relationships, and so on encountered difficulty during the extensive reorganization of modern western societies following the Industrial Revolution. Modernization has had a global effect on religious ethics. The pressures to adapt have been very strong, and ethical improvisation has been an important option in response to traditional patterns of ethical obligation.

In addition to this tension between tradition and the new demands of modernization a wider variety of ethical images is available to the individual. It is almost as if individuals are consumers in an ethical supermarket. A greater potential exists for drawing upon images of ethical identity that, without the extensive influence of mass media and communications, would otherwise be inaccessible. Many people find themselves experimenting with ethical obligations, as well as with new ways of responding. Ultimately, ethical responsibility may reside in the ability to respond with integrity to the challenges of living. The improvisational response is a legitimate, although perhaps unconventional, way of dealing with ethical obligation.

Rational Improvisation

The rational improvisations of western philosophical thought have pressured religious ethics to conform to the requirements of reason. Philosophical ethics in western thought has worked to provide independent criteria for good behavior. The entire tradition of philosophical ethics, from the ancient Greeks to the present, can be viewed as a series of experiments in defining rational criteria for the purpose of determining what is good in human experience. These criteria differ, however, from philosopher to philosopher. There is no consensus on exactly how such independent standards for human action can be determined, and there are even different definitions of the practical reason that would determine those standards. Nevertheless, many religious thinkers within the three major western traditions—Judaism, Christianity, and Islam—have felt compelled to adapt the norms of ethical obligation to fit one or another philosophical standard of practical reason. This represents a creative improvisation within these religious traditions, but it may also signify a weakening of the normative power of sacred authority over ethical behavior.

Reason and Sacred Authority

The challenge to sacred authority over ethics in western religious thought was posed by the Greek philosopher Plato in his *Euthyphro*. He asked a fundamental question regarding the authority that supports ethical norms within a religious tradition: Are ethical norms good because God commands them? Or does God command them because they are good? If the ethical norms of a tradition are good simply because a divine being commands them, then anything that a god might command would be good by definition. The norms for ethical action would depend solely on the will, whim, or caprice of that god. The most arbitrary rules and regulations could be commanded by a divine being, a religious text, or a holy prophet, and these ethical norms would be considered good simply because they were invested with sacred authority.

If, however, God commands certain actions because they *are* good, then there must be some independent set of criteria for determining good actions that God is following. Plato was convinced that this was the case and that it was possible for human beings to discern these independent criteria for good actions through their own rational abilities. Rational criteria for ethical behavior may, in fact, turn out to be consistent with the norms embodied in divine commands, religious scriptures, or exemplary prophets. But if objective standards can be discovered through reason, then perhaps there is no need for such sacred authorities in ethics. Ethics can be determined by reason alone.[13] Philosophical ethics is a tradition of western thought that has tried to produce a rational definition of the good: a single principle that could serve as a rational standard for determining good conduct. It will be important to briefly survey some of the most influential definitions that have been proposed in the history of philosophical ethics.

Ancient Greek Ethics

The ethical thought of Plato and Aristotle represents the most important contribution of ancient Greece to the tradition of philosophical ethics. They both subjected human conduct to rational analysis, but their conclusions were based on very different assumptions about what constitutes reason. For Plato, reason was the direct intuition of the eternal, unchanging, ideal forms of reality; for Aristotle, reason was a process of abstraction that distilled concepts from the changing flux of experience. With Platonic intuition one could know the essence of any object by rising above the play of appearances and rationally apprehending its eternal form. With Aristotelian abstraction, however, one could know the essence of an object only after encountering many particular examples of that object and abstracting from them basic features that they have in common. These different approaches to reason produced different rational criteria for determining what is good in human action.

Ethics of Plato   Plato understood the good as an eternal idea. Goodness was a timeless, unchanging, and universal form of reality. It exists independent of the world of appearances as an immutable precondition of any particular thing being good. Plato was convinced that the human mind is able to ascend from the world of particular things to a direct insight into this eternal idea of the good. In the world of things, human beings are deceived by sensory experience, perceptual illusions, opinions, and the basic deceptiveness of appearances. Through rational contemplation, however, the human mind can gain direct access to the eternal realm of ideas.

In his *Republic,* Plato expressed this theory in the image of the divided line. He proposed that there is a great division between the realm of things and the realm of ideas. Things are necessarily in a process of change, flux, and transformation. They are by nature impermanent. This is the world of becoming. Within the realm of things, Plato suggested, there are two kinds of knowing. First, there are illusions, such as the images produced by poets and painters, which are secondhand copies of actual things, or sensory illusions, such as the appearance of a stick that seems to bend in water, which deceives the knower. These illusions demonstrate the unreliability of perceptual knowledge. Second, there are opinions that human beings form based on their encounters with the perceptions of sensory experience. These are also unreliable kinds of knowledge. They are judgments based on deceptive appearances in the realm of things.

As the mind elevates itself from the deceptive involvement with appearances to the permanent, ideal forms of being, it begins to activate two other forms of knowing. First, the mind develops the capacity of rational thought, which enables it to work with the timeless precision of mathematical, geometrical, and logical principles. And second, the mind may ultimately achieve direct intuition, in which it sees directly the eternal archetypes of being—the unchanging ideas of the good, the true, and the beautiful. Contemplation of the eternal forms of reality, according to Plato, leads to a direct intuition of the good.

Ethical virtue in human conduct is assumed to be a direct result of seeing the eternal form of the good. A person who knows the good will act in ways that are good. The rational intuition of the good will naturally condition the behavior of anyone who has seen it. Desires and actions will inevitably come into harmony with its eternal and unchanging design. The implication of this theory is that if people do not act in ways that are good it is because they do not know the eternal form of the good. If they knew better, they would do better. For Plato, ethical virtue is a direct result of the philosophical exercises of rational contemplation. The direct intuition of the permanent essence of goodness will necessarily result in good action.[14]

Ethics of Aristotle

Aristotle rejected Plato's notion of an ideal good in his *Nichomachean Ethics*. Rather than a single form of the good, Aristotle insisted that human beings experience many different particular goods. The term *good* may be applied in different ways to different objects, or even in different ways to different qualities of the same object. A good horse is qualitatively different than a good man. In addition, to refer to a horse's good color, good size, good speed, and so on is to use the word *good* in different ways. Aristotle wanted to be able to identify the particular goods that are appropriate for each individual thing.

The goodness of any particular thing depends upon its own unique telos. *Telos* means end or goal or purpose. Each particular thing has its own telos by which it can be evaluated. The speed of a horse, for example, may be evaluated in terms of the purpose for which the horse is being used. Quickness may be good in a racehorse but bad in a plowhorse. Such value

judgments depend upon a rational consideration of its telos. Human behavior also has a general telos. The goal or purpose of human activity, according to Aristotle, is to produce a life of happiness. Actions that contribute to the fulfillment of the human telos are considered good actions; they are good because they are effective means for achieving the goal of human life. Aristotle refers to such good actions as ethical virtues.

Happiness is achieved through the rational ordering of attitudes, dispositions, and behavior through the cultivation of ethical virtues. Happiness is understood as rational moderation in action. Every virtue tends to be a mean between two extremes. The virtue of courage, for example, is a mean between the extremes of cowardice and foolhardy abandon. A courageous person has chosen a middle course between these two extremes and has developed an ethical virtue that will contribute to a happy life. Aristotle assumed that the supreme telos of happiness in human experience would be achieved in the balance, moderation, and order represented by ethical virtues. Aristotle proposed the ethical ideal of happy and virtuous human beings living a life of rational order and harmony.

In order to practice this ethical ideal, guidance is derived from the rational exercise of what Aristotle called practical wisdom. He separated the active life of practical wisdom from the contemplative life of theoretical wisdom. The knowledge gained from theoretical contemplation may be necessary for the development of virtues, but it is not sufficient. That would be like studying the science of medicine in order to be healthy. Health comes only from actions that produce health. Virtue therefore comes only from actions that produce virtue. While Plato felt that it was sufficient to know the single, eternal form of the good in order to produce good actions, Aristotle insisted that practical wisdom must be involved in assessing, measuring, and evaluating the many different kinds of goodness that may be experienced in the world of action.[15]

Enlightenment Ethics

The eighteenth century in western thought has been referred to as the Enlightenment. Philosophers celebrated the independent light of reason and tended to reject the influence of sacred authority. Philosophical ethics during this period was divided between two basic theories for determining independent rational criteria for human behavior. The first was deontological ethics. This approach evaluated behavior in terms of motives. It was concerned with the individual's inner sense of ethical duty, the awareness of right and wrong, and the workings of practical reason. The second approach was consequential ethics. Consequentialists evaluated actions solely in terms of their results. Only an action that produced good consequences could be considered a good action. The standards of evaluation that were used looked for measurable increases in human pleasure, happiness, and well being as indications of good consequences. These two philosophical approaches to ethics were developed during the Enlightenment, but they still have committed proponents today. Deontological and consequential ethics have exerted a powerful influence over the subsequent history of ethical reflection.

Deontological Ethics   The philosopher Immanuel Kant (1724–1804) was concerned with clarifying the philosophical issues surrounding ethical motivation. The first issue was the nature of the human will in the ethical process. In order to make moral choices, Kant insisted, the human will must be free to choose. It must be free of the influences of personal desires, social pressures, and any external control. The will must also be free from the binding demands of sacred authority, free to exercise practical reason in determining the best course for action. Kant focused on the rational motivation of human free will in making ethical choices. He declared that "nothing can possibly be conceived in the world, or even out of it, which can be called good without qualification, except a Good Will." [16] Goodness in Kantian ethics does not refer to actions and their consequences; it only applies to the free and rational motivation of the will.

The second issue Kant addressed, however, concerns the rational criteria to which the human will must conform in order to be considered good. Kant stressed that a good will is one that conforms to an inner sense of moral duty. His understanding of moral duty is suggested by two principles that he proposed in his major work on philosophical ethics, *Fundamental Principles of the Metaphysic of Morals*. The first principle is known as the categorical imperative. Kant suggested that we always act on certain maxims that guide our behavior; that is, there are certain reasons, or motives, or interests in the back of our minds when we act in certain ways that could be expressed in the form of a rule. Kant maintained that in order to act morally, we must always act in such a way that the maxim by which we act could be made into a universal law. Kant stated, "Act only on that maxim whereby thou canst at the same time will that it should become a universal law." [17] To determine if the maxim that informs our action is good, we might ask "Would I be willing to make this maxim a normative principle of behavior for everyone?" If the principle that guides a person's behavior could be made into a rationally acceptable rule for everyone's behavior, then that person is acting in a way that is consistent with the categorical imperative.

Kant's second principle of moral duty requires that a good will show respect for the integrity of other persons. Human beings are to be treated as persons of irreducible moral value. What has sometimes been called Kant's practical imperative insists that moral reason requires that we "treat humanity, whether in thine own person or in that of any other, in every case as an end withal, never as means only."[18] Human beings are to be treated as inherently valuable ends in themselves and never as means to be manipulated toward some desired end. This principle affirms the innate moral value of human beings. It reflects a basic disposition toward others that forms one of the conditions of a good will in Kant's deontological ethics. The deontological approach to philosophical ethics is concerned solely with the rational requirements of a good will. Kant's categorical and practical imperatives represent an inner sense of moral duty to which that will must conform in order to be good.

Consequential Ethics

Consequential ethics evaluates the moral status of actions by the results they produce. This philosophical position is usually called utilitarianism. It was first formulated by Jeremy Bentham (1748–1832), who was convinced that people basically try to act in ways that increase pleasure and avoid pain. He maintained that those actions that increase pleasure are by definition morally good. They produce good consequences to the extent that they increase the degree of pleasure in human experience. Bentham felt that utilitarian analysis was essential for ethics because it provided a way to calculate the projected consequences of actions and then measure the degree of pleasure or pain that would result. His approach was a variety of ethical hedonism in that it emphasized maximizing personal pleasure as an ethical goal, but Bentham also insisted that the pleasures of true happiness could only be realized if they were shared within a larger community of persons. For this reason, Bentham stated his utilitarian creed as "the greatest happiness for the greatest number."

John Stuart Mill (1806–1873) called this The Greatest Happiness Principle. As an influential utilitarian of the nineteenth century Mill elaborated on the basic themes of consequential ethics. He modified Bentham's quantitative calculations of pleasure by suggesting that intellectual pleasures were qualitatively superior to sensory or physical pleasures. Mill even imagined that utilitarianism could effectively replace traditional religions in providing the sacred norms for ethical action.

> *If we now suppose this unity to be taught as a religion, and the whole force of education, of institutions, and of opinion, directed, as it once was in the case of religion, to make every person grow up from infancy surrounded on all sides both by the profession and the practice of it, I think that no one, who can realize this conception, will feel any misgivings about the sufficiency of the ultimate sanction for the Happiness Morality.*[19]

The utilitarian happiness principle was not, of course, based on a concept of religious duty. Rather, it provided a method for rationally analyzing actions in terms of their projected consequences, and for rationally choosing the course of action that can be projected to produce the most positive results for the greatest number of people.

Expressive Theories of Ethics

Twentieth century philosophical ethics has been primarily concerned with the analysis of ethical language. This linguistic analysis of ethical statements is part of a larger concern with analyzing different types of discourse. The discourse of science, the discourse of religion, and the discourse of ordinary language all generate qualitatively different types of statements about the nature of reality. Scientific propositions are statements about reality that can be submitted to empirical testing; they can be verified or falsified by direct empirical experience. But religious propositions, including the prescriptive statements of religious ethics, cannot be tested in this way. They are non-sense statements because they refer to levels of sacred reality, meaning, and authority that are beyond empirical verification. Because religious statements are non-sense, however, does not necessarily mean that they are non-sensical. They may express emotions or preferences that play an important role in the ordinary experience of people who hold particular religious or ethical commitments.

The philosopher G. E. Moore (1873–1958) was convinced that the good was not something that could be proven or disproven through rational, scientific methods. The basic concept of the good was indefinable. The good is a simple thing, like the color yellow, that cannot itself be defined. If you do not know what yellow is, no verbal definition can possibly give you this knowledge. The good is precisely this kind of simple thing that cannot itself be defined. It is, however, a basic term that may be used in the definition of more complex things. G. E. Moore's position within philosophical ethics has been called intuitionism.[20] The good can only be known as it becomes evident to common sense. Moore was confident that common sense could reveal a basic awareness of the good, of right and wrong, of moral duty. However, these ethical perceptions could not be obtained, verified, or demonstrated through scientific investigation.

This separation of ethical and scientific thought cleared the way for an approach to ethics called emotivism. A. J. Ayer (born 1910), one of the most influential philosophers of twentieth century linguistic analysis, distinguished between descriptive statements and prescriptive statements. Descriptive statements make certain claims about the way things are; they describe the nature of reality. Such statements are subject to empirical, scientific verification, and therefore they represent the only legitimate form of human knowledge. Prescriptive statements, however, make certain claims about the way things ought to be. They are not a legitimate form of knowledge because they are neither true nor false; ethical prescriptions simply express emotions. Emotivism maintains that when people make ethical statements—such as "Always tell the truth," or "Honor your father and mother," or "Abstain from intoxicants as tending to cloud the mind"—they are expressing an emotional preference for certain kinds of behavior. Prescriptive statements have no basis in scientific knowledge about the way things are; they merely express emotional tastes, preferences, and interests regarding the way things ought to be.

This philosophical distinction between descriptive and prescriptive statements was also developed by the philosopher of ethical emotivism C. L. Stevenson (born 1908). Stevenson referred to the emotive character of ethical language as its magnetism. Ethical statements are dynamic uses of language: They not only express emotional preferences, but they are used to persuade, convince, or compel others to accept these preferences as legitimate. According to Stevenson, the persuasive power of ethical language does draw upon rational arguments and rational justifications in order to convince others. Descriptive statements about the way things are may be invoked in order to rationally justify a particular ethical preference and persuade others of its validity. Ultimately, however, all ethical discussions are expressions of moral choices that have been made on the basis of emotional preferences.[21]

In expressive theories of ethics, ethical norms are divorced from any necessary relation to legitimate knowledge about reality. However, this separation is foreign to any tradition of religious ethics. Prescriptive statements in religious ethics about what people ought to do are part of a larger mythic horizon that describes who people are and what they could be. Prescriptive statements exhort people to cultivate inner dispositions, perform certain actions, and demonstrate virtues that will allow them to realize who they are. These statements are part of a larger pattern of experience in which individual and collective behavior is brought into harmony with an embracing mythic vision of the way things are. Traditional ethical communities create a living context in which prescriptive statements reinforce mythic descriptions of reality.

A number of commentators view the lack of attention to the living context within which ethical virtues are developed as symptomatic of the breakdown in western philosophical ethics since the Enlightenment. By divorcing ethical norms from the context of sacred authority, Enlightenment ethicists tried to justify many of the same norms that had been handed down in the Christian tradition simply by reason alone. And twentieth century emotivism has explained ethical norms as expressions of emotion alone. These approaches to philosophical ethics ignore the fact that those ethical norms only made sense as patterns of experience, action, and virtue that were cultivated within living ethical communities. For this reason, the philosopher Alisdair MacIntyre observed "we have—very largely, if not entirely—lost our comprehension, both theoretical and practical, of morality."[22] A first step in recovering a sense of the vitality of ethical

practice may be in exploring actual, living ethical communities. MacIntyre noted that "we have to learn from history and anthropology of the variety of moral practices, beliefs and conceptual schemes."[23] This is particularly crucial in the study of religious ethics, where patterns of ethical action are a basic element in the holistic configuration of beliefs, practices, and experiences that comprise a religious tradition.

This brief survey of philosophical ethics has revealed some of the most important rational improvisations in ethical thought in the western philosophical tradition. After accepting that sacred authority for ethical standards of behavior was fundamentally irrelevant, these philosophical positions improvised new definitions for ethical standards and practices. These philosophical definitions of ethics, however, have limited value in the interpretation of ethics within religious traditions where sacred authority is an integral component of the ethical world that is generated by the tradition. Rational arguments and rational justification may nevertheless play an important role in the ethical responses to obligation within religious traditions. It will be important to consider the role of reason in comparative religious ethics.

Reason and Comparative Religious Ethics

The tradition of western philosophical ethics has entertained a number of different definitions of practical reason. Plato's contemplative intuition of eternal forms, Aristotle's rational abstraction of the telos in human activity, Kant's rational premises of moral duty, and Bentham's rational calculations of the projected consequences of actions all represented different assumptions about the role of reason in ethics. The role of rationality

in cultural traditions of ethics is further complicated by the question of whether or not there are universal laws of reason that are constant in all human experience. Are there basic standards of rationality—such as the principles of mathematics, the systematic reasoning of logic, or the principle of noncontradiction—that are common to all cultural traditions? Or does each cultural tradition produce its own distinctive criteria of rationality based on principles that only make sense within the context of that tradition?[24] If the pattern and process of rationality is truly culturally specific, then it would be impossible to evaluate the rationality of one culture in terms of what is considered rational or reasonable in another.

Recent studies in comparative religious ethics have argued that basic patterns of moral reasoning underlie all traditions and systems of religious ethics. Certain universal principles of reason come into play in the process of making moral decisions and taking moral actions. These studies contribute to the analysis of the role of rational reflection in religious ethics by applying basic categories of philosophical ethics to the comparative analysis of religious ethical systems. Fundamental patterns of moral reasoning emerge as the core of religious ethics. It is important to note, however, that authoritative guides for conduct in religious ethics may not always be produced by rational reflection, nor will they necessarily correspond to the requirements of philosophical reason. For this reason, these examinations of moral reason are of limited value in locating the full range of ethical experience in the history of religions. Nevertheless, we will consider some of the important contributions to the discussion of moral reason made by recent work in the comparative study of religious ethics.

Moral and Religious Reason

Ronald Green's philosophical analysis of religious ethics, presented in *Religious Reason: The Rational and Moral Basis of Religious Belief* (1978), attempts to demonstrate the "fundamental rational structures underlying religious belief."[25] Religion is defined as a necessary extension of the workings of human reason, and particular religions represent various "ongoing efforts to conform to reason's exacting demands."[26] Green begins by considering three basic kinds of reason, or what he refers to as three employments of reason. First, theoretical reason is employed to work out an objective and rationally acceptable picture of the world. It forms the basis for any rational knowledge of reality. Second, prudential reason is employed to make deliberative calculations regarding practical courses of action that can be rationally expected to maximize personal happiness, benefits, and well being. Prudent reason is concerned with furthering self-interests. Third, moral reason is employed in the rational selection of social rules that will support the whole community. Following Kant, moral reason defines a person's sense of duty in actions that affect other persons. The various moral rules—do not injure, kill, lie, cheat, break a promise, be unfair, and so on—are rational choices because they are required by the sense of duty defined by moral reason.

Religious Reason
A rational problem arises, however, when prudential reason comes into conflict with moral reason. Self-interest may often be in conflict with moral duty. There are situations in which people may advance their own interests by lying, cheating, and breaking promises, even though these acts violate the requirements of moral reason by injuring others. Why should people be moral when it seems to be against their own interests? It is precisely at this point, Ronald Green argues, that religious reason emerges to resolve this dilemma. Rational moral activity requires a set of religious concepts in order to be complete. "An independent and rationally constituted morality," Green suggests, "is compelled to resort to one form or other of religious beliefs in order to render its dictates coherent."[27] Religious beliefs that refer to an ultimate moral context beyond immediate human

experience provide a necessary supplement to moral reason.

Such religious beliefs in supernatural moral agencies—including concepts of eventual rewards and punishments for actions—are not used by religious traditions simply to make moral duty more compelling. They are necessary in order to make moral duty make sense. These beliefs, or their functional equivalents, are required by the inner workings of moral reason itself. Ronald Green maintains, "I can act rationally if I obey the moral rules and at the same time hold certain specific beliefs not supported by experience."[28] Moral reason itself requires that we posit some supreme causal moral agency beyond our immediate experience. That religious moral agency could be a personal god who rewards, punishes, and perhaps forgives human actions. Or it could be an impersonal cosmic principle, such as the notion of karma, that is responsible for the ethical consequences of action. Such nonempirical beliefs are necessary to complete moral reason. A problem arises here: If religious reason includes beliefs in supernatural rewards and punishments for action, behavior may be prudently conducted in order to achieve rewards and avoid punishments. Reason at this point ceases to be moral reason (in Kant's terms) and reverts back to prudential calculations of self-interest. Supernatural sanctions are simply factored into the calculations. But Green insists that moral reason requires religious beliefs to persuade people that moral obedience to duty is not against their self-interests. These religious beliefs are not fantastic flights from reason; they make morality rational.

Green's interpretation of religious ethics argues against any theory suggesting that religious beliefs that support ethical obligation are nothing more than irrational projections of human desires or irrational legitimations of oppressive social forces over human behavior. The requirements of religious reason are also the requirements of reason. They are "those beliefs which

each individual must hold if he wishes to be fully rational."[29] From this perspective, comparative studies of actual religious traditions can be made to evaluate whether or not they satisfy the requirements of religious reason. The capacity of these traditions for sustaining the demands of moral reason through supernatural religious beliefs can be assessed.

Limits of Religious Reason

A number of objections might be raised regarding this approach to religious ethics. First, it begins with a rather narrow definition of moral reason, which may obscure the variety of rational strategies that might be involved in the employment of reason within religious traditions. Kant's requirements for rational moral duty is simply one definition of ethical rationality. Ethical reasoning could be conducted by calculating the consequences of actions, by reaching contractual agreements within a community, or by conforming to the authoritative precedents set by exemplary sacred models.[30] These different types of reasoning may come into play depending upon the styles of rational improvisation employed by the tradition. The styles of reasoning that are actually used may not necessarily conform to a Kantian definition of moral reason.

Second, reason is not the primary motive for responding to obligation within a system of religious ethics. Reason may be given to justify a set of norms for ordinary behavior, but that does not imply that reason has somehow demanded, required, or produced these norms. Reason plays a more subsidiary role within the dynamic, experiential process of responding to a sense of obligation.

Finally, this approach to comparative religious ethics involves an implicit normative project. Traditions are evaluated on the basis of how well they conform to the requirements of Kant's moral reason. Some may be judged to be more successful than others. Certainly, this is evaluating religious traditions on the basis of rational criteria to which they may not necessarily subscribe. Although Green's interpretation is an important exercise in Kantian moral philosophy, it has limited application in the cross-cultural description and interpretation of religious ethics.

Religious and Moral Action-Guides

Another recent contribution to the philosophical analysis of the role of reason in comparative religious ethics has been made by David Little and Sumner Twiss. Their book, *Comparative Religious Ethics* (1978), presents a rigorous conceptual analysis of religion, morality, and law. They outline what they propose are the basic patterns of rational justification that underlie the employment of authoritative guides for action in religious ethics. Like Ronald Green, they also test their theory of religious ethics by means of detailed case studies of selected religious traditions. It will be useful to consider their definitions of religious and moral action-guides, as well as their theory of rational justification in systems of religious ethics.

For the purpose of analysis, Little and Twiss draw a basic distinction between religion and morality. Religious action-guides are defined as logically distinct from moral action-guides. Simply put, religion involves "sacred-regarding" and morality involves "other-regarding" guides for human action. A religious statement is one that expresses "the acceptance of a set of beliefs, attitudes, and practices based on a notion of sacred authority that functions to resolve the ontological problems of interpretability."[31] Religious action-guides are based solely on sacred authority. They support and warrant certain behavior by interpreting action within a sacred con-

text of meaning. A moral statement, however, is one that expresses "the acceptance of an action-guide that claims superiority, and is considered legitimate, in that it is justifiable and other-regarding."[32] Moral norms are concerned with the problems of interpersonal cooperation. They guide personal behavior in relation to other persons. Moral action-guides derive their legitimacy, not from appeals to sacred authority, but through processes of rational justification. By definition then, morality is logically independent of religion.

Practical Justification   The practical justification of moral action-guides requires providing convincing reasons for performing actions that would impinge on other persons. Any course of action that affects other people must be justifiable in terms of rational reasons. Little and Twiss maintain that there are two basic classes of justifying norms that are used in moral reasoning to validate actions: deontological norms and consequential (or what they call teleological) norms. They invoke the basic Enlightenment categories of philosophical justification for ethics. Actions may be rationally justified on the basis of whether or not they conform to moral duty (deontological ethics) or whether or not they produce good results (consequential ethics). Moral reason may take either course to justify a particular kind of behavior.

To illustrate the rational justification of action-guides, Little and Twiss propose a hypothetical situation in which a teenage boy, who is a member of a religious community, is about to strike his father. In a deontological ethical system, which is based on an authoritative sense of moral duty, a rational justification for why the boy should not hit his father could be provided in terms of a series of logical syllogisms:

> *1. Whoever has the power to create human beings has the overriding right to have what he*

commands obeyed, and what he forbids avoided by everyone (all human beings).

2. *God created human beings.*

3. *Everyone ought to obey what God commands, and avoid what He forbids.*

4. *God forbids dishonoring parents.*

5. *One ought not to dishonor parents.*

6. *Repudiating parental authority dishonors parents.*

7. *One ought not to repudiate parental authority.*

8. *Acts of striking parents repudiate parental authority.*

9. *One ought not to strike one's parents.*

10. *This man before you is one of your parents.*

11. *You ought not to strike him.*[33]

After listening to this series of logical deductions, which interweaves religious propositions and moral statements in a complex fabric of justification, the hypothetical teenage boy may have had time to cool off, or he may be angrier than ever, but he will have been confronted with a line of rational justification derived from the most basic authoritative norm of his religious community.

Little and Twiss do not claim that a person must go through such a series of logical deductions in order to make moral choices for behavior. The logical pattern of rational justification is implicit, however, and those who reflect on the norms that govern behavior should be able to reproduce such a series of rational inferences to validate their course of action. The emphasis on logical deduction, however, may obscure the aesthetic leaps that are often made in religious traditions to justify ethical authority. Christian ethics, for example, employs a number of powerful metaphors to symbolize the authority that justi-

fies specific ethical norms, rules, and values. Christ is the head of the church as the human head governs the body. The husband has an ethical authority in the family based on an analogy to Christ's role in the church. These are metaphoric leaps from one frame of reference to another that symbolize an aesthetic fit between different patterns of ethical authority.

When John Winthrop, the first governor of the Massachusetts Bay Colony, justified his ethical and legal authority to punish antinomians, dissenters, and heretics, he invoked the fifth commandment: "Honor your father and mother." The ethical authority of the magistrates was justified by a single metaphoric leap that made them the symbolic fathers of the entire Massachusetts community.[34] A series of rational deductions from the ultimate authority of God could certainly be constructed, as in the justifications offered to the teenage boy about to strike his father, but it would be an artificial translation of the immediate, compelling power of metaphor into the terms of logical reason. Such reasoning very well might come into play within a religious tradition, but it is one among many different symbolic strategies for justifying ethical norms.

Systems of Validation   Little and Twiss propose four basic systems for the justification and validation of ethical norms. However, these four ideal types of ethical systems can be reduced to the simple distinction between philosophical ethics and religious ethics. One system justifies action-guides independent of sacred authority; the other system justifies action-guides in terms of sacred authority.

The first is a purely *moral system*. Any ethical system that developed norms for evaluating human behavior, independent of sacred authority, would be such a moral system. This includes the entire history of philosophical ethics in the Western tradition that we just surveyed. Rational action-guides are generated, by whatever definition of practical reason, without regard for sacred authority.

The second is a purely *religious system.* Here there is no moral regard for other persons, but simply a concern with the personal relationship with sacred authority. "A purely mystical form of religion," Little and Twiss claim, "that had extruded all considerations of human material welfare would be an example of this system."[35] They cite no actual example of such a system. There is a good reason for this: No such system has ever existed. There is no example of a religion that does not have an ethical component involving norms for regarding others. Even a mystical, ascetic, and other-worldly religion that held to the principle "Avoid all contact with others" would still offer an other-regarding action-guide. Other people would be appropriately regarded by avoiding them. This definition of a purely religious system, therefore, has very little descriptive or interpretive value in the study of actual religious systems of ethics.

The third type is a mixed *moral-religious system.* In this system moral action-guides are worked out without reference to sacred authority, but beliefs in God, gods, or sacred realities are also adopted. These beliefs can be held, however, only if they are consistent with the moral norms that have been worked out by reason alone. Immanuel Kant, for example, was a moral philosopher who also believed in God; but this religious belief was irrelevant to his definition of the intrinsic demands of moral reason. This again is simply an example of an ethical system within the tradition of western philosophical ethics.

Finally, the fourth type is a mixed *religious-moral system.* In this system "other-impinging acts, together with whatever sacred-impinging acts there are in the system, are validated with a religious norm."[36] But the definition for this kind of mixed system that is offered by Little and Twiss is simply a description of the practical dimension of religion. Sacred-impinging acts are ritual, other-impinging acts are ethics. Both ritual and ethics are validated in religious traditions with reference to sacred norms. Every system of religious ethics in the history of religions can be located within this practical dimension of religion. The action-guides for ordinary behavior, including the appropriate measure of regard for other persons, are grounded in the same sacred norms that are demonstrated in ritual. Ritual and ethical action respond to the sense of obligation that is generated by the sacred authority of those norms.

Religious Ethics and Philosophical Ethics

The alternative to religious ethics is some variety of philosophical ethics. Whether a system of philosophical ethics allows for the existence of a divine being is ethically irrelevant. Ethical norms are generated solely through rational reflection. Rational improvisations independent of sacred authority define the conditions of ethical thought and action. These improvisations even set the terms under which beliefs in supernatural beings might be admitted into the system. Sacred authority can only be acknowledged if it already agrees with the prescribed rational principles of morality. We have defined morality as a harmony between desires and sacred norms. In philosophical ethics this harmony is achieved, not by adapting human desires to the obligations embodied in sacred norms, but by adapting sacred norms to the demands of reason. These are two antithetical ways of negotiating a sense of moral harmony in relation to ethical obligation.

The work of David Little and Sumner Twiss has helped to clarify what it means to use the categories of philosophical ethics in the comparative study of religious ethics. This brief summary has not even begun to suggest the precision and sophistication of their philosophical analysis of comparative religious ethics. However, a review of their work reveals two basic problems with such philosophical analysis in the comparative study of religious ethics. First, the concentration on philosophically rationalized ethics obscures the fact that there are many sacred norms that are not based on rational reflection that inform ethical action within religious traditions. This preoccupation with the categories of reason, as the comparative ethicist Frederick Bird has noted, "excludes many forms of authoritative guides for interpersonal conduct, like taboos, etiquette, and conventions, which have not been the object of such theoretical reasoning."[37] Sacred norms for ordinary behavior can be found in a variety of ethical models: catalogues of virtues, conventional advice, rules of customary etiquette, mythic descriptions of ancestors, and social role expectations. These models suggest some of the variations in which ethical norms might appear in religious traditions. Moral principles based on philosophical, rational reflection would simply be one variation. And such rational improvisation should probably not be considered the most important response to the normative obligations that are embodied in a religious tradition.

Second, the concentration on philosophically rationalized ethics distracts us from the fundamental aesthetic impulses that animate ethical action. Moral reason itself may be motivated by a more basic aesthetic quest for harmony between personal thoughts, feelings, and desires and an overarching sense of ethical obligation. We have noted that philosophical ethics achieves this internal harmony by modifying sacred norms so that they fit the desires of reason. Often a sense of harmony is achieved by rejecting the binding force of sacred authority entirely. But human beings who continue to act within the horizon defined by a religious tradition necessarily experience, to one degree of intensity or another, the inner tensions between personal desires and the sacred pattern of ethical obligation. An aesthetic sense of fittingness determines whether they experience dissonance or harmony in relation to the normative pattern of obligation. The aesthetic play of dissonance and harmony locates the essential character of ethical experience within the history of religions. And we are distracted from noticing the essentially aesthetic experiences of ethical dissonance and harmony when we are preoccupied with the categories of philosophical ethics.

Patterns of Response

Religious ethics does not simply define the obligations that govern ordinary human behavior; it requires a human response to obligation. Ethical response to obligation is not merely doing or failing to do what is obligatory. Responsibility is more than taking a set of obligations seriously enough to feel that they are personally binding. Ethical responses to obligation in the history of religions involve a dynamic range of qualitatively different ethical experiences in relation to the norms of a system of religious ethics. Chapter 2 has drawn a number of conclusions regarding these different responses to obligation in religious ethics.

––––––

1.   *Ethical responsibility is the ability to respond to obligation.* When actions match the pattern of obligation, there is harmony; when they do not match, fit, or conform, there is ethical dissonance. But the quality of experience in response to obligation depends on the dispositions of human desire that animate action. Different responses are conditioned by different disposi-

tions toward obligation. Ethical responses are the ways in which human beings respond to the sacred norms within a religious tradition that govern ordinary action.

The moral response is a harmonious alignment between personal desires and obligation; it is a response in which individuals conform to a pattern of ethical obligation because they want to act in such a way. It is a moral harmony between pattern and action.

The disciplined response brings behavior into alignment with obligation regardless of personal desires. It is a response that involves a certain degree of coercion. In a disciplined response to obligation, people will conform to normative patterns of action whether they like it or not. Legal obligations encourage this type of experiential response to obligation.

The antinomian response assumes for various reasons that obligation is not binding on a special group for whom ethical norms, rules, and values are felt to be irrelevant. Antinomians may respond in whatever way they want to obligation because they are beyond its binding control.

Finally, an improvised response to obligation adapts ethical norms, rules, and values to fit human desires. Improvisation adapts patterns to fit actions, rather than strictly conforming actions to match the patterns of obligation. Moral harmony may be experienced by aligning desires with obligation; but it might also be achieved by adapting the requirements of obligation to more easily conform to desires. These four modes of ethical response suggest the variety of experiential engagement with obligation in religious ethics.

———

2. *Independent rational criteria for ethics is a variety of the improvisational response to obligation.* Plato raised an important question for religious ethics when he asked: "Are obligations good simply because God commands them, or does God command them because they are good?" If obligations are good simply by virtue of the fact that a divine being commands them, then obedience to those commandments serves to demonstrate a harmonious relationship with that divine being. The Hebraic myth of the Garden of Eden, in which Yahweh commanded the first human couple not to eat from one tree in the garden, is often interpreted in this sense in Judaism and Christianity. The obligation not to eat from the Tree of the Knowledge of Good and Evil is regarded as purely arbitrary. But obedience to this arbitrary rule demonstrates a harmony between human actions and the divine will.

If it is assumed, however, that God commands certain actions because they *are* good, then there must be some independent criteria that God is using to evaluate actions. Rational improvisation strives to identify these independent criteria for good actions. This process makes sacred authority irrelevant to ethics. There is no need for the authority embodied in divine commands, sacred texts, or exemplary prophets if rational improvisation is able to arrive at the same normative obligations on its own. In this sense, rational improvisation is the independent effort of human reason to define ethical obligation without any direct reference to sacred authority.

———

3. *Western philosophical ethics has been a tradition of rational improvisation in ethics.* The goal of philosophical ethics is to achieve moral harmony by adapting, modifying, and reformulating ethical obligation according to the demands of reason. Enlightenment ethical theories have been dominated by two forms of rational improvisation: deontological ethics and consequential ethics. The first improvises obligation according to the demands of moral reason; it is an ethics of moral duty. The second improvises obligation according to calculations of the expected consequences of actions; it is an ethics devoted to increasing pleasure and avoiding pain. The irony of philosophical ethics, however, is that it tends to support the same kind of ethical rules against killing, harming, lying, cheating, and so on that were supported by sacred authority within religious traditions. Divorcing these rules from their sacred context separates ethics from its original religious function in the cultivation of virtues. Virtues are inner dispositions of desire in harmony with the sacred norms of an ethical tradition. In this sense, philosophical ethics has ignored the fact that ethical rules are epiphenomena of a deeper experiential harmony with sacred authority, which is the central concern of religious ethics.

_____

4.   *The categories of philosophical ethics do not adequately describe ethical experience in the history of religions.* Independent rational criteria for ethics, which take the form of moral reason, rational argumentation, and rational justification, have been used to analyze the normative guides for practical action in the history of religions.

This concern with reason perpetuates the division between (rational) morality and (irrational) religion produced by western philosophical ethics. Although it is clear that rational reflection on ethical obligation and action is important, it is only one aspect of the rich array of experiential responses to obligation that are involved in religious ethics. It is important to recognize that religious ethics is not simply moral reason or rational action-guides for human behavior. Religious ethics is an experiential process in which human beings strive to negotiate a sense of identity in relation to obligation, to cultivate, develop, and nurture certain inner dispositions of desire that might be regarded as virtues in ethical experience, and to engage the tension between dissonance and harmony in relation to obligation. The aesthetic tensions between dissonance and harmony are obscured by a preoccupation with reason in religious ethics. Dissonance and harmony are the experiential dynamics of ethical experience that animate ethical response to obligation.

CHAPTER

THREE

DISSONANCE

What happens when people do not do what they feel is required by obligation? How should we describe what people experience when their actions do not conform to the normative pattern of action that is established within a religious tradition? Rather than producing an inner sense of moral harmony, religious ethics often generates conditions of distress, tension, and anxiety when behavior does not match the ethical norms. People may often be in conflict with the sense of obligation. We will call this condition *dissonance*. Sociologists have analyzed the cognitive dissonance that arises when deeply held expectations are disproved by experience. The confusion and disorientation of cognitive dissonance may result when expectations of the way things should be do not match the actual experience of the way things are.[1]

Ethical dissonance involves this kind of mental conflict; but it also has an affective component. Dissonance involves the feelings of emotional uneasiness, disturbance, and turmoil that may result from a perceived conflict between people's actions and their sense of ethical obligation. These emotional tensions may be symptomatic of more pervasive ethical moods, attitudes, and dispositions. They may be affective signs of a deeper sense of ethical unworthiness, inadequacy, or self-disgust. Dissonance is a very common dimension of religious experience. It is analogous to the aesthetic experience of hearing two discordant musical notes, notes that simply do not go together. That experience of dissonant tones, of course, can only occur if there is already a trained sense of musical harmony by which the correspondence and conflict of particular notes can be evaluated. Ethical dissonance is experienced as internal discord because it is in conflict with an ideal system of ethical harmony. Dissonance and harmony necessarily define each other. Dissonance may be the single most important ethical experience because it symbolizes an immediate, dynamic, and personal involvement in the normative system of ethical harmony.

Emotional ambivalence about obligation is built into the experiential process of religious ethics. It may be that all emotions are mixed emotions: Certainty and doubt, tranquility and turmoil, obedience and rebellion—all are intricately intertwined in the human response to ethical obligation. The Christian church leader Augustine (354–430), described his struggle as a young man with the ethical demands of the Christian tradition in the autobiographical narrative of his *Confessions*. He felt that he was expected to live a life of sexual chastity, but this ethical demand was in tension with his personal desires. Augustine cried out in anguish to God: "Give me chastity and continence, but not yet."[2] There is an inevitable frustration of desires, emotional turbulence, and disturbance of the spirit inherent in the religious experience of obligation. Systems of religious ethics not only incorporate these emotions into patterns of ethical behavior, but they often find some positive value in what may seem to be a range of negative experiences.

The two major forms of dissonance produced by religious ethics are shame and guilt. These experiences of ethical dissonance both arise when behavior does not meet expectations. They emerge from an awareness of failure in relation to ethical obligation. These feelings of dissonance may be disturbing, yet, at the same time, they connect people dynamically with the experiential process of religious ethics. They indicate to what extent people have internalized the normative expectations of the ethical pattern, and they suggest the degree to which people measure their behavior by the internalized standards embodied in that pattern. It is almost as if the normative pattern of ethical behavior assumes watchful, ever-present eyes and becomes a kind of ideal spectator observing every human action. Ethical norms are not simply a pattern to be consulted in guiding human behavior. They are a source of potential disapproval and judgment experienced through shame and guilt.

Shame and guilt are involved to some extent in every system of religious ethics. Some systems, however, tend to cultivate one more than the other. Some anthropologists have tried to distinguish between shame cultures and guilt cultures in order to identify a significant difference between cultural systems that tend to cultivate the ethical experience of shame and cultural systems that generate ethical feelings of guilt. The anthropologist Ruth Benedict, for example, felt that this distinction was important. She observed that "a society that inculcates absolute standards of morality and relies on a man's developing a conscience is a guilt culture by definition."[3] *Guilt* is defined here as a reaction to an internalized critique of behavior. Guilt presumes the judgments of an ethically conditioned conscience on behavior that may be contrary to absolute ethical standards. *Shame* is a reaction to an external critique of behavior. It is a sense of chagrin, or embarrassment, for a public transgression. "In a culture where shame is a major sanction," Benedict continued, "people are chagrined about acts which we expect people to feel guilty about. This chagrin can be very intense and it cannot be relieved, as guilt can be, by confession and atonement."[4] Although the dissonance of shame cannot be relieved by ritualized public confessions of fault—because it is already public knowledge—it may, in fact, be eased by ritual forms of purification, or penance, or exchange, which restore the harmony of the community that had been disrupted by the shameful act. We will examine more closely the different qualities of ethical experience involved in shame and guilt before proceeding in Chapter 4 to consider the patterns of action that can restore ethical harmony that is disrupted by dissonance.

Religious traditions have developed strategies for locating and interpreting the experience of dissonance within a larger context of meaning. Ethical dissonance may be viewed as a variety of a more general and pervasive cosmic dissonance that permeates reality. It may be located within a larger symbolism of evil. Evil enters human experience in the forms of distress, suffering, and misfortune. But those experiences may be understood in terms of the symbolic economy of good and evil in the cosmos. Religious strategies for interpreting and making sense of the experience of evil provide general symbolic contexts within which ethical dissonance is perceived to have its ultimate significance. We will briefly consider the symbolism of evil in the history of religions as it relates to the ethical experience of dissonance.

Religious ethics, by the very nature of the confrontation between normative obligations and personal desires, generates dissonance. The ethical demands placed on ordinary human behavior often produce feelings of distress, tension, and anxiety. But religious ethics can also be seen as a creative response to dissonance. Ethical norms, rules, and values respond to the challenges of uncertainty, ambiguity, and conflict that arise at different stages of the human life cycle and within networks of social relations. There are experiences in life that characteristically produce dissonance, and religious ethics may offer a sense of comfort and security in knowing what to do in response to these dilemmas. Chapter 3 concludes with an outline of the varieties of situational dissonance that may be experienced in human life-cycle transitions and social relations.

Shame, Defilement, and Taboo

One context in which ethical dissonance appears in the history of religions is the complex symbolic relations defined by the sense of shame, the perception of defilement, and the ritual interdictions of taboo. A *taboo* is a prohibition of contact with certain persons, objects, or activities that are set apart. Any contact with something that is taboo is believed to be unclean. Contact becomes a source of defilement. Transgressing the ethical lines marked out by taboos renders the person unclean and impure, and defiled by contact with what is forbidden. The lines that separate what is clean and what is unclean are public knowledge. Any violation of taboo by crossing these lines is perceived as a dangerous disruption of the shared public order that binds the community together. Taboos do not simply operate in primal religions; they play an important role in any ethical system that relies on public distinctions between purity and defilement in ordinary behav-

ior. The defilement produced by contact with what is forbidden makes a person vulnerable to the ethical dissonance of shame.

Shame

Shame includes feelings of embarrassment, humiliation, abasement, disgrace, and dishonor in relation to ethical obligation. The etymology of the term reveals that it comes from a word meaning "to cover." The ethical dissonance of shame represents a desire to cover, or hide, some public transgression from disapproving public scrutiny. The first mention of shame in the Hebrew Bible occurs after Adam and Eve have violated the ethical obligation established by Yahweh. The primordial human couple eat the forbidden fruit from the Tree of the Knowledge of Good and Evil. Immediately after transgressing this perhaps purely arbitrary taboo they experience shame at their nakedness and try to cover themselves. Shame is both a feeling of distress and a desire to hide that distress from public view. It is a painful negative emotion arising from situations in which people perceive themselves as objects of disapproval, scorn, contempt, or ridicule. At the same time, shame may be a fear, dread, or anxiety that arises in anticipation of causing some offense against propriety, decency, and purity. In this sense, the experience of shame may function as an effective restraint on behavior.

The dissonance of shame may be incorporated within a system of religious ethics as an important internal guidance system for human behavior. In Confucianism, with its highly defined sense of ritual and ethical propriety (*li*), the experience of shame is considered a prerequisite for moral behavior. The dissonance of shame is a precondition for achieving moral harmony in ethical action. Confucius maintained in the *Analects* that "If you control the people (i.e. through discipline) they will still not have a sense of honor or shame. But if you lead them through virtue . . . then they will have a sense of shame and will attain goodness."[5] Here dissonance, in the form of a sense of shame, is viewed as an important ingredient in the development of moral virtue. Disciplinary manipulation of behavior to make it conform to the letter of the ethical law cannot produce shame. Shame can only arise spontaneously through a careful process of moral education. The awakening of shame, as a state of internal dissonance, is one sign of morality.

Mencius, another ethicist in the Confucian tradition, even went so far as to claim that dissonance was the beginning of moral virtue. The virtues of humaneness and righteousness begin in dissonance. Mencius declared that "the feeling of distress is the beginning of humaneness [*jen*];

the feeling of shame is the beginning of righteousness [*i*]."[6] The moral response to ethical obligation is not simply a matter of obediently accepting certain norms for behavior. Mencius suggests that a truly moral response depends on awakening the internal dispositions of distress and shame. The integrity of Confucian ethics consists precisely in embracing these experiences of dissonance in relation to ethical obligation.

Shame also played an important role in the ethical teachings of Socrates and Plato. Plato saw this internal restraint on behavior as one of the primary goals of ethics: "to infuse that divine fear we call shame." Alcibiades, one of the more recalcitrant students of Socrates, felt that awakening his sense of shame was an important contribution that his teacher had made to his ethical education. Alcibiades exclaimed:

> *There's one thing I've never felt with anybody else . . . and that is a sense of shame. Socrates is the only man in the world that can make me feel ashamed. Because there's no getting away from it. I know I ought to do the things he tells me to do, and yet the moment I'm out of his sight I don't care what I do to keep in with the mob.*[7]

Yet even when he is out of his teacher's sight, Alcibiades continues to experience the internal dissonance instilled in him by the ethical instructions and example of Socrates.

The ethical dissonance of shame, therefore, represents a state of inner distress at the failure to meet ethical obligations. But it is more than this: Shame functions as an internal ethical barometer for the measurement of ethical performance. It gives some indication of the degree to which obligation has been internalized in a person's sense of self. On a deeper level, this sense of shame presupposes powerful, primordial images of impurity. A shameful act is one that is impure, unclean, and therefore forbidden. The symbolism of defilement represents a very basic level of human ethical experience.

Defilement

The symbolism of defilement supports and sustains the ethical dissonance of shame. Defilement results from contact with whatever is classified as impure; it is symbolized as dirt or stain or pollution. A person may become defiled by coming into contact with those things that have been set apart from ordinary human involvements. The historian of religions Raffaele Pettazzoni defined defilement as "an act that evolves an evil, an impurity, a fluid, a mysterious and harmful something that acts dynamically—that is to say, magically."[8] The dynamic action of defilement produces an ethical infection, contagion, or pollution that contaminates the person who has associated with whatever may be proscribed from contact. Anyone who approaches such a defiled person may also become vulnerable to the contagious pollution of defilement.

Defilement is an objective violation of the ethical limits on ordinary human behavior. In other words, the stain of ethical impurity does not depend upon subjective intentions, but it results automatically from crossing the behavioral boundaries that set apart the clean and the unclean. The ethical rules of the Hebrew Bible, for example, clearly define the divisions between clean and unclean. The meat of certain animals is classified as ethically impure: the hare, the rock badger, the pig, and the camel. The ethical law states: "Of their flesh you shall not eat, and their carcasses you shall not touch; they are unclean to you." (Lev. 11:8) Even contact with the dead bodies of these animals is considered impure. Contact with lepers, menstruating women,

corpses, and so on are all classified as unclean. Regardless of the person's inner dispositions, motives, or intentions, contact with unclean things defiles that person with an ethical pollution.

There is an essential subjective aspect, however, to the symbolism of defilement. The prospect of defilement arouses feelings of ethical dread. Defilement can inspire fear, apprehension, or anxiety. The ethical dread of defilement, or impurity, involves a powerful emotional response to these symbols. As the philosopher Paul Ricoeur noted, defilement evokes a "half-physical, half-ethical fear that clings to the representations of the impure."[9] This fear originates in the perception of ethical vengeance that defilement invokes. The punishment for transgressing the rules of purity is felt to be inherent in the act itself: By doing an impure thing one becomes impure. Public disapproval and the symbolic vocabulary of purity reinforce the inherent sanctions of defilement. "Thus," as Ricoeur observed, "it is always in the sight of other people who excite the feeling of shame and under the influence of the word which says what is pure and impure that a stain is defilement."[10]

The vocabulary of purity and impurity, clean and unclean, defines the basic lineaments of an ethical order. Ethical purity is not medical hygiene, even though health and well-being may often depend on avoiding contact with whatever is classified as ritually or ethically unclean. Ethical purity is derived from maintaining the sacred order that organizes personal behavior, social relations, and the basic structure of reality itself. To be pure is to maintain everything in its place. Impurity is to be out of place. Dirt, stain, and pollution are simply matter out of place. As the anthropologist Mary Douglas has noted, impurity is an offense against order.[11] The fundamental order of an ethical community may be sustained by strictly observed classifications of purity and impurity. Demarcating the boundaries between the pure and the impure imposes an ordered system on what otherwise might be chaotic human experience. Rules of purity support a sense of living in an ordered universe.

These classifications also organize ethical experience. Belief in the danger of pollution and fear of contact with the unclean can provide powerful support for an ethical code of conduct. First, pollution beliefs can act as a deterrent against wrongdoing. Mary Douglas has observed that "certain moral values are upheld and certain social rules defined by beliefs in dangerous contagion, as when the glance or touch of an adulterer is held to bring illness to his neighbors or his children."[12] The danger of defilement can provide powerful reinforcements of ethical norms, rules, and values. Second, pollution beliefs intensify the seriousness of an ethical offense. Defilement does not simply expose a person to public shame and censure; it also makes that person vulnerable to all the danger, suffering, and misfortune that is felt to be inherent in ritual or ethical impurity. And third, pollution beliefs may reduce ethical ambiguities by providing a clear focus for ethical concern. The detailed classification of pure and impure acts reduces ethical confusion. If some ambiguity should arise, various rituals of purification may be performed that retrospectively define the specific defilement that must be cleansed. In all these respects, religious beliefs in purity and pollution define, support, and reinforce a pervasive sense of ethical order.

Purity and pollution beliefs are not the residual survivals of some primitive ethical mentality. They form the substratum of any system of ethical dissonance and harmony. As Paul Ricoeur suggested, "Dread of the impure and rites of purification are in the background of all our feelings and all our behavior relating to fault."[13] In the symbolism of defilement, ethical fault is represented as a stain, a taint, a contagious infection that results from impure conduct. Pure conduct maintains the ethical order that is felt to be in-

scribed in both society and nature. The boundaries of that order are drawn by those prohibitions that are represented by religious taboos.

Taboo

The experiential dissonance of shame is often the result of violating a taboo. Anthropologists discovered this term in use among the island societies of Melanesia. It has become a generic designation for anything that is set apart as forbidden. Taboo, however, is more than simply a prohibition. It involves the perception that certain objects, people, and situations are invested with a negative sacred charge; they are charged with the danger of defilement and should therefore be avoided. Taboos generally relate to boundary situations within human experience: the relations between male and female, the encounter with death, and the divisions between different social classes. In these situations, taboos mark out highly charged limits on human behavior in the interest of maintaining purity and avoiding defilement.

Sexuality involves careful ethical distinctions between purity and impurity. The prohibition against incest is an almost universal taboo in traditions of religious ethics. Restrictions on intrafamily sexual relations are the basis for complicated cultural distinctions between pure and impure relations between male and female. Standards of sexual decency, modesty, and propriety may all be surrounded by an intricate network of sexual taboos. Even within the ritual sanctions of marriage, sexuality may be limited by the force of taboo. Within some religious traditions sexual relations during menstruation, or just prior to ritual worship, or for a proscribed period of time after returning from battle may be a potential source of defilement. Sexual relations may be ethically organized within the space marked out by these taboos.

The human encounter with death is also mediated through explicit ritual taboos. Death is clothed in complex ritual actions that determine the proper ways of caring for the dying, disposing of the dead, and ensuring that the human community is protected from the defilement that death may represent. Certain contacts with the dying, with corpses, and with burial sites may be taboo. And improper conduct in relation to death may be seen as a powerful source of impurity. In the Hebrew Bible, for example, even contact with a clean animal that has died results in defilement. Those who touch the corpse must wash their clothing and remain classified as unclean until evening. (Lev. 11:39–40)

Finally, social classification systems within a society may distinguish certain people as a powerful source of defilement. A social hierarchy may identify certain groups of people as subclasses: groups of people within that society who are classified as impure. The *pariah,* or Untouchables, of traditional India, and the *eta* in traditional Japanese society, are examples of such social subclasses. These groups of people are usually employed in what are classified as impure occupations: sweeping streets, collecting garbage, tanning animals, and disposing of corpses. Because these classes are believed to be impure within the dominant system of social ethics, any contact with them by a member of a higher class is considered an occasion for defilement and shame.

The interactions among members of different social classes is carefully regulated in the traditional Hindu caste system by prescribed taboos. An upper class Brahmin must avoid any direct contact with lower class Untouchables; but even indirect contacts must be scrupulously avoided. A Brahmin may not receive food, tools, or money directly from the hand of an Untouchable. Even objects that they might touch at the same time are potential conductors for the charge of defilement. A Brahmin must not touch a stick, or a rope, or even a piece of straw that is in contact with an Untouchable. An observer of one Hindu community noted that "A Brahmin should not be in the same part of his cattle shed as his Untouchable servant, for fear that they may both step on places connected through overlapping straws on the floor." Fortunately, the ground is not considered to be a conductor of social impurity. If Brahmin and Untouchable should bathe in the same pond, the Brahmin "is able to attain a state of *Madi* [purity] because the water goes to the ground, and the ground does not transmit impurity."[14] The meticulous taboos that surround traditional Hindu social relations obviously help to maintain the unequal social statuses of the upper and lower classes. These occasions for shame, impurity, and defilement reinforce the ordered pattern of a hierarchical society.

Shame, defilement, and taboo operate in complex and interrelated ways to arouse, organize, and reinforce certain experiences of ethical dissonance. The prohibitions of taboo define the conditions of defilement under which a person might experience the ethical dissonance of shame. Certainly that experience of dissonance will vary in degree, intensity, and duration depending on the situations and circumstances in which it appears. But the fact that this form of dissonance arises at all, even in the dread of defilement that restrains behavior, indicates that the person is directly involved in an ethical system based on a strict division between purity and pollution.

Guilt, Judgment, and Sin

The second major type of ethical dissonance is guilt. Where shame is tied into a network of ethical relations based on the fear of defilement and the avoidance of taboo, guilt is a sense of distress, regret, and remorse that arises when a person stands accused of fault before the tribunal of ethical judgment. Actions, desires, and, more importantly, the person who performs those actions and holds those desires are all judged in terms of the demands of obligation. The dissonance of guilt arises when the person does not meet those demands. This failure to satisfy the requirements of ethical obligation is the defining characteristic of sin. Guilt, judgment, and sin provide a second symbolic context within which dissonance disrupts the ethical harmony that is supported by a religious tradition.

Guilt

The dominant imagery of guilt is not impurity, but a debt that is owed for failure to fulfill ethical duty. The word *guilt* is derived from *schuld,* which means a debt. Guilt is the failure to fulfill the conditions of a contract. It symbolizes an ethical liability. Guilt may be as objective as the determination of fault in a court of law; the individual's responsibility, culpability, and debt to society may be an objective social fact involving little emotional content. In religious ethics, however, feelings of guilt internalize that indebtedness resulting in intense feelings of inadequacy, contrition, and unworthiness. Guilt represents a sense of liability for failing to satisfy the specific requirements or absolute demands of obligation.

In religious ethics, guilt is a condition of dissonance that results from a tension between expectations and behavior. It is not, however, simply the feeling that one has failed to meet those expectations. Guilt may also be a powerful motivating force, a kind of internal guidance system, that directs human behavior into the pattern of obligation. It can be an ongoing impetus to modify behavior to conform to the demands set by the normative pattern of action. In this respect, the psychoanalyst Sigmund Freud called guilt "the most important problem in the evolution of culture."[15] Through guilt cultural traditions instill their patterns of ethical obligation in the innermost resources of personal conscience. Random personal desires are suppressed and the necessary adaptations to the requirements of social life are made. When people feel guilty, they are acknowledging that the demands of obligation are personally binding. Guilty people are affectively implicated in the set of normative judgments supported by ethical traditions. And those judgments are made intensely personal through the experience of guilt.

At the same time, however, guilt seems to be a debilitating, disempowering experience. Guilty people become liabilities to themselves. The feelings of inadequacy, anxiety, disapproval, and self-disgust that attend guilt may inhibit the individual's freedom of action and full participation in the religious community. Guilt may be symbolized as a burden that the guilty person carries, weighing upon the individual's conscience and impairing the ability to respond creatively to the ethical challenges of life. Therefore, guilt might represent either an internal reference point that guides action or an inner burden that inhibits action. These two functions may even alternate within the ambiguous texture of the dissonance of guilt.

A third and more subtle function of guilt is in providing a psychological buffer between the ethical norm and contrary actions. Guilt acts as a protective zone between the normative pattern of ethical action and behavior that contradicts the expectations contained in that pattern. If the ethical pattern, with its formative influence over the development of self-identity, contains expectations that a person does not lie, cheat, steal, commit adultery, and so on, and the person does in fact do these things, then an inevitable tension between pattern and action results. It is impossible to hold on to both the pattern and the action at the same time without experiencing some kind of dissonance. The pattern could be changed to fit the action, or the action could be altered to fit the pattern; either strategy could move toward an experience of ethical harmony. But as long as actions do not fit the ideal pattern, dissonance will be the necessary result.

Guilt is the glue that holds these two—pattern and action—together. It allows the individual to remain a viable member of a religious community that subscribes to a specific ethical pattern of behavior, while at the same time acting in ways that contradict that pattern. Guilt keeps that person in the game. Without guilt, even with all its debilitating dissonance, the individual would have to abandon the ideal ethical pattern. This would result in a dramatic alteration of that person's sense of identity, a disorientation of self-image, that could be even more disruptive than living with guilt. To experience guilt is to embrace the ideal ethical pattern, even while behaving in ways that oppose it. In guilt people can still own the pattern, even though their behavior may seem to disown it. The experience of guilt connects pattern and action, allowing people to share in the pattern, even when they do not conform to its required actions.

Judgment

The dissonance of guilt is an internal response to ethical judgment. Paul Ricoeur observed that guilt always appears "before God."[16] It is a feeling of fault, inadequacy, or unworthiness before the judgment of sacred authority. Within theistic religious traditions, a divine being who judges the ethical worth of each person holds the ultimate authority over human guilt. The throne of the divine king, the book of life, the recording angel, the scales of judgment—these are all powerful symbols that confront the guilty person within religious traditions.[17] Divine authority may distribute rewards and punishments according to ethical merit, and the ultimate standards of divine judgment may demand absolute condemnation of the guilty. Guilt feelings may be a proleptic punishment in anticipation of this final judgment.

In some traditions, however, the judgment of a person's ethical worth is symbolized as a subtle process of self-disclosure. The character of a person's conscience or consciousness is felt to be shaped by actions in this life. The quality of that personal character is revealed in death. Judgment is viewed as a process of self-judgment that is determined by the ethical quality of the conscience or consciousness that had been formed in life through the medium of action. For comparative purposes we will look at the symbolism of ethical judgment in two traditions—Zoroastrianism and Tibetan Buddhism.

Judgment in Zoroastrianism

Zoroastrianism was an archaic religious tradition of ancient Persia. Founded by the prophet Zarathustra (Zoroaster in Greek) sometime around the beginning of the first millenium B.C., Zoroastrianism became the state religion of two great Persian empires: the Achmaenian (around 540–333 B.C.) and the Sassanid (around 250–675 A.D.). Zoroastrianism continues to have around 150,000 adherents: The largest community today is in India and is known as the Parsis. The religion of Zoroaster was a cosmic dualism. It proposed that there are two gods: a good god of light (Ahura Mazda) and an evil god of darkness (Angra Mainyu). These gods of good and evil are engaged in a cosmic struggle for dominion over the world. But Zoroastrianism was also an ethical dualism. Ahura Mazda is the guardian of *asha,* the cosmic principle of goodness, truth, and righteousness; Angra Mainyu, however, upholds the cosmic principle of *druj,* which represents falsehood or the lie. Human beings were believed to be poised between these two ethical principles: asha and druj. Zoroaster exhorted his followers to conform to the ethical standard of asha in their thoughts, words, and deeds.

At death people are judged according to the ethical character of their thoughts, words, and deeds. That judgment is not determined by the supreme will of Ahura Mazda; rather, it is the result of a symbolic self-disclosure in the experience of the soul beyond death. Three days after death, the soul is conducted to a bridge that separates this world from the next. It is called the Chinvat Bridge, or the Bridge of Separation. On the other side of that bridge lies the Zoroastrian paradise: the House of Song that emits a boundless, radiant light. The ethical character of each soul will be revealed as it attempts to cross this bridge.

When a righteous soul, dedicated throughout its life to asha, begins to cross the bridge, it encounters the sweet fragrance from paradise. As it reaches the center of the bridge, it is met by a beautiful, radiant form. The Zoroastrian text describes this form as a lovely, young woman. When the soul asks who she might be, she responds "I am your *daena." Daena,* or con-

science, is that inner dimension of religion cultivated through thoughts, words, and deeds. The daena informs the soul that its thoughts, words, and deeds have made her beautiful. They embrace and proceed across the bridge into paradise.

When a wicked soul, dedicated throughout its life to druj, begins to cross the bridge, it encounters the foul stench from hell that looms as an abyss beneath the Chinvat Bridge. The text describes this smell as the worst punishment the soul will endure. Considering the severity of later punishments, this must be a very bad smell. As this wicked soul approaches the center of the bridge, it is met by an ugly, frightful apparition. The Zoroastrian text describes this form as a hideous old hag. When the wicked soul asks who she might be, she responds: "I am your daena." The soul is informed that its wicked thoughts, words, and deeds have made the daena uglier day by day, and that the soul's wickedness will cast them both into the abyss of hell. The soul tries to flee, but the daena embraces it, and they both fall off the bridge into the hell below.[18]

In this symbolic journey through the other world, the soul is judged on the basis of the ethical character of its conscience. That daena had been shaped by the quality of thoughts, words, and deeds during life, and it is revealed during the course of the soul's passage through death. The ethical character of the daena is symbolized in aesthetic terms: The good character of a righteous conscience assumes a beautiful form, the evil character of a wicked conscience assumes an ugly form. The ethical harmony of asha produces a beautiful daena, but ethical dissonance produces a hideous and frightening apparition. The aesthetic quality of the conscience is disclosed after death, and the ethical judgment of the soul is imagined to be a direct result of that self-disclosure.

Judgment in Tibetan Buddhism

During the first two centuries of the common era, Buddhism was introduced into Southeast Asia from India. By the sixth century a new variety of Buddhism had arisen in the Himalayan regions of Tibet. Several schools of Tibetan Buddhism emerged that supported elaborate mythological beliefs, new rituals and meditation techniques, and religious communities centered around the authority of an enlightened teacher. This teacher was known as the *lama*. Tibetan Lamaism flourished as one of the major forms of Buddhism in Southeast Asia until the emergence of Communist China disrupted traditional religious communities. Tibetan Buddhists were instructed in ritual meditation practices designed to awaken consciousness and achieve liberation from the karmic cycle of rebirth. One important text that was used as a focal point for meditation was the *Tibetan Book of the Dead* (*Bardo Thödol*). This text presents a visionary journey beyond death. It was designed to be read into the ear of a dying person, but its rich symbolic imagery was probably also a focus for meditation during life. It organized the Buddhist's expectations of what would be encountered during the passage through death. The judgment that took place on that journey was not based on the Buddhist's conscience; it was based on the quality of consciousness.

The *Tibetan Book of the Dead* suggests that the journey through death will be divided into three stages: (1) the moment of dying; (2) an interim stage of illusions; and (3) a final stage in preparation for rebirth. Because the Tibetans subscribed to the classical Buddhist assertion that there is no soul (*anatman*), they do not assume that there is some permanent self that passes through these stages after death. Yet the reverberating waves of consciousness set in motion during life will carry on through death, and consciousness will continue in death to encounter vivid images, perceptions, and experiences.

The challenge is to recognize that these after-death experiences are simply projections from consciousness. In that realization the consciousness may transcend the play of appearances and achieve liberation from subsequent rebirths.

At the moment of dying, the *Chikhai Bardo,* the consciousness encounters the radiant light and reverberating sound of Buddha nature. The consciousness is exhorted to recognize this pure light and sound as itself. If consciousness knows this undifferentiated Buddha essence as itself, it is liberated from future births. But consciousness will probably recoil in fear from the splendor of enlightenment, and retreat into the familiarity of its personal ego identity. At this point consciousness is propelled into the second stage.

In the *Chonyid Bardo,* the interim stage, consciousness beholds a dazzling array of illusions. First, it is met by five radiant divine beings: the merciful heavenly Buddhas. Consciousness is urged to recognize these gracious gods as itself. But the emotions of pride, anger, greed, lust, and so on will probably arise to alienate consciousness from this liberating realization. These are the dissonant desires that bind consciousness to a personal ego identity and prevent a full recognition of its inherent Buddha nature. Then a second set of illusions appears in the form of wrathful, avenging gods. The *Tibetan Book of the Dead* describes 58 angry, vengeful, blood-drinking deities, swinging axes, wreaking havoc, and violently attacking the consciousness. Consciousness is urged to recognize that these, too, are simply projections from itself. The evil deities, as well as the good deities, are merely projections of consciousness. But the truth behind these illusions will probably not be recognized. In suffering and anguish, the consciousness will be propelled to the final stage in the *Sidpa Bardo.*

The last stage in the journey through death prepares the consciousness for rebirth. Here consciousness will be subjected to judgment and punishment. It is confronted with the mirror of past actions and is punished, tormented, and tortured under the direction of a divine judge. Even at this point, consciousness might still achieve liberation by recognizing that mirror, judge, and punishment are all projections from itself. These punishments are not merely retribution for past actions; they are a program of educational shock therapy to refine, purify, and awaken consciousness. The experience of judgment and punishment depends entirely on the quality of consciousness. At this final stage consciousness will probably not recognize the truth of its Buddha essence, and it will begin to prepare for rebirth. The text suggests that consciousness starts to glow with the color corresponding to the world in which it will be reborn. This is the final disclosure of consciousness to itself before rebirth. That birth may occur in one of six worlds: (1) a fiery or icy hell; (2) a temporary heaven; (3) the ghost world (*preta-loka*); (4) a world of warrior-demons (*asura-loka*); (5) the animal world; or (6) the world of human beings. The judgment that determines the world in which consciousness will be reborn is solely the result of the quality of consciousness itself. It is attracted to the world that corresponds to its own level of enlightenment.[19]

Judgment of the dead plays an important role in systems of religious ethics. It symbolizes the absolute standards that measure human merit. In Zoroastrianism judgment measured the merit of a person's conscience; in the *Tibetan Book of the Dead* judgment measured the quality of a person's consciousness. What is impressive about these two examples of judgment is that the person's evaluation is revealed through a process of self-disclosure. A strong aesthetic sense operates in these judgments. A good conscience in Zoroastrianism is one that is in harmony with asha. A liberated consciousness in Tibetan Buddhism is one that is in harmony with its own Buddha nature. Actions, desires, or dispositions that disrupt that ethical harmony subject the con-

science or consciousness to punishment. The disruption of harmony in a system of ethical judgment may be classified as sin.

Sin

Judgment is the objective determination of sin; guilt is its subjective consequence. Sin is not simply a general sense of wrongdoing, but a very specific disruption of the ethical harmony that is sustained by a religious tradition. The perception of sin in the history of religions has taken three basic forms. First, the practical definition of sin is specific actions that are performed against ethical norms: the violation of specific ethical norms, rules, or laws. Second, the emotional definition of sin is contrary dispositions of desire: the cultivation of discordant feelings, attitudes, and desires. And third, the existential definition of sin is an alienation of the human spirit: a deep sense of separation from the ethical ideals that are embodied in a tradition. These three perspectives on sin tend to be interwoven within the ethical fabric of any religious tradition that is based on the judgment of human actions, desires, and dispositions. We can separate them, however, for the purposes of analysis. They represent three different aspects of the human engagement with sin and sinfulness in ethical experience.

Sin as Dissonant Action   To sin is to break commandments, disobey instructions, and behave in a way that contradicts some specific obligation. The normative pattern of a tradition sets the conditions for ethical action; sin breaks those conditions. The guilt of sin results from violating the specific conditions of a sacred contract. The conditional character of sin is often expressed contractually in religious traditions, in the form of "if . . . then" propositions. The ethical contract suggests that if certain acts are performed, then certain sanctions will be enforced. Punishments for sinful acts may be written into the terms of the contract.

A good example of this conditional character of sin is found in a text that appeared in the later Taoist tradition. The *P'ao-p'u Tzu* is a manual of religious ethics that outlines the conditions of the ethical contract. It consists of a long enumeration of sinful acts. If these acts are performed, then punishment will surely follow.

> *If they say one thing in people's presence and the opposite behind their backs . . . if they are cruel to subordinates or deceive their superiors . . . if they manipulate the law and accept bribes . . . if they destroy the public good for their selfish ends . . . if they shoot birds in flight or kill the unborn in womb or egg . . . if they overcharge or underpay . . . if they take things by force or accumulate wealth through robbery and plunder . . . if they love to gossip about peoples' private affairs . . . if they commit any of these evil deeds; it is a sin.*[20]

As the text continues, if an act is considered a sin it will be duly punished. The Arbiter of Human Destiny will reduce a person's life span on a kind of sliding scale, from units of 3 days up to 300 days, depending upon the seriousness of the offense. When all the days have been deducted from an individual's allotted term of life, then the person will die.

Sin may therefore represent specific acts in violation of a sacred ethical contract. The terms of that contract are made explicit in the normative pattern of action. Any specific violation makes a person vulnerable to judgment and punishment. Particularly in western religious thought, sin has this judicial character. A sinful act is an objective sign of guilt before the tribunal of divine judgment.

Sin as Dissonant Desire

These specific transgressions against ethical norms also involve a more profound opposition between human desires and the sacred authority implicit in those ethical norms. At this second level, sin is a disposition of human desire away from the perceived goals of the religious tradition. Sin directs human desires away from the feelings and attitudes that must be cultivated to properly respond to the demands of obligation. Just as moral harmony involves more than simply obedience, the dissonance of sin is more than simply disobeying the rules. Moral harmony requires an alignment between personal desires and the authority that animates obligation. Sin represents a disruptive dissonance between personal desires and the pattern of obligation.

Self-centered dispositions, such as pride, anger, greed, and lust, often define the more fundamental character of sin in systems of religious ethics. The standard list of sins developed during the Christian middle ages—The Seven Deadly Sins—were actually dispositions of human desire, rather than specific actions. These sins were more psychological dispositions than legal violations. The deadly sins—pride, anger, lust, sloth, greed, gluttony, and envy—were perceived as expressions of human desire that necessarily led away from God and toward a self-centered entanglement with the world. The Italian poet Dante Alighieri, in his *Divine Comedy,* referred to the Seven Deadly Sins as "misdirected love."[21] These misdirected desires separated human beings from the divine love that orchestrated the celestial harmony of the heavenly spheres. The sacred order of ethical harmony was disrupted by the dissonance of desire, and not simply specific sinful acts.

A similar perception of sin, as aberrant dispositions of desires, appears in Buddhism. We have already noted how personal desires were described in the *Tibetan Book of the Dead* as forces that bind consciousness to the limitations of ego identity. Within Buddhism the emotions of lust, greed, and anger are the conditions of human sinfulness that ensnare the human consciousness in the world of illusions, karma, and rebirth. They are self-centered dispositions of desire that inevitably produce suffering in human experience. Dissonant desires disrupt the ordered ethical harmony that represents a preliminary, and often necessary, first step on the path toward enlightenment.

Sin as Alienation

Finally, sin may appear as a fundamental condition of alienation that pervades human experience. The term *sin* is derived from a word meaning "to miss the mark." As the archer misses the target, people enmeshed in sin miss the pattern of action marked out by their religious tradition. The sinner might miss the mark, however, not through willful disobedience, or discordant desires, but because of a chronic disability that is felt to be endemic to the human condition. Human beings may perform sinful actions because as humans they can do nothing else. A basic alienation may prevent any possible alignment between human actions and their target. *Alienation* is to experience oneself as alien or other. It is to experience the deeply disturbing dissonance of being fundamentally *other* than one should be. Within some ethical systems, sin is perceived as something pervasive in human nature that makes people unable to do what they should do and be what they should be.

In many forms of Christian ethics, this fundamental alienation is defined by the notion of original sin. The unavoidable sinfulness of the human condition is felt to have been inherited from Adam. As Paul insisted, "one man's sin led to the condemnation for all men." (Rom. 5.18) That sinfulness has been transmitted through the generations to all human beings who, from the moment of birth, are alienated from God as part of the great fallen mass of humanity. Sinfulness is, therefore, understood as a pervasive resistance to the ethical pattern; it is an intractable inertia that operates in all human action. For this reason, Paul himself observed, "I can will what is right, but I cannot do it." (Rom. 7.18) By virtue of their fallen nature, original sin is understood to alienate human beings from achieving the pattern of ethical perfection through their actions.

Other religious traditions have developed different symbolizations for a pervasive sense of alienation that runs through human ethical experience. The ethical aspect of any religion may be viewed as a therapeutic program for analyzing, interpreting, and perhaps even curing this sense of alienation. The philosopher and psychologist William James once noted that every religion does two things: (1) it diagnoses the basic problem of the human condition; and (2) it proposes a cure.[22] A system of religious ethics may, in this respect, be a therapeutic enterprise that identifies the causes and heals the conditions of alienation. On the other hand, human beings might not feel alienated if they were unaware of the ethical pattern in relation to which they could experience themselves as *other*. A tradition of religious ethics holds up a certain pattern of ethical harmony against which dissonant acts and dissonant desires can be measured. It is within such ideal patterns of harmony that actions and desires are able to seem dissonant. Religions may, in fact, be therapeutic programs designed to cure the very sense of alienation that they produce.

Symbolism of Evil

Every religious tradition is confronted with the challenge of locating the experience of dissonance within the larger context of the universe, within a more general and inclusive mythic framework. How does a religious tradition account for sin, suffering, and misfortune in the world? How does it explain the undeniable fact that things do not appear to be as they should be? In the history of religious thought, this is the problem of evil. Evil is a fundamental dislocation in human experience that arises in misfortune, suffering, and death. There are ethical evils that occur when human beings perpetrate pain and suffering on each other, but in traditions of religious ethics, even physical evils, such as illness, disaster, and misfortune, may be given an ethical interpretation. All of the various forms of distress, disruption, and dissonance in human experience may be given an ethical content within a system of religious ethics.

Magical Realism

In small-scale, local, primal religions, the problem of evil has been approached practically; this has been called *magical realism*. Rather than trying to formulate abstract, general, or universal explanations for evil in human experience, magical realism inquires into the causes of evil in concrete situations. Misfortune is believed to have a definite cause. It may be the result of violating a taboo or it may be the result of a witch's curse. In either case, the immediate cause of a person's misfortune can be identified, and appropriate steps can be taken.

The anthropologist E. E. Evans-Pritchard documented the magical realism in response to evil among the African Azande. He observed that they do not pose the general, abstract question: "Why do people suffer?" Rather, they seek to identify the underlying cause of a specific misfortune within a particular situation. The Azande ask: "Why has the granary fallen on my brother and not on someone else's brother?" Here they are confronted with a very specific instance of misfortune. The Azande have highly developed beliefs in the magical power of witchcraft. The misfortune of one member of the community may have been caused by evil forces set in motion by another member of the community. They ask a second question: "By what means can I discover who practiced witchcraft against my brother, thereby causing the granary to fall on him?" Evil is highly personalized. Ritual techniques may be used to divine the responsible person. Once the witch is identified, a third question is asked: "What specific actions must I perform in order to wreak vengeance upon the witch?" The response to a particular incident of misfortune is to identify the cause and to take revenge.[23]

Vengeance is an important ethical response within magical realism. The harmony of the community that is disrupted by evil can only be restored through some corresponding reciprocal action. Acts of revenge are perceived as restoring the balance between people in the community that has been disturbed by some misfortune. The restorative action may take the form of a ritual counterattack against the witch. But the experience of misfortune could also require any number of other ritual responses: sacrifices, purifications, exchanges, and so on. These acts of restitution are practical methods of restoring the harmony that had been disrupted through an encounter with evil.

Religious Idealism

The notion of sin becomes highly developed in those religious traditions that seek to work out some rationalized, universal, and abstract symbolic context within which human beings might understand the experience of evil. This can be referred to as *religious idealism*. Religious idealism in the symbolism of evil appears as patterns of religious belief in which sin, suffering, and misfortune are located. It attempts to make sense out of the experience of evil. The sociologist of religion Max Weber suggested that there are three basic patterns of religious idealism that locate evil in human experience: monotheism, dualism, and monism.[24] Each system represents a different economy of evil. They identify the meaning and value of sin, suffering, and misfortune in relation to the sacred. These different patterns may appear in any religious tradition, but each tradition tends to develop one pattern as its primary strategy for locating evil.

In monotheistic systems, such as the ethical monotheisms of Judaism, Christianity, and Islam, sin is essentially disobedience. The perfect design of the universe established by its creator is understood to have been disrupted by the disobedient exercise of free will. The primordial human couple disobeyed the will of God and introduced dissonance into the world. This sin of disobedience is perceived to be the root of all evil in the economy of the universe. By locating evil in this way, these traditions are able to maintain an image of a divine being that is all powerful and all good. But the presence of evil within a monotheism would seem to suggest that God could not be both all powerful and all good. God might be all powerful and include evil in His nature, because evil appears in the creation for which God is solely responsible. Or God might be all good, but not powerful enough to produce an entirely good creation. By locating the origin of evil in the sin of disobedience, the mythic framework of monotheism is able to transfer responsibility to human free will turning away from God. Not only is the image of God maintained in its absolute goodness and power, but evil may even be incorporated in some greater design for a higher good.

In dualistic systems, such as the ancient Persian dualism of Zoroastrianism, or the Gnostic and Manichean dualisms of Hellenistic antiquity, sin is essentially materiality. The economy of the universe is divided between forces of good and evil, powers of light and darkness, that contend with each other over humanity and the human world. In this case, evil is not simply the perversion of the human will, but a real force in the universe. It is an independent antagonist to the good that is built into the nature of the cosmos. The world is understood to be presently under the control of the powers of darkness. To be involved in the material world, in the body and its desires, is to be ensnared in the powers of evil. Elements of dualism, in the imagery of demonic powers of darkness, are also at work in the monotheistic traditions of Judaism, Christianity, and Islam. To the extent that a monotheism identifies evil with a Satan, Devil, or Iblis, it has incorporated dualism into its basic understanding of evil.

Finally, in monistic systems, such as those developed in many forms of Hinduism and Buddhism, or in the Neoplatonism of Plotinus, sin is essentially ignorance. Any *monism,* derived from a term meaning "the one," sees unity behind the illusory world of appearances. Suffering, misfortune, and death, and all the manifold forms of dissonance, are basically illusions. Human beings experience dissonance to the extent that they lack the liberating insight into the unified, harmonious nature of reality. Everything is in a state of harmony, but the sin of ignorance obscures this basic fact. And the experience of evil that follows from this ignorance is simply a perceptual mistake. People must adjust their awareness in order to perceive the underlying cosmic harmony.

These three patterns of religious idealism define basic symbolic contexts for locating evil. Often they generate elaborate rational strategies for explaining the origin, meaning, and purpose of evil in human experience. These rational explanations of the causes and conditions of dissonance, however, do not alter the fact that human

beings inevitably experience distress, disturbance, and anxiety in their personal and social lives. We have suggested that religious ethics creates feelings of dissonance, in the forms of shame and guilt, in relation to the obligations embodied in sacred norms. But religious ethics also proposes specific strategies for responding to the experience of dissonance in the dilemmas of personal identity and social interaction. We will briefly survey those basic situations in which dissonance appears in the human life cycle and social relations.

Dissonance in the Human Life Cycle

Dissonance may be particularly acute during certain stages of the human life cycle, in situations when self-identity is in question. In times of dramatic change, times of growth or decay, individuals may experience uncertainty or anxiety about their identities. Ethical rules of the life cycle identify these feelings of dissonance and suggest a course of action for their resolution. Life-cycle transitions are intense periods of change that involve special ethical challenges for the individual and for the community of which that individual is an integral part. Religious ethics responds to these challenges.

The Challenge of Trust

Birth involves the challenge of creating a context of basic trust in which the infant can grow, develop, and form a sense of identity. In infancy, there may be an inherent dissonance between genetic nature and cultural nurture. The demand of the infant for immediate gratification

of desires, called in psychoanalytic literature the primary narcissism of infantile megalomania, comes up against the constraints of the infant's most immediate social environment in its relations with parents and siblings. The infant gradually acquires a sense of both the limits and potential of its power. That immediate community of significant others, however, also has the challenge of creatively introducing a new human being into its social world. Every birth calls upon a community to reaffirm its own self-understanding in order to introduce a new member.

Religious traditions respond to the life-cycle crisis of birth through both ritual and ethics. Birth rituals may isolate the mother and infant, and in some cases the father, from the rest of the community, and reintroduce them through purifications, naming rituals, circumcisions, and various other means of ritually marking the transition of a fully human being into the world. Along with these ritual actions, there are also ethical responses to the challenge of a new birth. Ethical rules relating to the practices of abortion and infanticide, as well as the ethical roles of family members in the care of the child, establish an environment of trust in which the child's self-identity may emerge.

The Challenge of Transformation

Adolescence involves the challenge of successfully making the transformation from childhood to adulthood. Here, dissonance may take the form of anxiety, uncertainty, or distress in assuming new social roles. It may appear in feelings of inadequacy before new social demands and in acts of rebellion at the prospect of new social responsibilities. Religious traditions respond to the life-cycle transition of adolescence through both ritual and ethics. Rituals of initiation focus the uncertainties that are involved in a changing sense of self-identity into dramatic rites of passage from childhood to adulthood. The child may symbolically die in the initiation ritual so that an adult may be born. With this new identity comes greater ethical obligation. Ethical rules that define this new sense of obligation may take the form of disciplinary training in the behavior, customs, and manners that are required for adult status in the community. Often, to be an adult is to act like an adult. Such ethical training defines those rules that guide and govern adult behavior.

Rebellion, delinquency, and deviance may also arise during the challenge of transformation. A system of religious ethics may develop creative responses to ethical deviance during the transition from childhood to adulthood. Among the Gururumba, for example, a young adult male who is of an age when he is expected to establish himself in the community, to take a wife and build a house, may find himself in a state of dissonance. He may become a "wild pig," perhaps as a result of being bitten by the spirit of an ancestor, and leave the community to live in the jungle, occasionally harassing the village, shooting arrows at the villagers, and displaying other antisocial behavior. The villagers leave food out for this "wild pig," with calm assurance that after a time he will return to the village, cured of his possession, and assume a legitimate adult role within the community.[25] Religious traditions develop a variety of ethical rules to respond to the challenges of transformation.

The Challenge of Tension

Sexuality involves the challenge of the tension between males and females in any society; and it involves the creative tension of human sexual instincts, drives, and desires. Dissonance may reside in unequal gender roles. There may be conflicts between the social roles of men and women, giving rise to a tension between different expectations and opportunities. Religious traditions respond to the tension between males and females through both ritual and ethics. Ritual separations of men and women are common in traditional patterns of worship, education, and work. Traditional systems of religious ethics propose different sets of rules, and thereby define different ethical obligations, responsibilities, and requirements, for males and females.

Religious traditions also respond to the creative tensions of human sexuality through ritual and ethics. Rituals of marriage define the accepted pattern for sexual relations, and they provide the basic ritual boundaries for classifying deviant sexual behavior. Extramarital sexuality, and various forms of what may be classified as deviant sexuality, are directly addressed by ethical rules within religious traditions. Ethical obligations in human sexuality seek to create a context in which sexual tension may be channeled into socially productive avenues.

The Challenge of Transcendence

Illness, aging, and death involve the challenge of transcendence in the face of ultimate human limit situations. These conditions that reveal the limitations of human consciousness, will, and vitality present the challenge of rising above or going beyond these limits and finding meaning in the degeneration of the human condition. Religious traditions respond to the life-cycle challenges of illness, aging, and death in ritual and ethics. Healing rituals provide a creative response to the uncontrollable contingencies of human life. They may dramatize a pattern of well-being in the face of physical, emotional, and mental suffering. Rituals of dying, the *ars moriendi,* give meaning to the decline of human vitality.

And funerary rituals affirm the ongoing connection between the living and the dead.

In religious ethics the question of transcendence in illness, aging, and death lies not so much in avoiding suffering as in suffering with dignity, meaning, or grace. The challenge of transcendence is to find ways to rise above the decay of the body. The ethics of medical care, as well as the ethical questions of euthanasia and suicide, all involve this underlying dilemma: the challenge of achieving some degree of transcendence in life-cycle situations that place human beings at the edge of their own mortality.

The various challenges of the life cycle are met by religious traditions with ethical rules. These rules provide guides for action in response to the dissonance of life-cycle transitions; they provide standards for right action at each stage of that process of development. The challenges of trust, transformation, tension, and transcendence suggest a basic structure for the ethical rules of the human life cycle in any religious tradition. In Part Two, we will examine the variety of these ethical rules.

Dissonance in Human Social Relations

The network of social relations that makes up any human community may also create dissonance. Expectations, desires, and basic human values may not be met within the social environment. This experience of social dissonance seems to be particularly prevalent in modern, industrial, western societies, where ritual has lost much of its cohesive power to provide a basis for ethical norms, rules, and values. Cut from its traditional roots in the power and authority of ritual, religious ethics has had to accommodate rapid

historical change, complex institutions of social organization, new technologies that have revolutionized human life styles, intense economic pressures of the marketplace, and escalating threats to human survival. New opportunities for the social dissonance of alienation, discontent, boredom, and anxiety arise in modern networks of social relations. And new challenges arise for religious responses to the difficult dilemmas of social relations.

The Challenge of Institutions

Institutions in modern, western societies are designed to provide services that hold the society together. Basic cultural values of health, safety, learning, communication, and so on are provided by corresponding institutions. Even in the most fundamental spiritual matters, a sense of the sacred is provided by a separate, differentiated institution called religion. The problem in this modern arrangement lies in the fact that these values are treated as though they were commodities that are produced, provided, and distributed by institutions. This passive relation between institutions and ethical values, implied in this institutional arrangement, often results in feelings of alienation from the very values that those institutions represent. The ethical challenge of institutions lies in recovering the power to create values through action, rather than imagining that they can be passively received from institutions.

The Challenge of Technology

Technology has produced a whole range of ethical dilemmas, from artificial life-support systems to unimaginable technologies of death and destruction. Technologies for extending the power of human action in the world have always existed, but perhaps for the first time in human history technology has become the primary basis for ethical action. Technology provides new challenges, but it also seems to have replaced ritual as the source of power underlying ethical decisions and practices. The question no longer seems to be how *should* we behave in order to correspond to the perfect pattern of action represented by ritual, but how *can* we behave in order to more effectively extend our technological control over the natural environment. Although technology may come under ethical review, its very presence and power set the conditions for ethical discussion. Technology calls into question the way ethical values are produced through human action.

The Challenge of Economics

Economics involves more than simply the exchange of goods and services; it is a total social fact that weaves together economic, social, ethical, and religious values in any pattern of human exchange. The religious dimension of economic patterns of exchange lies in the way the world of goods, their possession, distribution, and exchange, gives visible, tangible shape to the most fundamental worldview operating within a society. Exchange involves an implicit disposition toward the question of value. A society's social, ethical, and religious values may be demonstrated through its consistent patterns of economic exchange.

In modern, western economies, value is the result of scarcity. *Scarcity* is defined as that condition in economics when supply is inadequate to meet demand. Religious ethics addresses ethical dilemmas of economic inequalities, imbalances of wealth and poverty, and the meaning of material possessions. But on a more profound level, religious ethics explores the logic of desire. It could be that the perception of scarcity, and the experience of economic dissonance, arises, not when there is insufficient supply, but when there are excessive demands and expectations that cannot be met in the world of goods. This economic logic of desire extends to the total perception of values: To treat values as commodities is to build scarcity into the human experience of values.

The Challenge of Survival

Survival has always been an issue in religious ethics; it is the need to respond to threats to safety and security by uncontrolled forces of hostility, aggression, and violence. Religious ethics has addressed questions relating to warfare, the holy war, and the just war. It is strained to the breaking point, however, when confronting the unimaginable prospect of nuclear annihilation. For the first time in human history, people live with the possibility that their own deaths may coincide with the extinction of the species. Research is currently being done on a pervasive, shapeless, death anxiety, which many people experience while living under the shadow of nuclear weapons. Religious ethics in the nuclear age is beginning to explore the nature of this ethical crisis in the modern world. The value of survival may be the value upon which all other human values depend.

Any network of social relations necessarily embodies ethical values. In traditional societies ethical values appear to be embedded in the power and authority of myths and rituals. Ethical values are identified and reinforced through the sacred authority of the tradition. In modern, western, industrial societies, however, values are largely divorced from sacred authority. This is one definition of the term *secular* as it is used to describe modern societies. Ethical values are defined by institutions; they are produced through technology; they are acquired and exchanged through economics; and they are preserved through practical strategies for survival.

In relation to this powerful network of values, religion is one competing voice in the ethical debate, or it may appear as one competing institution in a struggle for ethical authority. Religious traditions, to the extent that they have become separate institutions in modern societies, are in competition with other social institutions for the attention, commitment, and ethical response of modern human beings. And yet, there may be more powerful and pervasive religious motives at work in the very social network that defines, produces, exchanges, and preserves ethical values. New myths and new rituals may in fact animate ethical values within modern social relations. In Part Three, we will look at the relation between religion and ethical values.

Patterns of Dissonance

Dissonance arises out of a conflict between expectations and behavior. Ethical dissonance is an inevitable sense of distress, disturbance, or turmoil caused by the failure to fulfill the demands of obligation. It is a sense of situational incongruity in ethical experience when human beings do not act in ways that they feel they ought to act. This experience of dissonance is often a negative, debilitating, and disturbing internal conflict, yet many systems of religious ethics strive to cultivate precisely that sense of dissonance. Dissonance reveals the extent to which people have internalized the demands of obligation in their sense of self-identity. Chapter 3 has drawn a number of conclusions regarding dissonance in ethical experience.

1.   *Shame and guilt are the two basic types of dissonance.* Shame arises in an ethical context that is structured by religious distinctions between purity and defilement. Shame is an inner sense of being defiled, polluted, tainted, or stained by violating the ethical boundaries that are established within a religious community. Shame is a public embarrassment, chagrin, or distress caused by violating the ethical order. It is deeply embedded in religious symbolism of impurity. The physical imagery of defilement symbolizes the ethical dissonance of shame. The danger of defilement and the avoidance of shame reinforce a shared ethical order. Dissonance represents a disruption of this order. The symbolism of purity, however, holds the potential for restoring order and resolving dissonance.

Guilt, on the other hand, is an experience of ethical liability. It is an ethical indebtedness before the tribunal of divine judgment. Guilt is a sense of basic unworthiness before the demands of obligation. Where shame is most often a matter of public knowledge, guilt may be a private experience of dissonance resulting from a failure to fulfill the expectations of a system of religious ethics. These two forms of dissonance, therefore, arise within specific contexts of religious belief. Shame emerges as an ethical defilement within the context of an ethical order marked out by taboos. Guilt emerges from ethical judgment that accuses, convicts, and condemns people of their sinfulness in missing the mark set by ethical obligation.

2.   *It is useful to distinguish between dissonant acts and dissonant desires.* Sinful acts are specific violations of ethical rules, laws, or customs. But these dissonant actions reveal more fundamental desires that are not in harmony with obligation. Dissonant desires are considered to be those human dispositions that are in conflict with the sacred authority invested in religious ethics. The

sins of pride, anger, lust, greed, envy, gluttony, and sloth are not specific actions; they are dissonant dispositions of human desire directed away from the sacred authority upon which ethical obligation is based.

3.   *Religious traditions place ethical dissonance within a larger symbolism of evil.* The symbolism of evil within a religious tradition mediates the experience of dissonance in ethical action. The symbolism of evil allows dissonance to be accounted for within the larger symbolic context of human pain, suffering, and misfortune. This symbolism of evil is not simply a way of explaining evil. Religions do strive to explain evil—as the result of uncontrollable forces, disobedience, materiality, or ignorance; but, more than this, the symbolism of evil mediates the experience of dissonance by allowing human beings to encounter misfortune, pain, and suffering in a meaningful way. In the Hebrew Bible, for example, when Job wrestles with his sufferings and his dissonance in relation to Yahweh, he does not receive a convincing explanation for evil. Yahweh appears out of a whirlwind to reinforce the majesty of God and the relative insignificance of human creatures in relation to the divine power. This is not an answer to the question of evil in human experience. Job does not receive a rational explanation for evil, but a new basis for accepting dissonance as an integral part of human experience. As Job repents in sackcloth and ashes, he demonstrates a moral harmony with the sacred power and authority of Yahweh. The symbolism of evil within any religious tradition provides both a way of placing dissonance in the economy of the cosmos and a way of accepting, mediating, and moving through dissonance in human experience.

4.   *Religious ethics both produces dissonance and responds to dissonance in the human life* *cycle and social relations*. Ethical obligation inevitably creates a certain degree of dissonance in human experience. The ritualized perfection of obligation is difficult to achieve in ordinary behavior, and this results in the experience of dissonance that grows out of the failure to meet obligation. In this sense, religious ethics, by the very nature of the tension between normative patterns and actual behavior, generates a certain amount of dissonance in ethical experience. But religious ethics also attempts to respond to the challenges, conflicts, and crises of personal identity and social relations. The developmental dissonance of change, transition, and ultimately degeneration in the human life cycle provide opportunities for religious ethics to respond to personal dissonance. The systemic dissonance of social interactions, conflicts of interest, and the demands of order provide opportunities to respond to social dissonance. The dynamics of dissonance in ethical experience, therefore, is two-fold: (1) dissonance arises out of a failure to meet the expectations that are embodied in ethical obligation, and (2) ethical obligations may take shape within religious traditions in order to respond to the dissonance that arises in personal development and social relations. A normative pattern of obligation both creates dissonance and holds the potential for resolving that dissonance in a pattern of ethical harmony.

CHAPTER

FOUR

HARMONY

Every system of religious ethics includes mechanisms for harmonizing dissonance. These strategies ease the dissonance inherent in the absolute demands of ethical obligation and achieve some degree of release from the tensions of shame and guilt. Techniques of harmonization complete the circle of ethical experience. They restore a sense of alignment between personal desires and ethical obligation. They bring behavior into a fully aesthetic pattern of closure. The tensions of emotional distress caused by the demands of obligation are channeled into creative avenues of expression through very specific, prescribed religious actions. One style of achieving harmony may become distinctive of an entire tradition of religious ethics; in other cases, a number of different approaches may be used together, or on different occasions, to achieve this condition of harmony through action. We will consider some of the

basic strategies for harmonizing dissonance before proceeding to explore specific ethical issues in the human life cycle and social relations.

Every society can tolerate a certain degree of dissonance in its ethical life. Along with ethical norms, there may be what have been called countermores. *Countermores* are transgressions of ethical norms that are expected, tolerated, and perhaps even taken for granted within a given society. The sociologists H. D. Lasswell and A. Kaplan have defined countermores as those types of behavior that are held by a community to be deviations from its mores, yet such deviations are fully expected to occur.[1] Bribery, for example, may violate an ethical norm, yet it is expected that some officials will give in to temptation. Countermores suggest the degree of flexibility through which a society can accommodate dissonance within its basic ethical system.

Although societies may be able to tolerate a

certain amount of dissonance in practice, individuals within that society may require mechanisms for restoring a sense of balance, alignment, and harmony with the ideal ethical pattern of the community. As long as the authority of obligation is acknowledged, and people act in ways that are contrary to its pattern, there will be strategies developed for harmonizing the dissonance that results. As the philosopher R. M. Chisholm observed, ethics is not simply establishing what we ought to do, "but also what we ought to do when we fail to do some of the things we ought to do."[2] In religious ethics, what people ought to do, when they do not do what they ought to do, is defined by ritual practices that serve to harmonize dissonance.

These strategies for harmonizing dissonance can be divided into two basic types: (1) practices designed to harmonize dissonant actions, and (2) practices designed to harmonize dissonant desires. The shame or guilt produced by actions contrary to ethical norms may be purged, released, or washed away through specific ritual processes for restoring harmony. Rituals of catharsis, purification, exchange, repentance, and confession may recreate the pattern of ethical harmony that had been disrupted by specific impure or sinful actions.

On a second level, strategies for achieving ethical harmony address the deeper dissonance of human desires. Strategies for harmonizing dissonant desires are not simply concerned with behavior; they involve those emotions, attitudes, and dispositions that disrupt a sense of ethical harmony. "What matters most in religious ethics," the philosopher of religion Donald Crosby has observed, "is not specific moral decisions or overt moral behavior, which affect only a relatively small part of day-to-day life, but an all-pervading harmony of appetites and passions in the inner man, so that one's inner dispositions are wholly attuned to and informed by the cosmic good."[3] The ethical strategies of detachment, asceticism, devotion, surrender, and unconditional love strive to bring human desires into a single regimen of ethical harmony. The strategies for harmonizing actions and the strategies for harmonizing desires sustain that pervasive sense of cosmic harmony toward which ethical experience is directed in any system of religious ethics.

Strategies for Harmonizing Actions

Some approaches to ethical harmony involve practices designed to counteract specific failures to meet ethical obligations. These strategies prescribe specific counteractions to eliminate dissonance and re-establish the necessary conditions for ethical harmony. Rituals of catharsis, purification, and exchange are particularly suited for eliminating the dissonance of shame, impurity, and defilement, while acts of repentance and confession are suited for discharging the dissonance of guilt. In all these strategies, however, ethical dissonance is dissolved and an overarching pattern of ethical harmony is reaffirmed.

Catharsis

Catharsis is a way of producing harmony by means of dramatic ritual techniques that release intense emotional energy. It is a ritual purging of the ethical dissonance produced by specific violations of a community's ethical norms. Aristotle, in his *Poetics,* viewed catharsis as a powerful emotional dimension in tragic drama. Through imitating life situations, the drama creates a context in which the audience experiences the intense expression of fear, anger, and violent emotions. The catharsis of drama releases negative emotional energy through acceptable social channels. By identifying with the dramatic presentation, the audience often finds expression for its own emotional tensions. Catharsis is the purging of those tensions.

Magical and ritual dramatizations become vehicles for the release of emotional energy in many religious traditions. Dramatic ritual celebrations of chaos, such as the new year festivals in some traditions, offer an occasion to suspend social conventions and ignore ordinary ethical obligations. These ritual celebrations of disorder temporarily release the tensions of obligation. The annual festival of Holi in Southern India is such a cathartic event. The celebration, dedicated to Kṛṣṇa, is held on the full moon of the vernal equinox. This festival was described by Major C. H. Buck of the Punjab Commission in 1917 as "the occasion of licentious joy, drunkenness, evil singing and dancing. Many persons lose all sense of respect for age, sex and religion—the foulest language is used, clothes are smeared with red powder [*kunkuma*] mixed with water, and this is squirted over everyone indiscriminately."[4] The Holi Festival breaks down social classifications, and in turn breaks down the boundaries of propriety, sobriety, and modesty. Distinctions between good and evil, clean and unclean, are dissolved. The festival is a public purging of ethical categories. In a society based on strict classifications of purity and defilement, this annual public catharsis plays an important role in releasing ethical dissonance. When order is restored again after the festival, people may have the sense of beginning their lives again renewed.

In catharsis personal emotional dissonance explodes in ecstatic or enthusiastic religious experience. *Ecstasy* comes from the word *ecstasis,* which means "out of the body." In ecstatic religious experience, through ritual dance, wild music, orgiastic frenzy, rhythmic chanting, or hallu-

cinogenic drugs, the individual steps out of the body, out of the confined, repressed, or disturbed bodily energies, and experiences a sudden radical freedom.[5] *Enthusiasm* comes from the word, *en-theos,* meaning "to have god within" or "to be in god." In enthusiastic experience, through spirit possession, mediumistic trance states, or the immediate rapture of the spirit, the intense power of the sacred may temporarily obliterate all vestiges of personal identity. The tensions of ethical obligation may be swept away by the energy of spiritual experience.[6]

In ecstasy and enthusiasm, dissonance is dispersed by a powerful discharge of energy. That purging of emotional energy is catharsis, which may have a powerful effect in releasing the tensions of ethical dissonance. People return to ordinary life with a renewed sense of vitality. They may have more energy to act and to respond creatively to the ethical obligations of everyday life.

Purification

Purification is the cleansing of guilt or shame through a specific pattern of ritual action. It is closely tied to the symbolism of defilement and stain. The ritual of purification itself may serve to define the sin or defilement that has been committed. It provides a specific counteraction to wash away that ethical stain. Many religious traditions practice a variety of water lustrations, ritual bathings, ceremonial cleansings, and other rites of purification to remove the defiling contamination of ethical dissonance.

Purification rituals are an important part of the religious practice in Islam. Water purification is prescribed before worship for the small pollutions that result from bodily elimination. The Muslim washes face, hands up to the elbows, feet, and ears; the Muslim sucks water up the nostrils, passes a wet hand over the head, and then is ready to enter into the ritual of prayer. Great pollution, caused by menstruation, sexual intercourse, or childbirth, requires a bath in which no part of the body remains dry. These purifications have nothing to do with modern notions of hygiene. In fact, if no water is available, the Muslim may perform these purification rites with dirt. Purification is a ritual technique that washes away the defiling effects of ordinary behavior and prepares the believer for the harmony of worship.

Baptism in the Christian tradition is both an initiation ritual, bringing the individual into the Christian community, and a ritual of purification for sin. Initiation and purification are in fact connected: In the symbolic death and rebirth of baptism the individual is purified of the stain of original sin that had been transmitted through all the human generations from Adam. There have been periods in the history of Christianity, however, particularly in the first four centuries, when baptism was understood as a mechanical ritual purification for all the specific sinful acts that have been performed in a person's life prior to baptism. This view of baptism accounts for the practice in some Christian communities of postponing baptism until late in life to wash away a lifetime of sins. The postponement also left less time after baptism for further sins. Although postponement did not survive as orthodox practice for Christian baptism, which became a ritual of purification for infants in most established forms of Christianity, it reveals some of the symbolic power of this ritual for dissolving the dissonance produced by specific sinful acts.

Purification is not only achieved through rituals of water; it may also be symbolized by rituals of blood. The Holiness Code (Lev. 19), one major formulation of religious ethics found in the Hebrew Bible, emphasizes blood sacrifice as a symbol of God's acceptance of the person who sacrifices: "When you offer a sacrifice of peace offering to the Lord, you shall offer it so that you may be accepted." The acceptance of the sacrifice implies the acceptance of the sacrificer, and the ritual purity achieved through an acceptable sacrifice erases the dissonance that results from specific failures in meeting an absolute ethical demand. The sacrificer is symbolically cleansed by the blood of the sacrifice.

The annual sacrifice of atonement required by Leviticus may be understood as a public act of ethical purification. The priest places the sins of the nation upon one of the sacrificial goats—the scapegoat—and it is taken out of the community to carry the sins of the people upon its head as it wanders in the desert. Specific sacrifices for atonement are also prescribed for the purification of priests, the temple, and the people of Israel. Sacrifice becomes a symbolic act of reconciliation between God and humanity. It is a way of releasing the dissonance that results from the radical difference between human and divine. Through rituals of purification, this dissonance is transposed into a closer harmony between human beings and God.

Exchange

Exchange is a strategy for reducing dissonance by performing actions that create ethical credit and reduce ethical debts. Exchange introduces a basic economic metaphor into the language of religious ethics. It suggests the possibility of literally paying off the wages of sin. The payment *redeems,* which literally means "buys back," the person from the shame of defilement or the guilt of sin. It reduces a person's ethical debt by means of a countervailing act of exchange.

This strategy of exchange was the basis for some of the more excessive practices of the sale of indulgences, which were part of the Roman Catholic ritual of penance in the later middle ages. An *indulgence* was a guarantee from the highest authority of the Church that in purgatory a person would be excused from suffering the punishment that was expected to result from sinful acts in this life. An indulgence could be obtained for oneself or for departed loved ones. This special dispensation could not technically be purchased; it was considered to be a free gift of absolution from the Pope. But conventionally, the issuing of an indulgence followed a donation to the Church.

The sale of indulgences in the early sixteenth century was one of the motives behind Martin Luther's break with the Catholic church. It was an impetus behind Luther's Protestant rejection of the whole sacramental system that organized religious ethics in the Catholic tradition. The Protestant Reformers claimed that indulgences were sold with exorbitant advertising slogans: "When a coin in the coffer rings, a soul from purgatory springs." Indulgence salesmen representing the authority of the Pope were said to have claimed that even if a man had deflowered the Virgin Mary he could obtain an indulgence. The sale of indulgences seemed to imply that it was possible to buy ethical justification. This was the background of Luther's assertion that justification was only the result of the free, unmerited gift from God; it was not something that could be obtained by ritual exchange. There were certainly abuses in the medieval system of indulgences. However, the strategy of exchange involved in the sale of indulgences, a practice long since discontinued by the Catholic church, is a fairly common feature in systems of religious ethics. The exchange demonstrates a commitment to the religious community that is believed to reduce ethical dissonance and increase ethical merit.

A similar attempt to harmonize the dissonance of sin through acts of exchange is found in Hinduism. In the text of the *Agni-Purana,* certain incentives were given for building temples. Again, ethical merit is demonstrated through acts of financial commitment to the religious community. Building a temple is perceived as a supreme

ethical act that produces ethical credit and cancels out the effects of sin. The *Agni-Purana* states: "He who attempts to erect temples for gods is freed from the sins of a thousand births." The evil consequences that follow from past sinful actions, according to the inexorable workings of the law of karma, are dispelled by the credit gained from erecting a temple. The strategy of exchange here also appears to produce somewhat extravagant claims: The construction of a temple for a deity, according to the *Agni-Purana,* may even dissolve the sin of murdering a priest.[7]

In many cases, a cosmic accounting system of merits and demerits measures ethical exchange. The social anthropologist Stanley Tambiah has described the role of ethical merit in a Thai village. In the popular Buddhism of this village it is generally assumed that every action either produces merit (*bun*) or demerit (*bab*). All actions can be assessed on the scale of merit and demerit. If at the end of life the Thai Buddhists have accumulated more bun than bab to their credit, then they can expect to go to a heavenly realm and remain there until all their bun has been spent. When their credit runs out, they will be reborn on earth. If, however, they have acquired too many demerits in this life, they can expect to go to a hell in order to "pay for their bab." They will only be reborn when their account has been balanced.

Various strategies are available in the popular form of Buddhism practiced in this Thai village for balancing the ethical account in this life. Bun may be gained through specific "merit-making acts." Tambiah has drawn up a list of these acts. They may be organized in order of importance, beginning with the acts that will generate the most merit. Merit producing acts include the following:

1. Completely financing the building of a temple

2. Becoming a monk

3. Having a son become a monk

4. Contributing money for the repair of a temple

5. Making gifts at an annual ceremony for the support of monks

6. Giving food to the monks daily

7. Observing every weekly fast-day at the temple

8. Strictly following the five ethical precepts[8]

What is interesting about this list is how many of the acts to gain ethical merit are forms of economic exchange: building temples, contributing to their maintenance, giving food and gifts to the monks, and so on. The list's least effective acts for producing merit are those five traditional Buddhist ethical precepts that are usually viewed as the standard of measurement for Buddhist ethics. Perhaps the ethical rules are least effective because they are simply expected to be observed in ordinary life, and the acts of exchange demonstrate an ethical commitment that is greater than the ordinary commitment expected of everyone in the community. However, the standard ethical rules do seem to play a rather subordinate role in a larger ethical accounting system of merit and demerit. And acts of exchange become an important strategy for reducing ethical demerits and increasing the ethical merit of a person within this Buddhist community.

Repentance

Repentance, a dramatic change in a person's behavior, is connected with a fundamental sense of forgiveness that erases the tensions of ethical dissonance. Many systems of religious ethics place the potential for forgiveness before the unrelenting judgment of ethical obligation. In some systems, divine release from the consequences of guilt may depend on an alteration in behavior. Forgiveness is understood as the result of a definite reversal in behavior. A change in behavior is a precondition for the restoration of ethical harmony in a tradition, such as Islam, where Allah is understood to respond to actions that are motivated by repentance. The Qur'an states: "He is all-forgiving to those who are penitent; All-forgiving, All-compassionate; and whoever repents and does righteousness, he only turns to God in repentance."[9] Penitent actions may counteract the sinful actions that are felt to deserve the judgment, condemnation, and punishment of God.

In other systems of religious ethics, however, this behavior change, repentance itself, is seen as the result, not the cause, of God's forgiveness. This is the case in the ethics of Luther, Calvin, and most Protestant theology; in these traditions the reversal in behavior, the ability to do good works, and the energy to respond effectively to ethical obligation are all the result of God's free and undeserved gift of grace. Still other systems, such as the Roman Catholic religious ethics of Thomas Aquinas, view repentance as the result of close cooperation between human effort and divine grace. In all ethical monotheisms the internalization of forgiveness, absolution from the strict application of divine judgment, eases the ethical dissonance of guilt. Repentance plays a central role in resolving the tension between behavior and the normative pattern of ethical action. It holds the potential for release from the dissonance of unworthiness, inadequacy, frustration, and despair before the absolute demands of ethical obligation.

Confession

Acts of repentance may be closely aligned with the ritual practice of confession within traditions of religious ethics. Confession is a means of bringing the inner tension of dissonance into the public arena. It makes a psychological fact social. Through confession, one may disperse the internal pressures of dissonance by bringing what is hidden out into the open. This ritual strategy seems to be particularly effective in dissolving the dissonance of private, personal feelings of guilt for particular sinful acts. Confession discloses the secret faults of conscience and makes them available for public absolution. The dissonance that is nurtured in private may be harmonized in the public ritual practices of the community.

In the Roman Catholic tradition, confession plays a central role in the ritual of penance. As the ritual practice of penance developed within the tradition, it became divided into three coordinated stages. The first stage is contrition. This is an intense inner awareness of dissonance. The individual feels guilt, remorse, and regret for having violated some ethical norm and wishes to correct the situation. Such private awareness, however, is not sufficient. It is necessary to make this private experience of ethical dissonance public. The second stage, therefore, is confession. Originally, the practice of confession in early Christian communities was a public declaration of guilt. The individual would stand up before the entire congregation and make a public admission of sin. Eventually the Catholic church institutionalized confession, making it a sacramental obligation to be performed only with a priest-confessor. Confession of private guilt is made before the public representative of the sacred authority embodied in the tradition. The third stage is penance. After hearing the con-

tent of the confession, the priest prescribes appropriate acts of penance to counteract the effects of sin. These acts may include the ritual recitation of sacred formulas, donations to the Church, acts of service to the community, or the commitment to go on a pilgrimage.

This ritual cycle defined by contrition, confession, and acts of penance represents a strategy for harmonizing the dissonance produced by specific actions that disrupt the pattern of ethical harmony. The ritual of confession has not been institutionalized within Protestant Christianity as such. But in the Methodist "assemblages of the dozens," beginning in the eighteenth century, public sessions of self-criticism and public declarations of sinfulness were encouraged. Such self-accusations became an important feature of Protestant revivalism, where public acknowledgment of sinfulness was often seen as a necessary precondition for a person receiving forgiveness and salvation.

Confession is also a ritual means of achieving ethical harmony in other religious traditions. In one Buddhist text, the *Mahavagga,* which describes the Buddhist monk's ethical obligations, instructions are given for a regular public confession of sin. The text describes how the Buddha arose from his meditation to institute the ritual of confession as a means for harmonizing the ethical behavior of his followers. He set the time for confession as the fast-day of the fifteenth day of the half-month. At that time, the monks should assemble, and their first order of business should be the public expression of their guilt or innocence.

The monks are instructed to listen to one of their learned elders reading from a text of Buddhist ethics. If they have sinned, they are to rise and reveal this fact. They are to make a public confession of that sin within the community. If they have not sinned, they are to remain silent, and their silence will serve as a testimony of their innocence. The monks are to listen to three readings of the text. At each reading they are given the opportunity to confess any sins of which they are aware. They are exhorted to make a public declaration of their sins as if they had been asked personally to confess before the group. If after the third reading they still have not confessed, their sin will be regarded as a conscious falsehood. This falsehood has such serious consequences that their sin is now referred to as a deadly sin. But if the monks do make a public declaration of sin, they will be purified. The *Mahavagga* states: "Therefore, if a monk remembers having committed a sin, and desires again to be pure, let him reveal the sin he committed, and when it has been revealed, all shall be well with him."[10] This ritual of confession is seen as a necessary self-disclosure that will free the Buddhist monk from the dissonance of sin.

The ascetic tradition of Jainism also practices the technique of confession in order to harmonize the dissonance that must arise from the extremely rigorous demands of the tradition. The Jain ethical ideal of perfect harmlessness (*ahimsa*) extends to all forms of life. Jaina ethics even includes prohibitions against inadvertently killing bugs while walking or destroying the invisible entities that inhabit air and water. Confession is an important way of harmonizing dissonance produced from being in constant danger of sin and impurity. The Jains are instructed to confess: "As long as I live, I confess and blame, repent and exempt myself from these sins, in the thrice threefold ways, in mind, in speech and in body."[11] Confessing in this way allows the monks to achieve some degree of exemption from the unavoidable harms that are caused by human actions. It resolves the inevitable ethical dissonance of striving to live within such rigorous demands for perfect harmlessness.

The laity within Jainism, who do not submit to the strict ascetic discipline of the monks, are also instructed to confess their sins. The first sin to be confessed is lack of proper respect for monks, whose heroic efforts in observing the ethical demands of the tradition are felt to transfer merit to ordinary people. This sin is followed closely by a list of the "day-to-day transgressions of mind, speech or body, through anger, pride, deceit or greed." The confession concludes with a declaration of the person's rededication to repentance: "Whatever offense I have committed I here confess, repudiate and repent of it and set aside my past deeds."[12] The ritual of confession in Jainism suggests that secret sins may not always be conscious. Sinful acts that harm other living creatures may have been performed unknowingly. Confession acknowledges that possibility and embraces even unconscious sins in its ethical harmony.

Strategies for Harmonizing Desires

Systems of religious ethics obviously must propose mechanisms for alleviating the dissonance produced by specific actions that violate the ethical norms, rules, and values of the tradition. However, more general strategies also appear within religious ethics for harmonizing the dissonance of human desires. These strategies are fundamental orientations toward action that focus moods, attitudes, and dispositions into a particular ethical style. They are not concerned with releasing the tension produced by specific impure or sinful acts, but with addressing the basic desires that motivate action in the world. The most common strategies for harmonizing desires try to bring all human experience under a single regimen of desire. Human desires may be unified in religious ethics through the strategies of detachment, asceticism, devotion, surrender, and unconditional love. These strategies for producing ethical harmony coordinate all the desires that animate action into a single ethical pattern.

Detachment

Detachment is an attempt to deal with desire by eliminating it. As an ethical orientation toward action, it encourages disinterest in the concerns of the world. In the ethical strategy of detachment, an individual acts without any regard for deriving personal benefit from action. This is the regimen of detachment encouraged by the discipline of action—*karma yoga*—in some forms of Hinduism. In the sacred text of the *Bhagavad Gītā,* Kṛṣṇa exhorts his disciples to act without any attachment to the results, or fruits, of their actions. "The action alone be thy intent," Kṛṣṇa instructs, "never its fruits."[13] Ethical action in this sense is simply the disinterested performance of the duties and obligations that are required by a person's station in life. Detachment in karma yoga implies that these duties and obligations are performed without any concern for personal benefits that might result. Desire is harmonized by acting without desire. In this way, people become free of the karmic cycle of cause and effect through which they are bound to the world of action.

The logic of desire in Buddhism suggests that the thirst, craving, and grasping after experience in the world is the basic cause of all human suffering. We may not get what we desire—and we suffer. Or we may get what we desire, but it dies, decays, or deteriorates in the normal course of things—and we suffer. Suffering results from attachment to objects, experiences, and relationships in the world of action. If a Buddhist should be so unfortunate as to fall in love and to feel an attachment to another human being, one form of Buddhism prescribes a meditation as an antidote

to this desire. The Buddhist is instructed to picture the face of the beloved as vividly as possible and then to imagine the flesh rotting, decaying, and melting away until only the skull remains. This is a sure cure for love's desire. In Buddhism, detachment is the extinction of desire. This is captured in the enigmatic term *nirvana,* which literally means "blowing out the flame" of desire. Detachment is a strategy for the liberation from the dissonance of human suffering. The cycle of grasping, losing, and suffering is broken through a supreme detachment.

In western thought also detachment may be recommended as an ethical orientation designed to harmonize human desires. The Greek Stoic philosophers prescribed an ethical attitude of *apathea.* They sought to cultivate a disposition of calm equanimity in relation to action in the world.[14] The Neoplatonic philosopher Plotinus also developed an approach to religious ethics based on detachment. The soul, which carries within it the light of divine reason, becomes evil when it is involved in the world, when it becomes entangled in the shadowy world of material desires. Eventually, the soul identifies itself with the roles it plays while caged in the prison of the body. Ethical virtue lies in detachment from the body. Plotinus explained the virtue of detachment in his *Enneads:*

> *The soul is evil to the extent that it is "mingled" with the body, in sympathy with it and judges in accord with it. And the soul is good and virtuous if this accord no longer has place and if it acts alone (such as thinking and being prudent), if it is no longer in sympathy with the body (this is temperance), if quit of the body it no longer feels fear (this is courage), if reason and intelligence control with ease (this is rectitude).*[15]

The classical virtues of prudence, temperance, courage, and justice are all united in this single ethical orientation: the detachment of the soul from the body. Plotinus defines this detachment of the soul as the likeness of God because it is ruled only by the divine intellect and is unaffected by bodily desires. This ideal of detachment provided an important ethical orientation that supported the development of the western mystical traditions within Judaism, Christianity, and Islam.

Asceticism

Asceticism is a strategy for controlling desire by disciplining the body. It is a denial of the flesh and the pleasures of the flesh. In this respect, asceticism is closely aligned with the technique of detachment. Unlike detachment, however, this strategy does not necessarily seek to leave the body. Asceticism disciplines, regulates, and controls the body. It focuses its primary ethical concerns upon the body and devises a regimen of work, study, and other disciplines to contain the body within a systematic network of controls.

The sociologist of religion Max Weber distinguished between two types of asceticism: other-worldly and this-worldly.[16] In the other-worldly varieties of asceticism, such as the ethical practices of monastic orders in Buddhism and Christianity, the monastery acts as a total institution for the discipline of the body. This monastery creates a carefully regulated pattern of work, study, and prayer. It systematically controls all the physical processes of waking, sleeping, and eating. And monastic asceticism denies any expression of sexuality. In such a comprehensive ascetic discipline, whatever physical activities that can be regulated will be subjected to disciplinary management. The vocation of the monk is to leave the world of ordinary society and submit to a rigorous discipline of the body.

In what Weber called this-worldly varieties of asceticism, which are most characteristically the Calvinist descendents of the Protestant Reformation, the discipline of the body is carried out in the situations and circumstances of everyday life. The Protestant work ethic insists that the Christian vocation is not to withdraw from the world of action, but to remain within ordinary social life. Within that context, however, the Christian is expected to submit to a rigorous discipline of the body. Work becomes the primary instrument of this ascetic discipline. The ethical value of work, as a vehicle for controlling the energies of the body, is essential to this type of asceticism. Disciplined activity, productive labor, and the utilization of human and natural resources set in motion a disciplinary regimen for the body. In the practices of this-worldly asceticism, the pleasures of the flesh are to be denied, although the Christian is still exposed to them in society. Desires become harmonized under this unified regimen of ascetic discipline.

Devotion

Devotion is a strategy that attempts to concentrate the multitude of human loves, longings, and attachments upon one sacred object. The object of devotion becomes the single focus of desire. The devotional strategy harmonizes all desires into the single-minded love and service of a personal deity. Every action becomes an act of devotional service to that god, and all the disparate desires that animate action are reduced to the simple harmony of devotion.

Within one form of devotional Hinduism, the devotee of Kṛṣṇa is expected to perform all worldly actions with a single-minded devotion to God. In this *bhakti-yoga,* or the discipline of devotion, every action is to be performed in loving service to Kṛṣṇa. In the *Bhagavad Gītā* Kṛṣṇa exhorts his devotees: "Whatever you do, or eat, or sacrifice, or offer, whatever you do in self-restraint, do as an offering to me. Thus you will be freed from the prison of deeds and their results, good and evil."[17] Devotion to Kṛṣṇa, expressed in even the most mundane actions of human life, becomes a way of unifying desire. Worldly action becomes infused with a constant attitude of devotion, as if the beloved divine presence was felt in every activity. In this way the strategy of devotion strives to harmonize the dissonance of conflicting desires and to define a path of escape from the karmic conditions that limit human freedom in action.

This attempt to unify desires is also found in western devotional traditions. The misdirected love of the Seven Deadly Sins, which Dante explores in the Inferno and Purgatorio of his *Divine Comedy,* are harmonized in Paradiso in his description of the beatific vision of Mary. In the center of the celestial rose, which Dante beholds at the summit of paradise, Mary is orchestrating a cosmic symphony of devotion. This directed love unifies all human desires. It harmonizes the dissonance of discordant desires so that Dante can describe his heart as "attuned to that love that moves the sun, moon and stars."[18] This devotional love of the heart is seen as the supreme virtue that aligns the human heart with that celestial harmony.

Devotion appears as a practical ethical orientation in the devotional Jewish movement known as Hasidism, which started in Eastern Europe during the eighteenth century. The ethical ideal of *devequt*—being with God—was an inner disposition of devotion felt to pervade all actions in the world. Everything was to be done with an awareness of the presence of God. The ideals of devotional humility, service, and even ecstasy were to inform every aspect of Hasidic life. The philosopher and interpreter of Hasidism Martin Buber called this inner disposition "the sacramentalization of the world."[19] To act as if every action is an interaction with God is to make a total ritual pattern of devotion of ethics. The strategy of

devotion strives for harmony through precisely such a single focus of desire.

Surrender

Surrender is the resignation of will. It is the act of giving up personal desires, wishes, plans, and intentions to some higher power. In this sense, surrender may be simply the other side of devotion, but the primary concern in the disposition of surrender is the renunciation of personal will to some more authentic source of willpower that is felt to operate in the world. Devotion may be involved in this ethical disposition of surrender, but it is not necessary. This strategy simply requires that all personal desires be harmonized by surrendering them to a more legitimate, powerful, or authoritative source of action, which is felt to be beyond ordinary desires.

Sometimes this more powerful, authentic source of action is perceived as a divine, supernatural agency. This is certainly the case in Islam, which literally means *surrender,* where the will of Allah is supreme. Many passages in the Qur'an suggest that the supreme will of Allah has predetermined everything that happens in his creation. The notion of predestination runs through many schools of Islamic thought. Predestination is also a theme developed in some forms of Christianity. The later writings of Augustine and the theology of John Calvin suggest that both salvation and damnation are ultimately predetermined by God. The primary ethical strategy that follows from this assumption is total submission to the will of God. In the ethical strategy of surrender, personal desires are irrelevant, as the person seeks only to submit to the desires of God that are expressed in the revelation of sacred scripture.

Other religious traditions provide examples

of surrender that do not assume the existence of a supreme being who governs the world of action. The ethical orientation suggested by Taoism, and some forms of Chinese Buddhism, is based on a principle of non-doing (*wu-wei*). In the ethical disposition of non-doing, there is again a surrender of personal desires to a more authentic source of action. Here, however, the individual surrenders to what is perceived as the natural rhythm that animates the universe. Non-doing is giving up striving or struggling or trying and simply going with the natural flow. The enigmatic poetry of the *Tao-te ching* suggests that when people surrender to the natural rhythms of the universe, they are able to flow through life in a state of balance, harmony, and equanimity. As water reaches its appropriate level by surrendering to the course of the river, human actions may take on an effortless, natural quality. Whether the more authentic source of action is the will of God or the rhythms of the Tao, surrender represents an ethical harmony with that source.

Unconditional Love

The strategy of unconditional love cultivates an ethical disposition toward the world that strives to harmonize all human actions and interactions in a love that is beyond the dissonance of desire. Regardless of situation or circumstance, all human beings are to be regarded with the same compassionate consideration. There is an impersonal quality in this ethical strategy. Personal preferences, likes and dislikes, are irrelevant. No conditions may intervene to limit the universal extension of this love to all persons. Love is seen as a unifying force, harmonizing self and other, which has the potential for bringing all action into a cohesive ethical harmony.

This love appears in the Hebrew Bible as a bond that unites a particular people. The people of Israel are commanded "To love all human beings who are of the covenant, as it is said: 'Thou shalt love thy neighbor as thy self.'" (Lev. 19.18) An unconditional bond of love is felt to unite the people of the covenant. But this unconditional love is not simply felt to unify the covenant community; many ethicists in the Jewish tradition have connected this love of neighbor with the instruction "To Love the stranger, as it is said, 'Ye shall love the stranger.'" (Deut. 10.19) The unconditional love of neighbor and stranger, those who are like us and those who are not like us, is felt to provide a basic harmony of human desire from which ethical behavior may proceed.

This love also appears to be the basis of Christian ethics: "You shall love God with all your heart, mind and strength; and you shall love your neighbor as your self." (Lk. 10.25–8) There is no question about placing conditions upon this love. In fact, many examples in the Christian New Testament concern those who seem to deserve love the least: those people who strike you on the cheek, take your coat, or make you walk a mile. The ethical strategy of unconditional love insists that this loving disposition toward others is independent of such external considerations. Love becomes canonized as the most important of the Christian ethical virtues in Paul's hymn to a love that goes beyond rational understanding:

> *Love is patient; love is kind and envies no one. Love is never boastful, nor conceited, nor rude; never selfish, not quick to take offence. Love keeps no score of wrongs; does not gloat over other men's sins, but delights in the truth. There is nothing love cannot face; there is no limit to its faith, its hope, and its endurance. (1 Cor. 13)*

An important distinction emerged in the Christian tradition between two kinds of love: *agape* and *eros*. While erotic love is motivated by personal desires, affections, and interests, agape is unlimited by such concerns. It is a divine love that fills the human heart and overflows into the world. When Augustine suggested that love is the ultimate ethical standard—"Love, and do what you will"—he considered this divine, unconditional love as a power in the human heart to harmonize all desires within an ethical pattern of action.

This emphasis on unconditional love as the standard for ethical behavior is sometimes called *agapism*. The philosopher Paul Ramsey called this Christian ethics of love pure-rule agapism.[20] He suggested that it is an exercise of love that presupposes the Mosaic law of the Ten Commandments, as well as a context of faith in divine authority over human actions. Yet, at that same time, unconditional love is a deontological ethical standard, a rule for conduct that is not dependent upon calculations of the projected outcome of actions. In this respect, pure-rule agapism is something like Kant's second imperative as a formula for ethical action: Human beings should never be used as means to an end, but always regarded as ends in themselves. The ethical strategy of unconditional love appreciates humans as beings of inestimable, irreducible, inherent value.

The philosopher William Frankena, however, has proposed that the ethical strategy of love might be called utilitarian agapism. He observed that the commandment to love is too ambiguous to work effectively as an ethical guide for behavior. It often gives rise to sloppy, romantic, affectionate sentiment, and it is not a realistic basis for determining the principles of justice that should apply in given social situations. Frankena suggested that what is really intended in agapism is a "benevolent commitment to promote good and justice."[21] This disposition of benevolence represents the quality of love that animates action, but the goodness and justice of those actions is determined by a consideration of their consequences.

In these considerations, it is important not to lose sight of the unconditional character of agape. Unconditional love does not depend on whether or not others may deserve it, nor is it concerned with furthering the practical interests of self or others. This love is primarily a disposition of the heart that is designed to harmonize the many different desires expressed through the medium of action. As an inner disposition, or attitude, it is perhaps similar to what the psychologist Carl Rogers has called unconditional positive regard.[22] As such, it may in fact be an impossible ideal, yet it remains one important strategy within some systems of religious ethics for trying to harmonize human action within a single regimen of desire.

Patterns of Harmony

Religious ethics is not simply a matter of knowing what one ought to do; it is also knowing what one ought to do when one does not do what one ought to do. The various religious strategies for achieving harmony strive to dissolve the dissonance of ordinary human failures to meet the demands of obligation. In this sense, the possibility exists within any religious tradition that ethical experience may be resolved in a harmonious alignment between human actions and the sacred authority of obligation. Religious ethics is not simply a pattern of action; it is a dynamic process by which actions and desires are harmonized with the sacred power and authority invested in ethical obligation. Chapter 4 has drawn a number of conclusions regarding patterns of harmony.

———

1. *Religious ethics begins and ends in ritual.* The process of religious ethics can be interpreted in three stages. First, the ritualized perfection of ethical obligation presents a pattern of action to which human behavior should conform. Second, the experience of dissonance indicates some degree of conflict between pattern and actions. Third, ritual practices are utilized to dissolve that dissonance. The experiential effects of dissonance may be expunged, erased, purified, fumigated, expelled, balanced, discharged, and resolved through specific ritual practices. These rituals of harmony are designed to dissolve ethical dissonance. Rituals of purification may wash away the dissonance of shame; rituals of confession may ease the dissonance of guilt. Within religious traditions, such ritual practices are an integral part of the ethical process that leads to a sense of moral harmony. These rituals of ethical atonement are not something added to ethics; rather, they fulfill the demands for ritualized perfection in human behavior with which ethical obligation begins.

———

2. *Rituals of harmony may not entirely resolve dissonance.* The ritual order may not be entirely congruent with the ethical order. Ritual strategies for harmonizing dissonant actions may still leave a remainder of ethical dissonance. The order of ritual harmony may not entirely resolve conflicts of dissonant desires in religious ethics. A second set of strategies, therefore, directly addresses the ethics of desire. The strategies for harmonizing desires may also involve specific ritual practices, but their goal is to bring all human desires under a single, unified regimen of desire. Strategies of detachment, asceticism, devotion, surrender, and unconditional love strive to re-

solve ethical dissonance and establish ethical order by bringing all desires under the domain of a single desire. Ethical order, therefore, is not simply a matter of adapting behavior to an obligatory pattern of action. Religious ethics also requires an attunement between desires and sacred patterns of action that will support a sense of moral harmony in ethical experience.

———

3. *Moral harmony in religious ethics is an attunement between desires and obligation.* An interpretation of ethical experience in the history of religions suggests that religious ethics is a complex, dynamic process of human involvement with the sacred obligations that govern ordinary, everyday behavior. In that encounter with obligation, desires are shaped, ordered, and harmonized. Or, they may be frustrated, confused, and ambiguous in their relation to obligation. This play of desire is at the heart of ethical experience in the history of religions. It may be useful at this point to simply recollect the essential ingredients in ethical experience.

First, a sense of obligation is provided, supported, and reinforced by the sacred authority of a religious tradition. Obligation has two basic dimensions: ritual and aesthetics. The ritual dimension of obligation presents the very notion of perfect action. Ritualized perfection in ethical norms, rules, and values is derived from the human ability to perform ritual patterns of action with reference to whatever is held sacred. Religious ethics is grounded in ritual, not only in the sense that ritual suggests the possibility that action can conform to a perfect pattern, but also in the sense that rituals of worship, prayer, meditation, and sacrifice cultivate certain dispositions that are necessary for the fulfillment of ethical obligations.

The aesthetic dimension of religious ethics emerges from the fact that ethical obligation requires human beings to fit their behavior to certain patterns, images, models, styles, and rhythms of action. These are all basic aesthetic categories in religious ethics. To the extent that the goal of religious ethics is a certain fittingness between pattern and action, religious ethics is more like aesthetics than logic. Obligation is fulfilled when there is an aesthetic harmony between normative patterns and human actions.

Second, the human ability to respond to ethical obligation reveals a variety of dispositions of desire in religious ethics. If moral harmony is an alignment between desires and obligation, then harmony can theoretically be accomplished by either adjusting desires to obligation or by adapting obligation to fit desires. The first strategy is a moral response; the second is an improvisational response. The moral response achieves harmony by cultivating inner dispositions of desire so that they fit the requirements of obligation. The moral response fulfills the demands of obligation, as Confucius said, in such a way that people may follow their desires and not oppose ethical obligation. Here the disciplined response is not regarded as sufficient for a full experience of moral harmony. Morality, in this sense, does not simply require that one do what one ought to do; it requires that one desire to conform behavior to the shape of obligation. It is also possible that obligation might be denied, inverted, or simply ignored. This would be the antinomian response. Although antinomianism is an important response to obligation, it tends to be a minority position within religious traditions. The more conventional process of achieving moral harmony in the history of religions is the work of attuning desires to the pattern of obligation.

Philosophical ethics in the western tradition, as a response to the sacred authority of obligation in religious ethics, has elements of both the antinomian and improvisational responses. Philosophical ethics is antinomian in the sense that sacred authority is believed to be ultimately irrelevant to ethical reflection and action. Rational categories for ethics deny, or ignore, sacred authority, and therefore propose indepen-

dent rational criteria for ethics that are beyond the hold of sacred obligation. Philosophical ethics is also improvisational in that moral harmony is achieved by adapting, modifying, and even creating ethical norms to match personal demands. These are not the demands of desire, however, but the demands of reason.

Rationality in philosophical ethics must be independent from both desire and sacred authority. Obligation is adjusted to independent sets of rational criteria for ethical action that are not determined by personal preference or religious tradition. Rational improvisation in western philosophical ethics has produced a number of conflicting and perhaps irreconcilable criteria for ethical action. Some ethical philosophers have concluded from these contradictions that ethical norms may after all simply be a matter of personal desires, taste, or preference. In the quest to define rational principles for ethics, however, philosophical ethics has ignored the fact that ethics in the history of religions has not been simply a way to determine proper actions, but a process of cultivating virtues, dispositions, and inner resources for behaving in ways that are in harmony with sacred authority. Ethical norms, rules, and values function within a process of harmonizing actions and desires with sacred authority. This is the context within which ethical experience takes shape.

Third, the path toward harmony in religious ethics is inevitably disrupted by dissonance. The dissonance of shameful or guilty actions reveals a deeper dissonance of desire. Ethical norms, rules, and values are religious instruments for patterning both actions and desires into the order of sacred authority. But the pattern of ethical harmony is often disturbed by dissonant desires, feelings, and emotions. This conflict of desire is perhaps the single most crucial experience in religious ethics. It is not a question of whether ethical norms produce a sense of harmony in knowing what ought to be done, or whether they produce a sense of dissonance through either failing or expecting to fail at what ought to be done. Ethical norms may generate any of these experiences. Ethical experience necessarily involves a fundamental tension between dissonance and harmony.

The experience of dissonance is integrated into a larger pattern of action that is supported by a system of religious ethics. It reveals the degree to which obligation has been internalized; it reveals the intensity of the personal desires that animate action; and it reveals the ideal pattern of harmony that allowed ethical dissonance to arise as dissonance in the first place. A sense of shame may be considered a precondition for ethical purity. A sense of guilt may be regarded as a precondition for ethical atonement. The dissonance of shame and guilt, in this respect, only arises within a religious context that embodies an ideal pattern of harmony. Dissonance is necessarily incorporated into the very nature of ethical experience in the history of religions as a vital prelude to harmony.

Finally, the potential for achieving moral harmony is reinforced in religious traditions through specific practical strategies for harmonizing actions and desires. The ritual and ethical order that informs human experience through these strategies aligns personal desires and religious obligation. In this sense, actions and desires may be experienced as fitting in relation to the sacred norms for ordinary behavior that are held within a religious tradition. This aesthetic sense of fittingness also provides the basis for whatever may be experienced as harmonious actions in personal behavior and social relations. In personal behavior, a sense of harmony may be supported by specific rules for right action, right conduct, or right behavior. Ethical rules that govern personal behavior particularly deal with the challenges of life-cycle transitions. Rules define right action during those transitions in the life cycle when personal identity is most in question. Part Two addresses ethical rules of the life cycle in traditional and modern religions. These rules provide detailed guidelines for right behavior in response to the ethical challenges of the life cycle. But they also provide a more basic sense of harmony in ethical experience. The process of ethical experience in the history of religions is a dynamic, dramatic, and ultimately aesthetic trajectory toward harmony within ethical patterns of action.

PART

TWO

ETHICAL RULES IN THE HUMAN LIFE CYCLE

*T*he human life cycle consists of a fairly constant set of challenges of transition—birth, adolescence, sexuality, and death—that are surrounded by ritual practices and governed by ethical rules in religious traditions. These may be marked out by ritual practices: birth rituals, adolescent initiation rituals, marriage rituals, and death rituals. These life-cycle transitions also present a series of ethical challenges that are addressed by customary practices, moral guidelines, and legal proscriptions. The customary, moral, and legal rules governing the dilemmas of life-cycle transitions constitute patterns of personal ethics within religious traditions. Many major issues in contemporary personal ethics occur in the liminal situations of life-cycle transitions. The dilemmas of abortion, infanticide, adolescence, adulthood, gender roles, sexuality, marriage, euthanasia, and suicide all raise questions of personal action, personal identity, and

personal involvement in a network of rules governing behavior in the transitions of the life cycle. Part Two explores the possible responses, suggested by illustrations from traditional and modern systems of religious ethics, to the most important challenges of personal ethics in life-cycle transitions.

Chapter 5 considers ritual and ethical patterns of action surrounding the event of birth. Birth rituals signify patterns of *classification,* which set the terms for acknowledging an infant birth as an authentically human birth, patterns of *care,* which indicate the parental responsibilities for the nurture of the child, and patterns of *community,* which initiate, introduce, or include the infant in the larger society. These issues of classification, care, and community arise in contemporary controversies over infanticide and, more intensely, over abortion. The abortion debate in particular can be interpreted as a conflict over the appropriate system of classification for what constitutes a human being, the appropriate measure of care in bringing children into the world, and the appropriate moral and legal responses on the part of the community, which contribute to a context of trust in which a fully human infant identity can emerge. The first chapter of Part Two, therefore, is called *Trust*.

Chapter 6 examines ritual and ethical patterns of action in response to the life-cycle transition from childhood to adulthood. Adulthood represents full participation in the ethical obligations and responsibilities of a community. In primal, archaic, and traditional religions, some type of formal initiation into adulthood was often an important ritual process that mediated this transition. The transition beyond childhood and toward adulthood has been more ambiguous in the modern world. To be an adult is to act like an adult. This involves often unexamined customary, habitual, and conventional rules for behavior. A close look at religious manuals for the discipline of children offers a genealogy of the rules that attempt to mold children into adults. This disciplinary transformation of children into adults focused almost exclusively on the body: table manners, bodily functions, physical purity, and so on. By conforming their bodies and bodily behavior into patterns of action associated with adulthood, children were transformed into adults in these systems of religious ethics. This second chapter of this section is called *Transformation*.

Chapter 7 explores the ritual and ethical patterns of action surrounding gender roles and sexuality. Marriage rituals reinforce culturally specific patterns in the relations between males and females and the socially sanctioned expressions of sexuality. Within traditional systems of religious ethics, gender roles have tended to systematically subclassify women. The ethics of obedience, which appears in different forms in religious traditions, imposes a set of rules upon women that requires obedience to male authority. In ancient China and India, for example, these

rules appear as the "three obediences": A woman must obey her father as a child, her husband as a wife, and her sons as a widow. The ethics of gender roles in traditional systems of religious ethics embodied a certain tension between male and female power. This tension has become more explicit with the changing role of women in modern societies. Human sexuality also involves dynamic tensions of instinct, desire, and energy within systems of religious ethics. Issues of contraception, the ethical status of pleasure, the discipline of sex, and alternative forms of sexuality are all addressed by systems of religious ethics. The rise of a modern science of sexuality, dedicated to the management of sexual behavior, reproduction, and even large-scale populations, has generated new tensions in human sexuality. This third chapter of this section, devoted to examining gender and sexual ethics, is called *Tension*.

Chapter 8, the final chapter of Part Two, considers ritual and ethical patterns that aspire to transcend the human limit situations of illness, aging, and death. Healing rituals in religious traditions specifically address the transcendence of human suffering, disability, and physical distress. The ethical consequence of traditional healing rituals often cultivates an attitude toward illness, aging, and death that places them within a larger pattern of transcendence; these rituals allow human beings to rise above or go beyond the apparent limitations of life, while at the same time enduring the suffering inherent in the human condition. Funeral rituals, cemeteries, and memorials for the dead signify images of transcendence, but healing rituals represent a potential for the living to transcend human limitations. Two major ethical issues that the living confront concerning death are the dilemmas of euthanasia and suicide. This final chapter of Part Two, therefore, examines ethical rules governing euthanasia and suicide as efforts to rise above, go beyond, or move through the ultimate limit situation of death. This chapter is called *Transcendence*.

CHAPTER
FIVE
TRUST

A sense of basic trust has been described by the psychologist Erik Erikson, in his research on the psychology of the human life cycle, as the foundation of self-identity.[1] In the earliest stage of life a sense of self emerges out of a context of trust: trust in others and trust in self. This basic trust provides a pervasive sense of confidence in a child's immediate environment of parents and family, and a confidence, safety, and security in an awakening sense of self. Of course, the potential for mistrust is always present, the lack of confidence that may grow out of frustrated needs, wants, or desires. Building a network of trust is the ethical challenge of infancy and early childhood. This challenge may be as simple as creating confidence in the regularity, continuity, and dependability of the natural and social world into which the child emerges. Confidence in the order of things is often carefully constructed through ritual and ethical action. Through action,

human beings attempt to create a perfect pattern of trust in response to the challenge of birth.

The most immediate environment in which infant identity emerges is, of course, the coordinated relations between infant and mother. Initially, this is a symbiotic relationship—living together. In this paradoxical situation, the infant is absolutely dependent and, at the same time, absolutely demanding. Psychoanalytic literature refers to the infant's absolute demands for the immediate gratification of desires for food, warmth, love, and so on as infantile megalomania. Infants apparently perceive themselves as the center of the universe, and mothers seem to be connected to them as self-contained support systems for the satisfaction of basic desires. In this earliest oral phase of development, infants do not seem to distinguish between themselves and an environment from which they receive satisfaction for all their needs.

It is only gradually that infants begin to perceive themselves as distinct persons. As they perceive themselves to be separate from the mother, a feeling of loss, or what is sometimes called "infant mourning," may arise. Desires are no longer immediately gratified on demand; they are now regulated by systems of training, routines of behavior, and negotiations in a world of conflicting desires. The basic elements of ethical action come into play in the situations of infancy and early childhood: the obligations of early childhood training; the different responses that infants make to these new obligations; the condition of dissonance, which takes the form of the repression of the most basic demands of desire in order to adapt to a social world; and, finally, the potential for harmony in building an environment of trustworthiness and mutual recognition.

We will examine the ritual and ethical responses to this challenge of creating an environment of basic trust. Birth rituals mark the entrance of a new member into the network of relations that define a human community. Ritual practices that surround the event of birth classify the infant, indicate the measure of care and responsibility that will be appropriate for raising the child, and signify that the infant is a fully human member of a human community. Borderline cases arise, however, when a fetus or an infant may be the product of human reproduction, yet for some reason may not be classified as a legitimate member of the human community. The ethical dilemmas of infanticide and abortion deal with these borderline situations. The religious rules governing infanticide and abortion attempt to define and reinforce a pattern of basic trust in response to the ethical challenges presented by the phenomenon of birth.

Birth Rituals

A religious community or tradition may surround the event of birth with ritual practices that serve three basic purposes. First, rituals dramatically signify that the infant is to be classified as a legitimate, complete, and fully human person. Second, birth rituals establish the context of care in which the infant's welfare, training, education, and so on will be provided. And third, these rituals openly facilitate the child's incorporation into a larger human community. These three functions of birth rituals—classification, care, and community—are central issues within religious traditions. Birth rituals are creative responses to the precariousness of human life in its earliest, and perhaps most enigmatic, stage.

In most societies, childbirth is considered an event of ritual impurity. Therefore, the mother is often separated from the rest of society. Perhaps she is removed from the village, secluded in a separate birthing hut, or isolated in a hospital. The expectant mother is separated from society, the family group, and perhaps other women in order to protect these groups from the danger perceived to be inherent in childbirth. After birth, rituals reintroduce the mother, along with the child, into the ordinary social world. Birth rituals form a cycle of symbolic actions that mark the entrance of a new human being into the community. This ritual process can be illustrated through a description of pregnancy and birth among the Toda of India.[2] This small community surrounds the process of birth with a cycle of ritual practices that highlights the basic ethical challenges of classification, care, and community that must be addressed in order to build a context of basic trust.

Rituals of Classification

The Toda live in a world that is structured by strict classifications of purity and defilement. This is the realm of taboo. We have noted that taboo operates in highly charged situations relating to sexuality, death, and otherness. Pregnancy brings together all three of these issues in the person of the expectant mother. When a woman becomes pregnant, she is forbidden to enter the sacred places. Such contact would be considered defiling both for her and for the community. In the fifth month of pregnancy the Toda hold a ritual ceremony—called "village we leave"—in which the woman goes to live in a special hut. She is carefully isolated from any contact with the dairy, which is the main economic industry of the community. This isolation signifies a ritual impurity associated with pregnancy and produces new boundaries that govern the expectant mother's behavior. Pregnancy is, therefore, governed by ritual classifications of purity and defilement.

However, these classifications do not simply apply to the mother: The fetus itself is a problem for classification. The fetus is obviously a product of human sexual reproduction, but there is some uncertainty regarding its status. It is a living organism, but in some sense it still may be considered as part of the world of the dead; it may be classified as not, or not yet, a fully complete, autonomous human person. The term of pregnancy is surrounded by important ritual taboos that create a protective boundary around this period of uncertainty and apprehension. These taboos mark the beginning of a system of classification

that will either accept or exclude the fetus as a human being. The classification of the mother and the fetus is the first stage of the ritual cycle of birth.

Rituals of Care

During the seventh month the Toda perform a special ritual called the Ceremony of the Bow and Arrow. This ritual is designed to determine who is to be the father of the child. We might think that paternity should already have been established as a biological fact, but the role of father is essentially a social fact: Who will be responsible for the care, support, and well-being of the child? Toda society practices *polyandry:* One woman may have a number of different husbands. The uncertainty that attends any pregnancy over the biological paternity is replaced by a ritual that guarantees the social paternity. The ritual Ceremony of the Bow and Arrow publicly acknowledges the responsibility of one adult male in the community for providing the necessary care for the new child.

In some societies that need to reinforce the social role of the father, there is a ritual practice called *couvade,* in which the father also goes into isolation during the mother's pregnancy, labor, and delivery. Although this practice may look something like sympathetic labor pains, it makes a public statement that the father is assuming responsibility for the care of the child. Sometimes, particularly in polyandrous societies, a question over the identity of the father will be settled by competitive couvade. Competing claimants to the title of father may all go into isolation, and they will try to make their case by convincing public opinion that they are the legitimate father. Determining responsibility for the care of the child is an important part of the ritual cycle of birth and is an essential ingredient in creating a context of basic trust.

Rituals of Community

Two or three days after the delivery, the Toda mother, father, and child go off to live in a special hut. There a set of rituals is performed. All three are believed to be tainted with an impurity called *ichchil*. Ceremonies are performed to protect them against the defilement of birth and the influence of the evil spirit (*keirt*). Finally, the family is permitted to return to ordinary life after drinking the prescribed sacred milk. These important ritual practices are designed to reincorporate the mother into the ordinary social life of the community. After the final rituals of purification and inclusion, the mother and her family are ready to be accepted as part of the community.

More important for the status of the child, however, are ritual practices designed to introduce the child into human society. The problem presented by the classification of the infant is resolved through rituals that acknowledge the humanity of the infant and guarantee its place in the human community. Sometimes these community rituals mark off a gradual process of development, as is the case in the traditional practices of the Ainu community of Japan. The Ainu assume that the infant gradually becomes a human being after birth. According to the tradition, the mother gives the child a body; the father gives it a soul. It takes 12 days for the soul to develop. During that period, the father will spend the first six days in a friend's hut and then the next six days in his own hut. After 12 days the child, having developed a soul, will be classified as a complete, autonomous person. The anthropologist Arnold van Gennep summarized this Ainu system of classification by observing that "it takes several days of

real life for the child to become an individual."[3] Once that time has elapsed, the child is acknowledged as a fully human member of a human community.

Another ritual practice within religious traditions that introduces the infant into the community of human beings is the naming ritual. By receiving a name, the infant is individualized, is given a unique, personalized designation. The infant is also socialized by the fact that the name places the infant within a network of social relations. A name communicates the child's gender, family, relation to ancestors, and any number of other important social facts. The ritual act of naming simultaneously acknowledges the child as a unique individual and as an integrated member of a human society. The name communicates a child's personal and social place in the community.

A variety of other ritual practices incorporate infants into the community of human beings. In the religious tradition of Judaism, for example, the ritual of circumcision, a religious and surgical operation performed on the male child eight days after birth, symbolizes the social fact that the child is a fully legitimate member of the community. In a symbolic sense, the covenant, or bond, between God and the people of Israel is physically inscribed on the male member of the male member. In the Christian tradition, the ritual of baptism also signifies the incorporation of an infant into the community. Infant baptism acknowledges the infant as a fully legitimate human being within the recognized ritual practice of the Christian church.

All of these birth rituals create an ideal pattern of action. They produce a ritual context for the development of basic trust in the lives of infants. The ritual practices of birth resolve uncertainties about (1) the classification of the fetus or infant, (2) the responsibility for the care and well-being of the fetus or infant, and (3) the social role of the fetus or infant within the community. The issues of classification, care, and community that are addressed by ritual behavior establish a context for responding to the two major ethical challenges of birth: infanticide and abortion. These ethical challenges are also dilemmas of basic trust in response to the event of birth within the human life cycle.

Infanticide

The anthropologist E. E. Evans-Pritchard observed that the seminomadic cattle-herding community of the Nuer practiced infanticide upon any abnormal, deformed, or monstrous birth. Within the classification system of the Nuer community, any monstrous birth will be classified as a baby hippopotamus. This is not to suggest that the Nuer literally believe that the deformed infant is a hippopotamus, but this classification implies that such an infant is not considered a legitimate member of the human community. It is classified as beyond the boundaries that define humanity. Once the infant has been classified as a baby hippo, the appropriate measure of care is indicated: The infant is gently placed in the river where it belongs.[4] Within the classification system by which the Nuer define the human community, the practice of infanticide is not considered to be a cruel destruction of an infant life; it is perceived as a necessary exercise of care that restores the nonhuman creature to its appropriate place in the natural order.

Western thought on the subject of infanticide has gone through two basic phases: first, the qualified acceptance of the practice in ancient Greece and Rome; and, second, the unqualified rejection of infanticide in the religious traditions of Judaism and Christianity. We will briefly review the ethical rules regarding infanticide in these two phases in the history of western religious ethics.

Infanticide in Ancient Greece and Rome

The destruction of infants, or allowing infants to be exposed to the elements, was a relatively common practice in ancient Sparta. The Spartan military society placed great value on physical strength. Any child that showed weakness, or disability, did not fit the ideal pattern of a human being and should not, therefore, be permitted to live. The ethical rules governing the practice of infanticide reinforced a cultural ideal of human perfection. Any infant that did not match this ideal was classified as fundamentally outside of the human community. The ethical practice of infanticide was perceived as a viable strategy for preserving the quality control of that community. Qualified support for the practice of infanticide is found in the writings of the most influential of ancient Greek philosophers—Plato and Aristotle.

Plato, in his *Republic,* suggested a number of conditions under which infants should not be allowed to live. He identified three basic categories of children that might be candidates for infanticide: (1) all children who have some physical imperfection, deformity, or disability; (2) children who are the offspring of "depraved citizens"; and (3) children whose parents are considered to be too old. According to Plato, all these children should be buried.[5] Plato indicated that abortion, or feticide, is preferable, as it is a more humane method of population control. But the killing of infants is considered an acceptable ethical practice under certain specific circumstances.

Aristotle also supported the practice of infanticide as a means of controlling both the quality and the quantity of the human population. To maintain an image of quality in the human community, Aristotle said that "nothing imperfect or maimed should be brought up."[6] Infanticide represents a kind of strategy for human quality control. As to regulating the quantity of human beings, Aristotle felt that population increases should be controlled to avoid poverty, social unrest, and other evils.[7] The number of children permitted to any family should be set by the state. Any children that are born, over the prescribed limit, should be terminated. Aristotle also preferred abortion to infanticide, but the practice of infanticide was accepted as a legitimate method of controlling the human population.

Ancient Roman society also practiced infanticide. According to Cicero, Roman law provided that deformed infants should not be allowed to live.[8] Seneca observed that "we destroy monstrous births, and we also drown our children if they were born weakly or unnaturally formed."[9] The ethical rules regarding infanticide described by these Roman, Stoic philosophers reinforce a basic cultural distinction between natural and unnatural births. Seneca also suggested that these rules were an act of reason—to separate what was useless from what would be useful. The practice of infanticide was thought to play an important role in this separation of the useful and the useless within the ancient Roman community.

The Roman father held the power of life and death over his children. This was referred to as the *potens patria*. As the one designated responsible for the care of his children, the father also had the legal right to expose or destroy newborn infants. Some attempts were made to modify this absolute power of the father on the part of Roman legislators. One Roman law exhorted the father to allow all his sons and at least the eldest daughter to live. This law not only reflects the different cultural values placed on male and female children within Roman society, but it also suggests that in the Roman practice of infanticide female infants were destroyed more often than male infants. Roman law also forbade the father from destroying any well-formed child until it had reached the age of three years. It was hoped that by this time the father's affection for the child would have developed to the point that the child would not be killed. The law continued to assume, however, that it was the father's responsibility to terminate the life of any infant that was, in the words of Seneca, "unnaturally formed." In other words, any infant that did not conform to the shared cultural pattern of natural form, proportion, and symmetry could be subject to infanticide. Once the infant had been classified as "unnatural," the prescribed method of care was to exclude it from the human community.

Infanticide and Christian Ethics

The Hebrew Bible suggests that the religious ethics of ancient Israel opposed the practice of infanticide. References are made opposing the infanticide that took the form of child sacrifice within some of the religious practices of the ancient Near East. Some evidence indicates, however, that child sacrifice was practiced in ancient Israel. Sacrifices to the god Moloch were performed in a valley outside the city walls of Jerusalem. (Lev. 18:21) The name of this valley in Greek—*Gehenna*—became a popular term for hell in the religious vocabulary of Hellenistic Judaism at the time early Christian communities were formed.

Authorities in the early Christian church were also strongly opposed to the practice of infanticide. The second century Church Father Justin Martyr opposed the Roman practice of exposing infants on the roadside for two reasons. First, if the infant lived it would most likely be used for immoral purposes such as prostitution, thievery, or slavery. Second, if the infant died of starvation or exposure, this practice should be considered murder.[10] To label infanticide "murder" was to call into question the absolute power over life and death attributed to the Roman father. It was to assume that the child did not depend upon the father for identity and that the child's status was not classified in terms of parental authority: The child was classified from birth, or perhaps even from conception, as an autonomous individual.

The status of the child in early Christian thought was particularly exalted by statements, such as those attributed to Jesus, that "You shall become as little children to enter the kingdom of heaven." The rejection of parental authority in the issue of infanticide is an interesting development in the light of a certain passage in the New Testament in which Jesus is quoted as destroying the power of the family unit and replacing it with a higher power. Jesus intended to "set a man at variance with his father, and the daughter against her mother." (Mt. 10.34) In this disruption of ordinary family relationships, the child is credited with a new, independent status in the kingdom of heaven: "Call no man your father upon earth: for no one is your father, which is in heaven." (Mt. 23.9) In practical terms, the child's independent status threatened the *patria potens* of the Roman father. With regard to infanticide, this new status challenged the notion that the father held life or death authority over his children.

The ritual practice that celebrated this independent status of the individual was the ritual of baptism. Water baptism served as a ritual of initiation into the community of the Church and the kingdom of heaven. It was a ritual of such symbolic significance that Augustine, as well as other Church leaders, was convinced that an unbaptized infant would be condemned to punishment in hell.[11] In Christian ethical reflection, the most basic conditions of an infant's identity were established by the ritual of baptism. It signified a central ritual classification: A baptized infant was assured a place in heaven; an unbaptized infant was only eligible for suffering in hell. Baptism, as a ritual classification, marked the boundary between eternal life and death. This ritual classification informed the Christian consideration of infanticide that is reflected in canon law. The Council of Metz (852), for example, ruled against the practice of infanticide. But, it further specified that the punishment for a mother would be more severe if she had killed an unbaptized child than if she had killed a baptized child.[12] The eternal consequences of killing an unbaptized infant were considered to be more serious because the child was deprived of any hope of heaven.

The issue of infanticide was involved in a second set of classifications in the legal reforms of the nineteenth century in Europe and America. Nineteenth century legal codes tended to distinguish between two classes of infants, based on the symbolic classification established by the ritual of marriage. Some infants were legitimate, others were illegitimate. In legal standards and practices during the nineteenth century, the death of an illegitimate child was not as serious as the death of a legitimate child. An unmarried woman who destroyed her illegitimate child was not in the same class as a murderer. The practice of infanticide was not by any means condoned, supported, or encouraged, but the ritual classification of legitimacy played an important role in the ethical, legal, and social thought concerning infanticide in the nineteenth century. Both European and American legal systems reflected this ritual classification in their treatment of the practice of infanticide.

In the modern world, infanticide tends to arise as an issue in population control and medical ethics. The government of modern China has attempted to control overpopulation by restricting families to one child. Reports from China suggest that it is not uncommon for a family that has reached its limit in children to practice infanticide on any subsequent births. Female infants are particularly vulnerable to infanticide. Strong economic, as well as traditional, pressures upon the Chinese family encourage having sons. A male child is felt to provide greater economic security for his parents in their old age; in addition, there are remnants of the traditional Confucian ideal that a son is necessary to carry on the obligatory rituals for the family ancestors. In either case, infanticide is apparently practiced as a method of population control. It is important to note how many of the ethical dilemmas of the human life cycle become reduced to issues of population control in the modern world.

The other area in which the issue of infanticide arises is medical ethics. A child may be born severely retarded, for example, and with any number of other birth defects that could be corrected by surgical procedures. Doctors and family are confronted with a dilemma: Should those defects be corrected to save the life of the child even though the child would live a severely disabled life? The medical technology itself has created this particular ethical dilemma. Without some extraordinary intervention, the child would most likely die. But such medical intervention is available. Families and physicians find themselves confronted with difficult decisions regarding the practice of infanticide.

The modern medical profession is not operating within a classification system in which deformed or disabled infants are classified as baby hippos and then gently restored to the river. And yet issues of classification are an important part of medical ethics. An infant may be classified as an autonomous, independent, human person worthy of preservation. But in some cases, the severely disabled infant may be classified as part of a parental unit, and doctors may follow the wishes of parents to allow such an infant to die.

Medical ethics functions within a difficult, and often ambiguous, system of classification. The ambiguity of classification in ethical responses to the human life cycle is revealed most intensely in the fiercely contested debate over abortion. Is the fetus to be classified as a human person? The opposing positions on this question reveal a basic conflict over symbolic classification. We will pay close attention to such issues of classification in surveying the various contemporary responses to the question of abortion.

Abortion

Abortion is a highly charged issue in the modern world, involving intense emotions, outrageous rhetoric, and legal battles. A line has been drawn between two opposing groups: pro-life and pro-choice. Behind these slogans lies a profound disagreement about what it means to create a context of trust in response to the ethical challenge of birth. The ethical debate revolves around this issue of creating a context of basic trust. There are the questions of classification: What does it mean to be a human being? When does human life begin? What is a person? There are the questions of care: What are the rights and responsibilities of parents, and particularly of women, in the process of reproduction? How are those rights and responsibilities related to those rights that the fetus may hold? Finally, there are the questions of community: How do we define the human community? Is it composed of all beings conceived through human biological reproduction? Or is the socialization process of loving, learning, and adaptation what constitutes the cultural character of the human community? To what extent should the community make the practice of abortion a matter of law?

The abortion controversy involves all these questions of basic trust. The participants in the debate have such different images of the nature of that trust that communication is almost impossible. One opponent of abortion stated the pro-life position succinctly: "One person's freedom to obtain an abortion is the denial of another person's right to live."[13] A representative of the pro-choice position, however, maintains that the woman's freedom, privacy, and conscience are the fundamental personal rights that are at stake. The state should not compel anyone to conceive or bear a child against her will. The ethicist Joseph Fletcher has discerned a central religious issue in this controversy. "Are we human beings," Fletcher asks, "stewards of God's gift of life ourselves responsible for producing lives carefully and creatively, or are we only subrational instruments of a reproductive process over which we may not exercise any control, i.e. responsibility."[14] The abortion issue has become a focal point for religious questions concerning personal roles, rights, and responsibilities in the creation of basic trust at the beginning of the human life cycle.

Abortion in Tribal Societies

Ethnographic reports of abortion practices in tribal societies reveal a variety of ethical responses to the issue of abortion. In many cases, it is forbidden. In many cases, it is practiced by means of abortifacient drugs, surgery, and other techniques for a number of specific, culturally defined reasons. We will consider a brief inventory of the more prevalent reasons for performing abortions that have been reported in tribal societies.[15]

Reasons of Health   Various medical justifications have been given for practicing abortion in order to maintain the health and well-being of women. Among the Purari, women practice abortion because they are afraid of the pains of childbirth. Mataco women customarily abort the first fetus because they believe that this will make future births easier. Women of the Ngaju Dyak abort if they believe they are pregnant with twins. These abortions are performed in the interests of the health and well-being of the mother. An interesting case of therapeutic abortion is recorded among the Dahomeya. If a pregnant woman should become ill, the fetus is made to stand trial. If the fetus is found guilty of having caused her illness, it will be aborted in order to cure the mother.

Reasons of Age   In some societies abortions are performed if the woman is considered too young to bear children. Often the age for childbearing is signified by an initiation ritual at puberty. In tribes such as the Owambo and the Masai, it is not permitted for an uninitiated girl to give birth; any pregnancy must be aborted. By contrast, women on the island of Formosa wait until they are 34 to 37 years of age before giving birth. They will abort any pregnancies—as many as 16 were reported for one woman—that occur when they are considered too young.

Old age is also a consideration for abortion. Chagga women abort all pregnancies that occur after their daughters are married. And older women in the Torres Strait abort their pregnancies to avoid the public ridicule that is directed toward elderly parents.

Reasons of Improper Paternity

Abortions are performed in some tribal societies, such as the Tikopia islanders, if the father's identity is unknown. Abortion is also practiced if the father is socially unacceptable, for various reasons. The Azande, as well as some other groups, require abortions if the father is not the woman's husband. The Wogeo are convinced that all pregnancies that occur before marriage are the result of several fathers and should be aborted.

Abortions are required if the father is too familiar, as is the case of the Gunantuna and the Sedang Moi, who perform abortions if the father is a close relative of the woman. Abortions are also performed if the father is too foreign, as is the case of the Tucuna, who perform abortions if the father is a stranger. A curious example of improper paternity has been described among the Jivaro of Brazil. They believe that demons may enter the body of a woman while she is bathing in the river and may cause her to conceive a monster. Those pregnancies that are thought to be conceived by demons are to be aborted.

Reasons of Economics   Many

groups who live a subsistence-level existence of hunting and gathering, nomadic wandering, or even small-scale agriculture abort for economic considerations. Extreme poverty has been reported as a cause for abortion among the Munda-Kohl. Gilbert Islanders abort because their soil is barren. And Malekula women abort so that they can continue working in the family garden. In times of famine, women of the Ngali and Yumu of Central Australia have been reported to abort in order to provide the fetus as food for their children. The woman herself will also eat the fetus out of hunger.

Reasons of Social Conflict   Inter-

nal conflicts within a marriage, family, or social group may result in the abortion of a pregnancy. Adultery, marital discord, and the hardships of raising children are often cited as motives for abortion in tribal societies. An intense form of social conflict may occur when the external influence of an alien society is experienced as oppressive. Women may abort their pregnancies to prevent children from being born into such a world. For example, mass abortions were practiced in the islands of the Antilles and Guam in response to the Spanish conquests of the sixteenth century.

This brief outline of reasons for abortion in tribal societies merely suggests the variety of motives that might animate the practice of terminating a pregnancy in any given social group. Many analogous medical, economic, and social considerations come into play in the decision to abort a fetus in modern western societies. These practical considerations are also informed by a long tradition of religious and ethical reflection on the classification of the fetus. We will examine the history of the fetus in western religious thought before turning to the positions on abortion that have been espoused by religious groups in modern America.

Classification of the Fetus in Western Thought

The practice of abortion in western societies has been informed by carefully considered systems of classification. The status of the fetus has been determined in relation to shared cultural images of what it is to be a human being. We have already noted that the Greek philosophers Plato and Aristotle preferred abortion to infanticide as a means of controlling both the quality and the quantity of the human community. The fetus itself, therefore, was not classified as a human person. It was the potential for life, but only when that potential had been actualized could it be considered a human person. The fetus was classified as prehuman in a fundamental sense.

The Hope of Life

This classification of the fetus as prehuman also informed the practice of abortion in the Roman Empire, where abortion was practiced rather extensively. Families too poor to afford more children, the wealthy who wanted to be free for a life of pleasure, and women who thought pregnancy would spoil their beauty all had recourse to abortion. The philosopher Seneca praised the exceptional virtue of a certain Helia because she never had an abortion "after the fashion of many other women, whose attractions are to be found in their beauty alone."[16] The fact that Helia was an exception indicates that abortion was common.

The practice of abortion was justified in classical Roman thought by a distinct line that divided the fetus from the infant; they were in two entirely different categories. The unborn fetus was classified as *spes animantis*—the "hope of life." The fetus was the pure potential for human life. This was very different from the classification *infans,* which represented an actual human life. The fetus, as *spes animantis,* was considered to be part of the mother. It was likened to a fruit that is part of the tree until it ripens and falls. The fetus did not have any status independent of the mother until after birth. At that point, of course, it came under the authority of the father. Ancient Roman thought, therefore, classified the fetus as a prehuman potential for human life. The termination of the *spes animantis* was not regarded as the destruction of an actual human person.

This classification of the fetus was adopted by the early Christian tradition, but a very different conclusion was drawn. The Church Fathers also classified the fetus as *spes animantis,* but the potential inherent in this hope of life was suffi-cient to qualify the fetus for an independent human status. The termination of pregnancy would, therefore, be considered murder. The second century theologian Tertullian summarized the early Christian position: "Prevention of birth is premature murder, and it makes no difference whether it is a life already born that one snatches away, or a life in the act of being born that one destroys; that which is to be a human-being is also human; the whole fruit is already actually present in the seed."[17] This was a dramatic improvisation on the Roman concept of *spes animantis*. Classifying the fetus as human denied the Roman assumption that it was part of the mother. As in the case of infanticide, Christian abortion ethics undercut the power and authority of the Roman family over the reproductive process. Tertullian's statement that the fetus should be classified as a human person, because the fruit already exists in the potential of its seed, anticipates the twentieth century arguments for human status of the fetus based on the fact that it possesses a full genetic code at conception. The conclusion drawn by the Christian church was that the termination of pregnancy was a type of homicide—the murder of a relative—and should be regarded as the murder of a fully human being.

The Ensoulment of the Fetus

The Christian tradition of ethical reflection on abortion introduced two other classifications: ensoulment and baptism. The first classification applied to the fetus before birth. In the fourth century, Augustine divided the development of the fetus into two stages. The first stage after conception was labeled *embryo informatus*. In this fetal development stage, the embryo was considered unformed because it had no soul. This classification was largely based on the mythic model of the creation of Adam. Adam's physical body was raised from the clay of the earth before it was ensouled by the breath of God. But the classification was also based on the perception that it was some time after conception that the fetus became animated. The unformed stage was believed to last 40 days for males and 80 days for females. At the end of this period, the fetus would become ensouled, and the formed embryo was classified as *embryo formatus*.

Augustine was convinced that the termination of an *embryo formatus* should be treated as murder punishable by death. The abortion of an ensouled fetus was considered a very serious offense because of the eternal consequences such an act would have on the unbaptized soul. The abortion of an *embryo informatus*, however, should be punished by a fine. This was not classified as the murder of a human person. "Because the great question of the soul is not to be hastily decided by unargued and rash judgment," Augustine maintained, "the law does not provide that the act pertains to homicide, for there cannot yet be said to be a live soul in a body that lacks sensation when it is not formed in flesh and so not yet endowed with sense."[18]

This distinction between different stages in the development of the fetus, reminiscent of the division of pregnancy into trimesters by the Supreme Court of the United States, found its way into the canon law of the Catholic church. The consensus throughout the middle ages was that abortion was homicide only when the fetus was vivified, ensouled, or formed. The abortion of an *embryo informatus* was a lesser offense against canon law.

Baptism and Abortion   We have already noted that the infanticide of an unbaptized infant was treated as a much greater crime than the killing of a baptized infant. Similar considerations, informed by the ritual classification of baptism and the eternal consequences involved, were applied to abortion. The medieval theologian Fulgentius stated that the ensouled fetus that dies in its mother's womb is "punished with everlasting punishment in eternal fire."[19] One medieval law code prescribed daily acts of penance for parents who performed abortions to correspond to the daily suffering of these unborn children in hell.[20] Within the ritual context of baptism, the termination of a *spes animantis* not only deprives it of the hope of human life, but also of any hope of salvation. The need for an ensouled fetus to be baptized intensified the Christian opposition to the practice of abortion.

This classification inspired nineteenth century Catholics to practice baptism *in utero* by means of a baptismal syringe. This curious *in utero* baptism could ensure salvation in the event that a miscarriage prevented baptism after birth. Although there have been a variety of attitudes toward infant baptism and different interpretations of the status of unbaptized infants in the future life, baptism clearly involves a ritual classification that has influenced attitudes regarding abortion in the Christian tradition. The concern for the projected eternal consequences of abortion underlies the traditional Christian opposition to its practice. These traditional considerations have been interwoven with arguments drawn from modern science and medical practice in the current debate over abortion in modern western societies. The central issue, however, remains the classification of human persons.

Protestant, Catholic, and Jewish Views on Abortion

In the United States the three major religious traditions—Protestant, Catholic, and Jewish—have taken public positions on the question of abortion. It is impossible to distill a single viewpoint from each tradition because there is so much diversity within each religious community. Each tradition has a spectrum of religious responses to the ethical challenge posed by abortion.

Jewish Responses

In Judaism, the Orthodox position on abortion maintains that it is a violation of the sanctity of human life. Abortion is prohibited by Jewish law. Exceptions are made, however, in cases where the mother's life or health is in immediate danger. In cases when abortion is medically indicated as the only means to save a woman's life or preserve her health, a decision for abortion may be made under the direction of a competent Orthodox rabbi. Rabbi Meyer Cohen, Executive Director of the Union of Orthodox Rabbis of the United States and Canada, has stated the Orthodox Jewish position on abortion:

> *Abortion, even when legalized by the state, does not cease to be a flagrant violation of the basic and fundamental religious and ethical principles. Human life, including the life of an unborn child, is one of the most sacred things. Mere human legislation cannot change that status. Considering the fact that the un-born child is innocent and defenseless, makes abortion doubly sinful and repugnant. Thus abortions are transgressions against religion and against humanity.*[21]

The Orthodox Jewish position, as expressed by Rabbi Cohen, classifies the fetus as human. Abortion, therefore, is viewed as a violation of the religious and ethical obligations that are binding on human interactions.

However, a case has also been made within the Jewish tradition for a more permissive attitude toward abortion. The Reform Rabbi Israel B. Margolis has argued for a more permissive ruling on abortion by referring to a passage from the Hebrew Bible that describes a pregnant woman who is caused to have a miscarriage as the result of blows suffered in a fight. (Ex. 21.21–23) In the biblical text, the miscarriage is treated as if it were a case of property loss and not the killing of a human being. The fetus was part of the mother, so damages are to be paid to her. The crime committed by fighting would only become a capital offense if the woman died.[22] This text seems to suggest that in the religious ethics of ancient Israel the fetus was classified as part of the mother; it did not have a separate legal existence.

This view of the fetus as part of the woman may be behind the attitude toward abortion expressed by the twentieth century Sephardic Chief Rabbi Ben Zion Uziel, when he observed that the fetus was prehuman. Since it is not a complete, living human being, it has no independent status. Just as a limb of the body may be sacrificed to avoid a worse malady, so the fetus may be destroyed for the mother's sake.[23] Abortion from this perspective would not be murder because the fetus is classified as part of the woman's body. These few examples of Jewish responses to the ethical issue of abortion suggest that diverse views are generated on abortion within the Jewish tradition. These positions are divided over whether the fetus is to be classified as human or as a nonhuman part of the pregnant woman.

Catholic Responses

The official Catholic response to abortion has revolved around the authoritative pronouncement on the subject by Pope Paul VI in his Papal Letter *Humanae Vitae* (1968). A special Papal Commission had been formed out of the second Vatican Council (1962–65) to study the question of birth control and report findings and recommendations to the Pope. The majority opinion of the commission favored reforming the traditional Catholic prohibition of artificial means of birth control. Pope Paul, however, responded to this suggestion by reaffirming the traditional doctrine that sex was only for the purpose of procreation and that any artificial, chemical, or mechanical means of interfering with procreation was a grave sin. In line with this, abortion was strictly forbidden. It was viewed as the taking of human life that was classified as beginning at conception. Abortion could only be considered in rare surgical operations in which the death of a fetus was an indirect, unavoidable effect of a medical intervention to save the pregnant woman's life.

Although the strict prohibition of abortion has been the dominant ruling of the Catholic church, liberal Catholic voices have called for a modification of the Church's position. Liberal Catholics may refer to the medieval theory of the ensoulment of the fetus in order to allow for therapeutic abortions in the earliest stage of pregnancy.[24] Or they may distinguish between morality and law, which would recognize the serious ethical issues involved but would make the decision for abortion (in the first 12 weeks of pregnancy) a matter of moral conscience rather than disciplinary legislation.[25] In this case, it is not simply the ruling against abortion that is at stake, but the freedom of moral conscience to make responsible choices regarding a major life decision.

Protestant Responses   As in the

other two major American religious traditions, the Protestant responses to the ethical issue of abortion vary considerably. Protestant views on abortion range from permissive to restrictive positions. The permissive approach supports the repeal of all laws that forbid the practice of abortion. The moderate position allows for abortions to be performed within certain legal and medical controls. The restrictive position supports legal prohibitions of abortion because it is classified as the destruction of a fully human life. Again, the issue of classification dominates the abortion issue.

The Permissive Position. The permissive view of abortion within Protestantism favors the removal of all laws that restrict women from terminating pregnancy. One Protestant denomination, the United Methodists, clearly stated this position in its *Population Crisis Resolution* (1970). Their resolution urged "that states re-

move the regulation of abortion from the criminal code, placing it instead under regulations relating to other procedures of standard medical practice. Abortion would be available only upon request of the person most directly concerned."[26] This approach elevates the authority of medical knowledge and practice over the traditional ethical images of the religious tradition. Women's rights are affirmed by allowing them the moral freedom to decide on abortion without legal restraints.

In the permissive approach, the personhood of the fetus is implicitly denied. In emphatic language, which has since been revised, the United Methodists maintained that the care and nurture given to a child is what contributes to quality of life. This quality of care is essential to what it means to be a human person. The population resolution continues:

> *Because life is distorted without the qualities of being wanted and loved, parents seriously violate their responsibility when they bring into the world children for whom they cannot provide. Since personhood is more than physical being, we affirm that the fetus is not a person but rather a tissue with the potentiality, in most cases, for becoming a person, also recognizing that personhood is not possible without physical form.*[27]

This permissive approach makes some important assumptions about the ideal image of trust within which parents should respond to the ethical challenge of abortion. First, it maintains the inalienable right of women to self-determination in the reproductive process. Second, tremendous confidence is placed in the technical competence of medical practice to set the terms for the time, place, and technique of termination. Third, the permissive approach to abortion is committed to the idea that human life is more than merely existence: It is a quality of experience. These assumptions define the basic grounds of trust from which moral choices about abortion can be made.

The Moderate Position. The moderate position on abortion within Protestant ethics recognizes these same assumptions yet seeks a greater measure of control in the practice of abortions. The American Baptist Convention drafted a resolution on abortion that is representative of this middle position. It distinguished an early stage of pregnancy, the first 12 weeks, in which abortion should be available on request. After that time, however, abortions should only be performed if one of three medical indications is present. The American Baptist Convention resolved:

1. That the termination of a pregnancy prior to the end of the twelfth week (first trimester) be at the request of the individual(s) concerned and be regarded as an elective medical procedure governed by the laws of regulating medical practice and licensure.

2. After that period the termination of pregnancy shall be performed only by a duly licensed physician at the request of the individual(s) concerned, in a regularly licensed hospital, for one of the following reasons as suggested by the Model Penal Code of the American Law Institute:

   (a) When documented evidence exists that this is a danger to the physical or mental health of the woman;

   (b) When there is documented evidence that the conceptus has a physical or mental defect;

   (c) When there is documented evidence that the pregnancy was the result of rape, incest or other felonious acts.[28]

This statement of the American Baptist Convention again places great trust in modern medical

practice to set the health standards that determine when a woman may obtain an abortion after the first 12 weeks. Medical classifications not only determine when an abortion would benefit the woman, but also the shared cultural standards of physical and mental perfection against which defects in the fetus are measured. The convention's final indication is a legal classification that assumes that the fetus is somehow different if it has been conceived through rape or incest. Some fetuses are thereby classified as more legitimate than others.

The permissive approach would disagree with the formulation presented in the resolution of the American Baptist Convention because the three indications for abortion after the first trimester submit the woman to a medical, legal, and bureaucratic inquisition to establish evidence of these conditions. These questions would be an invasion of her privacy, and they infringe upon her rights to self-determination in matters of procreation. The moderate approach, however, sees these criteria as necessary controls. Once acknowledging the right to terminate pregnancy, it seeks to set responsible limits on the practice of abortion.

The Restrictive Position. The restrictive approach opposes abortion on request at any time during pregnancy, including during the first trimester; it also questions the moderate position's assumptions that a number of conditions exist in which abortion would be an acceptable therapeutic medical practice. Abortion is to be prohibited except (perhaps) in cases in which the woman's life is directly threatened. The Protestant ethicist Paul Ramsey has argued against abortion on request. He emphasizes scientific advances in measuring movement, response, and brain activity in the fetus. He asserts that the EEG (electroencephalogram) is able to record distinctive brain activity at eight weeks. If this kind of scientific measurement is used in determining the moment of death, he asks, why should it also not be used in determining the moment of life?[29]

Other representatives of this restrictive approach claim that modern biology has established that human life begins at conception, when the full genetic pattern of human identity is present. The fetus should be classified as a fully human identity because it is the product of human conception.

This classification of the fetus specifies a different measure of care: the responsibility to protect the inalienable right of the fetus to life. The right to life, from this perspective, cannot be dependent upon whether or not the child is wanted. If desirability were the criteria for life, then any society could exterminate those types of people it did not like. Ramsey recalls the precedent set in ancient Roman law, where the *pater familias* had the absolute power of life and death over his children. Now, he suggests, the repeal of laws prohibiting abortion places the same absolute power over life and death in the hands of the mother. What was once classified as the property of the father is being treated as the property of the mother. For the restrictive approach, this kind of care is not appropriate for protecting the survival of human life.

Finally, representatives of the restrictive approach maintain that abortion is not a cure for the social problems of overpopulation, limited resources, and general welfare. The practice of abortion appears to be a symptom of the deeper problems of a sick society. Abortion is interpreted as the human community's failure to protect the weak, defenseless, and unwanted. It places the medical profession in a particularly problematic position. To treat abortion as standard medical practice puts physicians dedicated to preserving life in the position of causing death. According to Paul Ramsey, the liberal approaches treat abortion as if it were not an ethical problem at all, but simply a matter of medical practice.[30] The restrictive position on abortion not only seeks to highlight the ethical concern in the abortion debate, but also to make its own restrictions on abortion the rule of law.

The Supreme Court Decision on Abortion

The legal status of abortion was defined by the United States Supreme Court on January 22, 1973, in the controversial case of *Roe v. Wade*.[31] The seven-to-two majority of the Court attempted to clarify the constitutional issues involved in the practice of abortion in America. Since it was felt that modern science was unable to conclusively determine the beginning of human life, the Court was not in a position to rule on this issue. The Court did, however, devise a classification scheme that charted the development, not of biological human life, but of the legal human rights involved in the birth process. This classification of pregnancy into three trimesters defined three distinct stages in which the rights of the woman, the fetus, and the state may be determined.

In the first trimester the state could not interfere in the abortion decision. It was to be left exclusively up to the woman and her physician. During the second trimester, the woman's health becomes the concern of the state. During this stage, states may legislate where abortions may or may not be performed. The legislation can only be procedural; the decision for abortion still lies with the woman and her doctor. In the third trimester, the court determined, the fetus has a new status based on its viability. At this stage the fetus has a good chance of survival independent of the mother in the event of a premature birth. Therefore, the state has an interest in promoting this potential human life. The state may protect this life by prohibiting abortion, except in those cases where abortion is necessary to preserve the life and health of the mother.

The major constitutional issue at stake in the Supreme Court's decision on abortion was the woman's right to privacy. In defending the right of a woman's private conscience, the Court invoked the Fourteenth Amendment—which defined the concept of personal liberty and placed restrictions on state actions that deprived the individual of such freedom—and the Ninth Amendment, which reserves rights to the people. The Court ruled that there was a constitutional basis in personal liberty "broad enough to encompass a woman's desire whether or not to terminate her pregnancy." In considering the rights of the fetus, the Court rejected the notion that the state had a compelling interest in protecting life from the moment of conception. The Court observed that "the unborn have never been recognized in the law as persons in the whole sense." The legal classification of person is contingent upon live birth. A state's interest in protecting fetal life, therefore, cannot override the woman's basic right to privacy.

This right to privacy in the abortion decision is not without limits. A woman's power of decision is limited by the viability of the fetus. At this point, the state's compelling interest in protecting viable human life overrides decisions that might be made by the woman or her physician to terminate a pregnancy in the last 12 weeks. The Court stated:

> With respect to the state's important and legitimate interest in potential life, the "compelling" point is viability. This is so because the fetus then presumably has the capability of meaningful life outside the mother's womb. State regulation protective of fetal life after viability thus has both logical and biological justification. If the state is interested in protecting fetal life after viability, it may go as far as to proscribe abortion during that period except when it is necessary to preserve the life or health of the mother.

This statement still makes no reference to any rights of a fetus. The Court simply defined the terms under which a state might enter into the abortion decision. The third trimester is the period of pregnancy in which the state has a recognized legal right to protect the potential life of the fetus. It is only at this point that the fetus comes under the legal classification of a meaningful human life.

Pro-Life and Pro-Choice

The ruling of the Supreme Court in *Roe v. Wade* has, of course, generated a considerable amount of controversy. Ethical opinion on the issue of abortion has been polarized in recent years into two organized movements that define themselves as pro-life and pro-choice. They represent two fundamentally different ways of imagining the nature of basic ethical trust in the human birth process. The pro-life and pro-choice movements propose different ways of imagining classification, care, and community in the ethical issue of abortion.

Issues of Classification   The two movements begin with such opposing classifications of human being that almost no dialogue is possible between them. The pro-life group emphasizes the fully human status of potential life; the pro-choice group emphasizes the rights and responsibilities of actual humans. Pro-life proponents maintain that the fetus is human because of its potential; it contains at conception the genetic blueprint of human life and, therefore, is to be classified as fully human. John Noonan has presented this position in claiming that "once conceived, the being was recognized as man because he had man's potential. The criterion for humanity, thus, is simple and all-embracing: If you are conceived by human parents, you are human."[32] In the pro-choice position, however, the status of the actual, living woman is primary. Her rights and responsibilities in the reproductive process are affirmed. She has the responsibility to make important, and often difficult, decisions about when to have children. The fetus is not classified as human. The genetic pattern is like an architect's blueprint—a design to be followed, but not itself the completed house. Human identity emerges out of the specific social conditions of human culture and is not a simple biological fact.

The pro-life position responds to this classification by asking, If we do not draw the line at conception, where do we draw it? If a certain degree of socialization is necessary to recognize a life as human, then couldn't this argument for abortion also be used to justify infanticide? The *Roe v. Wade* decision involved precisely these difficult questions in drawing lines of classification in the birth process. However, the pro-choice position often relies on the perceptions and feelings of parents—which are generally different for a fetus than for an infant—as a control over extending their defense of abortion to an argument for infanticide. The different cultural perceptions of the fetus and the infant are embodied in laws, practices, and customs. Robert W. McCoy demonstrates these perceptions in rather outrageous hyperbole:

> *If fertilized ova were considered persons, we would require registration and burial for all spontaneously aborted fetuses. Will we abandon birth certificates in favor of conception certificates? Will birthdays be abandoned in favor of conception days? Will income tax deductions be allowed for all unborn? Will all physicians who perform abortions be put on trial for murder in the first degree?*[33]

These questions appear to be logical extensions of any classification of the fetus as a fully human person from the moment of conception. The pro-life and pro-choice movements are deeply divided over this issue of classification.

Issues of Care

The different systems of human classification represented by these two movements give rise to different conceptions of care. For the pro-life position, the quality of care indicated is the protection of human life from its conception. The care invested in protecting the weak, defenseless unborn is a measure of the care that an individual, or a society, demonstrates for life itself. The primary rights that must be cared for are those of the fetus. It is the responsibility of the living to protect those rights.

In the pro-choice position, the quality of care indicated is demonstrated by individuals responsibly bringing children into the world who will be wanted, loved, and nurtured in as positive an environment as possible. Individuals show this care through family planning, birth control, and loving relationships. But, in cases of last resort, abortion should be available to prevent children being born who will not receive this quality of care. The pro-life and pro-choice movements are also deeply divided over the definition of the appropriate measure of care that should be exercised in response to the ethical challenge of birth.

Issues of Community

Finally, these positions involve different ways of imagining the responsibilities of the human community in addressing the issue of abortion. The pro-life group feels that it is the responsibility of society to legislate the protection of fetal life. Society must enforce restrictive legislation that will not only make abortion illegal, but will define it as an act of murder. This legal extension of the pro-life classification of the fetus as a human person calls for a disciplinary response to the question of abortion. The pro-choice position maintains that such restrictive legislation has condemned women to the dangers of illegal abortions, has discriminated against the poor, and has resulted in the births of unwanted children. Such private decisions of personal morality cannot be regulated. Members of the human community should be able to make free and responsible choices about the abortion issue. Abortion calls for a moral response.

The pro-life and pro-choice movements are in fundamental disagreement over the nature of trust in the formation of a human community. More than a controversy over rights and responsibilities, the abortion issue brings into focus the central question of human identity: What is a human being? Two basic styles of response occur in answer to the question of what exactly constitutes a member of the human community. A quantitative approach is satisfied that the 46 chromosomes that make up the genetic inheritance of human beings provides the basic standard of human identity. Any entity with these genes counts as a human person. A qualitative approach identifies expressly human characteristics of awareness, self-consciousness, and rationality. It is one thing to be biologically a member of the species *Homo sapiens;* it may be quite another matter to be a fully human person. The ethical conclusions drawn from these opposing definitions of human identity are irreconcilable because they are based on different images of human community. They start from different images of what it is to be a human person. Perhaps the central ethical challenge of birth is precisely the need to clarify this image.

Patterns of Trust

The first challenge of the human life cycle is the task of creating a context of basic trust in which human identity may emerge. Ritual and ethical rules that govern the process of birth reflect a community's concern for creating this trust. Birth rituals act out the ritualized perfection of that context of trust; the ethics of infanticide and abortion define, embody, and extend that basic trust, which is felt to be appropriate to the earliest phase of the human life cycle. Chapter 5 has drawn a number of conclusions regarding the nature of ethical trust in response to the challenges of birth in religious ethics.

1. *Birth rituals create a context of basic trust.* The practices through which pregnancy, delivery, and birth are ritualized create a sense of trust that surrounds a human birth. Three elements of that sense of trust come into play. First, the rituals of classification that separate mother, child, and perhaps even father from the rest of society respond to a liminal situation in which the new life may be regarded as not yet fully human. The fetus may be classified as nonhuman, subhuman, prehuman, or human, but its status is often ambiguous. It may be classified as not yet one of the living, but not quite one of the dead. The birth process is often experienced as a time of danger, and the rituals of classification strive to bring the perilous situation of birth under control. Second, the rituals of care reinforce the social responsibility for the support, nurturance, and maintenance of a new life. Social patterns of paternity, maternity, and extended family may be identified by rituals that establish the environment of care within which the child will be raised. Third, the rituals of community introduce the new life into the society of human beings. Baptisms, purifications, circumcisions, naming rituals, and so on may acknowledge that the infant is a fully human member of a human community. These rituals of

classification, care, and community reinforce a sense of basic trust within which a human life takes shape.

———

2. *The ethics of infanticide and abortion also involve issues of basic trust.* The killing of certain infants has been regarded as an ethical practice in many human societies. It may be difficult to imagine that infanticide has been perceived as an expression of trust. But when a Nuer community classifies a deformed infant as a baby hippo—in other words, as not part of the human community—the care the community administers to that infant is regarded as an expression of the basic trust that is appropriate to maintaining the integrity of that community. The practice of infanticide in the ancient world followed this general pattern: Once the infant was classified as nonhuman, the appropriate measure of care was felt to be the exclusion of that being from the human community. To understand this process is, of course, not to condone infanticide; it is simply to acknowledge the conditions of possibility within which infanticide could be regarded as an ethical act within those communities that practiced it. The ethical issues of classification, care, and community support ethical rules regarding the practice of infanticide.

The same issues are involved in rules that govern the practice of abortion. The classification of what it is to be a human being is the basic point of departure for religious rules governing abortion. Three basic types of classification appear in religious responses to the challenge of abortion. First, the fetus may be classified as nonhuman. The ancient Roman classification of the fetus as *spes animantis* indicated that humanity was only a social fact after birth. Prior to birth, the fetus was regarded as part of the mother, as the fruit is part of the tree until it ripens and falls. Modern religious responses to abortion that stress the social responsibility for managing the reproductive process, the rights of women to make decisions about their own reproductive process, and the social context of care, nurture, and love within which true human identity emerges may involve such a classification of the fetus as nonhuman, subhuman, or prehuman. The measure of care indicated by this classification is the responsibility to only bring children into a world where they are wanted, loved, and supported to develop their potential for a fully human life.

Second, the fetus may be classified as fully human. The second century Christian theologian Tertullian inverted the Roman classification of the fetus by insisting that the fruit already exists in its seed. A human is also a human who is about to be one. Modern religious approaches that insist that any product of human conception is already fully human continue to uphold this type of classification. Opponents of abortion may insist that once the genetic code is in place, a human being exists. This classification of the humanity of the fetus may not stop at the one-out-of-three fertilized ova that have the statistical probability of implanting in the uterine wall; it may also extend to the problematic issues involved in the status of fertilized human eggs in test tubes. *In vitro* fertilization and embryo replacement suggest a new set of ethical challenges for any classification system that assumes the full humanity of any human *conceptus.* The measure of care indicated by this classification is the responsibility to preserve the life of all unborn.

Third, the fetus may be classified as a process of development. The Augustinian doctrine of the ensoulment of the fetus introduced this type of classification. A line was drawn between an unformed fetus and a formed fetus. Only the abortion of an *embryo formatus,* after 40 days for males and 80 days for females, could be classified as the termination of a human life. Modern religious approaches to abortion that make distinctions between stages in the development of the fetus continue this type of classification of the fetus. The Supreme Court ruling in *Roe v. Wade* divided the process of fetal development into three trimesters. Although the Court did not attempt to decide when, in fact, human life begins, it did provide a method of classifying the development of the fetus that protected the rights of women to self-determination over their own reproductive process in the early stages of pregnancy and protected the viable fetus in the later stages of pregnancy. The measure of care indicated by this classification is the obligation to draw responsible, careful lines in the process of gestation that will balance the rights and responsibilities of women, society, and the unborn.

The controversy over abortion has become so heated in modern, western societies that it is easy to overlook the fact that each of these three approaches to the classification and care of the unborn is an attempt to establish a context of basic trust in the birth process. They embody very different images of the pattern of trust that is required for a human community. When a community is in conflict over the pattern of ethical trust, it is also in conflict over those ethical issues that provide challenges to the basic trust within which human life emerges. The controversy over abortion is such a conflict over basic trust. It is a controversy that will not be resolved as long as these basic divisions exist regarding the definition of ethical trust at the earliest stage of the human life cycle.

––––––

3.   *In the issue of abortion, an important distinction may be made between customary, moral, and legal rules.* Abortions may be practiced within a community for any number of customary reasons: medical reasons, reasons of age, reasons of improper paternity, economic reasons, or social conflict. The rules that govern abortion in these situations may simply be a matter of social custom. However, the issue of

abortion intensifies when it becomes a matter of moral and legal rules. The distinction between moral and legal obligation is important in any analysis of the human response to the ethical challenges of the human life cycle. The challenges of personal ethics may be regarded as issues for moral decision, choice, and responsibility. In this sense, they may be considered issues that should be addressed by moral rules. On the other hand, a community may govern personal ethics through legal regulations. The challenges of the human life cycle may be regulated by laws that are backed up by force or the threat of force. Such legal rules necessarily involve an element of coercion, and they tend to elicit a disciplinary response to obligation. Where moral rules are extended by persuasion, legal rules are enforced by coercion.

One of the major ambiguities about abortion in the modern controversy is whether it is a moral or a legal issue. The legal arrangement in the United States since 1973, for example, has allowed for a certain degree of freedom for women to make personal and often difficult moral decisions about their own reproductive process. Within this arrangement, antiabortionists may make persuasive appeals to moral conscience. But women have the necessary freedom to make moral choices for or against the termination of pregnancy. A legal ban on abortion would take the issue out of the arena of moral choice and place it under the control of disciplinary regulation. A society that places a legal restriction on abortion is thereby enforcing one definition of trust in order to discipline the entire population. The ethical challenge posed by abortion, therefore, involves both the definition of rules, and the human ability to respond to those rules, in creating a context of basic trust.

CHAPTER

SIX

TRANSFORMATION

The transition from childhood to adulthood often represents a difficult transformation in identity. The pattern of ethical obligation that characterized the child's role is gradually—or in some cases suddenly—replaced by a new pattern. New standards of ethical expectation and behavior come into play. With this new sense of obligation comes a new status within the larger system of religious ethics. The social event of coming of age involves the individual in a network of new ethical responsibilities. There are new obligations, as well as new opportunities to respond creatively to the challenges presented by life-shaping situations. This stage of transformation focuses the process of growth in human life. The terms *adolescent* and *adult* both come from the Latin word *adolescere,* which means to grow. This growth is not simply the biological growth of puberty, but the process of maturation in response to ethical obligation. Religious traditions respond to the challenge of adolescence by discovering, through ritual and ethics, creative, productive, and meaningful avenues of action through which the energies of personal growth may be directed.

The process of growth is often characterized as a separation from parents and family. The process involves detaching from the network of ethical relations that defined the role of childhood and identifying with a larger community of adults. Sigmund Freud described this alternating process of disengagement and identification as the central task of maturity. "From the time of puberty onward," Freud noted, "the individual must devote himself to the great task of freeing himself from the parents; and only after this detachment is accomplished can he cease to be a child and so become a member of the social community."[1] To grow, in this sense, means to break the forms of life that gave shape to childhood in order to allow new shapes to emerge. Growth is a symbolic death and new birth, which is why many societies symbolize the transition from childhood to adulthood through rituals of initiation that act out the symbolic death of the child and the birth of the adult. These ritual practices are a good place to begin exploring the ethical challenges that are presented by that process of transformation that moves beyond childhood and toward adulthood.

Initiation Rituals

Initiation rituals, as they have been described in ethnographic accounts of the practices of primal religions, are performed around the time when the first signs of puberty appear. However, biological puberty does not mean social maturity. These rituals do not simply celebrate a biological event. They mark a transition into a new social realm of roles, rights, and responsibilities. They initiate the young person into the social world of adulthood. Initiation rituals usually have the following major features:

1.   *Initiation rituals are authoritative.* The elders of the community supervise and conduct the ritual practices of initiation. These practices not only carry the collective authority of the adults in the community, but also the cumulative authoritative weight of tradition. To be initiated is to enter into a new role within the network of authority that is defined by a social community and a religious tradition.

2.   *Initiation rituals are instructive.* The dramatic symbolic actions of the initiation ceremonies are accompanied by a process of instruction, education, and indoctrination in the myths, laws, and customs of the community. The initiate is introduced into the shared network of beliefs that are held by the community.

3.   *Initiation rituals are corporate.* Rituals of initiation tend to be conducted annually for a particular age group within society. All boys and girls of that age are initiated in groups.

4.   *Initiation rituals are exclusive.* The opposite gender is usually excluded from witnessing the initiation rituals that are designed specifically for males or females. Gender-specific initiation rituals indicate that different ethical roles, rights, and responsibilities are obligatory for men and women in the adult community. Parents are also usually excluded from participating in the initiation of their own children.

5.   *Initiation rituals are physical.* The ritual practices of initiation involve some kind of physical test, trial, or ordeal. Almost always, initiation entails some type of physical mutilation of the body that will act as a visible bond among the members of the community who share that particular physical mark of identification. The marking or scarring of the body may symbolize the

new ethical obligations that are binding on the person as a new member of the adult community.

These ingredients in initiation rituals contribute to a dramatic symbolic process that marks the transformation from childhood to adulthood. The ritual process of initiation channels all the potential dissonance, anxiety, and uncertainty of adolescence into a single symbolic event of transformation. The initiate is separated from the world of childhood in order to be ritually transformed into an adult. We will examine this ritual process more closely by drawing on representative examples of the initiation of boys and of girls.

Initiation of Boys

The initiation of boys in tribal societies can be illustrated through examples from aboriginal communities in Australia. Here initiation begins somewhere between the ages of 10 and 13. In some societies, the cycle of ceremonies, instruction, and ordeals may last over this entire three-year period. The initiate is separated from the world of childhood by being isolated from the women and children of the community. The boys are taken out in the bush, secluded in a special hut, and kept from any contact with the ordinary life of the community in order to begin the process of detachment from childhood roles. Often the mothers, and the women of the tribe in general, will mourn the initiate as if he were, in fact, dead. They may wear mourning clothes, wail, and cry, as if in grief at the death of their child.

The anthropologist A. W. Howitt described this process of detachment in the rituals of initiation within one society—the Murring of Australia. He noted that every aspect of the ritual

cycle contributes to making a dramatic transformation in the initiate's sense of personal identity.

> *The intention of all that is done at this ceremony is to make a momentous change in the boy's life; the past is to be cut off from him by a gulf which he can never repass. His connection with his mother as her child is broken off, and he becomes henceforth attached to the men. All the sports and games of his boyhood are to be abandoned with the severance of the old domestic ties between himself and his mother and sisters. He is now to be instructed in and sensible of the duties which devolve upon him as a member of the Murring community.* [2]

The finality of detachment, severing the ties of childhood, is followed by a new identification with the world of men. A period of instruction in the myths, rituals, and mysteries of the tribe introduces the boy into a new adult awareness.

In some initiation rituals, this instruction entails a certain demystification of the religious beliefs of the community. Many Australian communities will use the ritual device of the bull roarer to symbolize the powerful and terrifying voice of a god. At a crucial stage in the initiation ritual, the awesome, mysterious source of this sound will be revealed to the boys in its true form: a wooden noisemaker. Initiation involves the revelation of secret knowledge that is shared by the adult males in that society. This revelation is also accompanied by careful instruction in tribal law and the new responsibilities that are incumbent upon adult status in the community.

Finally, the ritual is sealed with an act of mutilation. A part of the body is marked, scarred, or excised. Often this ritual act takes the form of genital mutilation. The two most common forms of genital mutilation in Australian rituals of initiation are circumcision—in which the foreskin of the penis is cut off—or subincision—in which a cut is made into the penis. In these acts of ritual mutilation, the physical body becomes a social symbol of personal transformation and group solidarity. The body of each boy is ritually transformed to match the pattern or design of physical mutilation that is shared by all the male adults in the community.

Initiation of Girls

Young women may also go through initiation rituals symbolizing their social maturation. One illustration of female initiation ceremonies is provided by the African Sande, a women's religious society of Sierra Leone. This society conducts a long initiation process that involves both symbolic ceremonies and ethical instruction. A group of girls who have begun menstruation will be removed from their villages and will be taken to a secluded part of the forest. Here they will discard their childish clothes and put on special dresses. During the weeks that follow, the girls will receive instruction in the responsibilities of women. The older women will give them detailed information concerning childbearing, the raising of children, hygiene, nutrition, and medicine. The girls are carefully trained to fulfill the traditional roles of women in Sierra Leone. Their instruction even includes such ethical rules as "never reveal the faults of other women."[3] This period of instruction bridges the generations by establishing a sense of social cohesion within the community of women.

The initiation process concludes with a ceremony of physical mutilation. The girls celebrate the end of their training with music and dancing. They feast on the finest food available. Then each girl undergoes an operation in which the clitoris is surgically removed. This genital mutilation, called clitoridectomy, is performed in the female initiation ceremonies of a number of different societies.[4] It may appear as a cruel act of violence against female sexuality in male-dominated societies. Feminists have opposed its continued practice for this reason. But within the ritual context of traditional society in Sierra Leone, this genital mutilation produces scars that serve as visible proof that the young women have been trained in the ethical responsibilities considered appropriate for women within that society. After the operation, the young women who have been initiated into the Sande undergo a ritual of purification and are then reintroduced into the ordinary life of their village. They return with a new status: They are now eligible for marriage, childbearing, and all the roles, rights, and responsibilities that accompany adulthood for women in Sierra Leone.

Ritual Mutilation

How are we to interpret this emphasis on physical mutilation in initiation rituals? The frequency of scarring, incisions, and excisions in these ceremonies reveals several important aspects of the transformation from childhood to adulthood in these tribal societies. First, the ritual mutilation symbolizes the intersection between the physical body and the social body. The biological changes of puberty introduce new drives, impulses, and energies that are subjected to patterns of social control. Social control is worked out through the discipline, training, and management of the body. In initiation rituals, the body dramatically submits to social control by being scarred according to the demands of the shared, traditional practices of the community. As the anthropologist Mary Douglas has observed, "What is being carved in human flesh is an image of society."[5] The body itself is brought within the common regimen of a society by having the distinctive image of that social group literally inscribed upon it.

Second, this mutilation represents the image of adult responsibility. All adults of the same gender share a common image of identity carved into their bodies. This serves as a visible and tangible symbol of their adult status. Physical mutilation, therefore, signifies the rights and responsibilities of adulthood.

Third, the ritual mutilation involved in initiation ceremonies may serve as a means of discharging some of the dissonance of maturation. The painful processes of growth are crystalized into one ordeal of torture and blood. The violence of initiatory death and rebirth focuses the young person's desires into the pattern of an adult role. The psychoanalyst Bruno Bettelheim described this drama as "a conflict between man's instinctual desires and the role he wishes to play in society or which society expects him to fulfill."[6] Anxieties, uncertainties, and feelings of dissonance about this new adult role are focused into one dramatic ordeal from which the individual emerges as a new person. Physical mutilation may serve all of these functions in initiation rituals that propel humans beyond childhood and into adulthood.

Beyond Childhood

Modern western societies do not have such ritual means of marking the transformation from childhood to adulthood. Thus, the crisis of growth may be extended over a period of years in which the dangers and potentials of this transition are prolonged and perhaps never resolved. Certainly, there are important vestiges of initiation rituals in the *bar mitzvah* for boys (and *bat mitzvah* for girls) at age 13 in Judaism, or in confirmation within Catholicism, or in the many secular equivalents of rites of passage in graduations, driver's licenses, and drinking ages. But none of these symbols of transformation have the same sudden, compelling power of the tribal initiation ceremonies. As the periods of the life cycle become more diffused, the ethical responsibilities and obligations become less clearly defined within western societies. Nevertheless, analogous ritual and ethical processes are at work that also focus on the discipline of the body in the movement beyond childhood.

The Invention of Childhood

Our specialized vocabulary for life-cycle stages is a fairly recent system of classification. Although terms that are roughly equivalent to *child, youth,* and *adult* were in use before, it is really since the Industrial Revolution at the end of the eighteenth century that these terms have acquired the special meaning that they hold for us. The French historian Philippe Ariès, in his book *Centuries of Childhood,* has described the formation of a new social classification in western societies: the child. Prior to the eighteenth century, children "went straight into the great community of men."[7] The collective life of European communities was made up of people of all ages, and children were an integral part of the social and economic basis that supported those communities.

Gradually, children began to be set apart from the mainstream of society. Ariès refers to this as the invention of childhood. Children were isolated in institutions designed not only to educate them, but also to discipline them in conformity with ethical patterns of behavior. Schools not only introduced children into a world of basic information, but also into a regimen of discipline. "The school shut up a childhood which had been free," Ariès observed, "within an increasingly severe disciplinary system."[8] Rather than allowing children to enter freely into the adult world of work and leisure, pleasures and pains, the institution of the school separated children from their society so that they might be trained to be adults. During this period of ritual confinement, children learned to conform their behavior to the prescribed cultural patterns that would eventually enable them to be admitted into the world of adults. Ariès stated: "Each person had to resemble a conventional model, an ideal type, and never depart from it under pain of excommunication."[9] As in the initiation rituals of tribal societies, that ideal model was inscribed upon the body.

The discipline of the body in western societies is the point of intersection between the individual and the community. Social forces mold the body as if it were sculpture. The shape and movements of the body are conformed to an ideal type. Schools have been the primary institutions by which children have been disciplined in the regulation, management, and control over their bodily behavior. As this discipline is internalized, it becomes the visible manifestation of a social pattern of obligations in physical form. Body ethics has provided an important training in the disciplinary response to ethical obligation within the religious ethics of western societies.

The Discipline of the Body

The discipline of the body has become the central ethical issue in the transition from childhood to adulthood in western societies. This may be so obvious as to be overlooked. How do we know that people are adults? By the way they act. To be an adult is to act like an adult. The most immediate, basic, and pervasive arena of action is the body. Norbert Elias, in his *Civilizing Process,* has collected examples of religious manuals, educational guidebooks, ethical instructions, and so on that are directly concerned with the discipline of the body. These documents illustrate the ethical demands upon children by which "instinctual life must be rapidly subjected to the strict control and specific molding that gives our societies their stamp."[10] That mold is stamped on the bodies of children through specific obligations that are brought to bear upon bodily behavior. The central ethical obligation in the transformation of children into adults is conformity to these specific standards of bodily discipline.

The ethical discipline of the body governs its most basic functions: eating, sleeping, the processes of elimination, and the variety of bodily eruptions, such as belching, coughing, spitting, nose blowing, and flatulence. We will first consider some of the specific ethical patterns of ideal behavior that are found in the discipline of the body before interpreting the ethical significance of these patterns.

Table Manners   The discipline of the body in the act of eating communicates a person's social standing, class, and status. In the manuals of instruction for the eating habits of young men, the ideals of courtly customs—the habits of the upper class—were applied to the behavior of boys. A thirteenth century poem on courtly good manners made the following observations on proper conduct in eating:

If anyone is accustomed to loosening his belt at table, take it from me that he is not a true courtier.

If a man wipes his nose on his hand at table because he knows no better, then he is a fool, believe me.

I hear that some eat unwashed (if it is true, it is a bad sign). May their fingers be palsied!

It is not decent to poke your fingers into your ears or eyes, as some people do, or to pick your nose while eating.[11]

By the sixteenth century, it was assumed that adults did not do such things at table, but these same instructions were essential for the discipline of children. In 1530 the Christian humanist Erasmus wrote an important manual for the education of young men called *De civilitate morum puerilium* (On civilizing the habits of boys). Class distinctions in table manners remain an important ethical concern. Erasmus observed that "if you are seated with people of rank, take off your hat and see that your hair is well combed."[12] He devoted attention to the specialized uses of the implements of eating: the knife, the goblet, and the serviette or napkin. He also provided instruction on proper deportment while at the table: "Some people put their hands in the dishes the moment they have sat down. Wolves do that. . . ."[13] Table manners distinguished cultivated humans from wild animals.

By the eighteenth century, these ethical standards had become elaborated in manuals such as La Salle's *Les Règles de la bienséance et la civilité chrétienne* (1729). Good manners were perceived to be a basic Christian duty. La Salle showed the same concern for class distinctions at the table. He insisted that "it is for the person of the highest rank in the company to unfold his serviette first, and the others should wait until he has done so before unfolding theirs." La Salle also instructs in the use of the specialized instruments of eating: "It is against propriety to hold the fork or spoon with the whole hand like a stick; you should always hold them between your fingers. You should not use your fork to lift liquids to the mouth . . . it is the spoon that is intended for such uses." And there are demands on physical deportment while the child is within the sacred space circumscribed by the table: "It is improper to use the serviette to wipe your face; it is far more so to rub your teeth with it, and it would be one of the grossest offenses against civility to use it to blow your nose."[14] Table manners represent a ritual of order with everyone and everything in the proper place. The ritualized perfection of table manners creates a controlled environment that enforces a basic set of ethical demands for control over this most basic bodily activity of eating. The ethics of eating defines an ideal pattern of behavior in the disciplinary control of the body.

Natural Functions

The discipline of the bodily functions of elimination also provides a cultural symbol of adulthood in western societies. Erasmus, in his *De civilitate morum puerilium,* discussed the pattern of behavior appropriate for these functions in a serious, yet unashamed, manner. He observed that "it is impolite to greet someone who is urinating or defecating."[15] To perform these functions in private is a symbol of modesty. Erasmus also instructed boys to uncover only certain parts of their bodies in conformity to the virtue of modesty, because even if no one seemed to be watching, "angels are always present."[16] Yet he was not embarrassed to advise young boys on the subject of bodily eruptions.

There are those who teach that the boy should retain wind by compressing the belly. Yet it is not pleasing, while striving to appear urbane, to contract an illness. If it is possible to withdraw, it should be done alone. But if not, in accordance with the ancient proverb, let a cough hide the sound.[17]

Here the health of the boy is invoked as a motive for ethical behavior in relation to the body. Believing that restraint could lead to health complications, Erasmus advised a certain degree of relaxation of bodily control. But, this relaxation must be accompanied by a prescribed social deception. An implicit hierarchy of bodily eruptions is implied in the exhortation to "Follow the law of Chiliades: Replace farts with coughs."[18]

La Salle's manual of Christian civility is more rigorous in its prescriptions for modesty than Erasmus's and sets a decidedly more embarrassed tone. Modesty demands that you should cover all parts of the body except the head and the hands, that you should never touch those parts of the body that are normally covered, and that you should not look at those parts of another person's body "which Heaven forbids you to look at in yourself."[19] This ethical mood of embarrassment about body parts and functions even extends to discourse about the body. La Salle insisted that "It is never proper to speak of the parts of the body that should be hidden, nor of certain bodily necessities to which Nature has subjected us, nor even to mention them."[20] The unmentionable becomes enshrined in these codes of religious ethics. What should not be seen should also not be spoken.

This rigorous control over speech, which is itself a controlled bodily eruption, is reflected in a more restricted control of all bodily eruptions in the manual of La Salle. In place of the rather tolerant indulgence suggested by Erasmus, more rigid restraint was prescribed by La Salle on the matter of flatulence. "It is very impolite to emit wind from your body when in company," La Salle instructed, "either from above or from below, even if it is done without noise; and it is shameful

and indecent to do it in a way that can be heard by others."[21] There is no ethical hierarchy of uncontrolled eruptions for La Salle. All are considered shameful.

Nose Blowing

The *De civilitate* of Erasmus once again demonstrates a concern with the correlation between bodily behavior and social class in its treatment of nose blowing. Some methods are suggested to be more refined than others. Erasmus could place people on the social hierarchy simply by observing the way they blow their nose. A rustic would blow his nose on his hat or clothing; a tradesman would blow his nose on his arm; but a more refined gentleman would know that "it is proper to wipe the nostrils with a handkerchief, and to do this while turning away, if more honorable people are present."[22] The discipline of nose blowing becomes a symbolic index to a person's social standing.

La Salle also devoted a chapter of his manual on body ethics to the issue of nose blowing. This chapter is entitled "On the Nose, and the Manner of Blowing the Nose and Sneezing." Here La Salle set the limits on acceptable behavior in relation to the nose. For example, he insisted that "it is very impolite to keep poking your finger into your nostrils, and still more insupportable to put what you have pulled from your nose into your mouth."[23] The rules governing decency with regard to the nose, as well as the rules of respect for people around you, demand that you use a handkerchief, hide your face behind your hat, avoid making any noise, and never look into your handkerchief after blowing.

Spitting

Just as the nose becomes a focal point for cultural values of modesty, decency, and respect for others, the mouth also must be disciplined. Erasmus gave the following instruction on the topic of spitting:

Turn away when spitting, lest your saliva fall on someone. If anything purulent falls to the ground, it should be trodden upon, lest it nauseate someone.[24]

Erasmus was concerned with regulating the social effects of spitting in his body ethics. Spitting's direct effect should be regulated by avoiding any possibility that someone might be spat upon. Its indirect effect should be regulated by avoiding the possibility that someone's refined sensibilities might be offended by seeing spit.

La Salle also made some pointed comments about spitting. It should be regulated so that one does not spit too often or without need. If necessary, however, La Salle suggested that you should spit into a handkerchief, while turning slightly to the side, especially "when you are with well-born people, and when you are in places that are kept clean."[25] As in the case of nose blowing, you should never look into the handkerchief. The ethical management of saliva provided La Salle with a good indication of a person's breeding, respect for others, and social status. La Salle taught:

You should take great care never to spit on your clothes, or those of others. . . . If you notice saliva on the ground, you should immediately put your foot adroitly on it. If you notice any on someone's coat, it is not polite to make it known; you should instruct a servant to remove it. If no servant is present, you should remove it yourself without being noticed. For good breeding consists in not bringing to people's attention anything that might offend or confuse them.[26]

Again, body ethics involves a certain degree of social deception. A person of ethical refinement might be both offended and confused by encountering saliva out of place. The disciplinary management of such bodily products must follow strict rules of propriety to keep everything in its proper place.

Sleeping

Even the unconsciousness of sleep must be surrounded with conscious, ethical discipline. Erasmus expressed his concern that asleep, as well as awake, the demands of physical modesty must be observed. He exhorted his students: "When you undress, when you get up, be mindful of modesty, and take care not to expose to the eyes of others anything that morality and nature required to be concealed."[27] If the boy should have to share a bed with a comrade, he is instructed to lie quietly. "Do not toss your body," Erasmus demanded, "for this can lay yourself bare or inconvenience your companion by pulling away the blankets."[28]

La Salle also was concerned that boys preserve modesty in sleep. He maintained that you ought "neither to undress nor go to bed in the presence of any other person."[29] His comments on sleeping in the same bed as a comrade are even more stringent in their demands that the boys preserve modesty and avoid dangerously uncontrolled movements of the body. La Salle stated that "if you are forced by unavoidable necessity to share a bed with another person of the same sex on a journey, it is not proper to lie so near him that you disturb or even touch him; and it is still less decent to put your legs between those of the other. . . ."[30]

This ethical discipline of the body in sleep reveals the fears of uncontrolled bodily activity at the point where the body is farthest from the realm of conscious control. The response of such Christian ethicists as Erasmus and La Salle is to isolate the body as much as possible. The body is to be isolated from another's view, contact, and presence. In this way an ideal pattern of decorum, decency, and modesty can be maintained in Christian body ethics.

The Significance of Body Ethics

To isolate the body in this way is to invest it with a special power. It becomes a highly charged arena of ethical action. The body is always more than simply a body: It is a living symbol of ethical responsibility. The ethical patterns of table manners, natural functions, nose blowing, spitting, and sleeping become obligations to which the body must conform through the minute regulations of its actions. The body is either in a state of dissonance or harmony in relation to these ideal patterns of ethical behavior. Childhood seems to be an extended condition of dissonance in body ethics. Behind these patterns of harmony in body ethics are a number of specific ethical intentions. The significance of body ethics lies in the shared cultural motives that animate this discipline of the body.

Knowledge

Being an adult means knowing what to do. The specialized adult knowledge that is embodied in the discipline of the body reveals an ordered universe. The universe inhabited by the body is structured, organized, and constructed according to an ideal pattern. This pattern can be known. The specialized usages of things can be mastered. An adult can know, with a certainty seldom experienced in other areas of knowledge, that you wipe your fingers on a serviette and you wipe your nose with a handkerchief. The assured knowledge of such rules sustains a basic confidence in the order of things. This certain knowledge about what to do is a powerful motive force behind the discipline of the body.

Knowing what to do is also knowing what not to do. The creation of an ideal pattern of bodily behavior necessarily involves excluding some behaviors. But, this means that certain kinds of knowledge are also excluded. Many of the ethical instructions in the Christian manuals of bodily discipline exhort the child *not to look*: not to look at certain parts of the body, not to look at the handkerchief after blowing the nose or spitting, not to look upon someone urinating or defecating. The exclusion of certain kinds of knowledge is an important aspect of ordering the world in which the body lives. It is the cognitive equivalent of factoring out the variables and accidents of ordinary life in ritual. La Salle insisted that you should not call attention to spit on someone's coat, not simply because it would offend the person, but because it might also confuse the person. This point reveals the kind of knowledge that is embodied in body ethics: The harmony of the body consists in knowing what is and what is not to be known. When something that is not to be known intrudes on our awareness, both Erasmus and La Salle urge us to engage in deception in order to make that knowledge invisible.

Civility

Many strategies for disciplining the body presuppose classifications based on a vertical stratification of society. The civility of courtly manners was extended to the behavior of all social classes by the manuals of Erasmus and La Salle. Civility was a regimen of discipline imposed on all bodies. By the time of Erasmus, it was simply assumed that all adults conformed to this discipline. The rustics, the primitives, the uncivilized—these were the children. Children were congenitally lower class until they had been trained by the discipline of civility. This distinction between civilized and primitive behavior within the social classification system of Western Europe was transferred to other societies in the new world during the age of exploration. The "uncivilized" disciplines of the body practiced by other peoples made them appear childlike in the eyes of Europeans. One reason for this cultural prejudice was the fact that children had already been classified as barbarians in Europe. They needed physical discipline in order to become civilized.

Body ethics reinforce class distinctions. The major distinction, of course, is between human and subhuman. Often undisciplined body behavior was equated with the behavior of animals. Beyond this, civility meant the conscious recognition of class distinction in the ethical control of the body. Erasmus could identify people's social status by the way they blew their nose. Both Erasmus and La Salle reinforced class distinctions by recommending the subtle body language of turning aside in deference to people of a higher class. On the other hand, body ethics emphasizes signs of mutual respect in the disposition of bodies within a shared environment. Civility, as an ethical motive for action, means restraining private impulses in the public arena. The body language of civility, in giving up personal impulses in the interest of the public good, is a kind of calculated deception. The civilized body disguises flatulence with a cough; it trods upon spit so it does not nauseate anyone; it removes saliva from someone's coat without telling the person. The ethics of civility lies in a careful pretense that acts as if body functions are under constant and conscious control.

Purity

Body ethics exists in a world with highly structured boundaries between purity and defilement. The body is disciplined in the interests of ritual and ethical purity. In the manuals of Erasmus and La Salle, explicit religious motives are given for maintaining purity in body discipline. Erasmus insisted that boys should always maintain modesty, even when they are alone, because the angels are watching. La Salle reprimands children for looking at parts of another person's body that heaven forbids them to look at in themselves. These religious motives for maintaining purity in western thought are gradually superceded by notions of hygiene. Hygenic motives eventually dominate western thought regarding the health, well-being, and cleanliness of the body. Health concerns are, of course, present in the earlier religious manuals of body discipline. Erasmus believed that the wind in the belly should not be repressed because it might result in health complications. Later instructions in the hygenic purity of the body, as we find even in La Salle, emphasize restraint. Such restraint, however, will be formulated increasingly in terms of scientific, medical control over disease.

Purity is order; dirt is matter out of place. The discipline of the body attempts to ensure that everything is in its proper place. When something is not in its proper place, it is likely to be classified as dirty. For Erasmus and La Salle, wiping the nose with a napkin was dirty, but wiping it with a handkerchief was clean. Purity is achieved by maintaining this orderly control over behavior.

We operate with an elaborate repertoire of hygenic controls over behavior. Imagine a physical implement such as a toothbrush as it appears in different contexts: In the bathroom it is clean, but in the living room it is dirty. Purity may have little to do with protection from the invasion of microbiological organisms. In ordinary experience, germs may simply be a metaphor for disorder. Purity is largely an issue of place. To be out of place is to be exposed to shame. One of the most powerful motives behind the disciplinary control of the body is the desire to avoid the dissonance of shame. The potential for dissonance in bodily behavior can be avoided by keeping everything in its assigned place.

The Christian manuals in body ethics of Erasmus and La Salle suggest that the transformation from childhood to adulthood is a process of initiation in body discipline. Their recommendations for the control of body functions may not seem as dramatic as an ordeal of physical mutilation in an initiation ritual. But, these instructions in physical behavior effectively inscribe an ideal social pattern on the bodies of the children who are initiated into the rules of body discipline. To internalize these ethical patterns of body behavior is to move beyond childhood and begin the process of transformation toward adulthood.

Toward Adulthood

In preindustrial America, distinctions between age groups were rather loose. Generally, the term *infant* was used for the child still under the mother's care. This usually covered the years from birth to age six. *Childhood* extended from age 7 to about age 16, but the term could be applied to anyone under 18 or even 21. There were many variations and inconsistencies in terminology, but a general distinction was made among children, young men and women, and old men and women. These age classifications did not necessarily include an interim period between childhood and adulthood, filled with turbulence, ambivalence, and unique ethical dangers. The term for this interim period—*adolescence*—was popularized by G. Stanley Hall in his book *Adolescence: Its Psychology and Its Relation to Physiology, Anthropology, Sociology, Sex, Crime, Religion and Education* (1904).[31] The attention given to this interim stage in the life cycle may reflect massive transformations in American society after the Civil War: the shift from a rural agrarian society to an urban industrial society. The working family, in which children worked alongside parents in the fields and factories, began to disappear as the basic economic unit in American society. Industrial efficiency demanded workers who could fit into the machinery of production. The teenage years became a period of preparation—in education and discipline—for assuming a place in the working world.

Identification and Disidentification

Perhaps this stage in the life cycle has always had its special potentials and dangers. Erik Erikson maintained that identity formation is the essential task of adolescence. This is not simply a matter of self-recognition. Identity is formed out of the interchange of mutual recognition between an individual and a community. Identity formation during adolescence, as Erikson has defined it, is "a process by which a community recognizes a young person as distinct from other youth as having a style of his own."[32] In the terms of a simplified social psychology, there are two ways of knowing who you are: identification and disidentification. Identification is to recognize that I am *like* that. It is identifying the basic pattern of the self with a cultural image, a role model, or a social group. Disidentification is defining self-identity in terms of what you are not. It is recognizing that I am *not like* that. Every social environment presents an array of images for identification and disidentification. The period of adolescence may be a time of experimenting with such images of personal identity.

The central ethical challenge of adolescence is the need to respond creatively to rapid changes in identity. In a religious vocabulary, such a change of identity might be called *conversion*. The early psychologists of adolescence, such as G. Stanley Hall and Edward Starbuck, saw adolescence as a life-cycle stage that was particularly prone to religious conversion. Conversion itself was interpreted as an outgrowth of adolescence. It was seen as a religious response to the internal conflicts generated by biological maturation and new social responsibilities. Conversion was a way of defining oneself as an adult. These psychologists noticed that during the religious revivals of the early nineteenth century, with their enthusiastic preaching, tent meetings, and mass conversions, most of the converts were between the ages of 13 and 22. In the frontier revivals that swept the United States, conversion provided a means of making the transition from childhood to adulthood. The convert who stood in the assembly to give witness to an experience of conversion probably spoke for the first time as an adult in public. Full church membership that followed this conversion was a visible sign of adult status in the community.[33]

Conversion provided a way to form an adult identity by selecting one aspect of the personality at the expense of other aspects. In a sense, to be a child is to be pure potential. The child has the potential to choose any occupation, to marry any member of the opposite gender, and to be anyone. To be an adult is to move from the relatively unlimited potential of childhood, from the realm of infinite possibilities, to the finite, limited world of actual choices: to choose one occupation, to marry one mate, to be one person. Conversion is a mechanism for selecting one religious identity out of the theoretically infinite range of possible identities. It is an act of appropriation that makes that pattern of identity one's own. As a dramatic crystallization of personal identity, religious conversion establishes a model for other identity transformations that may occur during adolescence.

Youth

Traditionally, this transformation in religious identity would happen only once in a lifetime. Although there are examples of multiple conversions, and subsequent disillusionments, they have not been the norm. In recent history, however, beginning in the late 1960s, new patterns of conversion appeared in which young people went through a rapid series of identity transformations. Young people experimented with identities, allegiances, and various alternations in the process of identification and disidentification. The psychologist Robert Lifton referred to this process of identity transformation as the protean style. It is a style of identity formation emphasizing change, flux, and transition. The protean style is a response to two major cultural trends in modern American society. The first is a prevalent sense of historical dislocation in which many Americans felt cut off from the nurturing symbols, myths, and values of their collective past. The other cultural trend is the almost overwhelming flood of imagery through mass media in which a wider range of potential behavioral patterns are available than ever before.[34]

The explosion in possible identities that are available to the ethical imagination has been accompanied by a cultural tendency to prolong the period of adolescence. Within this extended adolescence is an interim stage of pure potential between childhood and adulthood. The psychologist Kenneth Kenniston referred to this interim stage as youth.[35] It is a separate stage, distinct from childhood, adolescence, or adulthood. The central ethical issue in youth is a tension between self and society. Compared to youth, adolescence has relatively conventional roles: rebel, truant, conformist, athlete, or achiever. Youth, however, represents a fundamental dissonance between an emerging sense of self and the existing social order. Youth is in conflict with the pattern of ethical obligations that are embodied in the prevailing network of social relations.

Erikson has observed that the main desire of youth is to find ideas, people, and causes that inspire faith. This recalls the traditional model of conversion. According to Erikson, youth has "a need for persons and ideas to have faith in, which also means men and ideas in whose service it would seem worthwhile to prove oneself trustworthy."[36] The stage of youth, as Kenneth Kenniston has defined it, is a period of social dissonance in which the emerging self, with its own potential, values, and sense of integrity, can find nothing in its adult environment worthy of faith, trust, or identification. So, youth finds itself in a state of positive disengagement—positive because the primary strategy of youth is to keep its own potential alive. The symbols of pure potential—change, movement, and experimentation—are perceived as ethical values in their own right. From this perspective, adulthood may not appear as the desirable culmination of the maturation process, but as the end of the vitality represented by youth.

These transformations in personal identity during the life-cycle stage of youth are accompanied by important changes in ethical responsibility. The ability to respond to a sense of obligation may undergo a process of development that can be outlined in three basic stages:

1.   *The preconventional stage.* In early childhood the response to ethical obligation is determined by relatively egocentric concepts of right and wrong. The child may be concerned with identifying the boundaries of ethical obligation in order to know what can be done without getting caught. Or the child may be concerned with determining those courses of action that lead to the greatest personal gratification of desires.

2.   *The conventional stage.* In later childhood, behavior tends to be determined by ethical conventions. Concepts of "good boy" or "good girl" become normative patterns for behavior. The shared standards of the community begin to become important as they are internalized by an emerging sense of self. The rules of law, custom, and morality tend to be perceived as objective, unquestionable, and based on the external authority of parents, community, or God.

3.   *The postconventional stage.* During the life-cycle stage of adolescence, the potential exists for a more independent response to ethical obligation. Erik Erikson called this the ethical stage. It is characterized by an expanding imagination of ethical possibilities. These possibilities may be in conflict with the pattern of obligation represented by social convention. Postconventional ethical imagination begins to be concerned with social contracts and personal principles. Moral choices may be based on agreements in the interest of the common good, and they may be expressions of a sense of personal integrity in creating standards for ethical behavior.[37]

The energy, enthusiasm, and interests of youth represent a potential for identity that cannot be controlled through discipline. The ethical issues that emerge during youth are issues of choice—about vocation, life styles, and personal involvement with the existing network of social relations. The ethics of choice necessarily involves a certain disposition toward experimentation, which does not mean simply calculating the advantages and disadvantages of possible courses of action. The ethics of choice requires a sensitivity to energy, enthusiasm, interest, attention, and even love—all qualities that cannot be forced, but must arise spontaneously in the process of action. In the ethics of choice, a person may carefully weigh the pros and cons of any decision and then throw out the results and do what is most interesting. In this spirit of experimentation, problems appear as challenges and mistakes appear as opportunities for learning and growth. The ethical stage represented by youth is a period that is primarily characterized by improvisation as the dominant style of response to ethical obligation.

Shared cultural images of adulthood consist of specific role models that provide adult behavior patterns. Becoming an adult means separating from parental models and beginning to identify with a range of cultural roles that are available in the larger social environment. These may be models set by cultural heroes, religious figures, or community leaders; these may be role models set by the range of occupations that are practiced in the adult world. The models are suggested by a limited repertoire of patterns, styles, and rhythms of behavior that are considered appropriate for adults. The internalization of any role model requires a certain balance between conformity and autonomy. The need to comply with the behavior rules of a given role model competes with maintaining a degree of detachment for ongoing improvisation within the framework that the model provides.

Every system of religious ethics contains certain assumptions about adult roles that define ethical maturity. Often these are traditional roles, set by time-honored patterns of behavior, rigid in their inexorable demands for conformity and relentless in their exclusion of any who depart from their design. In one sense, a society recognizes maturity in conformity to cultural expectations within the adult roles of work, marriage, and family. But in another sense, maturity implies a certain independence from cultural stereotypes. Rather than conforming to comfortable expectations, a mature adult can create a more open, undefined, and ambiguous lifestyle that re-

mains responsive to opportunities for change, learning, and growth. This tension between conformity and autonomy presents the central ethical challenge of the transitional stage of the life cycle during the period of youth.

Ethical Burden

Ethical obligation in adulthood is often symbolized as a burden in religious traditions. Adults carry the heavy weight of ethical responsibility. They are burdened by the full demands of obligation. Tseng Tzu, one of the students of Confucius, observed in the *Analects* that the burden of humanity is a heavy weight to bear.

> *The True Knight of the Way must perforce be both broad-shouldered and stout of heart; his burden is heavy and he has far to go. For humanity [jen] is the burden he has taken upon himself; and must we not grant it is a heavy one to bear? Only with death does this journey end; then must we not grant that he has far to go?*[38]

The obligation to cultivate and sustain the ethical virtue of jen is described as a heavy burden that the Confucian adult must carry on the long journey toward death. Conscientious training in Confucian ethics is required to support the weight of obligation.

The definition of an adult in the tradition of Islam also involves this image of the burden of obligation. Adults (*mukallafun*) are legally and ethically responsible. They have achieved physical maturity and are of sound mind. They may enter into contracts, dispose of property, and be subject to criminal law. The mukallaf is fully responsible for carrying out all the religious commands and obligations of Islam. As an adult, he is "responsible for bearing the burden [*taklif*] laid upon him by God."[39] The image of ethical obligation as a burden is very common in systems of religious ethics. When the Christian New Testament records Jesus describing the nature of the responsibility that is placed upon his followers, it is symbolized as a burden. An ironic note is struck, however, when Jesus declares that "My yoke is easy and my burden is light." (Mt. 11:30)

One way of bearing the burden of adult obligation is to keep a childlike quality alive. The Confucian sage Mencius saw this as one of the virtues of Confucian ethics. "The great man," observed Mencius, "does not lose his childlike heart."[40] Of course, Jesus urged his followers to become like little children in order to enter the kingdom of heaven. A childlike response to adult obligation is not a case of arrested development, even though this might be suggested by the Protestant Reformer John Calvin's statement that "in this life we are never men." Rather, it is to recognize life as a process of change in which there is always potential for new growth. The pure potential of the child remains a vital response to the ethical obligation of adulthood.

Augustine suggested this perspective when he contemplated the potential for change in human nature. A human person is not a stationary object, but a living force of change. Augustine asked, "What, then, am I, my God? What is my nature? A life that is ever varying, full of change, and of immense power. . . . This is the great force of life in living man, mortal though he is."[41] Although Augustine was convinced that humans are limited by their mortality, he nevertheless believed that they possessed some spark of the divine creative power. The only thing permanent in human nature seems to be this force of change. The capacity to change, adapt, and respond creatively to life situations may reveal human nature at its best. The creative disclosure of self-identity in a process of change is the primary ethical challenge of transformation.

Patterns of Transformation

The challenge of adolescence in the human life cycle focuses the transformation of a human being from childhood to adulthood. This is not simply a biological process, but a social transition beyond childhood and toward adulthood. Ritual and ethical rules that govern this social process may embody basic religious responses to transformation. That change may be sudden or gradual, but it signifies the assumption of new ethical obligations that are regarded as appropriate for the various social roles of adulthood. Chapter 6 has drawn a number of conclusions regarding the nature of this ethical transformation in response to the challenges of childhood, adolescence, youth, and adulthood in religious ethics.

1.   *Initiation rituals mediate the transformation from childhood to adulthood.* Rites of passage from childhood to adulthood play an important role in effectively separating people from the world of the child and introducing them into adult social roles. This ritual transformation focuses all of the potential dissonance regarding new adult roles, rights, and responsibilities into one dramatic ritual process. That process is often acted out as if it were a symbolic death and rebirth; it is a symbolic transformation that results in the birth of a new identity. Adult identity is often signified through the ritual mutilation of the body. In these cases, a shared image of society

is literally inscribed on the body. The ritual muti-lation, cutting, or scarring of the body serves as a physical emblem of adulthood within a community of adults who share that same marking. With this new adult status comes new ethical obligations, responsibilities, and rights.

---

2.   *Body ethics in western societies also involve ethical issues of transformation.* The discipline of the body in religious ethics transforms physical behavior into a normative pattern of action. Body ethics trains physical behavior so that it conforms to cultural images of adult behavior. In this sense, to be an adult is to act like an adult. An adult acts in a way that demonstrates a disciplined, conscious control over the body. That control becomes an internal guidance system that conforms bodily behavior to body ethics. Physical behavior in eating, natural functions, nose blowing, spitting, and even sleeping all come under this disciplinary management of the body. Adults adapt their behavior to a disciplinary pattern of body ethics; children and wild animals do not. Body ethics, therefore, is one way of marking out the transformation from childhood to adulthood.

Body ethics reveals the extent to which western societies organize ethical behavior on the basis of distinctions between purity and de-filement. The ethical order within which the body is disciplined corresponds to clearly defined boundaries of pure and impure behavior. The eighteenth century Christian ethicist La Salle revealed this relationship between ethical order with the order of purity when he cautioned young boys not to act in ways that might offend

or confuse others. An offense against the ethical ordering of physical behavior confuses the categories of purity and impurity. As long as the body performs what is classified as pure and avoids what is impure the ethical order of physical behavior is maintained. Body ethics demonstrates a knowledge of the order of purity by sacrificing private impulses in the public arena. Public rules of physical purity, whether they are reinforced by notions of physical hygiene, fear of defilement, or the watchful eyes of the angels, discipline bodily behavior in body ethics. By mastering this ethical discipline of the body, a child moves beyond childhood and toward adulthood.

---

3.   *Adulthood represents the full burden of ethical responsibility.* Entering into adulthood, a person assumes the full weight of ethical obligation that is incumbent upon a human being within any system of religious ethics. The possibility always exists, however, that the burden of adult obligation may be met with a degree of youthful spontaneity, enthusiasm, and improvisation. The challenge of the transformation from childhood to adulthood lies precisely in this need to keep alive some of the childlike potential in the ability to respond creatively to ethical obligation. Patterns of transformation in religious ethics respond to the often ambiguous transition from childhood to adulthood in a variety of ways. But the creative potential in this transformation consists in the ability to maintain a balance between the freedom to improvise and the necessity to carry the ethical burdens of adult obligation.

CHAPTER

SEVEN

TENSION

Religious ethics enters into the deepest inner tensions in human experience. It responds to those tensions that generate the strongest irrational power in personal life: the tension of gender differences and the tension of sexual energy. Systems of religious ethics produce ideal patterns of action for both gender and sexuality. Gender is the basic biological distinction between male and female; it is given a specifically social character within religious ethics. The two genders are almost always assumed to have different ethical roles, rights, and responsibilities. Sexuality encompasses the entire range of human sexual desires and the expressions of those desires in human interaction. Sexual activity is carefully shaped by traditions of religious ethics to conform to ideal patterns of sexuality. The pleasure, discipline, and knowledge of sex is an important concern of religious ethics. The two genders—male and female—are like the positive and negative poles of a battery: a difference, a

creative tension, a potential for generating energy. Religious traditions attempt to channel this energy through ritual and ethics into normative patterns of action.

In most societies the ritual of marriage is the ideal pattern of action that determines the range of expectations for the relationship between the genders and the expression of sexuality. We will consider both the ritual classifications and the ethical obligations that are associated with marriage in the history of religions. Within this context, gender differences in traditional patterns of religious ethics have been reinforced by the subclassification of women. We will also examine the ethical obligations proposed for males and for females in religious ethics.

Finally, the ethics of sexuality involves three basic issues. The first issue is the ethical response to the pleasures of sex. Religious traditions have developed a range of obligations that govern the experience of pleasure in human sexuality. The second issue is the ethical response to the discipline of sex. Disciplinary rules governing sexuality determine the types of sexual behavior that are proper and improper within a system of religious ethics. The third issue is that the modern, scientific appropriation of sex as a means for population control has given rise to new ethical issues: genetic engineering, artificial insemination, and medical control over the reproduction process. Religious ethics addresses the ethical issues of pleasure, propriety, and population control in an attempt to respond to the challenges of sexuality in human experience. These issues are part of a basic ethical project in which religious ethics directs the creative tension of human sexuality into normative patterns of action.

Marriage Rituals

Marriage rituals symbolize a socially legitimate sexual union. As a public event, marriage represents the social affirmation of a more or less permanent relationship. It acknowledges certain explicit rights and responsibilities that apply to the relations between spouses. Marriage also defines the grounds of ethical trust between spouses and their children. As a rite of passage in the human life cycle, Arnold van Gennep noted, "marriage constitutes the most important of the transitions from one social category to another."[1] Individuals are separated from their previous social category, within one family unit, and are incorporated into a new family pattern. This transition represents a leap in the cycle of generations, setting the social conditions for the creation of new life. Those conditions are socially acknowledged and often religiously sanctioned, and form a normative marriage pattern. We will reflect briefly on the variety of those patterns in human societies.

Marriage Patterns

Almost every imaginable marriage pattern has been approved by some society at one time or another in human history. The calculus of possible cultural permutations in the marriage pattern is not exhausted by the monogamous relationship between one man and one woman. Varieties of polygamy have also been sanctioned within systems of religious ethics. These ritual patterns of marriage incorporate a community's primary classification of male and female genders; these patterns also create the basic ritual context for the legitimate expression of human sexuality.

Polyandry   Polyandry is one variety of polygamy: a marriage pattern involving multiple spouses. In this case, polyandry is a marriage of one woman with more than one man. A wife may have several husbands. Often this is an arrangement attributed to economic hardship, in which the economic unit of the family must be supported by the labor of several men. Sometimes polyandry is the result of a surplus of men in relation to women. This situation may even be caused by the practice of female infanticide, which reduces the number of women in the community. Often the multiple husbands are brothers, as was the case among the Toda of India. As we noted in Chapter 5, the Toda needed to perform a special ceremony during pregnancy in order to determine which of the woman's husbands would assume the social role of father. It has been suggested that the practice of polyandry among the Toda grew out of the fraternal benevolence of elder brothers; they were willing to share their wives with their younger brothers. However, this marriage pattern seems to have been a response to the shortage of women in the community brought on by the practice of female infanticide. The Toda are reported to have thought so little of women that they often had female infants trampled to death in buffalo pens. The Toda women had no choice in husbands, but had to accept all of the brothers in marriage.[2]

A variation of polyandry appears in the arrangements of *levirate* marriage in ancient Israel. If a husband should die without leaving any children, it was incumbent upon his unmarried brother to take over the conjugal responsibilities. Children produced from this union would be legally considered the offspring and heirs of the deceased elder brother. The biblical story of Onan reinforced the importance of the levirate rule in ancient Israel. Onan was called to fulfill the ethical duties of levirate marriage after the death of his elder brother. But, instead of conscientiously trying to conceive a child with his sister-in-law, Onan "spilled his seed upon the ground." And Yahweh punished him with death. The narrative of Onan does not necessarily illustrate the evils of masturbation or *coitus interruptus*. The sin of Onan was a specific violation of the obligations of levirate marriage.[3]

The levirate marriage is also mentioned in the Christian New Testament when the Sadducees posed a problem to Jesus concerning the eternal consequences of such an arrangement. If a woman had been married to seven brothers in succession by the custom of levirate marriage, whose wife would she be in heaven? His answer suggested the provisional nature of marriage itself in Christian thought: "In heaven they are neither married nor are given in marriage." (Mt. 22.23–33; Lk. 20.27–40; Mk. 12.18–27)

Polygyny

Polygyny is a second variety of polygamy. It is the marriage of one man with more than one woman. This marriage pattern appears when there is a surplus of women, or when a culture produces men who fear dying without children, or when power within a social group is demonstrated by having many wives and children. A statistical survey of global marriage patterns reveals that more societies practice polygyny than practice an exclusive form of monogamy. Those polygynous societies are smaller in total population, however, and the majority of them practice monogamy in addition to allowing polygynous marriages. In social groups where women outnumber men, polygyny allows more women an opportunity to bear children. In polygyny, men may find the advantages of variety, access to sex during taboo periods of pregnancy, lactation, or menstruation, and a supply of cheap, dependent labor supplied by multiple wives.

There are examples of polygyny in the Hebrew Bible. The patriarch Jacob had two wives: Rachel and Leah. But he was outdone by King Solomon, who is reported to have had 700 wives and 300 concubines. The institution of concubinage was common in the ancient world. In addition to a legally recognized wife or wives, a man might also have concubines attached to his household. Any offspring would be legally recognized as part of his family. The patriarchs Abraham and Jacob both had children by their wives' handmaidens, and these children were recognized as legitimate by their fathers.

The Qur'an established polygyny as the standard marriage pattern for the tradition of Islam. Muhammad specified that the Muslim may take as many as four wives. This was an ethical response to the surplus of women, largely the result of the influx of captives taken in war. The man was only to take as many wives as he could afford to provide for, up to the maximum limit of four wives. The husband is instructed to treat each of his wives equally, but the Qur'an notes, almost as an aside, that he will probably not be able to do this successfully.[4]

Monogamy

Monogamy is a marriage between one man and one woman. It is an exclusive marriage pattern. Monogamy may have some practical advantages of economy, efficiency, and rationalization. The monogamous nuclear family provides relatively simple kinship patterns and clear lines of inheritance and descent. Like any marriage pattern, monogamy defines a socially sanctioned ritual context within which gender roles are defined and sexuality is legitimately expressed. Christianity arose in a Hellenistic cultural environment that practiced monogamy as its standard marriage pattern. This pattern became enshrined in western religious thought regarding marriage. By establishing exclusive, monogamous marriage as an ethical obligation, aberrant forms of sexuality are automatically defined. Threats to the socially sanctioned pattern of marriage have intensified as the relatively inflexible institution of monogamous marriage has been subject to boredom, extramarital sexual relations, and increasingly higher divorce rates.

Exogamy and Endogamy

Traditions of religious ethics are usually very clear about who you can and cannot marry. Marriage partners are determined by rules of exogamy and endogamy. Rules of *exogamy* determine which prospective spouses are to be excluded as potential marriage partners by virtue of the fact that they are classified as too familiar. This excludes, in most cases, members of the immediate family group. Rules of *endogamy* determine which prospective spouses are to be excluded because they are classified as too different. Endogamy rules out certain potential marriage partners by virtue of their social class, nationality, or race. The rules of exogamy and endogamy identify legitimate mates by ruling out those who are classified as too similar or too different, too familiar or too strange.

Exogamy

Exogamy creates a special classification of members of the opposite gender who are forbidden as marriage partners because of a real, assumed, or conventional bond of kinship. The taboo that applies to incest is precisely such an exogamous classification. Incest taboos are cultural restrictions on sexual relations between sisters and brothers, between parents and children, and perhaps between other members of a culturally defined extended family. The taboo against incest is an almost universal ethical rule. One exception is the ethical rule that encouraged brother-sister marriages in the Zoroastrian tradition of ancient Persia.[5] But in the few other cases in which incestuous marriages were practiced, as between members of the ancient Egyptian or traditional Hawaiian royal families, these arrangements were not permitted for ordinary people within those societies. Incestuous marriages demonstrated the power of royalty to transcend the ordinary rules that applied to the conventional marriage pattern and were binding upon the rest of society.[6]

The incest taboo has had a tremendous power and persistence in religious ethics. Three basic reasons for the almost universal taboo against incest have been suggested. First, the incest taboo is a cultural mechanism that serves the interests of natural selection. It is a cultural means of avoiding the negative biological effects of inbreeding. Many taboos against incest in primal religious ethics are accompanied by warnings that monsters would be born from such a union. These warnings may be supported by the findings of a recent research study of 18 infants born from incestuous sexual relationships: 12

were born from brother-sister unions and 6 from father-daughter unions. After 6 months, it was determined that only 7 of the 18 infants were fit for adoption. Five had died, two were mentally retarded, one had a bilateral cleft palate, and three were considered to have borderline intelligence with an IQ below 70.[7]

We may find it difficult to imagine tribal societies making decisions about marriage based on considerations of genetics. The suggestion seems to be that social groups have simply responded to the biological problem of inbreeding by means of the rule against incest. Edward Westermarck, in his *History of Human Marriage,* proposed that primitives identified the genetics of inbreeding with familiarity. Human beings developed an instinctive aversion to sexual relations with anyone who had been part of the close, familiar household of childhood. This cultural aversion to familiarity in marriage relations served the interests of natural selection by avoiding the hazards of inbreeding.[8] It may be, however, that the cultural avoidance of familiarity in marriage patterns served other more immediate psychological and social functions through the incest taboo.

The second reason for the rule against incest emphasizes the role that this taboo plays in psychological adaptation. Psychoanalytic literature has seen the incest taboo as an adaptation to conflicts within the nuclear family. One perspective explains the horror of incest as a reaction formation, a psychological mechanism in which people feel a strong aversion for something that they actually desire. According to Sigmund Freud, the aversion to incest was the result of the repressed instinctual desire that children feel for the parent of the opposite gender. Other psychological perspectives have suggested that the incest taboo is the result of a learned avoidance of relatives through unsuccessful sex play in childhood. Or, the horror of incest may be analyzed as simply an internalization of parental instructions, prohibitions, and sexual fears. In all of these psychologi-

cal perspectives, the cultural rules against incest are related to basic sexual instincts, drives, and desires that contribute to the formation of personal identity.[9]

Regardless of genetic problems created by inbreeding, or psychological drives that may animate the horror of incest, a third reason for the incest taboo identifies the rule's important social functions. One social function is role maintenance. Incest would disrupt the network of social roles that are developed in systems of kinship classification. It would create problems of identity, create confusion in the lines of authority, and disrupt the delicate balance of roles, rights, and responsibilities that are built into family relationships.[10] A second function of exogamy that appears in the incest taboo is social reciprocity. Rules that prohibit marriage within a family unit commit the family to giving up what may be regarded as its most valuable property: women. The exchange of women among kinship groups opens up the family to a larger network of reciprocal social relations. This may be the basis of all cultural exchange. Incest taboos, as a basic rule of exogamy, force family units to enter into the social ties created by marriage with other family units. The prohibition of incest sustains the reciprocal network of cultural exchange that makes social relations possible.[11]

Endogamy

In contrast to the rules of exogamy, which open up the family unit to a greater field of social relations, the rules of endogamy place limits upon that field. Some prospective marriage partners are excluded from the field of potential mates by virtue of the fact that they are classified as too different, foreign, or strange. The rules of endogamy encourage marriage within particular social, ethnic, or religious groups by prohibiting marriage to partners outside those groups. The boundaries of endogamy define the cultural territory within which marriage is to be permitted.

Endogamy involves horizontal classifications that exclude potential marriage partners for reasons of race, nationality, or religion. These classifications rule out the possibility of marriage with adjoining social groups that, for one reason or another, appear to be too different. In ancient Greece, particularly in the city-states of Athens and Sparta, marriages with spouses of a foreign race were illegal. In ancient Roman society, the marriage of a Roman citizen with a foreign woman was invalid. Any children produced from such a marriage would be classified as illegitimate. Some adjoining communities, however, had been granted the special privilege of *conubium* with Rome, which would allow for marriages between members of those communities and Roman citizens.[12] These classifications in these ancient societies defined the rules limiting marriage in terms of nationality.

Religion has also been a divisive and limiting factor in marriage ethics by establishing rules of endogamy. Many traditions prohibit marriage outside the boundaries of the religious community. Jewish law, for example, does not recognize the marriage between a Jew and a non-Jew. The early Christian community was concerned with promoting endogamous marriages within the Church. Paul insisted that Christians were not to marry heathens. (1 Cor. 7:19) Islam specified that a marriage between a Muslim woman and a Christian man was not permitted. A Muslim man, however, could marry a Jew or a Christian (but not a heathen) if he was moved by love or if no Muslim women were available. These endogamous rules reinforce the horizontal divisions that separate adjacent religious communities in marriage ethics.

Endogamy may also be governed by vertical classifications based on social class. Class endogamy restricts prospective marriage partners to members of the same social class. Captain Cook, on his voyage to the Pacific Islands, reported that a Tahitian woman was forbidden to marry a man from a lower social class; any children produced from such a union would be killed. The rigid caste and class hierarchy of traditional India prohibited intermarriage among social classes. In ancient Roman society, the marriage between low-class plebians and upper-class patricians was forbidden by law until 445 B.C. Even after that time interclass marriages were discouraged by social convention. These examples only suggest the extent to which vertical classifications within a society may limit the range of potential marriage partners. The social classifications also reinforce the boundaries of the exogamous social group within which marriage is permitted.

Marriage as an Ethical Obligation

Most religious traditions suggest that marriage is a pattern of ethical obligation that is required of all people. There are some exceptions. The marriage ethics of the most rigorously ascetic form of Jainism requires that its adherents renounce all sexual pleasures "either with gods, or men, or animals." One Buddhist text counsels that "a wise man should avoid married life as if it were a burning pit of coals."[13] But, for the most part, religious traditions view marriage as an obligation. Marriage is viewed as an essential requirement for all fully functioning members of the religious community.

In some societies, to be unmarried is to be not fully human. Edward Westermarck recorded that among the Santals, a single man was classified as "no man."[14] A system of religious ethics may hold that marriage and the production of children are basic religious and ethical obligations. Among the Futana of the Western Pacific, it was reported that marriage was necessary in this life to ensure a happy future life after death. Unmarried people would receive special punishments in the next world. The islanders of Fiji are said to have believed that those who die in an unmarried state will be met on the road to paradise by the god Nangganangga and be smashed to atoms.[15] Such an expectation would certainly encourage a person to fulfill the ethical obligation of marriage.

Marriage is viewed as an ethical obligation in some of the religious traditions of the East. The *Laws of Manu,* for example, maintained that marriage is a religious duty. A family is necessary for performing all the essential religious observances in this life, and it will also be necessary for performing the required prayers for the dead that will benefit the deceased in the next life.[16] The religious traditions of ancient China also viewed marriage and family as essential for the performance of rituals for the dead. The Confucian sage Mencius summarized the Confucian ethics on marriage by insisting that it was a serious sin to die without having produced sons through marriage.[17] Sons were necessary to perform the regular rituals for departed ancestors, to worship at the ancestral tombs, to care for the ancestral tablets, and to conduct all the traditional rituals for the dead. To die without sons would break this chain of ritual observance. It would condemn such a man, as well as his ancestors, to an unfortunate existence in the other world. The ritual and ethical obligations of marriage suggest that these ancient societies perceived the family as an ongoing link between the living and the dead. Marriage represented the ethical obligation to maintain this continuity.

Western religious traditions have also viewed marriage as an ethical obligation. The sacred texts of Zoroastrianism specify that marriage, with children, is the highest ethical achievement of humanity. "The man who has a wife is far above him who lives in continence; he who keeps a house is far above him who died without children." The text informs Zoroastrians that the first question they will be asked by the angels will be, "Have you left a substitute for yourself in the world?"[18] According to the Orthodox code of Jewish law, the *Shulchan Aruch,* a man who does not marry, is considered guilty of bloodshed. In not producing children, he has diminished the image of God on earth and caused the divine presence to withdraw from the people of Israel. A man who does not marry will have no part in the next world.[19] In Islam, marriage is an ethical obligation of such central importance that the Prophet declared, "When a man marries he has fulfilled half of the religion."[20]

Christianity has had a particularly ambivalent attitude toward the institution of marriage. On the one hand, Christians inherited the image of divine approval for marriage from the Hebrew Bible. Marriage is part of the design for human life, that male and female should become one flesh and that they should be fruitful and multiply. (Gen. 2:24; 1:28) On the other hand, the Christian New Testament suggests that marriage is a rather provisional, temporary, and conditional arrangement. This provisional character of marriage is suggested by the observation attributed to Jesus that the inhabitants of heaven will neither be married nor be given in marriage.

Partly in the interest of reconciling these different tendencies, Paul worked out a hierarchy of human sexuality in his New Testament letters. For Paul, "it is better to marry than to burn," but it is even better to be celibate. (1 Cor. 7:9) Marriage is a provisional accommodation for human desires, procreation, and companionship. Although celibacy is the ideal ethical pattern for human sexuality, marriage is accepted as a compromise. "It is good for a man not to touch a woman," Paul instructed, "nevertheless, to avoid fornication, let each man have his own wife, and let each woman have her own husband." (1 Cor. 7:1) Paul elevated virginity to an ethical status that had a profound effect upon the development of the

Christian tradition. He proposed an ethical rule that specified, "He that gives [his virgin daughter] in marriage does well; but he who does not give her in marriage does better." (1 Cor. 7:38)

The effect of this ethical ideal of virginity is seen in the ethics of the Church Father Tertullian, who insisted that it is far better neither to marry nor to burn with desire.[21] Tertullian saw little difference between marriage and fornication. Both gave in to the sexual lusts of the body and should be avoided. Later in the tradition, the medieval theologian Thomas Aquinas exalted virginity by placing it at the pinnacle of his scale of goodness. Aquinas even quantified this scale by assigning marriage an ethical value of 30, widowhood 60, and virginity 100.[22] Virginity was interpreted as the supreme symbol of ethical purity.

Leading theologians of the Eastern Orthodox Church, such as Gregory of Nyssa and John of Damascus, imagined that Adam would have remained a virgin if he had been obedient to the will of God. The loss of virginity is associated with Adam's fall into sin. The reproduction of the human species would have been carried out in the Garden of Eden by a process of vegetation that would have produced innocent and immortal human beings.[23]

Theologians of the Western Church did not go quite this far in eliminating sexuality from their vision of God's plan for human beings. However, they were clear that God only intended sexual expression for the purpose of procreation; it was an act to be performed without pleasure. Many theologians imagined that sex in the primordial garden was without desire, lust, or pleasure before the fall. The consensus in traditional Christian theological ethics held that marriage was an acceptable arrangement for two reasons: to continue the propagation of the human species and to place a restraint on the indiscriminate exercise of lust.[24]

Divorce

Systems of religious ethics may also make provisions for terminating the marriage relationship. Usually divorce is very carefully restricted. The *Laws of Manu* stipulates the rules for divorce from a traditional Hindu marriage. A husband can set aside his wife for a number of specific reasons. First, a man may divorce his wife at any time if she is rebellious, quarrelsome, diseased, mischievous, wasteful, or drinks liquor. These grounds for divorce reveal something of the ethical obligations that were binding on wives. Second, a man may divorce his wife in the eighth year if she has not borne children, in the tenth year if all the children she has borne have died, and in the eleventh year if all the children she has borne have been daughters. The divorce timetable suggests the importance placed on a wife producing children, and more specifically, producing sons, in traditional Hindu marriage ethics. The *Laws of Manu* offers no provisions for a legal separation initiated by the wife. She has no legal basis to obtain a divorce. The text only suggests that she may go so far as to "show aversion" toward a husband who is mad, impotent, or suffering from venereal disease.[25]

Similar limits are placed on the rights of women to initiate a divorce within western ethical traditions. In ancient Roman law, according to Plutarch, a wife could not leave her husband. But a husband could divorce his wife on the following grounds: drinking wine, committing adultery, counterfeiting his keys, or poisoning the children.[26] The Hebrew Bible specifies that a husband was entitled to divorce his wife if he "found some uncleanness in her." (Deut. 24:1) A wife, however, could not legally separate from her husband.[27] Gradually, Judaism—as expressed in the Talmud—began to allow for conditions under which a woman could sue for divorce: if the husband refused to perform his conjugal duties; if he continued to live a disorderly life after marriage; if he proved to be impotent after 10 years of marriage; if he suffered from an intolerable disease; if he left the country forever. The woman could sue for a divorce under these conditions, but it still might be difficult to obtain.[28] In Islam, a husband could divorce his wife simply by declaring three times: "I divorce you."[29] The rules for divorce in traditions of religious ethics emphasize a disparity between the rights of males and females. The ethical rules of marriage and divorce support implicit, and often explicit, double standards in determining the ethical roles, rights, and responsibilities of men and women. This tension between the genders is a basic challenge in any system of religious ethics.

Gender

Traditional systems of religious ethics tend to embody classifications of human beings that elevate men and subjugate women. With this subclassification of women, traditional forms of religious ethics also impose a qualitatively different sense of obligation: the obligation of obedience. In examining the tension between male and female genders, we must be attentive, not only to the different social roles that are assumed to be appropriate for men and women, but also to the different ethical rights and responsibilities that correspond to these social roles.

The Subclassification of Women

The subclassification of women runs throughout almost all traditional systems of religious ethics; it is simply assumed that women play a subordinate role in the ethical drama of human life. Plato suggested the subclassification of the female gender by placing women in the same category as children and servants.[30] The ethical rights and responsibilities of women are gauged on this lower, dependent, and subservient level. In all the pursuits of humanity, women were considered inferior to men.

In western religious thought, the subclassification of women was tied to the imaginative mythic connection between women and sin. The first creation story in Genesis suggests that women and men were created simultaneously during the last stage of creation. (Gen. 1–2.4a) But in the second story in Genesis, first the male (Adam) and then subsequently the female (Eve) were created. (Gen. 2.4b–4) This already introduces a note of subclassification in the secondary derivation of the female from the male. The story of the fall of this primordial couple from paradise has been interpreted both within Judaism and Christianity as the event that brought sin into the world, and woman has often been held responsible for sin. A Hellenistic Jewish text, *Ecclesiasticus,* declared that Eve was the origin of sin, suffering, and death. "Of the woman came the beginning of sin, and through her we all die." (25.24)

Woman being to blame for original sin became a common theme in Christian thought. "Adam was not deceived," according to one New

Testament letter, "but the woman being deceived was in the transgression." (1 Tim. 2:14) The integrity of the male is maintained by emphasizing the temptation, weakness, and sinfulness of the female. The ethical liability of this one woman was felt to have been passed down through the generations to all women. That caustic Christian ethicist Tertullian, who railed in his sermons at the immodest fashions, outrageous hats, and immoral manners of women in second century North Africa, reached new heights of invective in his attacks against women. Tertullian confronted women with a rhetorical question: "Do you not know that you are each an Eve? The sentence of God on this sex of yours lives in this age; the guilt must of necessity live too. You are the devil's gateway. . . ."[31] Woman was imagined to be the medium through which sin entered the world, and women were considered the vehicles that continued to carry that sin.

Attitudes toward women in the Christian tradition based on the mythic narrative of Eve filtered into religious ethics. Women were not perceived as independent moral agents, but often as merely occasions for temptation and sin. Serious questions were asked about the ethical status of women. The sixth century Church Council of Macon even went so far as to debate the question of whether or not a woman is a human being.[32] In addition, there is some evidence of ambivalence about the status of women in the future life. The apocryphal *Gospel of Thomas* indicates in its last verse that females must first be made male in order to enter into the kingdom of heaven.[33] The Eastern Church Fathers St. Basil and St. Hilary agreed that women in heaven would be shapeless, sexless beings.[34] All of these themes contributed to a basic subclassification of women in Christian thought. Such strategies of subclassification are common in religious ethics; they result in a separate set of ethical obligations that are binding on women.

The Ethics of Obedience

By subclassifying women, systems of religious ethics emphasize a single ethical obligation required of women: obedience. The primary obligation for women is that they be obedient to men. The ethical rights and responsibilities for women are defined in terms of this basic obligation of obedience to men.

The ethics of obedience can be found in the ethical systems of eastern traditions. In Confucian ethics, for example, the proper relationship between the genders is specified when Confucius observes that "man is the representative of Heaven, and is supreme over all things. Woman yields to the instructions of man, and helps to carry out his principles." Males are characterized by active roles, females by passive roles. Women can do nothing on their own, but are dependent on the guidance of men. As we noted earlier, Confucian ethical thought standardized this dependence of women on men as the three obediences: "When young, she must obey her father and elder brother; when married, she must obey her husband; when her husband is dead, she must obey her son."[35] Throughout her life, the woman is subject to the dominance of male authority. Her basic ethical obligation is this obedience.

The *Laws of Manu* proposes a traditional Hindu version of the three obediences. A Hindu woman's life cycle is also divided into three phases of obedience to males. "In childhood she is subject to her father; in marriage to her husband; in widowhood to her sons."[36] A woman is never to be independent. The *Laws of Manu* promises that she will be exalted in heaven for her obedience. But a woman will be punished for disobedience by being reborn in her next life as a jackal.[37] The ethics of obedience exemplifies the ethics of place: The supreme obligation for women embodied in the three obediences is that she must know and keep her place in the sacred order of things.

A similar preoccupation with the ethics of obedience is found in the gender ethics of ancient Greece and Rome. According to Aristotle, a wife has a religious duty to conform her behavior to the instructions and the example of her husband. "The well-ordered wife," Aristotle declared, "will justly consider the behavior of her husband as a model for her own life, and a law to herself, invested with a divine sanction by means of the marriage tie." Aristotle even went so far as to insist that in submitting herself to the rule of her husband "the wife ought to show herself even more obedient to the rein than if she had entered the house as a purchased slave."[38] Roman law put precisely this kind of master-slave marriage relationship into effect. Marriage under *manus,* or *in manum viri,* legally transferred the father's authority over his daughter to the husband.

In the religious traditions of the ancient Near East, obedience was also considered the primary ethical rule for women. Zoroastrians were able to identify a woman who had fulfilled her ethical obligations because she was "well-principled and obedient to her husband." An evil woman, however, was defined as "ill-principled and disobedient to her husband."[39] The Hebrew Bible indicates that women ought to be subservient to men, as Yahweh cursed the woman after the fall: "Thy desire shall be to thy husband, and he shall rule over thee." (Gen. 3:16) An ideal pattern of female behavior is enshrined in the popular tribute to the ethical virtues of women that appears in the Book of Proverbs. This hymn of praise—"A Woman of Valor"—represents an ethical model for wives. A good wife is described as "more precious than jewels." She is trustworthy, strong, dignified, wise, kind, and hardworking. She works with willing hands. She rises while it is still dark to provide food for the household. She supervises the servants, purchases land, plants a vineyard, gathers wool and flax, spins and weaves, clothes the household in scarlet, clothes herself in linen and purple, and makes garments for sale. She works by lamplight through the night. This remarkable, industrious woman is duly appreciated by her family: "Her children rise up and call her blessed." Her husband praises her: "Many women have done excellently but you surpass them all." (Prov. 31:28–29)

New Testament ethics also encourages appreciation for the efforts of women. A husband should love his wife as his own body. (Eph. 5:28) He should honor her as the "weaker vessel." (1 Pet. 3:7) But the lines of authority between males and females are clearly drawn. Paul refers to the creation myth in order to delineate the proper ethical relationship between man and woman. Clear priority is given to the male. "Man is not of the woman; but woman is of the man. Neither was the man created for the woman; but the woman for the man. For this cause ought the woman to have power on her head." (1 Cor. 11.8*ff*) The authority of man over woman, and her ethical obligation to obey the man, is justified by the mythic image of the origin of male and female genders. The male came first; the female came after for the purpose of serving his needs. The ethical law for women is obedience: "As the church is subject unto Christ, so let wives be to their husbands in every thing." (Eph. 5:23)

Beyond Obedience

Two recent responses to the ethics of obedience for women in the history of religious ethics are noteworthy. The first response is from the feminist perspective. One of the most powerful representatives of the feminist response to gender discrimination in religious ethics has been the theologian Mary Daly. In 1968, she attacked sexism in religious language in her influential book,

The Church and the Second Sex. In this text, Daly laid a foundation for a feminist response to the ethics of obedience. Christian ethics can be seen as an attempt to legitimate the power interests of a patriarchal society. The ethical ideals of female passivity, subservience, and inferiority support the male power structure. The prospect of rewards and punishments in a future life ensures female conformity to male expectations in this life. Daly called for a reform in the language of Christian theology, liturgy, and ethics that would begin to remove this built-in gender bias.[40]

Daly's recent book *Gyn/Ecology* makes a much more radical claim: The subclassification of women is part of a larger reign of terror perpetrated by men upon women. It is symptomatic of the violence done to women within male-dominated societies. The ethics of obedience is part of an ongoing attempt to harness female sexuality, fertility, and reproductive power in the service of male interests. In this book, Mary Daly has abandoned any hope of reforming traditional patterns of religious ethics. She no longer is working for constructive changes from within the tradition. Rather, she encourages women to disengage themselves from all interactions with men. In forceful language, she urges women to separate themselves from men—to refuse to work with them, to refuse sexual relations with them, to refuse to associate with them. The ethical integrity of women depends upon their independence from men. From this perspective, the ethical obligation incumbent upon women is certainly not obedience: It is the creation of self-sufficient life styles independent of men.[41]

Another interpretation of the ethics of obedience is provided by Ivan Illich in his book *Gender.*[42] Illich contrasts two kinds of social organization. One he calls the gendered society, in which roles are differentiated, and the male and female genders occupy separate, but equal, spheres of interests, tools, wisdom, and power. The other form of social organization Illich refers to as the sexed society. In a sexed society, males and females are transformed into unisex, interchangeable economic units in the industrial machinery of production. Modern, western industrial societies have eliminated the traditional roles of gender. They tend to treat males and females as relatively interchangeable in economic terms. Both genders can theoretically occupy the same place on the assembly line. A gendered society, however, maintains a carefully synchronized division of labor, in which males and females occupy different, yet complementary, spheres of influence. Illich expresses a certain nostalgia for preindustrial social arrangements in which work was organized along the lines of gender.

An example of a gendered society can be suggested by the Orinoco Indian who reported to the missionary Father Gumilla that men may be responsible for hunting and fishing, but women handle agriculture.

> *When the women plant maize the stalk produces two or three ears; when they set the manioc the plant produces two or three baskets of fruit; and thus everything is multiplied. Why? Because women know how to produce children, and know how to plant the corn so as to insure its germinating. Then, let them plant it; we do not know so much as they do.*[43]

This division of labor is based on gendered occupations that cooperate in preindustrial societies to support and sustain life. Rather than seeing this division as a sexist discrimination against women, Illich prefers to see it as a social arrangement that is sensitive to the creative contrasts between men and women. From this perspective, the emphasis on the obedience of females in traditions of religious ethics is overdrawn. The actual ethical dynamics of traditional preindustrial societies allowed for the development of specialized spheres of male and female interests, influence, and power.

Separate ethical standards for male and female genders is certainly a major feature of religious ethics. The normative pattern of action within a religious tradition may require different standards, expectations, and roles for males and females. This separation is a fact of life in traditional societies. It is represented dramatically by the institution of purdah, which is prevalent in the Muslim world and South Asia. *Purdah* literally means "curtain." It is the practice of secluding women and enforcing high standards of female modesty. Purdah is observed by both Hindu and Muslim women. The Hindu purdah is based on systematic rules of avoidance between a woman and her male relatives, which begins with marriage. For Muslims, it is a curtain that separates a woman from contact with men outside of her most immediate kinship group beginning at puberty.[44] It is difficult to determine whether purdah is simply a social mechanism by which females are dominated by male power interests, or if there is some independent realm of female power that is generated behind the curtain. This practice does suggest, however, the extent to which the tension between male and female genders forms an essential ingredient in a traditional pattern of religious ethics.

Sexuality

Human sexuality involves mysterious drives, desires, and powers that come under the purview of religious ethics. Religious traditions attempt to channel the creative tensions of this sexual energy. The energy of human sexuality is intimately related to knowledge in the history of religions. The Hebrew word *yeda*—to know—can mean both knowledge and sexual intercourse: Adam *knew* Eve. The knowledge that is invested in human sexuality can be divided into three major areas. First, the art of sex cultivates the knowledge of pleasure, companionship, and love in human sexual expression. Second, the discipline of sex is concerned with controlling the exercise of human sexuality by identifying proper and improper forms of sex and then punishing those who engage in that which is improper. Third, the science of sex seeks to understand sexuality within the context of modern medical practice and to manipulate the mechanisms of sexual production in the interests of population control. These three kinds of knowledge—pleasure, propriety, and population control—provide different modes of access to the power of human sexuality, and they each involve different ethical challenges.

The Art of Sex

The art of sex may bring to mind those ancient manuals devoted to sexual pleasure, such as the *Kama Sutra* of India or the pillow books of traditional China and Japan; or perhaps it may recall more recent manuals such as *The Joy of Sex*. Certainly, these texts represent formulations of a certain type of knowledge about erotic experience. These avenues of information reflect important cultural values about sexual identities, expressions, and experiences. However, the art of sex is also an important issue in religious ethics. Sexual ethics is also concerned with identifying the place of pleasure within a larger pattern of ethical action. Western religious ethics has been particularly concerned with defining those rules that govern the relationship between pleasure and procreation in human sexuality. We will briefly survey the ethical positions on this issue that have emerged in the Jewish, Catholic, and Protestant traditions in order to suggest how religious traditions respond to the art of sex.

Judaism

In Judaism, marital relations have been understood as a religious duty. Sexuality within marriage, however, has not been viewed simply as fulfilling the duties of procreation: Companionship and self-fulfillment in sexuality have traditionally been regarded as experiences of intrinsic ethical value. The Hebrew Bible indicates this viewpoint by requiring a special deferment from military service during the first year of marriage, so that a man might "rejoice with his wife." (Deut. 24:5) The tradition maintains that it is a husband's responsibility to provide for his wife's sexual needs and that he should be sensitive to the feelings of his wife. Sexual relations are the duty of the husband, but they are the privilege of the wife. Marital intercourse for pleasure is fully justified within the tradition.[45]

Some rabbinic authorities have emphasized the motive of pleasure in sex. The thirteenth century Rabbi Isaiah Da Trani maintained that contraception is permissible in order to pursue pleasure; the nineteenth century Rabbi Hayyim Sofer ruled that the more a contraceptive device interfered with the pleasures of sexual intercourse, the less acceptable was its use.[46] More conservative positions in the tradition have emphasized the ethical duty (*mitzvah*) of procreation as the primary purpose for marital relations. Such relations should result in a minimum of two children, but more would be desirable. However, a more liberal current in the Jewish tradition exists that holds "the legitimacy of pleasure as a function or objective of marital relations."[47]

Separating the motive of pleasure from the duty of procreation raises questions about birth control. The birth control device that is discussed in the Jewish tradition was called a *mokh:* a tampon used before and during intercourse, or a postcoital absorbent. The Talmud specified that a mokh is to be used by (1) a minor, because it was feared that she might become pregnant and die, (2) a pregnant woman, to avoid any complications with her pregnancy, and (3) a nursing mother, because it was feared that she might become pregnant and be forced to wean her child too soon.[48] These categories of women were permitted to use birth control in the interests of pursuing pleasure and preserving health. Therefore, sexual pleasure was permitted even though it would not be for the purpose of reproduction.

The practice of *coitus interruptus* acquired negative associations from the biblical story of Onan, who "spilled his seed upon the ground" in order to avoid the mitzvah of procreation. Judaism tended to interpret this as a rule against all nonprocreative emissions of semen: masturbation, sodomy, as well as coitus interruptus. A more permissive ruling within the tradition, however, specified that the intention of the practice of coitus interruptus is what is important. If the intention is to avoid fulfilling the obligations of procreation, it is forbidden; but if the intention is to experience pleasure, then the practice is acceptable.[49] In general, Judaism has viewed the intention behind the practice of birth control as the primary consideration in determining whether it is to be permitted or not. If birth control is practiced to avoid the duty of procreation, or to avoid pregnancy so as not to mar the wife's beauty, then it is considered improper. But if the intention of the married couple using birth control is to avoid hazards to the wife's health, or to pursue pleasure, then its use is considered proper.

Catholicism

The Catholic tradition, from its most ancient formative period, has seen procreation as the only justification for sexual relations in marriage. Sexual expression should only be for procreation, and, as many Church Fathers insisted, without pleasure. The fourth century Saint Jerome even viewed sexuality as a disease, a "minor epilepsy," which needed to be cured by a chaste, celibate life. More recently, however, the Roman Catholic church has begun to place more emphasis on the role of love and companionship in marital relations. *Humanae Vitae* (1968), the encyclical of Pope Paul VI that defined church doctrine on human sexuality, recognized both the procreative and the unitive purposes of marriage. In the unitive function of marriage, husband and wife "attain their human perfection" through what is described as "a very special form of personal friendship."[50] An appreciation for the unitive dimension of sexuality begins to recognize the value of pleasure in marital relations.

However, *Humanae Vitae* restates the traditional Roman Catholic position that sex is only legitimate when it is open to the possibility of procreation. The encyclical states, in the strongest possible language, that any artificial methods of interfering with the reproductive process—either chemical or mechanical—are expressly forbidden. Sexual relations within marriage are described as "noble and worthy." But they are not legitimate for pleasure alone, because "each and every marriage act must remain open to the transmission of life."[51] The unitive pleasures of sexual relations cannot be separated from the ethical obligation to keep every sexual act open to the possibility of conception.

The Catholic community has voiced widespread opposition to the Papal encyclical prohibiting birth control. A survey of Catholic women in 1970 showed that 60 percent were opposed to the ban on birth control and only 16 percent supported the official church position.[52] This put many Catholics in a state of dissonance in relation to the Church. A number of Church leaders, particularly American Catholic theologians, have disagreed with the Papal stand against birth control. Such opponents have argued that the encyclical places an "over-emphasis on the biological aspects of conjugal relations as ethically normative."[53] They have encouraged Catholics to question the authority of *Humanae Vitae* and to "responsibly decide according to their conscience that artificial contraception in some circumstances is permissible and indeed necessary to preserve and foster the values and sacredness of marriage."[54] This call for improvisation in traditional Catholic sex ethics suggests that the sacred value of marriage might not lie exclusively in its openness to the biological process of procreation.

Protestantism

The leaders of the Protestant Reformation of the sixteenth century denied the spiritual superiority of celibacy as a sexual life style. Martin Luther not only broke with the Catholic Church over theological doctrine, but also over a sexual ethics that exalted virginity, celibacy, and the monastic life. It was no accident that the former Augustinian monk married shortly after leaving the Church. Luther spoke of the dangers that were inherent in suppressing sexual desire. "It necessarily strikes into the flesh and blood and becomes a poison," he said, "whence the body becomes unhealthy, enervated, sweaty and foulsmelling."[55] The Protestant Reformers Martin Luther and John Calvin both emphasized the spiritual value of human companionship in married life.

Protestant sex ethics allows for a practical separation between the unitive and the procreative purposes of marriage. Where official Catholic sex ethics views these two functions as combined in any legitimate sexual act, Protestant ethicists have justified the pursuit of pleasure, companionship, and love in sexuality, independent of procreation. An official statement of the United Church of Christ made this clear when it observed that, "Sex is good: not alone because the sexual act is the means of setting new human life in motion. Sex is good as a form of unity and communication between persons."[56] The United Presbyterian Church in the United States has also issued a public statement on sex ethics that departs from traditional approaches to sex that, in its terms, emphasize "restraint, prohibition, legalism and the definition of limits." This Presbyterian statement counters these limitations by announcing the "Christian calling to glorify God by the joyful celebration of and delight in our sexuality."[57] The emphasis on pleasure as a legitimate value in human sexuality has been accompanied in mainstream Protestant sex ethics by a concern for the issues of population control. Responsible reproduction has been encouraged through birth control, family planning, and small families.

The issue of birth control in religious ethics arises when the value of pleasure in sexual relations is freed from the obligation of procreation. Pleasure is given a legitimate ethical status. In both Jewish and Protestant ethics there are times when birth control methods are permitted to allow for the intimate companionship of marriage without requiring that it be open to procreation. The official position of the Catholic church, however, has insisted that the unitive values of sexual relations should never be divorced from the natural reproductive process. In this case, the pleasures of sex must always be tied to the responsibilities of procreation. Any restraints that religious traditions impose on the pleasures of human sexuality place sex within a network of ethical obligations. Those normative patterns of action within which sexual experience is organized by a religious tradition are most clearly revealed in the discipline of sex.

The Discipline of Sex

Traditions of religious ethics embody ideal patterns of human sexuality. Departures from these normative patterns create a condition of dissonance between the individual and the tradition. In order to restore a sense of ethical harmony in human sexuality, systems of religious ethics may prescribe certain acts of penance that will atone for dissonant sexual behavior. The medieval Catholic church, for example, developed guidelines for the discipline of sex in the form of manuals called Penitentials, which were disciplinary catalogues of sins of the flesh.[58] These catalogues were used by priests in hearing confessions for the purpose of determining the relative seriousness of various sexual acts. The seriousness of the act was reflected in the severity of the prescribed punishment. The primary form of punishment was fasting: abstaining from food and drink (except bread and water), sexual relations, and any form of self-indulgence. But the Penitentials might also prescribe other acts of penance, such as corporal punishment or the singing of psalms, to atone for dissonant sexual behavior. One Penitential ruled that seminal emission was a sin. It required a punishment of 7 days of fasting if it was involuntary, but 20 days if manually assisted. A monk who masturbated in church was required to fast for 30 days in penance. Contraception, including all nonprocreative sexual activities, was often considered to be almost as serious a sin as homicide. The discipline of sex embodied in these manuals attempted to enforce the normative pattern of sexual behavior in medieval Catholic sex ethics.

Other traditions also developed similar penitential systems for the discipline of sex. One traditional Chinese text presented an inventory of ethical merits and demerits that would be accrued from different types of sexual acts.[59] In order to quantify the severity of sexual misdeeds, it specified precisely the number of demerits that would result from various types of forbidden sexual behavior. (See Table 1.)

In this Chinese catalogue of illicit sexual behavior, a higher number of demerits is awarded for sudden, unexpected acts of passion than for premeditated sexual acts. This suggests that the rules for sexual behavior value disciplined control of the passions. The different classifications of women also reveal a social hierarchy in this penitential system. Thus, the penitential rules reinforce the value of control and the relative values of different social classes.

This Chinese source also contains a catalogue of other types of behavior with sexual connotations. The corresponding demerits for these actions are also enumerated. (See Table 2, p. 164.)

This quantification of sexual behavior provides detailed information about the propriety of sex. It is a knowledge based on the meticulous regulation of all aspects of sexual behavior. Everything related to sexual desire, including speech, gestures, and thoughts, is carefully controlled through the discipline of sex. That discipline covers sexual conduct both within the legitimate institutions of marriage and outside its ritually defined boundaries.

Discipline within Marriage

We have already noted that the earliest tradition of Christian sex ethics disciplined sexuality within marriage by insisting that it was only permitted for the purpose of procreation. This stipulation placed definite limits upon the frequency of sexual relations between husband and wife. The Church Father Athenagoras, for example, exhorted men and women to observe discipline in marriage by invoking the image of a farmer who plants his seeds into the ground and then awaits

TABLE 1

	DEMERITS		
	RAPE	**SPONTANEOUS ACTS OF PASSION**	**PREMEDITATED ILLICIT INTERCOURSE**
Married woman	500	200	100
Servant's Wife	200	100	50
Widow or Virgin	1000	500	200
Nun	too many to count	1000	500
Prostitute	50	100	20

the harvest. The farmer does not keep sowing more seed upon the ground.[60] If sexuality is only for reproduction, the marital relations of husband and wife must be guided by the example of agriculture.

Medieval Christianity placed a set of ritual restraints on sexual relations in marriage. One manual instructed married couples to abstain from sex during the seasons of fasting, especially for the duration of Lent, and during times of religious festivals. In addition to this abstention, however, they should abstain from sex on Thursdays (in memory of the arrest of Jesus), on Fridays (to honor his death), and on Sundays (in celebration of the resurrection). Saturday should be set aside to honor the Virgin Mary. And married couples should abstain from sex on Mondays in commemoration of the dead. This ritual calendar for the discipline of sex left only the Tuesdays and Wednesdays that did not fall on feast or fast days.[61] Even within the ritually sanctioned pattern of marriage, therefore, sexual relations are controlled by disciplinary obligations.

Extramarital Sex

Most systems of religious ethics restrict sexual expression outside of the ritual institution of marriage. An ancient Chinese legal code defined any extramarital sex as a criminal offense. If such sexual relations were by mutual consent between unmarried adults, the prescribed punishment was 70 blows. The corporal punishment was only slightly more severe if the woman was married.[62] The *Laws of Manu* insisted that strict chastity should be maintained outside of marriage.[63] The Hebrew Bible also specified that premarital sex was forbidden. (Lev. 19:29; Deut. 23:18) However, the Torah does provide instructions for how such a situation should be handled if it occurs. Should a man have

TABLE 2

BEHAVIOR	DEMERITS	BEHAVIOR	DEMERITS
Lewd dreams	1	*Having lewd thoughts about women in the streets*	10
If they result in lewd actions	5		
Singing frivolous songs	2	*Associating with friends who go whoring and gambling*	50
Studying such songs	20		
Keeping erotic pictures (per picture)	10	*Going to the theater*	1
		Taking part in a play	50
Touching women's hands by accident	1	*Telling women dirty stories*	20
With lustful intent	10	*If they are told to awaken the women's sense of shame*	none
To help in an emergency	none		
But if such help arouses lust	10		

sexual intercourse with a woman who is not married, he is instructed to take her as his wife. If her father refuses to give his consent, the man must pay money equivalent to the marriage dowry for virgins. (Ex. 22:16*ff*) Christian sex ethics traditionally banned any form of extramarital sex as an extension of its ethical ideal of virginity. The medieval theologian Thomas Aquinas even held that kissing was a forbidden act for the unmarried.[64] Such boundaries reinforce the ritual pattern of marriage that is supported within a religious tradition as the only legitimate arena in which sexuality might be expressed.

Adultery

Adultery explicitly violates the ritual institution of marriage. Systems of religious ethics generally forbid it in the strongest terms. Considerations of social status, however, may enter into a tradition's ethical evaluation of the act of adultery. One Chinese ethical code, for example, specified that a slave who commits adultery with the wife of a free man shall be punished more severely than a free man would have been punished for committing the same act.[65] In traditional Hindu sex ethics, if a man of one of the three upper classes commits adultery with a working class woman, the punishment is banishment. If a worker, however, should commit adultery with a woman of one of the upper classes, the punishment is death.[66] The relative severity of the act depends to a considerable degree on the social status of the persons involved.

These social classifications do not explicitly appear in Jewish and Christian religious laws regarding adultery. The act is treated with the highest seriousness regardless of the social classes of the adulterers. This severity is supported by the fact that the injunction against adultery is one of the Ten Commandments. In the Hebrew Bible, the penalty of death is specified for a man who has committed adultery with another man's wife. (Lev. 20:10; Deut. 22:22) In addition, medieval Christian legal codes prescribed death for the

adulterer, or adultery was considered as serious as other crimes, such as murder, idolatry, and sorcery, which were also punishable by death.[67] Jewish and Christian law, in these cases, consider adultery a capital offense.

Homosexuality

Sexual relations between persons of the same gender have been considered in a variety of ways within traditions of religious ethics. The Chinese legal code of the *Ta Tsing Leu Lee* treated homosexual acts between consenting adults as a criminal offense to be punished by 100 blows. Homosexual acts performed on an adult without consent, or with a child under 12 with or without consent, were treated as a capital offense.[68] The *Laws of Manu,* however, treated homosexual acts as a minor offense to be punished by public embarrassment. Homosexual acts were classified along with other unorthodox sexual acts. The *Laws of Manu* specified that "a man who commits an unnatural offense with a male, or has intercourse with a female in a cart drawn by oxen, in water, or in the day time, shall bathe, dressed in his clothes."[69] The shame of such a public display was considered appropriate punishment for these sexual acts that were classified as unnatural.

Homosexual love achieved a considerable degree of support in ancient Greece. The Spartans valued the relationship between *inspirator,* an older man, and his younger *listener.* The young man looked to the elder as a model and pattern for life. Plato's *Symposium* pays special tribute to the ethical value of homosexual love, which was believed to instill virtue in young men through love. Herodotus suggested that the love of boys was a custom introduced into Persia from Greece.[70] But the Persian religious tradition of Zoroastrianism shows no sympathy for homosexuality. The adamant opposition to homosexual relations in Zoroastrianism set the tone for the general attitude toward homosexuality in the ancient Near East and in western religious thought.

Homosexuality was considered a capital offense for which there was no forgiveness. Homosexual behavior was to be punished with death in this world and was believed to be punished with eternal torments in the next world. Even someone involuntarily involved in a homosexual act was liable to be put to death. One Zoroastrian text went so far as to suggest that homosexuality was a more serious sin than killing a righteous man. The prescribed ethical response to homosexuality was specified in detail:

> *There is no worse sin than this in the good religion, and it is proper to call those who commit it worthy of death in reality. If any one comes forth to them, and shall see them in the act, and is working with an axe, it is requisite for him to cut off the heads or rip up the bellies of both, and it is no sin for him.*[71]

Although proscriptions against homosexual relations may not be phrased in such vivid terms, the western traditions of religious ethics have placed severe limits on homosexuality.[72]

The discipline of sex produces one kind of knowledge about sex; it is a knowledge about the limits of human sexual behavior. The discipline of sex factors out some kinds of behavior and gives an aura of exclusive religious legitimacy to a select repertoire of sexual acts. An ideal pattern of action is embodied in the discipline of sex, which strives to bring powerful sexual desires under conscious social control. This control seems to be a losing battle and a common source of dissonance. We can only assume that these rules regulating sexual behavior would not exist if the practices they prohibit did not themselves exist. In the discipline of sex, ethical rules reveal the actual sexual practices of the social environment. The pervasive intention of the discipline of sex, however, is not simply restraint: Discipline controls human sexual energy in order to channel it into reproduction. There is a reproductive

politics in the discipline of sex, an ongoing political struggle to harness the power of human sexuality in order to populate the world with more people who are "like us." This political interest in the power of reproduction motivates traditions of religious ethics to prohibit any form of sexuality that diverts sexual energy from this social goal. The concern with reproductive politics surfaces in modern sex ethics through scientific controls over sexual behavior.

The Science of Sex

The science of sex involves a different kind of knowledge than either pleasure or propriety. Although science may serve these goals, it offers a more independent realm of knowledge, defined by scientific medical discourse, practice, and power. The science of sex is knowledge about the biological process of reproduction, a concern with the mechanics of sexual instincts, organs, and genetics. Sexual desire is translated into physiological terms, managed within the context of scientific medical practice, and harnessed to the political interests of population control. In modern western societies, the science of sex has generated two major sexual issues with both religious and ethical implications: (1) the medical discipline of sexuality and (2) the medical ethics of genetic engineering.

Medical Discipline of Sexuality

The scientific medical profession in modern western societies has come to fill many of the roles traditionally ascribed to religion. In the area of human sexuality religious ethics made judgments about behaviors that were right or wrong, moral or immoral, legal or illegal; medical practice makes judgments about behaviors that are normal or abnormal. The ethical pattern of normal behavior plays a powerful role in medical practice in its ability to set guidelines for behavior based on claims of scientific knowledge about sex. The science of sex may set standards for what *ought* to be, based on a claim to direct scientific knowledge about the way things *are*.

One dramatic illustration of the medical control of sexual behavior is found in the nineteenth century discovery of "masturbatory insanity."[73] Masturbation was considered a sin in medieval Penitentials. The anonymous eighteenth century author on the topic of masturbation captured this in the title of his book: *Onania, or the Heinous Sin of Self-Pollution* (1710). Onanism was a sin because it violated the supreme Christian pattern for permitted sexuality: It was a sexual act for pleasure, not for procreation. By the nineteenth century, however, what had been a sin became a disease. Masturbation could be diagnosed and treated like any other disease. The physician Benjamin Rush, in the first American textbook of psychiatry (1812), maintained that the "solitary vice" produced such medical conditions as "seminal weakness, impotence, dysury, tabes dorsalis, pulmonary consumption, dyspepsia, hypochondriasis, loss of memory, manalgia, fatuity and death." Europeans were also concerned with the medical diagnosis of masturbation. In 1816, the French physician Esquirol claimed that "it is recognized in all countries as a common cause of insanity." And Sir William Ellis, superintendent of a British asylum, asserted in 1839 that "by far the most frequent cause of fatuity is debility of the brain . . . in consequence of the pernicious habit of masturbation."[74]

The medical profession proposed three basic responses to this scientific diagnosis of the disease of masturbation. First was medical intervention in the form of various surgical techniques. Circumcisions were recommended for males, clitoridectomies for females. The medical literature contains descriptions of surgical opera-

tions to insert a metal ring in the foreskin of the penis. Medical intervention also took the form of various patent medicines that promised to chemically control masturbation.

The second response was a variety of physical restraints, ranging from devices designed to tie the hands of children during sleep to the use of autoerotic chastity belts for both males and females. These physical restraints represented a marriage of scientific knowledge with technological ingenuity to produce technical solutions for new scientifically defined medical problems.

Third, the medical profession encouraged a program of ethical education. There was a concerted effort to educate both parents and children about the medico-ethical dangers of masturbation. Ethical instructions on the discipline of the body were based on claims to authoritative knowledge about the evils of masturbation. A guide to childraising written at the turn of the century called *What a Young Wife Ought to Know* gave instructions for disciplining the sexuality of children:

> *While yet very young, they can be taught that the organs are to be used by them only for throwing off the waste water of the system, but that they are so closely related to other parts of the body that handling them at all will hurt them and make them sick.*[75]

This combination of medical and ethical assumptions tried to provide scientific standards for disciplining sexuality in the interests of health and hygiene. Where the earlier manuals of Erasmus and La Salle controlled behavior by reminding children that the angels are always watching, the science of sex disciplined children's behavior by threatening illness.

When these medico-ethical instructions were directed at children, they reinforced scientific notions about ethical responsibility in reproduction. In *What a Young Boy Ought to Know,* an ethical manual also written at the turn of the century, the author insisted that

> *the consequences which result from masturbation do not stop with the boy who practices it. . . . When a boy injures his reproductive powers, so that when a man his seminal secretion shall be of an inferior quality, his offspring will show it in their physical, mental and moral natures.*[76]

The medical interest in "masturbatory insanity" soon subsided. However, the motives that inspired it persisted in western societies through attempts to define normal behavior, to provide expert medical opinion on proper behavior, and to pursue an authoritative scientific discipline of the body. The ethical concern of a manual like *What a Young Boy Ought to Know* is with human reproductive powers; it is not a concern with pleasure, or simply with propriety, but with the scientific calculation of the effects of abnormal behavior on the human population. The science of sex produced an abiding concern with the relation between reproduction and population. Scientific knowledge of genetics, heredity, and natural selection in reproduction offered a new set of ethical challenges for the science of sex.

Medical Ethics of Genetic Engineering

Eugenics is a science that investigates ways to improve the genetic inheritance of the human species. At the same time, however, eugenics has taken form in social movements, government policies, and even legislation designed to regulate reproduction in the interest of that improvement. Two kinds of eugenic proposals have been made. First, what is called negative eugenics would prevent the reproduction of people who are regarded as unfit by scientific standards. Second, there have been proposals for positive eugenics, which would encourage the reproduction of those people who are considered most fit. Eugenics is the use of science as an instrument of social policies designed to promote the betterment of the human race. It is a modern, scientific, medical, and technological approach to the ancient ideal of human perfectibility. But the science of eugenics has been vulnerable to social prejudices, racism, and bigotry in the assumptions about what kinds of people ought to survive, reproduce, and contribute to the gene pool of the human species.[77]

The term *eugenics* was coined by the nineteenth century Social Darwinist Francis Galton. He applied Darwin's theory of natural selection—the survival of the fittest—to the evolution of the human species. Extending this scientific concept to human beings, going farther than Darwin would have himself, Galton saw the potential for taking conscious control over the direction of human evolution. "If a twentieth percent of the costs and pains were spent in measures for the improvement of the human race that is spent in the improvement of the breed for horses and cattle," Galton declared, "what a galaxy of genius might we not create."[78] A science of eugenics might supervise the breeding of human beings to eliminate undesirable traits and ensure the increased reproduction of desirable traits. Galton's dream of scientific mastery over the process of reproduction, and the evolution of the human species, seems to be almost within the grasp of scientific medical practice. Eugenics has taken four basic forms in modern medicine.

1. *Birth Control.* Artificial contraception for eugenic reasons limits the reproduction of undesirable genes. It may place restraints upon reproduction in order to breed out certain traits from the human gene pool. On a voluntary basis, this may be a response to a new kind of ethical obligation: the responsibility for not passing on certain diseases, deformities, or disabilities to fu-

ture generations. Involuntary birth control, however, such as the laws passed in the United States during the 1920s that required the sterilization of all mental patients, represents the intervention of the science of eugenics in the formation of social policy.

———

2.   *Biogenetic Surgery*. Techniques of genetic surgery that are being developed within medical science give rise to new ethical problems. Surgical intervention in the genetic code, such as a cure for infertility, may be viewed as an elective medical treatment. Yet it may also be a case of playing God with human inheritance. Genetic engineering gives Francis Galton's dream of human perfectibility a new force, but the ideal pattern remains a question for ethical reflection and not simply a matter of technical manipulation of the genetic code.

———

3.   *Artificial Insemination*. This technique employs positive eugenics to encourage the reproduction of certain genetic traits. Whether in test tube or *in utero,* the eugenic technique of artificial insemination assumes that certain desirable genotypes should be multiplied as much as possible. Sperm banks may be established to preserve and transmit the genes of supposedly superior males, and their genetic inheritance may be multiplied in future generations.

———

4.   *Cloning*. From a botanical term for "cutting," cloning is an asexual means of reproduction—a scientific technique for copying a desirable genotype. Proponents of this reproductive technology claim that cloning has the advantage of increasing similarity, uniformity, and harmony in the human population by creating people who are genetically alike. Cloning may multiply proven excellence in human beings. The potential disadvantages of cloning, however, lie in a

loss of diversity and innovation that make human life interesting. In addition, how do we classify any mistakes, or mutations, that might result from a cloning operation? Are they human, subhuman, or parahuman?

Eugenics introduces a range of new ethical challenges in human sexuality. One response has been to seek a scientific definition of the "ethics of genetic duty." H. J. Muller, for example, has painted a very dark picture of the genetic future of the human species. Because modern medicine has allowed people with certain diseases to live and reproduce—people who otherwise would have died before reproducing—their genes have been maintained and multiplied in the human gene pool. This has resulted in what Muller has called the deteriorization of our genetic load. The future holds the promise of "a lot of hopeless, utterly diverse genetic mutations." The only hope, Muller has suggested, is conscious, scientific, and medical intervention in the process of reproduction. Human reproductive responsibility is conscious management of this shared genetic inheritance through both positive and negative eugenics. Muller asserts:

> *Although it is a human right for people to have their infirmities cared for by every means that society can muster, they do not have the right knowingly to pass on to posterity such a load of infirmities of genetic or partly genetic origin as to cause an increase in the burden already being carried by the population.*[79]

———

From this perspective, a science of sex holds the potential for managing the human population through eugenics.

Christian ethicist Paul Ramsey has recognized the ethical imperatives of population control and eugenics, while at the same time insisting on a reaffirmation of traditional religious values in human sexuality. The standard that Ramsey has used to evaluate the scientific techniques of eugenics restates the traditional Christian position, found in *Humanae Vitae* and elsewhere, that the unitive and procreative aspects of sexuality should always be held together. Ramsey has insisted on "the requirement that there be no complete or radical or 'in principle' separation between the personally unitive and the procreative aspects of human sexual life."[80] Any medical or scientific effort to depersonalize reproduction should be avoided. For this reason, Ramsey has approved of the voluntary attempts in negative eugenics to take responsibility for limiting the transmission of undesirable genes; but he has disapproved of any of the techniques of positive eugenics that take reproduction out of the loving, personal, and ultimately human context of the sexual relationship and make reproduction a matter of scientific manipulation. His response suggests the humanizing potential of religious ethics as it confronts the challenges posed by new techniques developed in the medical science of sex.

Patterns of Tension

The tensions in human experience created by gender differences and human sexuality create special challenges for religious ethics. The ethical rules that govern gender and sexuality strive to create a ritualized perfection in gender roles, marriage patterns, and sexual behavior within the ethics of the human life cycle. These rules attempt to bring the tensions of gender and sexuality into harmony with ethical patterns of action. The ideal of harmony in gender ethics and sexual ethics aspires to transform these tensions into creative forces that will support well-ordered, positive, and productive human interactions. Chapter 7 has drawn a number of conclusions regarding the nature of ethical responses to the tensions of gender and sexuality in religious ethics.

1. *Marriage patterns create a ritual context in which tensions between male and female genders, and the tension of human sexuality, are channeled.* Human marriage patterns establish ritually sanctioned interactions between the genders. The marriage ritual is also a rite of passage from the unmarried state, in which the person may still be defined by the family ties of child-

hood, to a new status within a marriage pattern. The person may at this point become part of the nucleus of a new set of interlocking family relations. The rules of exogamy and endogamy determine which potential mates are excluded and which are included. The various marriage patterns—monogamy, polygyny, and polyandry—suggest the variety of socially sanctioned marriage arrangements that have been established in the history of marriage. Although some religious traditions—particularly those based on monastic orders, ascetic practices, and withdrawal from the social world—may establish rules against marriage, the ethical obligation of marriage is required in most religious traditions. Marriage serves as the model of ritualized perfection that governs the relations between men and women in religious ethics.

2. *Women have been subjected to the ethics of obedience in traditional systems of religious ethics.* The ethics of obedience was formulated in the traditional religious ethics of India and China, for example, as the three obediences that are incumbent upon women. Women must be obedient to their fathers when children, obedient to

their husbands when married, and obedient to their sons when widowed. This pattern of obedience weaves a fabric of disciplinary constraints on the behavior of women through the course of their entire life cycle. The ethics of obedience may also be embodied in rules of *purdah,* enforced standards of female modesty, and cultural constraints on female roles in the larger network of social relations.

Two interpretations of the ethics of obedience have been suggested. One insists that these gender-specific obligations are the result of patriarchal domination of women in traditional societies. The obligations are symptomatic of a violent subclassification of the female gender in traditional systems of religious ethics. A second interpretation suggests that gender differentiation in social roles, rights, and responsibilities in traditional religious ethics supported an interlocking system of male and female roles that were both essential for the survival of preindustrial societies. Behind the veil, so to speak, women created their own unique domain of female responsibility, authority, and power that was integral to the survival of the traditional community. If both of these interpretations are correct, then women created that domain of independent power in spite of the almost universal tendency toward the subclassification of women in male-dominated systems of religious ethics.

———

3.   *Sexual ethics involves the issues of pleasure, propriety, and population control.* Systems of religious ethics strive to direct human sexual energy into normative patterns of action. First, the art of sex in religious ethics is concerned with the ethical significance of pleasure in human sexuality. This necessarily raises issues about birth control practices that would separate the pleasure of sexuality from its procreative function. A variety of attitudes toward pleasure can be found in religious sexual ethics: Pleasure may be denied, pleasure may be tied to procreation, or

pleasure may be regarded as a legitimate value in itself. Religious rules regarding birth control tend to be directly related to the prevailing attitude toward sexual pleasure in any system of religious ethics.

Second, the discipline of sex in religious ethics is concerned with establishing rules of propriety in sexual behavior. Discipline covers sexual behavior both within and outside the socially sanctioned patterns of marriage. Disciplinary rules for proper sexual behavior create the norms by which alternative sexual expressions are defined as abnormal. The reproductive politics of many traditions directs human sexuality into the procreation of children and restrains, controls, and disciplines all other forms of sexuality.

Third, the science of sex continues this emphasis on disciplinary control of the human population, but exercises control through the medical management of human sexuality and reproduction. The scientific management and social engineering of the reproductive process is perhaps most evident in the ethical challenges posed by genetic engineering. The science of sex in the modern world covers a wide range of human behavior as scientific, medical expertise has been invoked to define normal and abnormal as if they were ethical judgments on human sexuality.

———

4.   *Sex ethics is governed by customary rules, legal rules, and moral rules.* Much of sexual ethics in human communities merely follows customary practices that are taken for granted as if they were simply the natural order of things. In no other area of human experience are the customs of others so quickly classified as unnatural as in this area of sexual customs. The discipline of sex implies that sexual behavior is entangled in a network of legal restrictions, prohibitions, and taboos that are reinforced by punishment. Penitential systems of religious traditions indicate the

relative seriousness of various deviations from the legal rules governing sex within these traditions. We must remember, however, that these laws would not exist if the practices that they try to control did not occur. The legal regulation of sex in religious ethics struggles to bring the diversity of human sexual behavior into a common, shared pattern of discipline.

Moral responses to the challenges of sexuality, as in other areas of ethical responsibility, require a certain degree of freedom to make ethical choices. The tensions of sexual desire are an intense source of dissonance when they conflict with prevailing patterns of ethical obligation within a community. Moral harmony may be achieved by attuning desires to the pattern of obligation, or it may be accomplished by renegotiating obligation to more nearly approximate desires. This latter, improvisational strategy characterizes the revolution in sexual ethics that has occurred in modern, western societies. The renegotiation of obligation in sexual ethics may confront the resistance inherent in customary attitudes, the disciplinary regulations of legal codes, and the censure of moral conventions. But however sexual identity is negotiated, human beings are posed with the challenge of directing the creative tensions of sexual desire into ethical patterns of action.

CHAPTER

EIGHT

TRANSCENDENCE

One of the most important functions of religion is therapeutic. Religious traditions take responsibility for the spiritual, mental, emotional, and physical well-being of human beings. They provide resources for rising above, or going beyond, the limitations of human consciousness and will that are inherent in illness, aging, and death. We will refer to this movement above and beyond human limits as *transcendence*. Religious traditions provide reservoirs of images, techniques, and practices for transcending human suffering. Often the transcendence of human suffering is a way through suffering. Rather than trying to avoid suffering, religious traditions cultivate ways of suffering with dignity, integrity, and a sense of purpose. Religious paths through suffering reveal a creative potential for generating a sense of meaning and power in the confrontation with human limit situations.

Healing is such an important function of religion that, it has been observed, "no religion has survived that does not heal."[1] Modern medicine's hegemony over healing in western societies makes it easy to forget how important healing rituals have been within religious traditions. We will briefly consider healing rituals as patterns of action designed to transcend the suffering of illness. Two ethical issues stand at the end of human life: euthanasia and suicide. *Euthanasia,* or mercy killing, is one possible response to unrelenting suffering in illness, old age, or the process of dying. As in the case of abortion at the beginning of life, euthanasia involves questions of ethical classification, care, and community. If a life can be classified as not worth living, what is the appropriate measure of care that should be administered by the human community? We will explore the question of euthanasia in some detail. Finally, suicide holds the potential for the sudden termination of human life. The philosophical essayist Albert Camus declared that "there is but one truly serious philosophical problem, and that is suicide."[2] Suicide also poses a problem in any system of religious ethics. The possibility of terminating life calls into question its ultimate meaning and significance. The response to this question may define the nature of transcendence within any system of religious ethics.

Healing Rituals

Every society seems to have three basic approaches to healing. The first approach is through pharmacopia. Healing practices involve a wide range of medicines—plants, herbs, minerals, and so on—and traditional wisdom regarding their use. Native American Indian medicine was reputed to have a highly developed and effective pharmacopia. In 1714, an early historian of North Carolina observed that "cures performed by Indians are too numerous to repeat."[3] The Puritan church leader Cotton Mather was convinced that God had carefully placed remedies all over the earth, and that the Indians had discovered them to perform "cures many times which are truly stupendous."[4] John Wesley, the founder of Methodism, commented on the health and healing techniques of the Native Americans. He noted that their diseases were "exceedingly few" and their medicines were "quick, as well as generally infallible."[5] These observations suggest that modern medical practice has not been the only provider of effective medicines.

A second set of healing techniques involves direct intervention with the body through performing surgery, treating wounds, setting broken bones, and so on. Various kinds of surgery have been practiced. There is even evidence of primitive brain surgery, or *trepanning,* as a form of medical intervention. Among the human skulls excavated at Lachish, dated around 800 B.C., three had been trepanned. Part of the skull had been removed, the patient survived, and there was evidence of new bone growth. Before the invention of anesthesia in the 1840s, surgery was a technique of last resort. Due to the pain, surgeons were valued for their skill in getting in and out of the body quickly. Even without anesthesia, however, traditional societies have long practiced various forms of intervention in their healing techniques.

The third type of healing practice is ritual. Healing rituals are symbolic actions that creatively respond to the human limitations of disease, illness, and suffering. Rituals create a larger context of symbolic action within which the prescription of certain medicines, the performance of certain surgical interventions, and the natural healing of the body are felt to make sense and to perform their special healing power. Rituals of healing act out ideal patterns of action for human health and well-being.

Healing Rituals in Two Primal Religions

Healing rituals practiced by the Navaho and the Tewa of North America illustrate the symbolic actions of diagnosis and treatment in their response to illness. In Navaho healing rituals, various techniques are used to discover the cause and nature of a person's illness. The healer may run his hands around the person's body with a trembling, vibrating motion; or the healer may gaze into the sky, at a particular constellation of stars, praying and chanting until the secret of the illness is revealed; or the healer may "listen" to the patient's body until sounds or voices are heard that reveal the nature of the illness. These ritual techniques of diagnosis disclose the disruption of the natural harmony of elements that has caused the person to become sick.

The prescribed methods of treatment aim to restore a sense of balance, harmony, and proper relationship between the patient and the elements of nature. The Navaho call this ideal, harmonious relationship "beauty." This beauty is a perfect ethical, aesthetic, and even medical sense of harmony. The ceremony that is performed to restore a person to beauty lasts from two to nine nights depending on the nature of the illness. During this time, the *hatali,* or singer, sings over the patient to restore health, balance, and harmony through music. Other healing techniques are also used: sweat and emetic treatments, purifying baths and hairwashing, fumigation with pungent and fragrant herbs, herbal medicines, and sand paintings. But all of these techniques are orchestrated within a basic ritual format designed to restore the patient to a state of harmony by means of ritual singing. Within this ritual context the other medical techniques are felt to have their power to restore the patient to health.[6]

The Tewa of the Rio Grande Pueblo Indians formed healing societies called the Bears. The Tewa believed that bears were natural healers because they were able to pull foreign objects out of their flesh and apply healing dressings of mud to their wounds. The Bear Societies in the Tewa community were responsible for diagnosing and treating illness. Most commonly, the cause of illness was revealed to be the effects of witchcraft or evil spirits. Medical treatment was designed to counteract this evil contact. The Bears touched the body of the patient to feel the sickness. They massaged the body forcefully and applied herbs. During the healing ceremonies, the Bears would go into a trance and suck rags, stones, or other intrusive objects out of the patient's body. They would go outside into the darkness and battle evil spirits. They would chant, "be a man" and "be a woman." All these efforts were to counteract the effects of some evil contact and restore the balance within the patient's body that had been disrupted.

The Tewa held regular healing ceremonies for the entire community—preventative rituals of healing, designed to protect the group from contact with evil forces. The Bears would put on special bear paws that covered their arms, and they would move around the group touching, hitting, and slapping everyone. Tewa rituals of healing, in both diagnosis and treatment, were based on symbolic ritual actions of physical contact. The positive contact provided by the healers of the Bear Society acted against those forces that were felt to disrupt the health, well-being, and harmony of the Tewa community.[7] Healing rituals generally provide a dynamic symbolic context within which the health of individuals and the community as a whole may be restored. The Navajo and Tewa healing practices illustrate the therapeutic potential for transcending illness through healing rituals.

Healing Rituals in Western Religions

Western religious traditions have also developed specific ritual formats for healing. Within these symbolic contexts, illness is both diagnosed and treated. Traditional ritual approaches to healing in the history of western culture can be classified in four basic formats: inquisition, invocation, isolation, and integration.

Inquisition   Inquisition was a common ritual format for healing in the ancient Near East. As a ritual practice, inquisition consists of asking a series of questions in order to determine the causes of illness. Assyrian inscriptions from ancient Mesopotamia (900–600 B.C.) suggest that disease was not only perceived as a punishment for human sin, but it was the very image of sin itself. The same word, *shertu,* was used for both sin and disease. If a person should break any commandment of the gods, both physical and spiritual impurity resulted. The impurity of sin was felt to insinuate itself into the body. Sin was sickness but sickness was also the outer manifestation of sin. This diagnosis of illness as a condition of both ritual and ethical impurity is illustrated by the prayer of a sick man.

> *Impurity has befallen me. In order that thou may judge my case . . . I have prostrated myself before thee . . . . Tear out the malignant disease from my body; destroy all evil in my flesh and in my muscles. Let the disease of my body, of my flesh, and of my muscles flee from me, and let me behold the light.*[8]

The causes of this sinful condition, including both its ethical impurity and its physical suffering, could be determined by means of a ritualized inquisition into the specific nature of the sins that had been performed. The diagnostic ritual of inquisition consisted of a long series of questions: "Have you incited a son against his father?" "Have you used false scales?" "Have you said yes when you should have said no?" This inquisition inquired into the nature of the sin that had taken form in a physical malady. If the answer to any of these questions was yes, then appropriate rituals of expiation—such as sacrifices for ritual purification—could be performed to restore the ritual, ethical, and physical harmony of health. Once the ethical dissonance of sin was revealed through the ritual of inquisition, it was believed that this harmony could be restored.

Invocation   Rituals of healing based on the invocation of a higher power are a common feature of the Hebrew Bible and the Christian New Testament. Transcendent spiritual powers are called upon to bring about healing. In the Hebrew Bible, the general diagnosis of all illness attributes the responsibility directly to God. In the Torah, God claims, "I kill, and I make alive; I have wounded and I heal." (Deut. 32:39) Treatment for disease consists of prayer, entreaty, and even (as in the case of Job) an absolute surrender to the mysterious power and authority of Yahweh. Healing may result from the worshipful invocation of this divine power.

The Christian New Testament suggests a different diagnosis of disease. Evil spirits, demons, and possessions are felt to be responsible for illness. The primary form of treatment is *exorcism.* The earliest miracles attributed to Jesus in the Gospel of Mark, for example, are exorcisms: driving out unhealthy influences by invoking divine power and authority. The New Testament develops an elaborate demonology of the powers and principalities of this world who inflict human beings with spiritual and physical suffering. The image of Jesus as a magician, exorcist, and healer was common in the ancient world.[9] The example of Jesus informed Christian rituals of healing through the invocation of sacred power.

Isolation   Ancient Greek medical practice was supported by a number of ritual practices. Ritual sacrifices were performed for the purifying of people in their relationships with the gods. Ceremonial ablutions, such as the ritual cleansing of the people of Thebes ordered by Oedipus in Sophocles's *Oedipus Rex,* suggest the practice of public healing rituals. But the most distinctive ritual format in ancient Greece was isolation. Patients would be isolated in the healing temples of Asclepius. They would bathe in the healing springs, take herbal medicines, and

sleep in the temple. While in this medical isolation, the patients would pay special attention to
their dreams, which were felt to hold the key for
their own healing process. The interpretation of
dreams, with the help of the priests of Asclepius,
and the prescription of treatments derived from
the symbolism of dreams, were basic to ancient
Greek rituals of healing. These were healing
practices conducted in ritual isolation.[10]

Integration

Finally, a ritual format for
healing that had far-reaching effects on the development of western medical practice was the
search for physical balance through the harmonious integration of the elements. Earth, air,
fire, and water must be in harmony in order for
health to be maintained. Illness could be diagnosed as an imbalance of the different properties
associated with these elements. Alcmaeon of
Crotona, who flourished around 500 B.C., is credited with the belief that "health is maintained by
the equilibrium of the physical qualities: the
moist and the dry, the cold and the hot, the bitter
and the sweet and others. The predominance of
one of them causes disease. . . . Health, on the
other hand, consists in the well-balanced combination of physical qualities."[11] The ritual techniques used in ancient Greek medicine were designed to create an integrated symbolic balance
among these various elements in the body.

A second kind of integration was the balance
between human and divine dimensions of illness. Ritual divination to determine the causes of
disease, and ritual purifications in its treatment,
could both be employed because illness was felt
to be simultaneously human and divine. In his
treatise on *Airs, Waters and Places,* Hippocrates
asserted that diseases are not simply physical in
nature. "It appears to me," he said, "that these
affections are just as much divine as all others,
and that no disease is either more divine or more
human than another, but that all are equally di-

vine, for each of them has its own nature, and
none of them arises without a natural cause."[12]
The diagnosis of the natural causes of disease,
which was revealed in the imbalance of the natural elements, was integrated with a sensitivity to
the sacred dimension of human maladies, illness,
and suffering. A dimension of transcendence was
discerned in the very experience of disease itself.

These healing rituals established perfect patterns of action in response to the limitations on
human consciousness and will that are acutely
present in disease. Disease arises as a condition
of ethical dissonance that needs to be harmonized through ritualized medical practices. To
treat illness as part of a ritual process is to invest it
with meaning, to give sickness, infirmities, and
disabilities their ethical significance. Disease may
be a symbol of ethical transgressions, demonic
influence, or personal imbalance.

There has been considerable interest in recent medical ethics in the possibility of redefining our concepts of illness and health. Modern
medical practice has isolated the body as if it
were a machine. By treating the body as a machine, the doctor appears as a mechanic who
fixes it when it breaks down. In this mechanical-
biological model of disease, health is defined as
simply the absence of physical symptoms. But
new efforts at redefining health, such as the definition proposed by the World Health Organization in 1979, emphasize holism and well-being.
Holism implies that the health of a person includes all of the physical, social, psychological,
and environmental dimensions of human life.
Any concept of health needs to take all of these
aspects into consideration. Well-being is a concept used to define health in positive terms.
Health is not defined in negative terms as the
absence of symptoms, but as a condition of positive well-being. These assumptions about health,
and what it is to be healthy, provide a preliminary
foundation for medical ethics. Traditional healing rituals attempted to produce a multidimensional context within which a sense of well-being

might emerge. Healing involved practices to restore harmony for the whole person. Healing rituals are practiced on the body, but they encompass the psychological, social, environmental, and spiritual dimensions of human life in a transcendent pattern of well-being.

Euthanasia

Healing practices are dedicated to preserving, maintaining, and sustaining human life. However, there may be situations in which it is considered necessary to cause someone's death. *Euthanasia* is the painless inducement of death in order to relieve intolerable pain and suffering. Euthanasia has been described by its proponents as mercy killing, death with dignity, or a beautiful death. It is seen as a positive response that allows a person to transcend the limits of illness, aging, and the death process at the end of the human life cycle. Both inside and outside the medical profession, defenders of euthanasia have seen it as a viable response to unrelievable pain, irreversible coma, or the agonizing suffering of a terminal illness.

There has also been strong opposition to euthanasia in modern, western societies. Laws prohibit its practice. Euthanasia may be classified as a form of murder, or suicide when it is voluntary, and the western religious traditions tend to see euthanasia as a violation of the sanctity of human life. As an ethical issue, euthanasia has generated considerable controversy. In a sense, euthanasia is a kind of death control, analogous to birth control at the beginning of the life cycle. Just as abortion raises questions about human responsibility in the beginning of human life, euthanasia raises analogous ethical issues at its end. There is a pro-life position on euthanasia that insists that human life is always worth living, regardless of the pain and suffering that might have to be endured. Euthanasia, therefore, would never be considered an acceptable practice. And there is a pro-choice position that would allow individuals, families, and physicians greater freedom to make responsible decisions about the termination of a life that is felt to be unendurable. The same issues that divide the pro-life and pro-choice positions on abortion—classification, care, and community—highlight the differences between opposing sides in the euthanasia debate.

Euthanasia in Traditional Societies

Although the issue of euthanasia is generally treated as an ethical problem of modern medicine, the practice of euthanasia was common in many tribal and traditional societies. Euthanasia was practiced in many Native American tribal groups. When a father could no longer make a productive contribution to the society of the Gallinomero, a native tribe of California, it was expected that his life would be terminated by his sons. According to one description, "the poor old wretch is not infrequently thrown down on his back and securely held while a stick is placed across his throat, and two of them seat themselves on the ends of it until he ceases to breathe."[13] This practice was common among nomadic tribes where survival depended upon mobility, and the aged and feeble were a burden to the community. Euthanasia was not practiced by the Iroquois, for example, who resided in permanent, settled villages. But a large number of the wandering tribes apparently did practice some form of euthanasia. It was reported that "among the roving tribes of the wilderness the old and helpless were frequently abandoned, and, in some cases, hurried out of existence as an act of greater kindness than desertion."[14] An accepted practice among these migratory communities was to abandon the aged and infirm when they were too weak to keep up, when there was insufficient food to support them, or when the intention was to put an end to their lingering misery. Any of these reasons could support the practice of euthanasia.

Examples of euthanasia that have been reported from the island communities of Melanesia are justified by shared cultural and religious values these societies place on strength, vigor, and vitality in life. Bishop Codrington reported that the Melanesians buried old people alive. He noted that "there was generally a kindness intended." The aged Melanesians would request their friends to put them out of their misery. It was considered a disgrace to the family of an aged chief if he was not buried alive.[15] Among the Fiji islanders, sons would show their filial respect and affection for their fathers by burying them alive. This practice was consistent with a general contempt for any sign of physical weakness in a community of warriors. They believed that human beings enter the next life with the same powers they possessed at the moment of their death. Thus, there was an incentive to die while still possessing full consciousness.[16]

Euthanasia and Modern Medical Practice

Euthanasia was not widely encouraged or practiced within western religious traditions. There is the folk tradition of the Holy Mawle, a kind of club that would hang on the back of church doors in England to be used by a son on his old, decrepit, and useless father to put him out of his misery. But in western religious ethics, euthanasia has not been an accepted practice. Euthanasia does appear as a controversial ethical issue in modern medical practice for at least two reasons. First, artificial medical techniques have increasingly been able to maintain the vital signs of life, while the patient may linger in intense pain, irreversible coma, or a prolonged process of dying. The very success of medical techniques has raised new problems at the end of the human life cycle. Second, euthanasia becomes an issue whenever people want to assume a more direct control over their lives and deaths. The practice of euthanasia may allow for a more conscious control over the termination of a human life.

We must distinguish between voluntary euthanasia, in which a person may decide for various reasons—incurable disease, insufferable pain, or insurmountable debilitation—that death would be preferable to life, and involuntary euthanasia, in which some agency or institution with social authority may make that decision. Voluntary euthanasia suggests that life and death can be brought under the direct control of the individual. It permits self-determination in the time and place of a person's own death. Involuntary euthanasia, however, represents a form of external social control that is exercised upon an individual. Even when involuntary euthanasia is ostensibly for the person's own good, it still involves difficult decisions by governments, physicians, or families to terminate that life. This distinction between voluntary and involuntary euthanasia is the first important consideration in evaluating the status of euthanasia in medical ethics.

A second distinction can be made between active and passive methods of euthanasia. In active euthanasia, physicians might administer lethal injections, chemicals, or other fatal means in order to bring a life to an end. This involves the doctor in a direct action that causes death. In passive euthanasia, doctors simply do not intervene with certain life-saving techniques and thereby allow a terminal patient to die who might otherwise have been kept alive. Passive euthanasia is an act of omission, but it omits those extraordinary life-support systems in modern medical practice that can keep a patient alive when vital signs would have stopped without them. Such extraordinary means of sustaining life signs have become so common in modern medical practice, that death does not occur when the angel of death arrives, but when the doctor pulls the plug.

These distinctions between voluntary and involuntary, active and passive, can be combined to reveal the four basic varieties of euthanasia that confront modern medical ethics.

------

1.   *Voluntary Active Euthanasia.* This is a death that is decided upon and carried out by a patient. The action may be taken in consultation with a physician, but it is an elective death chosen by the patient. Individuals exercise choice in the time, manner, and conditions of their own deaths. Reasons for voluntary active euthanasia may include intolerable suffering, unrelievable pain, or a fear of being a burden to family. But for whatever reasons, the person makes a decision that death would be preferable to life and makes arrangements for death.

------

2.   *Voluntary Passive Euthanasia.* In this form of euthanasia, people make a decision, either while suffering from a terminal illness, or in advance in the form of a living will, that they do not wish to be kept alive through extraordinary medical techniques. Preferring death to a continued existence in a vegetative state, the person may request that no heroic medical measures be taken to sustain life. The individual makes a voluntary decision to allow death to take its natural course without extraordinary medical interventions.

------

3.   *Involuntary Active Euthanasia.* This has been referred to as "mercy killing." It is a decision made by physicians or family to bring about or hasten a person's death in order to relieve the agonies of prolonged suffering. The slow, painful process of some terminal diseases may be accelerated to shorten the dying process. Or, people in irreversible comas may be killed if there is no hope that they might recover consciousness. Although such a death may not be the choice of the patient, it may be decided by relatives, doctors, or medical policy that death is in the patient's own best interests.

------

4.   *Involuntary Passive Euthanasia.* In this form of euthanasia doctors may simply allow a patient to die when there is no prospect that the person will recover. This decision may be made by medical staff when there is nothing else that can be done to restore the patient to health. Often proponents of active euthanasia will see this passive approach as undesirable. Even though efforts may be made to make the patient as comfortable as possible, this often results in a slow, agonizing dying process. This agony could be avoided, they contend, by taking direct action. Lethal drugs could be administered that would relieve the dying of their pain and misery. Such direct action would not simply put life to an end, but it would put the painful process of dying to an end. Medical professionals dedicated to preserving life, however, have been reluctant to initiate death, and euthanasia, in the form of passive involuntary euthanasia, may appear to be more acceptable because it does not implicate doctors in the taking of life.

These four varieties of euthanasia are simply possibilities to be confronted in medical ethics. It should not be implied from this that all the forms of euthanasia are actually practiced in the medical profession. There has been a considerable controversy in modern, western societies regarding the ethical status of euthanasia. Legal codes continue to prohibit any form of active euthanasia. The controversy over euthanasia involves fundamental questions about the nature and value of human life. There are basic disagreements concerning the place of euthanasia within an ethical pattern of action at the end of the human life cycle.

The Euthanasia Controversy

The euthanasia movement began in Britain in 1936 with the introduction of a bill in Parliament to legalize voluntary euthanasia. Cultural luminaries, such as George Bernard Shaw, H. G. Wells, and Julian Huxley, endorsed the proposed legislation, and it received support from representatives of every Christian denomination except the Roman Catholic church. The bill proposed that voluntary euthanasia should be permitted with the following qualifications: Euthanasia should be allowed for (1) persons over 21 years of age; (2) who are suffering from an incurable and fatal disease; (3) who are in severe pain; and (4) who sign a form, in the presence of at least two witnesses, requesting euthanasia.[17] After extensive debates, the bill was defeated by a vote of 35 to 14. Active voluntary euthanasia remains illegal in British law.

The Euthanasia Society of America was founded in 1938. This organization also had the support of public figures and some religious leaders, but it has not been able to get legislation passed in Congress that would permit euthanasia. Charles Potter, the founder of the society, saw euthanasia as a type of death control, an effort to take responsibility for the process of dying, which was analogous to the kind of responsibility implicit in birth control. In 1938, Potter observed, "We have been for years active in the

birth control movement and since that fight is largely won, we feel free to transfer some of our efforts to the euthanasia enterprise."[18] Potter's views suggest that the proponents of euthanasia saw it as part of a larger ethical project to achieve a greater freedom to exert conscious control over the challenges of the life cycle. The birth control movement and the euthanasia movement were both efforts to change legal codes to allow for individual freedom of conscience, personal responsibility, and self-determination in these life and death issues. Many of the same religious, philosophical, and ethical arguments in the birth control and abortion debates are also engaged in the controversy over the practice of euthanasia.

Issues of Classification   A central issue of classification is at stake in the euthanasia controversy: Where do we draw the line between life and death? There was a time when this seemed to be a fairly easy classification to make: Determining the moment of death was simply a matter of checking the vital signs of respiration, heartbeat, and pulse. A doctor could certify that a person was dead by putting a mirror up to the nostrils, listening for a heartbeat, and feeling for a pulse. If these vital signs were absent, the person could be classified as dead. Even with this degree of certainty, however, mistakes could be made. The nineteenth century custom of installing bells in coffins so that the "deceased" would be able to get someone's attention upon suddenly waking up under ground gave expression to a fear that there might be a margin of error in the diagnosis of death.

In modern medical practice, extraordinary technological means for sustaining the vital signs of biological life, even when brain activity ceases, have blurred the line between life and death. Is human life defined by respiration, heartbeat, and pulse? Or is human life to be defined by the presence of neurological activity in the brain that makes consciousness possible? The development of artificial life-support systems has created a new classification of death: brain death. A person may be declared dead if there is no brain activity. This condition provides for the possibility in modern medical practice that the patient could be classified as dead, even though the vital signs may still be functioning. To disconnect such a person from artificial life-support systems is a form of passive euthanasia based on the classification of brain death.

A second issue of classification is at the center of the controversy over active euthanasia. Are there certain conditions under which a life may be classified as not worth living? The defenders of euthanasia insist that life belongs to the individual. It is the responsibility of individuals to take conscious control over their own process of living and dying. As Joseph Fletcher stated this position, euthanasia is "the right of spiritual beings to use intelligent control over physical nature, rather than to submit beastlike to its blind workings."[19] This intelligent control over nature is seen as one of the important rights and responsibilities of being human: People have the right to dispose of their lives as they see fit. The dignity, responsibility, and self-determination of being a human being includes the right to decide that, under certain conditions, death would be preferable to life. Again, as Fletcher has observed, "death control, like birth control, is a matter of human dignity. Without it persons become puppets. To perceive this is to grasp the error lurking in the notion—widespread in medical circles— that life as such is the highest good."[20] The biological life signs of breathing, heartbeat, and circulation are not the highest values in human life. The value of a human life, from this perspective, lies in a certain quality of experience. Therefore, it is possible to imagine a life not worth living.

Opponents of euthanasia insist that there is no life that is not worth living. From a theological perspective, Arthur J. Dyck has opposed euthanasia by classifying human life as a gift from God.[21] Life does not belong to the individual.

Choices may be made about how to live it, but not about whether or not to live it. These ultimate choices are attributed to a divine agency that transcends ordinary human life. The decision to cause one's own death is not an individual right, but the prerogative of God. Dyck has argued against euthanasia by citing the commandment "Thou shalt not kill" as a prohibition of self-killing. Voluntary active euthanasia would therefore be classified as suicide and would be forbidden by this extension of the commandment against killing to any intentional self-killing.

The defenders and opponents of euthanasia hold two very different images of transcendence. The defenders of voluntary active euthanasia argue that this conscious control over the dying process represents the human right to transcend the limitations imposed by the natural, physical, and even animal level of human existence. Euthanasia rises above the constraints placed on human freedom by the natural course of dying. The opponents of active euthanasia, however, imagine transcendence to lie beyond human control. Human beings must simply accept the transcendent will of God, or nature, in the time and place of death.

Issues of Care   The controversy over euthanasia also involves different assumptions about the quality of care that is appropriate for a person who is dying. The quality of care that defenders of euthanasia feel is indicated is compassion for people who are painfully and terminally ill. Euthanasia is seen as an expression of this compassion for people who are victims of unrelievable suffering, the loss of mental faculties, or a vegetative existence, alive only through the extraordinary techniques of respirators, intravenous feeding, and other life-support systems. In these cases, the highest quality of care may be to allow that person a death with dignity. Care is demonstrated by a conscious decision to control the dying process through a simple, painless, and direct intervention. The defenders of euthanasia argue that it is a measure of care that should be applied to people who would die regardless of medical treatment. If the intention is to relieve suffering, why not hasten the process in order to avoid a slow, agonizing death? In this sense, the intention behind euthanasia is not to cause death, but to terminate suffering and shorten the dying process as an expression of care for a person in unrelievable pain.

Opponents of euthanasia maintain that suffering people need the support of others to endure their lives, not encouragement to bring about their deaths. Suffering does not make a life less worth living; it does not make a life less worthy of being cared for, supported, and sustained. The argument against the practice of euthanasia, again expressed by Arthur J. Dyck, insists on "the intrinsic worth and equal value of every human life regardless of its stage or condition."[22] This reverence for human life is the ideal that should motivate medical practice dedicated to preserving, protecting, and prolonging every human life. Such a position, however, requires some sense of the intrinsic value of suffering in human life. Here also different images of transcendence are involved. The defenders of euthanasia argue that suffering may be transcended by consciously bringing it to an end. Its opponents, however, argue that human beings transcend suffering by enduring pain and demonstrating the acceptance, patience, and personal character that represent the ultimate nobility of being human. The appropriate quality of care indicated is, therefore, a supportive environment within which this transcendence may emerge.

Issues of Community
Those who promote euthanasia maintain that the primary responsibility of the community lies in protecting the rights of individuals to make free decisions about their own deaths. Currently, there is no legislation in the United States permitting the practice of voluntary active euthanasia. Euthanasia tends to be classified in criminal codes as an act of suicide. Suggested legislation, such as the proposed British Euthanasia Act of 1936 or the Voluntary Euthanasia Act of 1969, may provide some guidelines for changes in the laws governing euthanasia. There is also a need for clearly defined rules governing the practice of involuntary euthanasia in medical practice. Active involuntary euthanasia, which would cause death through direct medical intervention, remains a practice prohibited by medical policy. The medical community requires a recognized consensus on the length of time a patient's body should be kept alive after brain death has been determined.[23] A clearer classification of the line between life and death might allow doctors to end the suffering of patients, and families, in those terminal cases in which consciousness is irrecoverably lost, yet the patient's vital signs continue. In any event, the community can support the rights of individuals to respond in a variety of ways, with freedom, dignity, and self-determination, to the ethical challenge posed by their own deaths.

Opponents of euthanasia maintain that the primary ethical responsibility of the community is the protection of life. A common argument against euthanasia is the suggestion that it is a thin wedge inserted into a community's commitment to protect life, and that soon the practice of euthanasia will generate disrespect for human life. It is often feared that euthanasia will lead to the involuntary killing of classes of people whom the community may not consider worthy of living. This point is suggested in Leo Alexander's reflections on medical practices in Nazi Germany. The extermination of people considered undesirable by the state, according to Alexander, "started with the acceptance of that attitude, basic in the euthanasia movement, that there is such a thing as a life not worthy to be lived."[24] The lives not worth living broadened to include the socially unproductive, racially unwanted, and eventually all non-Germans. The problem with this analogy is that Hitler's Germany sought the involuntary extermination of undesirable people for what was perceived to be the good of the community; the euthanasia movement desires the freedom for a voluntary, compassionate, and humane death when it is perceived to be for the good of the individual. Nevertheless, opponents of euthanasia maintain the nonnegotiable value of every human life and the responsibility of the community to protect that value by prohibiting the practice of euthanasia.

The euthanasia controversy reveals fundamentally different responses to the ethical issues of classification, care, and community at the end of the human life cycle. Defenders of euthanasia insist that members of the human community should be free to choose this option in order to transcend the lingering pain, suffering, and debilitation of the dying process. In this regard, euthanasia may be interpreted as an act of healing, a pattern of action in the interest of a person's ultimate well-being in the face of death. Opponents of euthanasia, in seeing this practice as a violation of the fundamental obligation to maintain life, interpret such a pattern of action as suicide. This raises questions about the role of suicide within religious ethics. Within religious ethics, are there situations in which suicide has been interpreted as a positive act of transcendence in relation to human limits?

Suicide

Suicide may provide the ultimate challenge to any system of religious ethics. The possibility of self-destruction calls into question the most basic ethical concerns for the meaning, purpose, and value of human life. When we contemplate suicide, we are confronted with the central question of human existence: to be or not to be. Suicide places before us the option of not being. A person contemplating suicide is looking into the face of death, and the images of death that the person holds play an important role in assessing the meaning of suicide for that person.

Images of Death

Human beings may confront the image of death throughout the course of the life cycle. It may be the case that the way we imagine death gives shape to life: It organizes priorities, forms expectations, and gives ultimate significance to the course of any life. Sigmund Freud maintained that it was impossible for human beings to imagine their own deaths. He held that death was the total and complete extinction of the human person. Whenever we try to imagine our own death, we find ourselves somehow still there in our imagination. We survive in imagination as a spectator at our own funeral, a disembodied spirit floating through space, surviving in a heaven of material pleasures or lingering in a hell of physical pains. The failure of the human imagination to conceive of the absolute emptiness of extinction convinced Freud that we are unable to accept the fact of our own death. In the unconscious depths of the human psyche, each of us is convinced of our own immortality.

Sigmund Freud felt that this unconscious resistance to imagining death left human beings with two choices: acceptance or avoidance. We may consciously assent to a scientific acceptance of death as the extinction of human life, or we may avoid acknowledging death through a variety of imaginative projections of survival. Any belief in the survival of the human personality after death was simply assumed to be a failure of reason and nerve. Freud interpreted beliefs in immortality as fantasy projections based on the unconscious resistance to imagining personal nonexistence. He included all religious responses to death within this category of unconscious resistance to imagining death. They were interpreted as strategies of avoidance. Beliefs in an afterlife, visionary journeys through the realms of the dead, and theories of the survival of the human soul were all, according to Freud, imaginary ways of avoiding the fact of death.

Recent psychological theory in the Freudian tradition, however, has begun to attribute a more positive role to religious responses to death. Imagination is not simply an avoidance of death; it may be a creative response to human mortality. Religious responses to death provide legitimate ways of transcending the limits of the human life cycle. The psychologist Robert Lifton has outlined four basic creative responses to death. He refers to these imaginative responses as four modes of symbolic immortality.[25] Symbolic immortality in one form or another is an integral part of the human experience of death. It demonstrates the ways people seek to transcend the limits of the ordinary human life cycle; it creates a sense of continuity in human life with that which precedes birth and follows death. The four modes of symbolic immortality can be identified in the following brief descriptions.

1. *Biological Immortality*—the sense that human identity is necessarily connected with an unbroken biological chain that links ancestors to offspring. In biological immortality, human beings transcend the limits of an individual life cycle by living on through children.

2. *Creative Immortality*—the sense that human identity is part of a larger, ongoing historical community. The human creations of the past are alive in us, and we transcend the limits of our life cycle by living on in the hearts and minds of others.

3. *Natural Immortality*—the sense that human identity is fundamentally connected with its natural environment. We are part of the elements, rhythms, and process of nature. Human beings transcend their personal life cycles by living on through nature.

4. *Religious Immortality*—Although the other three forms of symbolic transcendence may have religious dimensions, the fourth form includes religious images and mythic visions of human survival after death. These images of immortality are not simply strategies for avoiding death; they are creative responses to human limit situations that allow those who hold them to die with a fully human integrity.

These images of symbolic immortality create a deep sense of connection between the human self and a larger reality within which the self is always alive. They affirm the larger symbolic connections within which human identity is located. Suicide may represent a broken connection. To destroy one's own life may break the network of biological, creative, natural, and religious connections that provide life with its uniquely human meaning and significance.

In some cases, however, suicide may be a response to an overwhelming sense that those connections are already broken. It may be an ethical response to an experience of dissonance at the perceived meaninglessness, futility, or disorder of life. The poet Antonin Artaud maintained that suicide was a transcendent act of will in the sense that it imposed a self-determined order, control, or design on the disorder of human life. "By suicide," Artaud declared, "I reintroduce my design in nature, I shall for the first time give things the shape of my will."[26] From another perspective, however, this willful act of self-imposed order appears to deny the transcendent connections that provide the most basic context of meaning for human life. However suicide is understood, it is a pattern of action that raises the most fundamental issues of human identity and responsibility. Suicide may be a response to an intolerable, disordered, or chaotic life situation, but is it the most creative response that is available? It will be important to reflect on the place of suicide within traditions of religious ethics.

Religious Suicide

Suicide has appeared within some traditions in the history of religions as a legitimate ethical response in a number of very specific situations. Religious suicide has taken four basic forms: ritual, revenge, release, and revolution. Each form of suicide places the act of self-destruction within a larger context of religious meaning and significance. In these cases, suicide is interpreted as a pattern of action that affirms certain values of life in the act of a self-imposed death.

Ritual   Perhaps the best documented example of ritual suicide in the history of religions is the practice of *seppuku,* or *hara-kiri,* in traditional Japan. The warrior ethics of the Japanese *samurai* demanded strict discipline, absolute allegiance, and purity of conduct. The ethics of the samurai was a rigorous military code of obedience to a war lord. The samurai warriors were obligated to act in ways that upheld the honor of their order and avoided the dissonance of shame. A number of different situations might produce an intense sense of shame. If the warrior disobeyed the commands of a superior, if he committed some criminal or treasonous act, or if he should fall into enemy hands, the samurai would bring dishonor upon himself. This dishonor was symbolized as the impurity of defilement.

The response to this ethical defilement was a formally structured ritual of self-sacrifice. The suicide ritual of seppuku was an opportunity to achieve self-purification and to restore a sense of harmony within the samurai pattern of ethical action. With the prescribed gestures, posture, and demeanor, the warrior would plunge a knife into his abdomen, opening up and exposing that part of the body that represented the center of spiritual power and purity. By this superhuman act of self-sacrifice, it was believed that the samurai restored a fundamental ethical harmony that had been disrupted by his shameful actions. Seppuku in traditional Japan represented a purification ritual through self-sacrifice.[27]

Another example of ritual suicide is found in the custom of wife sacrifice that was practiced in traditional India. The ritual of *sati* required a widow to throw herself upon the inferno of her husband's funeral pyre. Sati was not simply performed because a wife was expected to join her husband in death; it was also connected to prevailing notions that a woman without a husband was an anomaly in the social system. Widowhood violated the ethical obligation that required women to be married. For a woman to be unmarried was seen as a disgrace. One text of the ancient Vedas described the experience of hell as similar to being a woman without a husband.[28] To be without a husband is to be radically out of place in the network of social relations that make up traditional Hindu society. Sati was a form of ritual suicide designed to avoid the shame of being out of place in the social order.

Revenge   A common motive for suicide in the history of religions is revenge. The Hebrew

Bible relates the story of the hero Samson and his battles against the enemies of Israel. Taken captive by the enemy, Samson with his tremendous strength managed to pull down a temple upon himself and countless Philistines. The Bible suggests that in this one suicidal act he killed more of the enemy than he had killed in his entire career. (Jud. 16:28–30) Considering that Samson had been very efficient in disposing of Israel's enemies prior to this event, his act of suicidal revenge must have taken many Philistines along with him.

The motive of revenge often animates suicides in tribal societies.[29] Two factors are important in revenge suicides: first, a belief that the spirit of the deceased will survive to torment the living; and, second, the existence of social penalties that will be imposed on the person accused of provoking the suicide. Revenge suicides tend to be justified, therefore, in both religious and legal terms. They may be referred to within tribal communities as killing oneself *upon the head,* or *on the neck,* of another person. The anthropologist Malinowski described revenge suicides as an attempt to achieve justice. In these cases, suicide "is performed as an act of justice, not upon oneself, but upon some person of near kindred who has caused offense. As such it is one of the most important legal institutions among the natives."[30]

These suicides are understood as a type of post mortem retaliation, a way for people to seek revenge on someone who has done them some wrong. Among the Ashanti of the African Gold Coast, the practice of revenge suicide was supported by certain social pressures. "If a man kills himself on the head of another, the other must kill himself also, or pay twenty ounces of gold to the family of the suicide."[31] Among the Yoruba, a heavy fine must be paid to the suicide's family by the person who provoked the suicide of revenge. "To commit suicide in the presence of another is one of the ways the Yorubas have of revenging a gross insult offered to him by that person. This is called dying on the neck."[32] Revenge suicide is therefore seen as an act of retribution upon the living in these tribal societies.

Release

Suicide is sometimes imagined to be a form of release from the troubles of life. It may be a liberation from life's bondage, a rest from the weariness of life's journey, or a final entry into the peace of extinction. In an ancient Egyptian text called the *Dispute Over Suicide* the author contemplates his own self-destruction as a welcome release from life:

> *Death is in my sight today*
> *Like the recovery of a sick man* . . .
> *Like the longing of a man to see*
>   *his house again* . . .
> *After many years of captivity.*[33]

This notion of suicide as a welcome release from the troubles and tribulations of life was adopted in ancient Greek thought by the Epicureans and Stoics. These schools in ancient Greek philosophy held that death was simply the end of existence. They were convinced that there was nothing to fear on the other side of death's door because there will be no one there to fear anything. In nonexistence there can be neither fear, nor pain, nor any experience at all. Death was therefore a release from experience itself.

The Epicurean poet Lucretius, who ended his own life through suicide, recommended that life should be fully enjoyed. But if at some point life should cease to be enjoyable, then suicide provided the option of bringing that life to an end. Lucretius maintained that "if one day, as well may happen, life grows wearisome, there only remains to pour a libation to death and oblivion. A drop of subtle poison will gently close your eyes to the sun and waft you smiling into the eternal night whence everything comes and to which everything returns."[34]

The Stoics placed certain restraints on the

practice of suicide. They felt that it should be permitted, but only as a carefully reasoned response to a person's situation. Suicide was not something to be performed out of despair, but only out of a commitment to maintaining a personal integrity and rational self-determination that would choose the time, place, and circumstances of death. The philosopher Seneca expressed the Stoic ideal of suicide when he observed that "as I choose the ship in which I will sail and the house I will inhabit, so I will choose the death by which I leave life. In no matter more than in death should we act according to our own desire."[35] In Stoic ethics, suicide may be performed as a rational act of self-determination that releases the individual from the irrational contingencies of accident, suffering, and incapacitation.

Revolution
A number of examples of suicides in the history of religions were performed as revolutionary acts of defiance against oppressive forces of social opposition. Revolutionary suicides have been performed by groups of people who would rather die than surrender. The American revolutionary patriot Patrick Henry is remembered for exclaiming, "Give me liberty, or give me death!" There have been a few cases in which religious groups have actually chosen mass suicide rather than surrender their freedom. The Jewish Zealots who held out against the Roman armies on top of the fortress of Masada preferred death to surrender. Their mass suicide was a revolutionary act against Roman authority. Their leader Eleazar exhorted them to perform this revolutionary mass suicide by declaring that "it is death which gives liberty to the soul and permits it to depart to its own pure abode, there to be free from all calamity."[36] His words provide evidence of the motives of both liberation and purity for the act of revolutionary religious suicide.

In the seventeenth century, many of the Russian Orthodox faithful were excommunicated, persecuted, and killed for refusing to cooperate with certain changes in the Russian Orthodox ritual practice. Those who resisted these changes came to be called Old Believers. In response to what the Old Believers perceived as an oppressive alliance between the Russian church and state, many of them committed suicide, in groups of 1000 to 2000 at a time, by locking themselves in houses, barns, or monasteries and setting the building on fire. As many as 20,000 Old Believers died in mass suicides during the seventeenth century. The practice was occasionally revived. The most recent case of the mass suicide of Old Believers occurred in 1896. For the Old Believers, collective suicide was seen as a revolutionary act against the authority of the Russian church and state. As one Old Believer declared, "We would rather die than give up the old ways."[37]

The most dramatic recent example of a revolutionary act of mass suicide occurred on November 18, 1978, in the agricultural community of Jonestown in the jungles of Guyana. The religious commune, led by the charismatic Jim Jones, was under investigation by a congressional delegation. It was the visit led by United States Congressman Leo Ryan that served as a catalyst for the self-destruction of the Jonestown community. Jim Jones apparently felt that he was being besieged by his three most dangerous enemies: (1) the United States government, represented by an official congressional delegation; (2) the media that he felt was hostile to the Peoples Temple; and (3) a group known as the Concerned Relatives accompanying Congressman Ryan, who were perceived by Jones as traitors to his movement. Jim Jones's response to this situation was to initiate the mass murder-suicide of 913 men, women, and children who lived in the Jonestown community.

This incomprehensible act of violence displayed many of the attributes associated with religious suicide in the history of religions. First, it was a ritual. The mass suicide, or what Jones called the white night, had been rehearsed a number of times in mock-suicide sessions that demonstrated loyalty to Jones and the community. Second, it was an act of revenge: The mass suicide was performed as an act of vengeance upon the government, media, and traitors to the movement, who Jones insisted had provoked this final act. The mass suicide was seen as an act that would cast blame on the enemies of the community. Third, it was presented to the community of Jonestown as an act of release. The members of the community were exhorted to step over, across, or through the door of death as a final liberation from their suffering, poverty, and misery in the world. Finally, the very term *revolutionary suicide* was used by Jones to describe this act. "We didn't commit suicide," Jones wanted the world to know, "we committed an act of revolutionary suicide protesting the conditions of an inhuman world."[38] This one act of violence drew upon all the justifications for suicide that have been offered in the history of religions. Jim Jones brought about the revolutionary suicide of Jonestown as a ritual of revenge and release against what he perceived to be overwhelming forces of opposition to his community.

Religious Ethics of Suicide

Most religious traditions have forbidden the practice of suicide. The justifications of ritual, revenge, release, and revolution have not been supported by most ethical traditions. Suicide appears as a basic contradiction to the impulse for preserving life that animates most systems of religious ethics. In ancient China, for example, Confucian ethics held that suicide was unthinkable because human beings owe their life to heaven and are therefore responsible for the care and preservation of life as if it were a precious gift. Life does not belong to the individual to dispose of as he or she sees fit. The Taoist text *Yu Li* maintained that suffering in hell was destined for those who commit suicide "in a trivial burst of rage, or fearing consequences of a crime."[39] Suicide was not seen as a legitimate release from the human condition. Exceptions were made, however, for those who killed themselves in the interests of loyalty, filial piety, or to preserve chastity. In these cases, suicide actually served some higher ethical value and therefore was allowed.

In traditional Hindu ethics, suicide was considered a serious crime for a Brahmin. It was strictly prohibited as a denial of the inherent value in life. There were certain provisions, however, for a kind of religious suicide. One popular account of Hindu customs outlines five methods of self-sacrifice that are considered consistent with Hindu ethical and devotional practices. You might commit suicide by (1) starving, (2) covering yourself with cow dung and setting it on fire, (3) burying yourself in snow, (4) cutting your throat where the river Ganges meets the Jumna, or (5) bathing in the water where the Ganges meets the sea, confessing all sins, and then praying for alligators to come and eat you.[40] It is difficult to know how extensively such self-sacrifices were practiced in popular Hinduism. These acts of suicide are described as devotional sacrifices offered as gifts to the gods.

Buddhist ethics strictly prohibits suicide as an extension of its ethical injunction against killing. Suicide was not considered a legitimate means for achieving the extinction of human desires represented by nirvana. There have been cases within the tradition, however, such as the self-immolation of Buddhist priests in Vietnam, in which self-destruction was performed as a revolutionary act of protest against social injustice.

In the Hebrew Bible, six suicides are mentioned. They are simply described without any moral condemnation. The Jewish tradition, however, came to extend the commandment against killing to the prohibition of self-killing. Suicide was defined as a crime against God. The first century historian Josephus opposed suicide as a crime against God and nature: "Suicide is repugnant to that nature which all creatures share, and an act of impiety towards God who created us."[41] In Judaism human life is regarded as a gift from God, and any destruction of this gift would be a serious violation of the duties that are owed to its creator. The rabbinic tradition in Judaism demonstrated this strong disapproval of suicide by not performing the standard funeral and mourning ceremonies for the deceased if that person had taken his or her own life.

The persecution of the early Christian communities in the Roman Empire resulted in the martyrdom of many Christians who chose death rather than betray the community. Popular accounts of the deaths of these Christian heroes, or athletes as they were called, provided an ethical pattern that encouraged many other Christians to choose death rather than betrayal of their faith. Many of the earliest women saints of the tradition were canonized for defending their virginity with death. They allowed themselves to be killed rather than give up their chastity. The fourth century Church Father Jerome applauded this variety of suicide for the preservation of virginity. Young women should kill themselves before surrendering their chastity. But Augustine, in his *City of God,* argued that suicide was never justified. He presented four arguments against its practice. First, suicide destroys hope. The religious life is dedicated to the openness of hope; it represents possibilities of change, repentance, and self-transformation. Suicide closes off these possibilities, and is therefore a denial of the ethical virtue of hopefulness that permeates a truly Christian life. Second, suicide is murder. It is covered under the commandment against killing and is therefore a very serious sin. Third, suicide does

not under any circumstances atone for sin. Human beings cannot erase their sins by eliminating themselves. Suicide is never a productive response to the dissonance of sin. Finally, suicide may be regarded as an action that is symptomatic of the greatest human sin: pride. It is an act that denies God the power over human life and death that belongs to Him as Creator. In Augustine's thought, pride was the root of all sin. Suicide was a demonstration of self-centered human pride in performing an action that should only be performed by God.[42]

Similar arguments against suicide were developed by the medieval Catholic theologian Thomas Aquinas in his *Summa Theologia,* written in the thirteenth century. According to Aquinas, suicide was a serious crime against self, society, and the sacred duties owed to God. First, suicide was a crime against self. It was an action that was contrary to the *caritas,* or unconditional love, which every person owes to self and others. Suicide is a denial of that unconditional love that people owe to themselves. Second, suicide was a crime against society. The act of self-destruction is not only detrimental to that person, but it disrupts the community of which that person is a vital part. Suicide deprives that community of a person whose very existence makes an incalculable impact on friends, family, and acquaintances. Society is impoverished by any act of suicide. Finally, suicide was a crime against God. The act of suicide usurps God's power to dispose of human life and death; it is therefore the ultimate act of rebellion against the will of a God that commands life.[43] These three arguments of Thomas Aquinas summarized the powerful motives for the aversion to suicide in the Christian tradition. Suicide violated the sanctity of the self, the community, and sacred authority. But the emphasis on suicide as a crime gave rise to a variety of Christian social practices designed to punish suicides: post mortem excommunication, refusal of religious burial, and even the medieval practice of public humiliation of suicides by dragging their bodies through the streets.

Ethical Responses to Suicide

When we contemplate suicide, we look into the face of our own deaths. The images we see reflected there may be the many facets of human life itself. We may see the joy and the sorrow, the pleasure and the pain, that is interwoven in the complex fabric of human experience. We may be confronted with our own emptiness and our own fullness. The temptation of suicide may be its promise for imposing a self-determined order upon the ambiguities of life. The conflicts, tensions, and disorders of life may be reduced by a single, self-imposed act of closure in suicide.

Ethical responsibility in religious ethics is itself a kind of order that defines the normative pattern of human experience. Like suicide, it reduces the contradictions of life to a single design. But ethical responsibility is also an ability to respond creatively to the complex, ambiguous, and often contradictory challenges of living. It may require a certain degree of openness to dissonance, conflict, and contradiction in order to maintain its own responsive integrity. Ethical responses to suicide within a tradition of religious ethics may take a number of different forms.

1.   *The Moral Response.* The ethical norms of most religious traditions insist that suicide is a violation of the sanctity of human life. A moral response to these norms seeks to align personal desires with a pattern of action that affirms life as an inestimable sacred value. Not simply refraining from self-destruction, it signifies a commitment to actions that affirm the living values of the self, the community, and the sacred authority within which self and society derive their meaning. In this sense, the supreme obligation of religious ethics is always to affirm life in the face of death. Even those traditions that permit suicide as a legitimate moral response only allow acts of self-destruction if they are perceived as supporting some higher human value that is felt to make life worth living. The moral response to suicide, therefore, invests personal desires in the most fundamental ethical values that sustain human life.

2.   *The Disciplinary Response.* Ethical rules against self-killing are often supported by sanctions, reprisals, and punishments that reinforce an ethical response based on discipline. Within a religious tradition that forbids suicide, people may submit to this disciplinary rule because they are motivated by the fear of punishment in hell or the hope of heaven. These disciplinary constraints on behavior are intensified by social sanctions against suicides. The punitive treatment of the bodies of suicides in medieval Christianity must have discouraged the practice of suicide and reinforced a disciplinary response to its prohibition.

3.   *The Antinomian Response.* The philosopher David Hume, in his essay "On Suicide" in 1777, represented a widely held antinomian position on suicide in the modern world when he maintained that there are simply no divine or natural laws that govern the human freedom to choose death. Hume argued that human beings are free to do what they will with their own lives. In creating the world, God may have set up unchanging natural laws that govern the universe, but those laws do not in any way restrict the freedom of human beings to pursue their own self-preservation or their own self-destruction. "The life of a man," Hume suggested, "is of no greater

importance to the universe than that of an oyster."[44] Whatever meaning might be found in being alive is largely self-created. In this antinomian response to suicide, therefore, the prospect of self-destruction is left entirely to the discretion of the individual.

———

4.   *The Improvised Response.* An ethical response that is willing to improvise within the situations and circumstances of life may see suicide as a real possibility. But a truly improvisational response would insist on placing suicide alongside as many other creative responses as possible. Improvisation calls for creative response-ability. Often when people contemplate suicide, they have the sense that the world has narrowed down to two, and only two, choices: Either some intolerable life situation must go away or I must go away. Life has been reduced to an either-or proposition. This constriction of the horizon of life to an either-or opposition already signals a deathlike loss of imagination, energy, and response-ability. The willingness to improvise in response to the ethical challenge of suicide begins with the recognition that life necessarily involves three or more choices. One of these choices may always be suicide, but with the expansion of possibilities a new sense of response-ability may enter into experience. Self-destruction may not appear as the most attractive available option.

Patterns of Transcendence

Ethical patterns of life in response to illness, aging, and death hold the potential for an experience of transcendence in the face of human limit situations. Rising above, going beyond, or moving through limits allows the ethical imagination to realize its potential for transcendence. The ethical issues of healing, euthanasia, and suicide all elicit creative resources with which a context for the experience of transcendence may be formed through ethical patterns of action. Chapter 8 has drawn a number of conclusions regarding the challenge of transcendence in confronting the ultimate limit situations of the human condition.

———

1.   *Rituals of healing create a context for transcendence.* Healing rituals confront the human limit situations of illness, disease, and degeneration with sacred patterns of action that act out a drama of ritualized perfection for the human experience of the body. Rituals of healing provide a creative, imaginative, and symbolic context for the transcendence of illness. The body is incorporated into symbolic patterns of action that both diagnose illness and enact a pattern of well-being. The diagnostic and therapeutic rituals of the Navaho and the Tewa suggest that religious rituals of healing involve body, mind, feelings, and imagination in a total ritual process that affirms the well-being of the patient and the community. From the perspective of modern medical practice, these rituals appear superstitious and ineffective. But these practices would not have been continued if they were not therapeutically effective in maintaining and restoring well-being whenever it was disrupted by illness.

Western religious traditions have also developed ritual formats for healing. These ritual contexts invested illness with religious meaning and significance. The practices of inquisition inquired into the ethical significance of disease; the practices of invocation evoked transcendent religious powers to intervene in the healing process;

the practices of isolation awakened the healing power of dreams and imagination; and the practices of integration sought to restore a balance within both the human and divine forces that constitute well-being. These rituals of healing were creative attempts to imagine illness as part of a larger physical, ethical, and spiritual process of healing. They sought to transcend the limitations of illness by incorporating it in the ritualized perfection of healing. The imagination of illness may be regarded as a precondition for medical ethics. These rituals of healing suggest that illness can be imagined as a meaningful part of a larger pattern of action that affirms health, well-being, and transcendence even in the face of human limits.

------

2.   *The ethics of euthanasia and suicide also involve basic ethical issues of transcendence.* Euthanasia and suicide go to the heart of ultimate questions regarding the meaning and value of human life. In euthanasia, the question arises: Are there conditions under which a life could be classified as not worth living? Defenders of the right to euthanasia point to conditions of unrelievable pain, unbearable suffering, or irrevocable loss of consciousness as limitations on the meaning and value of human life. A conscious decision to terminate such a life would not be regarded as defeat, but as an act of transcendence that rises above the physical limits of pain, suffering, and impairment to maintain the dignity of human life. Opponents of euthanasia, by insisting that no human life is not worth living, must develop an ethics of human suffering. They must propose that suffering has an inherent value, or can be invested with meaning and value, that ultimately enhances, enriches, or ennobles human life. Religious approaches to suffering provide ways of moving through suffering, rather than avoiding suffering. Opponents of euthanasia may also see suffering as an opportunity for transcendence; it is a transcendence of physical limits that

is demonstrated by the ability to move through suffering in a supportive environment of family, friends, and loved ones.

The ethical issue of suicide also engages the challenge of transcendence. Suicide may be viewed as a transcendent release from the ordeals, trials, and tribulations of life. Suicide may be interpreted as the one moment, as Artaud suggested, in which the individual imposes a pattern of his or her own design upon the disorder of ordinary life. There is a vestige of transcendence in such a self-willed control over the otherwise uncontrollable forces of life and death. When Albert Camus claimed that suicide is the only truly serious philosophical issue, he recognized that whatever meaning and value human beings experience in life is created in the face of the imminent possibility of their own deaths. The potential for self-destruction intensifies the human potential for self-affirmation, self-realization, and the transcendence of even self-imposed limits on the human life cycle. To turn from suicide is to return to the creation of meaning and value within the patterns and processes of life.

------

3.   *The human response to death is also a response to life.* Imagining the end of the human life cycle provides opportunities for affirming, or reaffirming, transcendence in the face of human limit situations. Human beings seem to be unique among animal species in their awareness of their own mortality. Religious approaches to death need not be regarded, as Freud seemed to regard them, as imaginary avoidance mechanisms for denying human mortality. Rather, they can be seen as creative, imaginative, and ultimately human ways of engaging death with integrity. Human integrity in facing death is revealed in the way that the meaning human beings attribute to their own deaths reflects back on the meaning of life itself. Even if death is felt as something to be feared, it may still be invested with a meaning that reflects on the value, significance, and purpose of

life. The ethics of euthanasia and suicide are ultimately approaches to death that strive to reaffirm the meaning and value of life. Defenders and opponents of these practices are both attempting to define the terms of transcendence in human life by which death can be faced with integrity. These ethical challenges at the end of the human life cycle reveal the potential for transcendence that may, in fact, permeate the entire course of a truly human life.

The variety of ethical rules that govern personal ethics in the human life cycle supports deeper constellations of ethical values. The rules for right action, right conduct, and right behavior serve underlying ethical values of goodness in human action. Good actions are regarded as good because they sustain certain experiences that human beings feel they need, want, and desire. Good actions sustain the experience of values. The values seem to be inherent in certain patterns of action that are valued by a religious tradition, society, or community. The ethics of death provides human beings an opportunity to reaffirm, or re-evaluate, the ethical values of life within their personal experience. In a larger sense, those values are not simply embodied in a process of personal development, but they are shared within a network of human social relations. Part Three is concerned with identifying, analyzing, and interpreting the ethical values of social relations.

P A R T

THREE

ETHICAL VALUES IN HUMAN SOCIAL RELATIONS

*H*uman social relations necessarily involve ethical challenges in the definition, production, exchange, and preservation of values. The ethics of social relations within any human community evaluates those organized social institutions that are dedicated to the service of values, those techniques for producing, actualizing, or realizing values, those social systems for the exchange and distribution of values, and strategies for the collective reinforcement, protection, and preservation of values. In the modern world, crucial issues of social ethics have arisen in relation to questions of value concerning the role of institutions in mass societies, behavioral patterns of work and leisure, the emergence of a pervasive technological ethos, the impact of technology on the natural environment, the role of goods, money, and economic exchange in human social relations, the problem of scarcity, and the ethics of violence, war, and the prospect of

nuclear destruction. These issues have become focal points for the ethics of social relations in the modern world.

Part Three is an interpretive analysis of ethical patterns in modern social relations from the vantage point of the history of religions. It is an archaeological excavation of patterns of ethical action in the modern world and patterns of ethical value in what might be called the modern worldview. The arena for ethical action constructed by modern institutional arrangements, technology, economic exchange, and strategies for collective survival can be analyzed with reference to characteristic, traditional patterns of action in the history of religions. The type of comparative analysis pursued here is temporal comparison. Traditional and modern patterns of action in the service of ethical values are juxtaposed to allow accute ethical dilemmas of modern social relations to appear in a new light. This section explores the major issues of value in the ethics of social relations.

Chapter 9 outlines the ways in which a pervasive worldview in modern, western, industrialized societies is embodied in social institutions. Any worldview has two basic dimensions: (1) orientation in time and space, and (2) the classification of persons as "like us" and "not like us." The arrangement of institutions in modern societies can be interpreted to reveal how social institutions embody these two dimensions of a worldview. There are modern institutions of orientation, which perform many of the functions of traditional religions in orienting human beings toward the experience of values. And there are modern institutions of exclusion, which are designed to eliminate those persons from society who have been classified as "not like us." In this respect, religion in the modern world is not simply a separate, distinct institution in competition with other economic, political, and social institutions over the definition of ethical values; rather, religion, or a religious worldview, exists as the pattern of powerful symbols, myths, rituals, and ethical values that permeates the entire network of social relations. Specialized scientific, educational, medical, legal, economic, and political institutions perform many of the traditional functions of religion in orienting human beings toward the experience of values. Prisons, asylums, and other institutions of exclusion perform the functions of traditional rituals of exclusion in reinforcing a sense of Us by excluding Them from full participation in the arena of values. Social institutions, therefore, embody a network of ethical values. They may also frustrate the experience of values by treating values as commodities to be defined, produced, and distributed by institutions, thereby putting human beings in a passive position in relation to the experience of values. The experience of values is the central ethical dilemma posed by institutions in the modern world. Chapter 9 is called *Institutions*.

Chapter 10 examines the pervasive role of technology in the modern world and the technological ethos in the modern worldview. Traditional attitudes toward the value of human action have tended to designate three spheres of action: ritual devoted to the value of meaning, work devoted to the value of utility, and leisure devoted to the value of pleasure. If all human action can be seen as performed in the interests of meaning, utility, or pleasure, then the modern technological ethos can be interpreted as an orientation toward the value of human social action that factors out questions of human meaning and pleasure in the exclusive interest of technological usefulness. Technical efficiency, rationalized organization, systematic exploitation of resources, and utility for its own sake have emerged as self-justifying practical values in this technological ethos. The power that has been generated by this technological ethos, and that has been supported by trends in traditional, western environmental ethics, is one of the most influential forces shaping ethical patterns of action in the modern world. Alternative ethical resources within traditional religions have been called upon, and post-industrial ethical orientations have emerged, to address the challenge posed by the *technopower* that pervades the modern worldview. Chapter 10 addresses the meaning and value of technology as one of the most crucial ethical issues of modern social relations. This chapter is called *Technology*.

Chapter 11 is concerned with the possession, exchange, and distribution of values in human social relations. One important index to social value is found in the world of goods. Goods are not simply good for having, consuming, or displaying: They are a meaningful communication system that symbolizes the shape of the human social world and locates persons within that world. The exchange of goods brings human beings into socially patterned interaction, cooperation, and competition. The pattern of market exchange in modern, western, industrialized societies, which seems to have transformed all human beings into "economic animals" whose value can be measured in monetary terms, is only one pattern of economic exchange in human societies. A comparison of systems of economic exchange based on reciprocity, redistribution, and a market economy reveals the different ethical principles and ethical patterns of interaction that are possible in human economies. Religion enters the ethics of economic exchange through patterns of action that address economic inequalities through acts of charity, through analyses of the significance of scarcity, and through different appreciations of the meaning of material wealth. On a deeper level, religious patterns of action are implicated in economics to the extent that exchange is a total social fact involving social, political, religious, as well as purely economic factors. Very different religious orientations toward value are inherent in patterns of economic exchange based on reciprocity, redistribution, or a market economy. Chapter 11 interprets the religious ethics of goods, exchange, and scarcity to develop an appreciation of these differences. This chapter is called *Economics.*

The final chapter of Part Three, Chapter 12, explores the religious ethics of violence, war, and the nuclear age. Here the concern is with strategies for the reinforcement, protection, and preservation of the collective values at stake in the survival of a social group. This chapter returns to a more broadly based, comparative survey of religious ethics in the analysis of traditional ethics of military violence, war, and warfare in the history of religions. Sacred warfare in some religious traditions reinforces a sense of the sanctified order of the world through military ceremonials, decorative weapons, and rules of martial etiquette. Sacred war appears as a ritual enactment of patterns of social order with respect to some larger sense of cosmic order. Holy warfare in other religious traditions serves to carry out the will, designs, and work of a transcendent god. In holy wars the ethical intention is not simply to reinforce order, but to eliminate evil by eliminating those persons who are perceived as obstructing the will of God. Sacred war and holy war represent two basic ethical orientations toward military violence that have appeared in the history of religions. A third orientation is suggested by those systems of religious ethics that have placed constraints on the exercise of military violence by proposing independent criteria of justice that must be met before legitimately engaging in warfare. Just war theory in western religious thought can be analyzed as an attempt to place ethical limits on the acceptable conditions for entering into war and conducting warfare. Finally, the prospect of nuclear war, destruction, and annihilation has posed new problems for ethical imagination in the modern world. Chapter 12 considers ethical responses to the nuclear age, responses confronting a challenge that not only involves the reinforcement, protection, and preservation of human values held by a particular social group, but also a threat to the survival of humanity and, by extension, all human values. This final chapter is called *Survival.*

CHAPTER

NINE

INSTITUTIONS

Institutions are organized patterns of social action in the service of values. Social institutions are designed to produce the basic values that human beings feel they need, want, or desire. They are collective social projects for the production of the goods that are valued by any given society. Ethical values in human social relations can be identified in the network of institutions designed to affirm, reinforce, or provide those values. These institutions give tangible form and structure to the underlying ethical values supported by a community. We will analyze the relation between institutions and values in order to enter into an interpretation of ethical values in human social relations.

The pattern of institutions supports a society's most fundamental worldview. A *worldview* is that basic perspective from which people perceive, interpret, and imagine the world they inhabit. As the anthropologist Robert Redfield noted, a worldview is "the way a man, in a particular society, sees himself in relation to all else."[1] The shared worldview of a community is embodied in its institutions. In modern societies, social institutions have become highly differentiated. Institutions of education, labor, science, government, medicine, and so on fulfill different specialized functions. This specialization has had important consequences in shaping modern worldviews and in creating the context in which ethical values are experienced in human social relations.

Even religion has become isolated as a specialized institution in the modern world; religion has become simply one specialized institution among many in modern societies. This differentiation of religion from the rest of society has contributed to the sense that religion has lost much of its traditional power in the modern world. And yet the power of religion, in terms of an underlying and pervasive worldview, may be diffused through the entire pattern of social institutions. Specialized institutions of science and learning, health and healing, work and leisure, government, law, and nationalism perform many of the basic social functions that were once performed by traditional religions. In this sense, it is possible to recognize visible and invisible religion in the modern world. Religion is visible as a specialized institution, and it may be visibly embodied in a variety of religious associations, organizations, and movements. But a religious worldview, with a rich vocabulary of symbols, myths, and rituals, invisibly pervades the pattern of modern institutions to the extent that they perform social functions that have been ascribed to religious traditions.

The underlying religious worldview that pervades modern social institutions can be identified in terms of the basic ethical values to which these institutions are dedicated. Two types of institutions support the modern worldview and reinforce its most basic ethical values: institutions of orientation and institutions of exclusion. Institutions of orientation correspond to that dimension of a religious worldview that orients human beings to their world. These institutions give shape, structure, and design to the human world of values. The institutions of religion, education, labor, science, government, and medicine provide a basic orientation toward ethical values in human social relations. Each specialized institution is designed to produce a specific set of values. The problem that arises in modern institutions, however, is this very notion that values are commodities produced by institutions. Values are treated as if they were goods to be created, produced, and distributed by institutions. This places human beings in a passive orientation to values. The central ethical challenge common to all these institutions of orientation is the question of responsibility for ethical values. Are values

commodities that can be acquired from institutions? Or are they experiences that can only be generated through personal patterns of ethical action?

The second type of social arrangement that reinforces the ethical values of the modern worldview takes the form of institutions of exclusion. Institutions of exclusion correspond to that dimension of a religious worldview that classifies people. Any religious worldview makes distinctions between Us and Them: Some people are classified as "like us," while others are classified as "not like us." Traditional religions have employed a variety of rituals of exclusion in order to exclude people who are "not like us." These rituals remove people from society who are not fulfilling what are considered to be legitimate social roles. Excommunication, banishment, and even execution have been employed as ritual acts of exclusion. By excluding people who do not fulfill legitimate social roles in the community, a society reinforces its own identity. By excluding Them, we reinforce a sense of Us. The primary institutions of exclusion in modern societies are the prison and the asylum. We will consider the ethical values in human social relations that are reinforced through these institutions of exclusion.

This exploration of the ethical values invested in social institutions is an exercise in worldview analysis. The pattern of social institutions in modern societies can be analyzed to reveal a fundamentally religious worldview. This worldview is a way of looking at the world that is shaped by these institutions. The modern worldview, therefore, is embedded in specialized institutions of orientation and exclusion. Analysis of these institutions may help to clarify ethical values—those goods that are inherent in human action—as they are experienced in modern social relations and as they are often frustrated by the very institutions that are designed to produce them.

Religion, Institutions, and Values

Religion as Worldview

Worldview may be useful as an alternative term for *religion*. Every religious tradition necessarily embodies a worldview. And that worldview shapes the way in which persons look at themselves in relation to everything else. Worldview has this comprehensive capacity to organize every aspect of human belief, action, and experience. A worldview is more, therefore, than simply a way of looking at the world. It sets the stage for action. A worldview is the living context in which human actions make sense to the very people who are acting and to the community in which they act. A worldview determines the context within which a community is able to make ethical judgments regarding what is, and what is not, good action.

Religion as Worldview

Since the worldviews of various traditions, cultures, and communities differ, human beings actually inhabit very different worlds. Yet, every worldview necessarily defines the relationship between self and environment in terms of two basic dimensions: (1) orientation in time and space, and (2) the classification of people. The identification of these two necessary aspects of any worldview—orientation and classification—provides the basis for an exploration of the relation between ethical values and institutions in the modern worldview.

First, it is important to recognize that a worldview defines the basic arena of human action in space and time. Worldviews orient human beings within the spatial and temporal coordinates of their world. "Every worldview," the anthropologist Robert Redfield observed, "includes some spatial and temporal dimensions . . . man is necessarily oriented to a universe of extension and duration."[2] This orientation in time and space locates people within a meaningful universe. It provides a sense of that universe's center and boundaries, its shape, contours, and textures, its movement and direction. This sense of temporal and spatial order in a worldview overcomes what the historian of religions Mircea Eliade has called "the vertigo brought on by disorientation."[3] A sense of orientation is necessary for human beings to act in a coherently ordered world, and a sense of orientation in time and space is the first ingredient in any worldview.

Second, a worldview provides a symbolic vocabulary for classifying people. A worldview involves a classification system that identifies, categorizes, and separates people into different types. In the words of Robert Redfield, a worldview classifies "groupings of people, some intimate and similar to oneself, others far and different."[4] Some people are classified as similar, others as strange, foreign, and fundamentally different. This process of classification Redfield calls "the essential distinction between Them and Us."[5] Some people are classified as "like us." Other people, whether within a given society, or residing outside its boundaries, are classified as "not like us." This classification of people categorizes not only foreigners as not like us. Even within a single network of social relations, a worldview sets the terms by which members of the community may be judged by their different, strange, or deviant behavior to be fundamentally "not like us." This systematic classification of people is the second basic ingredient in any worldview.

When a community shares a common religious tradition, that tradition provides a shared worldview for orientation in time and space and the classification of people. The community is unified by that shared, common worldview. In the modern world, however, traditional worldviews have come under tremendous pressures of social, economic, and political changes in human social relations. All people in modern, western, industrialized societies may not share the same worldview, but they all come under certain social pressures that have had a formative effect in the modern world. These pressures have informed what we might call the modern worldview.

The Modern Worldview

There is some controversy over the use of the term *modern* to characterize a society. The term should not suggest that modern means better, or that modernization is a necessary, or inevitable, process of development. The modern world is also made up of many traditional, or antimodern, movements that resist the forces of social change. However the term is used, any analysis of modern social relations will have to seriously consider two dominant forces that have had a dramatic impact on human worldviews: urbanization and industrialization.

Urban social arrangements are not new, but they dominate modern societies. The city is at the center of the modern world, and its power embraces vast territories within the elaborate network of its domain. *Civilization* (from the Latin word for city) in the modern sense means the extension of the domain of the city over all forms of rural, agricultural, or village life. Modern cities have their own builtin ethical order. Urban space requires a high degree of standardization, conformity, and efficiency. It depends for its very existence on the efficiency of its networks of sanitation, transportation, and communication. The city demands a high standard of uniform efficiency as its primary criterion for collective ethical action in human social relations.

Urban time requires a precise regulation of human rhythms. The sociologist Georg Simmel observed that urban interactions are so complex, diverse, and varied "that without the strictest punctuality in promises and services the whole structure would break down into inextricable chaos."[6] The urban cosmos is maintained through a stable, impersonal, and universal time schedule. The regulated rhythms of urban time eliminate irrational, instinctive, and spontaneous impulses in the interests of an ethical order of punctuality, calculability, and exactness. Since the Industrial Revolution, urban space and time have dominated western societies. Most people are either located in or are dependent on its distinctive ethical order. It has been noted, for example, that America was born in the country and moved to the city.[7] Modern social relations in America have come under the domain of the urban ethical order.

Industry plays a central role in the modern universe. The Industrial Revolution revolutionized more than simply the machinery of production. Industrialization dramatically altered the traditional network of social relations, the character of the family and the household, and the conception of what it is to be an individual. The central ordering principle of industry is mechanization. The sociologist Max Weber was concerned with the effect of industrialized mechanization on the ethical status of human beings. In mechanized labor "the individual is shorn of his natural rhythm as determined by the structure of his organism."[8] The standards of industrial efficiency gradually came to dominate all other ethical considerations, and the human being began to appear as "only a single cog in an evermoving mechanism which prescribes to him an essentially fixed route of march."[9]

This image of the individual as a single element, an interchangeable part, in the social machinery conflicts with notions of the modern individual as a free moral agent who is able to make choices from a range of options. Max Weber perceptively pointed to this contradiction. In the modern worldview the standardized, regulated, and mechanical individual is assumed to be the pinnacle of a long process of human evolution. Weber observed, however, that unless some unexpected changes occur "mechanism will produce only petrification hidden under a kind of anxious importance. . . . Specialists without spirit, libertines without heart, this nothingness imagines itself to be elevated to a level of humanity never before attained."[10] Urban space and time, along with the industrialized mechanization that supports their distinctive rhythms, have established the primary arena for ethical action in the modern world.

Other factors have contributed to this process of modernization. An inventory of these factors would have to include mass communication media—with the explosion of available information, particularly through television, which has replaced religious symbols, myths, and rituals as the principle mode of communication; standardized education—with a priority on the technology of literacy, the development of specialized skills, and technical, scientific, and quantitative approaches to knowledge; and pluralism—with the ongoing collision of religious and secular ideologies threatening the stability of local, particular, or traditional religions. These developments have all disrupted traditional religious worldviews. In combination, they create what the sociologist David Martin has called "an alien environment for traditional religion."[11]

This tension between traditional religions and modernity has been pointed out in strong terms by Ernest Gellner:

> *The intellectual advances of recent centuries have corroded the inherited belief-systems beyond recovery: the widening of horizons, the flowing together of so many "forms of life" into one Babel-like and rapidly evolving civilization, have also made unacceptable the old, local, particularistic, asymmetrical faiths (except as sentimental links with the past).*[12]

Gellner's choice of words is significant: Traditional religions are peceived as asymmetrical because they do not fit the rationalized, uniform, and efficient symmetry demanded by modernization.

For all this dramatic change, and in spite of the apparent displacement of traditional religions, religion persists in the modern world more than might be expected. The disruption of traditional religious forms has been accompanied by a diffusion of a religious worldview and ethos throughout a range of social institutions. Although institutions have gone through dramatic realignment, basic human, ethical, and religious values have remained fairly constant. These values are now being served by social institutions of education, labor, science, government, and medicine, which are not labeled "religious," yet nevertheless serve ethical values that were once the province of traditional religions. We will look more closely at the relation between institutions and the ethical values of human social relations.

Institutions and Values

Institutions are social systems that organize material and human resources in the service of values. They are relatively stable practices, relationships, or organizations concerned with accomplishing social goals. In this sense, institutions are necessarily involved in the process of valuation. They operate with implicit, and often explicit, sets of norms, objectives, and values. Institutions are committed to realizing those values that are held to be good within a network of social relations. The anthropologist Bronislaw Malinowski defined an institution as a group of people united for a common purpose, with (1) some degree of systematic organization, (2) support from a material base to its operation, and (3) a system of ideas, or an ideology, from which it forms plans to carry out its purpose.[13] From Malinowski's functionalist point of view, institutions are believed to fulfill individuals' basic needs within a social system. An institution's primary function is to enable people to realize their values in action.

At the same time, social institutions draw people into specific roles, organized patterns of behavior, and structured interactions that correspond to the values represented by the institution. The sociologist Erving Goffman has noted that "every institution captures something of the time and interest of its members and provides something of a world for them; in brief, every institution has encompassing tendencies."[14] Institutions encourage people to need, want, and desire certain values by means of this encompassing tendency to create the world in which they act. Institutions of education, for example, may fulfill the need for advanced training, credentials, or degrees that the institutions themselves have created within the larger network of social relations. Social institutions are in the business of values, whether they fulfill basic human needs, or whether they in fact create the needs for the valued services they provide.

Institutions also serve to frustrate the realization of values. Many institutions seem to be counterproductive. They do not satisfy the needs, wants, or desires that they are intended to satisfy. This is particularly the case with modern institutions—religion, education, labor, science, government, and medicine—when they no longer are groups of people united in a common purpose, but social organizations that have taken over the responsibility for the production of val-

ues. As providers of the things that human beings need, want, or desire, institutions tend to treat these values as if they were commodities. Values are treated as if they were goods that could be created, manufactured, and distributed by institutions. This places human beings in a passive relationship to values, as if people were consumers of the goods they desire from institutions. Basic ethical values are not commodities; they are experiences: an experience of the sacred, an experience of historical continuity, an experience of vitality, an experience of knowledge, an experience of order, security, and safety, an experience of health. These ethical patterns of action in modern social relations tend to be treated as if they were commodities to be provided by institutions.

When modern human beings do not experience these basic ethical values in human social relations—when they do not experience what they feel they need, want, or desire—they tend to conclude that the institutions did not deliver the values. Institutions of religion have failed to produce a sense of the sacred, education has failed to produce learning, law has failed to produce order, medicine has failed to produce health, and so on. However, these basic values—the satisfaction of human needs, wants, and desires—can only be experienced through action. They may be experiences inherent in a pattern of ethical action. For example, to experience the value of love it is necessary to act in ways that are loving. Love is not a value that can be created, produced, and distributed by an institution as if it were a commodity. This may also be true of other ethical values.

What would it mean to be responsible for values? We have considered several different meanings of the word *responsibility*. First, there was the sense in which responsibility meant to take ethical obligation seriously: To feel bound to an ethical obligation is to feel responsible, to internalize its requirements and demands. Second, there was the sense in which responsibility meant the ability to respond creatively to the ethical challenges posed by the situations and circumstances of life; it is the ability to respond in a variety of ways to the demands of obligation. A third sense of the word suggests the possibility of taking responsibility for experiencing values as goods that are inherent in a pattern of ethical action. Values are not external goods to be acquired from institutions, but they are internal goods inherent in action. The challenge of taking responsibility for the experience of values is the central issue posed by institutions in the ethics of modern social relations.

Institutions of Orientation in Time and Space

In order to clarify the relation between values and institutions in the modern worldview, we must examine in detail those institutions that give visible, tangible, and concrete shape to the modern orientation in time and space. These institutions orient human beings toward ethical values within the temporal and spatial dimensions of human experience. This worldview analysis suggests that modern institutions correspond to traditional values that they are designed to serve.

The corresponding values and institutions can be outlined as in Table 3 below.

This chart outlines the different dimensions of temporal and spatial orientation that are governed by institutions in the modern worldview. Each modern institution addresses a basic ethical value that traditionally has been within the domain of religion. This suggests the underlying structure of a religious worldview that pervades these various institutions.

TABLE 3	TRADITIONAL VALUES	MODERN INSTITUTIONS
Orientation in Time		
COSMIC TIME	Experience of the Sacred	Religion
HISTORICAL TIME	Experience of Continuity	Education
BODY TIME	Experience of Vitality	Labor
Orientation in Space		
COSMIC SPACE	Experience of Knowledge	Science
GEOGRAPHICAL SPACE	Experience of Order	Government
BODY SPACE	Experience of Health	Medicine

Modern institutions are designed to produce a range of basic human values, but it will be important to remember that these values are experiences that are integral to an ethical pattern of action. The values are ingredients that contribute to an experience of ethical harmony in social action. To treat these values as commodities, however, introduces a sense of scarcity, lack, or deprivation into the human experience of values. Assuming that a value (such as learning) is a commodity that can only be obtained from an institution (schools, colleges, and universities) implies that the value is not abundantly available through immediate action. In modern societies, values of health, order, knowledge, vitality, continuity, and even a sense of the sacred are treated as scarce commodities controlled by institutions. This accounts for the counterproductivity that is endemic to modern institutions; the counterproductivity of institutions is a direct result of treating values as commodities that can be produced by institutions. If values are goods that are inherent in a pattern of ethical action, they cannot be acquired from institutions, but can only be experienced through a direct involvement, participation, and commitment that takes an active responsibility for the experience of values. We will explore these institutions of orientation in more detail.

Orientation in Time

We experience the flow of time in a number of different ways. Some times move fast, others slow. Sometimes we waste time, lose time, or kill time. Some times are special times and seem to remain alive in our memories; other times are forgotten. Our most immediate experience of time is in the rhythms, movements, and life of our bodies. This is *body time*. There is also a sense of time shared by the collective memory of a group of people, a sense of the group's continuous existence, important past events, and illustrious ancestors. This is *historical time*. Finally, we may have some sense of the rhythms of the universe, perhaps its beginning and end, perhaps its eternal pulse. This is *cosmic time*. These three dimensions of time are involved in the temporal dimension of any worldview.

Cosmic Time

A religious worldview provides a sense of renewal, regeneration, or rebirth, in and out of the flow of time. This renewal of time is accomplished through patterns of ritual action that set out special moments of sanctified time in holy days, festivals, and celebrations of the sacred calendar. It is also achieved through the various rites of passage during the course of the human life cycle. Often these rituals reenact, recapitulate, or refer to cosmic creation myths, and they allow the celebrants to step out of the ordinary flow of time to participate directly in the creative power of that sacred time. Religious ethics also offers an orientation to cosmic time by supporting a basic conviction that human life has a *telos*—an end, a purpose, a goal—to which human actions in the world are ultimately leading.

The traditional value in this process of orientation in cosmic time is an experience of the sacred. It is an experience that transforms ordinary time into sacred time. The present value in the experience of sacred time is that it transforms human experience of the flow of time to produce a sense of regeneration. The projected value of the experience of the sacred lies in the potential for some kind of salvation, the transformation of time into eternity.

The modern institution designed to provide this value is religion. One problem in analyzing modern religion is that this distinctive, specialized institution—religion—goes by the same name that is also used to designate a worldview, a life style, or a system of meaning and value in other cultures. This is no accident: Most societies do not have a term for religion as a separate institution. The institutionalization of religion is the result of the specialization, differentiation, and segmentation of all aspects of culture in the modern world. Religion takes on the character of any other institutional organization within modern societies. Religions become bureaucratic institutions dedicated to administrative rationality and criteria of efficiency. The model for modern institutional religion may be those late nineteenth century urban evangelists in America who boasted of the relative cost-effectiveness of their conversions. The efficient religious organization was able to save souls like an efficient business produces commodities. Institutionalized religion has become one of the largest business operations in modern America.

The sociologist Bryan Wilson observed that the "commodity of religion" is advice about, and training in, the necessary steps for salvation.[15] In other words, the business of religion is providing an experience of cosmic time in the promise of eternal salvation. The problem with treating this value as a commodity is that when people do not experience the present value of sacred time, or lose confidence in the institution's ability to produce the projected value of future salvation, they conclude that religion has failed. The failure of religion in the modern world has been documented by a number of indicators: a decline in membership and attendance, fewer church marriages, baptisms, and confirmations. These indicators have been used to provide statistical evidence of a certain institutional decline in religion within modern societies. Wilson has pointed to a decline in religious participation and religion's decreased effect on the human life cycle.[16] The sociologist Charles Glock has concluded that religious ethics has less and less influence on secular, nonreligious structures of value in the modern world.[17]

This sense of failure, decline, and ineffectiveness suggests a degree of counterproductivity in the institution of religion. The value of sacred time cannot be distributed as if it were a commodity; it requires a high degree of direct involvement, participation, and engagement with actions that immediately transform the experience of time. Perhaps this is why various forms of religious enthusiasm—what the psychologist Robert Lifton has called experiential transcendence—through entertainment, sporting events, mind-altering drugs, ecstatic dancing, speaking in tongues, and exotic religious practices have been so popular as means of transforming the experience of time of modern individuals.[18] These enthusiastic experiences are survivals of traditional ritual strategies for experiencing sacred time through action in the here and now. They may be attempts to recover the immediacy of an experience of sacred time as an ethical value.

Historical Time

The traditional religious process of orientation in historical time provides a community with a shared, collective identity by generating a sense of continuity with the past and a projected continuity with the future. A sense of historical time is located in a community's collective memory and its collective hopes and aspirations. Orientation in historical time is achieved through the recollection of mythic stories of gods, founders, and culture-heroes, which illustrate the ways of the ancestors. Most traditional ethical instruction takes this form. The Hebrew Bible, for example, illustrates the power of sacred history in the religion of ancient Israel. Every year the 12 tribes gathered at a shrine for a covenant renewal ceremony. The renewal of the covenant that bound these tribal groups together in a common identity began with the recitation of the sacred history of the patriarchs, the captivity in Egypt, the exodus of the people of Israel, and their triumphant entrance into the promised land. (Josh. 24) To give the 12 tribes a common story was to give them a shared identity that would transcend any present differences.

The value in this process of orientation in historical time is an experience of continuity, the sense that every individual within that community shares in a creative continuity between the past and the future. Personal identity, therefore, transcends the limits of the life cycle and connects with ancestors and offspring who share in this common, continuous, and, to a certain extent, immortal cultural tradition. This experience of continuity is a basic ethical value within human social relations.

The institution in modern societies that is designed to provide this value of continuity is education. Education is that social institution that indoctrinates young people into the shared cultural myths of the past and introduces them to skills that allow for a continuity of the cultural tradition into the future. Past and future meet in the educational process. This quasireligious function of modern educational institutions has prompted the historian of American religion Robert Michaelsen to ask: "Is the public school religious or secular?"[19] The public school movement, which received its greatest impetus in the 1870s during a period of rapid immigration, indoctrinated new Americans into the myths, rituals, and ethics of a common civil religion. Immigrants from many different ethnic, cultural, and religious backgrounds were given a common identity by being initiated into American values through the public schools. "The common school," Michaelsen noted, "has been the primary center in and around which this common religionizing has gone on."[20] The public school appears to be the established church of American civil religion, the institution designed to provide this basic value of historical continuity. Institutions of education were formed to produce "a kind of homogenizing effect in which all differ-

ences would disappear in one great nationalistic faith, and in its church, the public school."[21]

Educational experience, therefore, is more than simply learning information and skills; it is an initiation into the historical continuity of a shared tradition. Many observers, however, feel that the commodity of learning is not being produced by public institutions of education. Malcolm Muggeridge, for example, has complained of the failure of education to produce the values for which it was designed: "Education, the great mumbo-jumbo and fraud of the age, purports to equip us to live, and is prescribed as a universal remedy for everything from juvenile delinquency to premature senility. For the most part, it only serves to enlarge stupidity, inflate conceit, enhance credulity. . . ."[22] The problem with institutions of education lies in treating learning as a commodity that could be produced by an institution. Learning only occurs through the active participation of the learner. It requires an awakening of interest, attention, enthusiasm, and even love. Learning involves an active participation in a continuous cultural tradition that cannot be forced, disciplined, or manipulated. This experience probably cannot even be given, but seems to be something caught like a spark. One critic of public education has called for a "disestablishment" of educational institutions.[23] Compulsory educational institutions may work against the kind of free, moral response that is necessary to participate fully in the living continuity of a historical tradition.

Body Time   Traditional religions cultivate distinctive orientations toward the body. The awareness, energies, and rhythms of the body are molded according to ideal cultural patterns. In ritual, the rhythms of the body are regulated in sacred patterns of physical action: kneeling, bowing, or prostrating in positions of prayer, practicing certain postures (such as the *asanas* of yoga), movements (such as the flowing rhythms of the

Chinese sacred martial art of *Tai Chi Chuan*), or gestures (such as the *mudras* of Tantric Buddhism). These patterns of action all cultivate a structured awareness of the body. Religious ethics channels the energies of the body into social behavior patterns. Like the disciplined body ethics we examined in Chapter 6, religious ethics patterns the movements of the body, the standards of distance and proximity between bodies, and the normative rhythms of sleeping and waking, work and rest.

The value in these temporal orientations to the rhythms of the body is the experience of vitality. It is the value of life itself. Life is not something abstract; it is lived out in the detailed actions of the body: its movements, its rhythms, its energy. Sigmund Freud was once asked if he could describe the secret of a happy life. His answer was simple: work and love. The vitality of life is derived from experiencing the body through useful and pleasurable activity. The value of life itself is supported through work and love in human social relations.

The modern institution designed to support and sustain the vitality of human life is labor. Modern human beings work in order to live; but often they live in order to conform to the demands of work. Institutions of employment, based on the model of wage labor, have become the dominant means of regulating the rhythms of the body. Modern institutions of labor place strict demands on the performance of the body in ways that guarantee regularity, repetition, and efficiency of movement. The goals of industrial, administrative, and rational efficiency have placed the body in a unique situation. Body time has undergone a profound mutation. A common standard of time regulation has come to be shared by both employers and employees. As the historian Asa Briggs has noted, with the advent of the Industrial Revolution "time, which had acquired a new significance for the employer, had to acquire a new significance for the employee."[24] Time became defined by a common

regimentation, discipline, and coordination of the body. E. P. Thompson has described how work-discipline produced a specific orientation toward body time, "by the division of labor; the supervision of labor; fines; bells and clocks; money incentives; preachings and schoolings; the suppression of fairs and sports—new labor habits were formed, and new time discipline was imposed."[25] In this time discipline, a new sense of the body's movements, rhythms, and energies was enforced through institutions of labor.

An important reversal occurred through the mechanization of labor in the relation between the body and its tools. Where tools may once have been extensions of the body's own energy, they now molded the body to their own demands. The movements, rhythms, and energies of the body had to conform to the requirements of the machine. "It is no longer the body's movement that determines the implement's movement," as Hannah Arendt has observed, "but the mechanism's movement which enforces the movements of the body."[26] Body time becomes regulated by the machine, and the experience of vitality in physical action becomes increasingly mechanical. Perhaps this discipline of the body is one of the major reasons for the boredom, frustration, and alienation reported in the modern workplace. The mechanization of body time separates work from love. It isolates the value of usefulness from any pleasurable experience of the body's own vitality in action. Modern institutions of labor tend to discipline body time in the interests of utility, but to the exclusion of pleasure.

In the temporal dimension of the modern worldview, body time is regulated by institutions of labor, historical time is provided by institutions of education, and cosmic time is mediated by religious institutions. These institutions structure the three levels of temporal orientation in the modern worldview. They provide the primary arenas for their corresponding ethical values to be either experienced or frustrated. Next, we must examine those institutions of orientation that relate to the spatial dimension of the modern worldview. Modern orientations in space provide the second dimension that needs to be analyzed in this interpretation of ethical values in the modern world.

Orientation in Space

We experience space in a number of different ways. In some places we feel at home, in others we are out of place. We may feel we need space, or feel lost in space, or maybe just "spaced out." Some spaces are special, others are ordinary. Our most immediate experience of space is that dimension given to our world by our bodies. We may be in shape, out of shape, or in bad shape. This is *body space*. There is also a sense of the space that is shared by a community. A network of social relations may have centers around which its life revolves and boundaries that set its limits. It may also create a sense of what lies beyond those boundaries. This is *geographical space*. Finally, there is some sense of the larger shape and pattern of the universe, a sense of the extension of things from the smallest to the largest, from the highest to the lowest. This is *cosmic space*. As in the experience of time, these three aspects of spatial orientation are interwoven in a worldview. We will examine the relation between values and institutions within the spatial orientation of the modern worldview.

Cosmic Space　　One traditional function of religion is to provide a sense of where human beings fit into the scheme of things. A religious orientation locates the place of human beings in the cosmos. What is the ultimate shape of the universe that human beings inhabit? That orientation in cosmic space is very different,

for example, if the sun is a god (as it was for the Egyptian Pharoah Akhenaton), or if the sun revolves around the earth (as it did in the Ptolemaic cosmology), or if the sun is at the center of the universe (as it was for Copernicus), or if the sun is an obscure star at the edge of the Milky Way. Cosmic space represents the most basic ordering of things. Often this ordering is found in creation myths. That order may be *cosmocentric,* such as the creation story in Genesis that describes the cosmic order imposed upon the waters of chaos (Gen. 1.1–2.4a), or that order may be *geocentric,* such as the earth-centered order suggested by the creation story in Genesis that describes how a desert became a garden for human beings to inhabit. (Gen. 2.4b–4) In any case, this ordering represents a basic sense of orientation in cosmic space.

The value in this spatial orientation is knowledge. This knowledge is not simply information; it is a knowledge of the human place in the cosmos. To know one's place in the cosmos is to have a place on which to stand. This knowledge is fundamental to a sense of confidence, security, or awareness that human beings live in a meaningfully ordered universe. The knowledge of spatial orientation also implies that this universe can be measured. It can be measured, as Plato observed, in terms of quantity (number, proportion, and geometrical relations) and in terms of quality (worth, value, desirability, and a general ordering of goods in the universe). This knowledge allows human beings to measure, evaluate, and assess their place in the cosmos.

The modern institution designed to realize this value is science. Science is primarily a method; it is a means of acquiring knowledge about the universe through experimentation. The experimental method depends on specific techniques of measurement, quantification, and the verification of experimental data. But science is also a set of institutional values. The sociologist Robert Merton has analyzed the ethics of modern science in terms of four institutional values that support modern scientific practice. The first value is universalism. Scientific knowledge must be subject to universal criteria. Its truth claims must conform to impersonal, generally accepted, and uniform criteria of judgment based on observation and previously confirmed knowledge. The second value is communalism. Science is a corporate enterprise. The results of research are shared within the scientific community without concern for personal advantage or profit. The third value is disinterest. Scientific knowledge requires objectivity, detachment, and intellectual honesty in its experimental methods. Finally, the fourth institutional value in modern science is skepticism. The results of experimentation must be submitted to logical scrutiny and possible disconfirmation. Only that which has been demonstrated, measured, and quantified can be admitted into the body of legitimate scientific knowledge.[27]

These ethical imperatives embodied in the institution of science overflow into the prevailing worldview of the society that supports it. Science itself becomes a powerful force in the modern worldview. The French philosopher Auguste Comte expected that religion would eventually be replaced by positivist science, and many scientific perspectives on religion have been affected by this assumption. In the modern worldview, science encourages a prevalent orientation toward the cosmos that might be called scientism. Sidney Hook has described this scientific orientation in the modern worldview as "the wholehearted acceptance of scientific method as the only reliable way of reaching truths about the world of nature, society and man."[28] This knowledge of the cosmos, society, and humanity serves the purpose of extending science's domination over nature. Scientific theory is inherently practical in its usefulness for controlling, manipulating, and dominating the natural environment.

Scientific techniques of knowledge and control, however, are unable to provide qualitative knowledge of values in human orientations to the cosmos. The preoccupation of quantification as the only legitimate basis for knowledge in scientific method tends to exclude any consideration of qualitative values. As the institutional values inherent in science become transposed into the modern worldview and diffused throughout society, they are particularly devoid of standards for assessing the value, worth, or desirability of our knowledge. Scientific knowledge about the splitting of atoms, for example, is essentially neutral regarding the uses to which such knowledge may be put. The accumulation of scientific knowledge has its own momentum, and ethical reflection on the value of scientific knowledge lags behind the impetus of scientific and technological innovations. Human beings in the modern world have more data, but they are not sure what to do with it to actualize the most basic ethical value of knowledge in knowing where they stand.

Geographic Space

Every religious tradition has its spiritual geography. This orientation in geographic space yields a sense of the center and the boundaries of the world in which human beings act. Various centering devices may be used, such as altars, trees, mountains, temples, sanctuaries, and churches, to provide a focal point for geographic orientation in a religious worldview. The story of the Achilpa, an Arunta tribe of nomadic food gatherers and small-game hunters in Australia, is a favorite of historians of religion in illustrating the power of symbolic centers to organize a community's internal sense of geographic space. The Achilpa tribe carried a sacred pole that, according to tradition, had been fashioned and sanctified by the god Numbakula. They used the pole as a ritual device to direct their wanderings, moving as a group in the direction it pointed. When this pole was broken, the group was so disoriented that it wandered around aimlessly and then lay down to await death.[29]

Just as important as the sense of center in

providing geographic orientation is the sense of periphery. A community's limits may be set by various marking devices, natural boundaries, and borders. Its limits may also be reinforced through ritual warfare that unifies a group within a shared geographic space against a common enemy outside its boundaries. These devices define the group as a unique, self-contained community by affording a sense of geographic orientation in space.

The value in this form of spatial orientation is order. As Simone Weil remarked, "Order is the first need of all."[30] A community maintains an internal sense of order through the social organization of families, kinship systems, classes, hierarchies, and rulers. The internal order of a society monitors the distribution of resources, goods, and services. This internal order within a geographic area defines a system of justice. In defining the boundaries among societies, regulating their interactions, and providing protection from external dangers, an external geographic order is also established. This external ordering represents a system of security. Justice and security are the two aspects of the value of order in the ethics of human social relations.

The modern institution designed to provide the value of order is government. The modern state is that form of government that has emerged out of a long evolution from societies based on kinship to societies based on territory. A state is the organized, structured, and institutionalized power that is enforced upon a territory. The political power of the state is derived from the fact that it is the only social institution that can legitimately exercise violence, or the threat of violence, in order to control the geographic territory within its domain. Increasingly, the state has assumed the aura of ultimate authority, power, and legitimation that once belonged to religion. The state has assumed ultimate legal authority over human behavior, and it has assumed the authority to demand the ultimate sacrifice of

its citizens to protect its own interests. The historian J. D. Mabbot has defined the state in terms of the spatial order it enforces over a territory. A state is "an association distinguished by (a) territorial limits, (b) inclusiveness within those limits, (c) the power in its officers to exercise force and the fear of force as instruments of policy, and (d) the possession by its officers of ultimate legal authority."[31] We must keep these elements in mind when considering the institutions of justice and security that enforce order within the state.

The value of justice, in the ordering of the internal space of the state, is provided by the institutions of law. The anthropologist Bronislaw Malinowski suggested that law is simply the rules, customs, or habits of a community which are organized in explicit codes.[32] But, law is more than merely a system of rules. Law is always supported by the use of force. Legal rules are backed up by force or the threat of force. As Robert Redfield insisted, law is "the systematic and formal application of force by the state in support of explicit rules of conduct."[33] Legal institutions enforce a certain pattern of justice within the geographical domain of the state. They enforce a particular distribution of resources, rights, and responsibilities that correspond to that pattern of justice.

The question of social justice in the internal ordering of resources, rights, and responsibilities within a state encounters a problem of authority that is analogous to the role of divine commands in religious ethics. Is a pattern of distribution just simply because a state commands it? Or must a state conform to some independent criteria of social justice? Recent debates on social justice have revolved around two conflicting theories: (1) a theory of justice based on equality and (2) a theory of justice based on the right of entitlement to property. Both theories represent independent criteria for social justice against which a state's internal ordering of geographic space may be evaluated.

In his influential book *A Theory of Justice* the

philosopher John Rawls maintained that justice must be based on equality. He presented this notion of justice in a formula: "Each person is to have an equal right to the most basic liberty compatible with similar liberty for others."[34] When inequalities do arise, they should be distributed throughout the society so that they are to the advantage of the whole. Equality is, therefore, the primary principle that should guide the distribution of resources, rights, and responsibilities within a pattern of social justice. Robert Nozick, in his *Anarchy, State and Utopia,* responded that the only basis for justice in society is not equality, but entitlement. Everyone should be free to acquire, possess, and transfer ownership of property to which they are rightfully entitled. "A distribution is just," according to Nozick, "if everyone is entitled to the holdings that they possess under the distribution."[35] A just order in such a society would protect the right of ownership over private property and would not interfere with the individual's right to dispose of that property in any way he or she saw fit. Justice would not take the form of an equal distribution of resources; it would lie in the inalienable entitlement to acquire, own, and dispose of property.

One theory of justice begins with equality, the other with entitlement. Both, however, assume that institutions can be arranged so as to support these independent criteria of justice. Rawls and Nozick have produced arguments that are internally consistent and compelling to support their ideal patterns of social justice. But the fact that they have been able to produce such compelling, yet incompatible, arguments suggests the ambivalent status of justice in the modern worldview. The internal ordering of modern states does not necessarily depend on such ideal patterns of social justice; rather, it depends on the arbitrary exercise of force to maintain control over the population that inhabits the geographic space within its domain. Defining a pattern of justice, therefore, becomes a struggle within the context of the institutions of legal control that order a network of social relations.

The value of security, the ordering of the external space of the state, is also achieved through force, or the threat of force, in the form of military institutions. Military forces, often referred to in modern states as institutions of defense, are used to maintain a sense of security regarding the boundaries of the state. Military institutions also employ violence, and the threat of violence, to carve out a sense of order, safety, and security in geographic space. We will explore the ethics of military power in more detail in Chapter 12; at this point, it may be important to simply note that military institutions also generate ambivalent attitudes toward the basic value they are designed to serve. Institutions dedicated to preserving national security may also heighten insecurity about the order, safety, and stability of geographic space. The general posture assumed by these institutions in defending national borders, identity, and prestige seems to be: "Pray for peace, but prepare for war." Institutions devoted to mobilizing military power may contribute to an increased sense of insecurity. The result of escalating military power in the modern world, as observed by Winston Churchill, is the current reign of mutual terror that pervades the geographic space of international politics in the nuclear age.

Body Space

One important traditional function of religion is to define the space of the body by creating a sense of its physical, emotional, mental, and spiritual well-being. Rituals of healing provide a specific organization of the space that is defined by the human body. We have already seen how religious traditions create contexts for achieving an experience of the body in healing rituals. The major patterns of action in the healing rituals within western religious traditions were inquisition, invocation, isolation, and integration. Each of these ritual contexts offered a way of working out the experience of dissonance and harmony within the space of the body. The primary value invested in these orientations toward the body is health; it is a sense of well-being, wholeness, and harmony within the space of the body.

The institution in modern societies designed to produce the value of health is scientific medical practice. Religion has given over the responsibility for maintaining the health of the body to the profession of scientific medical practice. Scientific medicine has self-consciously divorced itself from religion. The discourse, knowledge, and power of medical practice have claimed independence from religious ritual. Yet, there are traces of the ritual formats of healing in modern medical practice. Modern versions of traditional western rituals of healing may account for much of what is often experienced as counterproductive in modern medical institutions.

------

1.   *Inquisition has become observation.* Medical practice is conditioned by a basic ritual format: the observation of symptoms. The trained gaze of the physician diagnoses illness by the appearance of symptoms and determines a healthy recovery by their disappearance. Traditional healing practices in Europe and America employed various different senses: tapping the bones and body, listening to the heartbeat, smelling the patient to detect diabetes or typhoid fever, and even tasting the urine to detect sickness or health. But modern medicine has isolated vision as the dominant sense in its ritual of healing. Medical observation provides the standard of diagnosis, and the rituals of healing attack any appearance of symptoms. Medical practice is governed by a visual orientation that includes clinical observation, the microscope, and the X ray. Diagnosis is a knowledge that comes from *seeing* what is wrong, and healing is achieved when doctor and patient can *see* a difference. The

emphasis on vision in medical practice has tended to exclude other ways of symbolizing health through harmony, balance, or positive contact. Also, the treatment of observable symptoms has been preferred over various practices of preventative medicine, holistic healing, and public health measures. Medical observation provides the first ritual context for healing in modern medicine.[36]

------

2.   *Invocation has become professionalization.* The power and authority invoked in modern medical practice is that of an organized, licensed, and accredited medical profession. The medical profession did not always enjoy the unquestioned respect that it seems to today. At one time in American history, a medical career was socially suspect; it did not carry social power, authority, or prestige. In the early nineteenth century, J. Marion Sims, who would become one of America's most prominent surgeons, met resistance when he told his father of his decision to pursue a medical career. Sim's father exclaimed, "If I had known this I certainly would not have sent you to college . . . it is a profession for which I have the utmost contempt. There is no science in it. There is no honor to be achieved in it; no reputation to be made."[37] Even as late as 1870 a medical journal observed that when a young man of potential chooses a medical career, "the feeling among the majority of his cultivated friends is that he has thrown himself away."[38] The professional status of medicine rose largely because of social factors, such as licensing, regulation, and education requirements, which elevated scientific medical practice at the expense of other approaches. Medicine acquired a social authority as a profession that it invokes in its rituals of healing.

------

3.   *Isolation has become confinement.* Modern medical practice is based on a ceremonial institution of exclusion: the hospital. The sick are

systematically separated from society, excluded from the occupations of ordinary life, and isolated from normal interactions with family and friends. The ritual of confinement not only excludes the patient from society, but it shields society from directly encountering the ill, the disabled, or the deformed. The hospital reinforces a pattern of ritual purity in the rest of society. Perhaps this motive of ritual exclusion, separation, and confinement was one reason that the hospital, rather than public health movements, became the preeminent medical institution in the modern world. Public health measures, in changing living conditions, promoting sanitation, purifying water supplies, and improving nutrition, were largely responsible for decreases in infant mortality, lengthened life spans, and better health. Yet the hospital, rather than public health departments, became the social institution with status, power, and vast financial resources in the modern world.[39] The symbolic value of ritual confinement plays an important role in the social status attributed to the hospital as a modern institution.

———

4.   *Integration has become alienation.* The integration of human and divine, spiritual and physical, as dimensions of health (the ideal in ancient Greek medical practice) has given way to an alienation between mind and body in modern medical practice. The healing enterprise has become exclusively physical, as if the body were a machine that has broken down and needs to be taken to a mechanic for repairs. The average person is considered inadequate to perform self-maintenance or repairs. It is necessary to have the training, credentials, and recognized expertise of a medical doctor. The ritual approaches to healing in modern medical practice are often counterproductive because they tend to alienate people from the knowledge and power that is appropriate to their own bodies.

What is the knowledge and power appropriate to the body? Modern medicine suggests that it is knowledge and power that is invested in scientific discourse about the body: the languages of biology, physiology, chemistry, anatomy, and so on. But, as medical discourse has become more sophisticated, and its practices have become more technically complex, this language is increasingly beyond the imagination of the average person. Yet, it is precisely this discourse that sets the terms for the discussion of ethical issues of life and death in medical practice. The ethical imperative facing modern medical practice is to develop a discourse that is imaginable, an approach to the rituals of healing that engages the imaginative energy of the patient. This approach has been the traditional power of rituals of healing. They have provided ways to imagine illness as part of a larger ethical pattern of action. Rituals of healing offer ways of imagining the afflictions of the human condition as phases in the rhythmic alterations between dissonance and harmony. The secret to being healthy all the time may be to redefine health in such a way that it includes being sick. Healing rituals have traditionally provided the resources for making this imaginative integration.

Institutions of Orientation

These institutions in the modern world—religion, education, labor, science, government, and medicine—represent the basic structure of a worldview. They structure human experience in time and space on personal, social, and even cosmic levels. These institutions provide a collective sense of orientation in time and space that has been a primary function of a religious worldview in traditional societies. To this extent, they represent the visible outline of a quasireligious worldview that has had a pervasive influence on human experience in the modern world.

That orientation in time and space is also an orientation toward values. Each institution is designed to serve some basic value that people feel they need, want, or desire. But the primary orientation toward values that is supported by each institution is a passive relationship between an institution and its clients. Human beings are regarded as consumers of values that are created, produced, and distributed by institutions. The assumption that values can be produced by institutions is an illusion. Values are experiences that are generated, cultivated, and nurtured through action; they are valued experiences in action, not commodities to be acquired from institutions. In this sense, medicine cannot produce health, education cannot produce learning, religion cannot produce a sense of the sacred, and so on; these values can only be experienced by direct involvement in actions that are healthy, educational, and felt to be sacred. This applies to all the institutions in modern societies that orient people toward ethical values. An experience of values begins when human beings take responsibility for cul-

tivating values in action. This may be what traditions of religious ethics refer to as virtue in social relations.

Although they cannot produce values, institutions may be structured to allow people more freedom to experience values. A utopian network of social relations would not be one in which all human needs, wants, and desires were provided by institutions. Rather, it would be a network of social relations with sufficient flexibility for active involvement, participation, and commitment to experiencing values in human action and interaction. Such an ethical order would only be imaginable if human beings took responsibility for their own experience of values. The ethical order of modern institutions, however, encourages a passive orientation toward values. The prevalent sense of scarcity, lack, and deprivation in the experience of values within modern societies may be the result of this passive orientation toward values that is inherent in the major institutions of the modern world.

Institutions of Exclusion

The second dimension of any worldview is the classification of people. A worldview categorizes people into Us and Them. Some people are classified as fundamentally other. These others may not even be considered fully human because they do not fit the definition of humanity that is established by Us. Institutions that support this classification of otherness seek to exclude Them from society. Institutional barriers may be erected in order to keep Them out. Such institutions offer a tangible structure for the classification of people within any worldview. They reinforce a sense of

collective identity by excluding all otherness from the ordinary network of social relations.

The Classification of People

The construction of external institutional barriers attempts to exclude people who are classified as foreign, strange, or different. Sometimes these differences are considered so great that these others are classified as subhuman. Reports of classification systems in some tribal groups reveal this tendency to subclassify all others. The Marind-Anim of South New Guinea, for example, are said to refer to themselves as real human beings (*Anim-Ha*), but they refer to others as *Ikim-Anim*—"strangers who are there to be killed."[40] The Yanomamo of Southern Venezuela call themselves "the first, finest, and most refined form of man to inhabit the earth." Other people are classified as *naba,* or subhuman.[41] This tendency of a religious worldview to subclassify other people prompted the sociologist Max Weber to observe that religions develop two standards of ethical behavior. One standard applies to relations with people within the community (*Issenmoral*), and a separate standard governs behavior in relation to those who live outside the boundaries of the community (*Aussenmoral*). Various institutions of exclusion may be employed to keep these others out, or to dictate the terms of adaptation by which they might be allowed in, to become one of Us.

Internal classifications of people may establish institutional barriers among different classes of people within a society. An important example of internal classification is the class system of traditional India. The internal classification of people into a rigid hierarchy provided the ethical order of social relations. The elaborate caste system, with its specific obligations, occupations, and life styles incumbent upon each group, was based in the four Hindu social orders, or *varnas*. Each varna was identified with a different color: white for the *Brahmin* (poet-priest), red for the *Kṣatriya* (warrior-ruler), yellow for the *Vaiśya* (trader-agriculturist), and black for the *Śūdra* (servant-laborer). The first three classes were the twice-born (*dvijas*) who underwent religious initiation and were allowed to participate in the basic rituals of the tradition. The last group was generally excluded.

Each varna was assigned different ethical ob-

ligations, responsibilities, and rights—its own *varnadharma*. For the Brahmin, it was study, teaching, officiating at sacrifices, and accepting charity; for the Kṣatriya, it was the protection of subjects, nonattachment to sense pleasures, and the giving of charity; for the Vaiśya, it was tending cattle, practicing agriculture, carrying on trade, and giving charity; for the Śūdra, however, the primary obligation was to serve the other three classes. The institutionalized barriers among these social classes not only reinforced different ethical duties, but served to exclude the lower caste groups from full participation in both religion and society. Servants and laborers were classified as fundamentally inferior by the internal classification system of traditional Hindu society.[42]

Sometimes an internal classification of people is based on race. The subclassification of blacks in the European Christian worldview, for example, was occasionally justified by the biblical narrative of Noah's curse of his son Ham in the book of Genesis. (9:18–27) According to the story, the descendents of Ham were cursed by Noah to be "servants of servants." His lineage was to be forever subservient to the descendents of his brothers, Shem and Japheth. As the slave trade expanded in Europe and America, Europeans invoked this myth to argue that black Africans were descendents of Ham, while "civilized" Europeans were descendents of Shem and Japheth. This gave Europeans a mythic warrant for the subclassification and enslavement of black Africans.[43] Such myths of otherness operate in religious worldviews to differentiate types of people and to justify different ethical standards of behavior toward them. The mythic subclassification of blacks in America allowed them to be included in society, but only if they were confined within the dehumanizing institution of slavery. They were, therefore, excluded from fully human status within the network of social relations that supported that institution.

Rituals of Exclusion

Religious communities have exercised a number of ritual techniques to exclude people from their community's space. The major rituals of exclusion are excommunication, banishment, and execution. Traditional religions have used excommunication as a ritual of exclusion. This is a particularly powerful ritual sanction when it is backed up by sovereign political power. An example of religious excommunication, supported by political power, is found in the Edict of Emperor Theodosius (380), which classified all non-Catholics as heretics punishable by law. The edict read:

> *We command that those persons who follow this rule shall embrace the name of Catholic Christians. The rest, however, whom We adjudge demented and insane, shall sustain the infamy of heretical dogmas, their meeting places shall not receive the name of churches, and they shall be smitten first by divine vengeance and secondly by the retribution of Our own initiative, which We shall assume in accordance with divine judgment.*[44]

This royal excommunication excluded all heretics from communion with the Christian church. *Heretic* comes from a Greek word meaning "to choose." From the perspective of any orthodoxy, heretics are believed to have made the wrong choice regarding religious doctrine, practice, or association. Excommunication excludes them from the community. Notice that those heretics excluded by the Edict of Theodosius are not simply condemned for unorthodox beliefs: They are classified as abnormal, mad, and insane. Heretics are excluded because they are perceived as fundamentally other.

Banishment is another ritual of exclusion. This form of social death can be illustrated by the choice that was offered to Socrates when he was found guilty of corrupting the morals of Athenian youth through his teaching. The Athenian state presented him with the choice of banishment or death. In social terms, they are roughly equivalent. Both banishment and death effectively remove the person from the community. Banishment, as a strategy of exclusion, was used by Christian nations to expel Jews from England in 1290, from France in 1306 and 1394, from Spain in 1492, and on numerous other occasions in the long history of European Christian anti-Semitism.[45] In these cases, the Christian response to the otherness of Jews was to exclude them from society.

Finally, capital punishment has been used as a ritual of exclusion. The execution of people classified as heretics, witches, or social deviants offers a particularly powerful method for a community to reinforce its system of classification. The line between Us and Them within a society may be drawn by violent rituals of punishment, torture, and execution. As Kai Erikson has observed, "morality and immorality meet at the public scaffold, and it is during this meeting that the line between them is drawn."[46] Execution obviously excludes a person from the community; it also reinforces both the ethical standards of the community and the authority to judge anyone who violates those standards. Such acts of exclusion support the ethical integrity of Us by eliminating one of Them.

In modern western societies the primary ritual mechanism of exclusion is confinement. The French historian Michel Foucault pointed to the great confinement of different classes of people, who were excluded from French society by being locked up in the Hôpital General of Paris in 1652, as an important event in the history of ritual exclusion. Beggars, thieves, prostitutes, madmen, and the poor were all excluded from society in a common regimen of confinement.[47] The two great classifications of otherness that emerged from institutions of confinement in modern western societies have been criminality and insanity. These two classifications now define the outer limits of fully legitimate human identity. They are the boundary definitions of what counts as human in the modern worldview. Criminality and insanity are the definitions of deviance that give shape to modern notions of normal identity. The two institutions of confinement designed to exclude individuals who fall into these two classifications are the prison and the asylum.

The Prison

The prison is the primary institution of exclusion in modern societies. It is an institution of confinement that attempts to exclude from society all those individuals who are not perceived as fulfilling legitimate human roles. The primary goal of the prison is simply exclusion in the form of confinement. The sociologist Erving Goffman has noted that most of the time prisons "seem to function merely as storage dumps for inmates."[48] Goffman suggests, however, that prisons are social institutions constructed to serve more specific ethical goals. "They usually present themselves to the public," Goffman has observed, "as rational organizations designed consciously, through and through, as effective machines for producing a few officially avowed and officially approved ends."[49] Prisons are social institutions of exclusion that are designed to serve a set of cultural, ethical, and (in an important sense) religious values.

The sociologist Donald Cressy has defined these values in terms of the institutional goals of the prison. Prisons are intended to serve four basic institutionalized values: (1) incapacitation, (2) retribution, (3) deterrence, and (4) reformation.[50] The prison is a social institution designed to prevent the criminal from acting in society, to exercise ethical judgment on the criminal, to discourage potential criminal activities, and to change the moral character of the criminal. These social values inherent in the prison are analogous to important religious patterns of action in social relations. The institutional goals of the prison play a critical role in reinforcing the modern worldview.

Incapacitation as Exclusion   We have already seen that rituals of exclusion can be important social mechanisms for reinforcing the identity of a religious community. Exclusion maintains a sense of the community's integrity, uniformity, and limits. The incapacitation of the criminal by the ritual of confinement is precisely such an act of exclusion. It is also a social death.[51] It is an exclusion that does not apply simply to those who do not adhere to the ethical standards of the community, although the population of prisons is largely comprised of people who have not conformed to the dominant work ethic of society. The ritual of exclusion is extended over those people who are classified as impure. The prison protects society from contact with this symbolic impurity represented by the criminal.

Nineteenth century prison reforms occurred in the same urban environment that was actively promoting public sanitation movements. "The sewer and crime," as Louis Chevalier has noted, were "the two by-products of urban life."[52] It is no accident that metaphors for criminality were drawn from the imagery of filth, refuse, and impurity associated with the sewer systems of modern cities. Geoffrey Parsons has collected numerous examples from nineteenth century ethical literature on crime, law, and order to demonstrate that "sewage and drains were guiding metaphors for those who depicted the deviants of this time."[53] Images of impurity and danger were woven together in the popular imagination when visualizing the criminal in modern, industrial cities. The criminal was symbolized as "moral filth," "moral refuse," "a vast dung heap of ignorance," "foul wretch," "slime," "offal," "dregs," and "moral debris." Dirty, disorderly mobs of criminals were imagined to linger around the city in "stagnant pools," or perhaps to "ooze in a great tide" through its streets. The ghettos in which criminals were believed to live were described as "poisoned wells," "sinks of iniquity," "plague-spots," "cess-pits," and "moral miasmas."

When a nineteenth century moralist noted that a city "reeked" with crime, the observer was reflecting the power of the sewer image to connect physical and ethical characteristics in a single emblem of impurity. This impurity was perceived as dangerous and had to be disposed of by removal from society. As Geoffrey Parsons concluded, these images of ethical impurity reveal a preoccupation with "dangerous refuse: particularly the unemployable human refuse of an unpredictable economic system."[54] The ritual institutions of confinement, therefore, were viewed as a means of symbolically sanitizing society from contact with this impurity. These institutions performed an essentially religious function in protecting society from the danger of defilement.

Retribution as Divine Judgment

As an exercise in ethical retribution, the institution of confinement demonstrates a society's power over life and death. This is an absolute power and authority to exercise judgment over human beings, a power similar to that displayed in the Edict of Theodosius, which was derived "from the heavenly judgment." The power of judgment, punishment, and retribution reinforces the absolute, almost divine power of the state. This power is infused in all public institutions designed to control deviant behavior. This display of power in penal institutions, as R. A. Scott has noted, serves to revitalize the entire social system:

To contain and control deviance, and thereby master it, is to supply fresh and dramatic proof of the enormous powers of the social order. The visible control of deviance is one of the most effective mechanisms by which a social order can tangibly display its potency. The act of harnessing things which are dangerous helps to revitalize the system by demonstrating to those who live within it just how awesome its powers really are.[55]

The awesome power of judgment, punishment, and retribution, in the ritual expulsion of evil from the human community, reinforces the power of the social order. In its symbolic control over the dangerous forces of evil, the social system achieves a religious legitimacy.

Deterrence as Magical Control

The belief that prisons serve as a deterrent to crime, even in the face of contradictory statistical evidence, exemplifies the exercise of magical controls over the social environment. Not everyone classified as criminal is confined. Some are out in the world, driving over the speed limit, cheating on income taxes, and jaywalking. But the threat of punishment, reprisals, and retribution, represented by the prison, is supposed to exert a mysterious control over behavior outside its walls. The prison represents an attempt to create an ideal, perfectly regulated and controlled social institution that will have a magical effect on the rest of society.

In the modern worldview, the prison is felt to have two magical effects on the larger society. First, the ritualized perfection, discipline, and order represented by this institution is intended to spill over into the ordinary human interactions in society. By mysteriously affecting behavior outside its walls, the prison is designed to encourage potential criminals to imitate its disciplined order in their ordinary behavior. This is sympathetic magic, in which like is felt to produce like.

The total institution is hoped to produce a normative pattern of order that will be imitated by the larger network of social relations. The prison becomes the normative symbolic pattern of order in modern societies, as Michel Foucault noted, where "prisons resemble factories, schools, barracks, hospitals, which all resemble prisons."[56] The prison is also felt to exert a magical control on behavior through contagious magic, based on contact, or the fear of contact, in which crime will be deterred through the invisible influence of institutions of confinement. This magical control over human behavior is a powerful symbolic motive behind the prison as a social institution in the modern world.

Reformation as Religious Conversion

The reformation, rehabilitation, or resocialization of the criminal is essentially a form of religious conversion. It is an attempt to convert the criminal to a new pattern of beliefs, practices, and experiences. The reformation of character is aimed at converting the criminal's moral conscience, behavior, and life style to the dominant ethical pattern represented by the modern worldview. "The translation of inmate behavior into moralistic terms suited to the institutions avowed perspective," as Erving Goffman has observed, "will necessarily contain some broad presuppositions as to the character of human beings."[57] In other words, the conscience and behavior of the criminal is to be reformed to match the presuppositions of what it is to be a human being.

Prisons are experiments in conversion. However, the prisoner is often forced to internalize the ethical values of guilt, judgment, and punishment in ways that are counterproductive to the expressed goals of the institution. As Richard McCleery has pointed out,

after an offender has been subjected to unfair or excessive punishment and treatment more degrad-

ing than prescribed by law, he comes to justify his act which he could not have justified when he committed it. He decides to "get even" for his unjust treatment in prison and take reprisals through further crime at the first opportunity. With that decision he becomes a criminal.[58]

The very institution designed to convert an offender into a productive member of society may succeed in converting that person into a committed criminal. The prison, as a social institution designed to exclude Them from Us, may convert offenders of the social order into permanent members of Them.

The Asylum

The mental asylum is also an institution of exclusion from society by means of confinement. The asylum excludes those people who are classified as mentally ill. In this classification of mental illness, norms derived from modern medical practice are applied to mental states and social behavior. Mental illness has three basic categories: (1) physical abnormalities, such as syphilis of the brain, or toxic psychosis resulting from acute alcoholism; (2) personal difficulties, such as fears, depressions, traumas, and stress; and (3) antisocial acts. The last two categories of mental illness, although they may be evidence of real suffering and social conflicts, are only diseases in a metaphorical sense. But the asylum, and the practice of institutional psychiatry, extends medical classification, management, and control over these areas as well.

Like the prison, asylums exclude people through confinement who are perceived as not fulfilling legitimate human roles in society. One observer has suggested that "state mental asylums are the 'Indian Reservations' for America's non-criminally labelled poor, old, black, latin and female populations."[59] In modern societies, insanity has become a second classification of otherness for excluding certain people within a common regimen of confinement.

Recently, a large body of what is sometimes called "antipsychiatry" literature has emerged to question the medical assumptions of psychiatry in the modern worldview. One ardent critic of institutional psychiatry, Thomas Szasz, has repeatedly called for a perspective on the asylum that would place it in its social context. He has analyzed the social function of the asylum in the modern world. The dominant majority within any given society classifies certain groups of people as deviant, or in the case of the asylum, classifies people as mentally ill, in order to set them apart as inferior, to control, persecute, or even destroy them. Szasz has suggested that institutional psychiatry performs precisely this function of classification. It distinguishes between Us and Them, between self and other, in terms of medical classifications of mental health and mental illness. According to Szasz, "Institutional psychiatry fulfills a basic human need—to validate the Self as good (normal), by invalidating the Other as evil (mentally ill)."[60] Institutional psychiatry uses the medical classifications of normal and abnormal to identify good and evil mental states, attitudes, and behavior.

In reinforcing shared cultural standards of normal behavior, the asylum, like the prison, provides a compelling ritual and institutional demonstration of the power of the ethical order inherent in the modern worldview. The asylum represents, as Thomas Szasz has insisted, "an intellectually meaningful, morally uplifting, and socially well-organized system for the ritualized af-

firmation of the benevolence, glory, and power of society's dominant ethic."[61] By ritually excluding the abnormal from society within an institution of confinement, the asylum affirms the norms of modern society. An ethical order is sustained and reinforced by excluding all those who for some reason do not fit within its design.

These institutions of exclusion can be interpreted by analogy with traditional institutions. Erving Goffman has compared the prison to the monastery, as a total institution for regimentation of behavior, mortification of the body, and reformation of character. And Szasz has compared the asylum, and institutional psychiatry, to the Inquisition: "Medicine replaced theology; the alienist, the inquisitor; the insane, the witch. The result was the substitution of a medical mass-movement for a religious one, the persecution of mental patients replaced the persecution of heretics."[62]

The prison and the asylum have a fundamentally religious character in the modern worldview, and not simply because they can be compared to traditional religious institutions. These institutions of exclusion perform the essential religious function of the classification of people. They represent the visible outlines of a classification of people in the modern worldview that defines what counts as Us and excludes all who are classified as Them. The prison and the asylum are the imaginary boundaries of a prevailing myth of normal identity in modern social relations. An interpretation of the function of these institutions of exclusion in the modern worldview would suggest, as H. J. Muller has noted, that "historians of the future will point out that we too lived by myths."[63]

Patterns of Institutions

The pattern of institutions within any society reveals a collective commitment to values. Institutions are organized social efforts dedicated to the production of values. They are established in the interests of defining, producing, and distributing the goods that people feel they need, want, or desire. The French sociologist of religion Emile Durkheim imagined that religion provided an all-embracing sense of shared values in traditional societies that held human beings together as a community. This unifying function of religion, Durkheim contended, had been reduced with the complex differentiation of institutions in modern social arrangements. Religion has been limited to a single institution in modern societies, but the traditional religious function of generating over-arching values has become diffused through a variety of institutions. Institutions of education, medicine, science, and so on play essentially religious roles in the modern world by giving tangible outline to a uniquely modern, quasireligious worldview. Chapter 9 has drawn a number of conclusions regarding the social ethics of institutions in the modern world.

---

1.   *Some institutions orient human beings toward values.* The first dimension of any worldview is a sense of orientation in time and space. Institutions in the modern world structure this orientation within the temporal and spatial coordinates of human experience. Institutions of medicine and labor structure the experience of the body; institutions of the state and education structure the experience of the world; and institutions of science and religion structure the human experience of the larger cosmos that human beings inhabit. These institutions of orientation in time and space pattern the human experience of purpose, meaning, and value in action. Ultimately, they embody a network of values that are felt to make life worth living.

The central problem with modern institutions, however, is their tendency to treat values as if they were commodities to be created, produced, and distributed by institutions. This not only places people in a passive relation to the things they need, want, and desire, but it also builds a sense of deprivation into the experience of values. When people do not experience values, they simply conclude that the institutions have failed to deliver. But if values are goods that are integral to action itself, then they cannot be passively received from institutions. Values can only be generated by an active commitment to those activities, interactions, and experiences that are regarded as valuable. The primary ethical challenge posed by modern institutions is this need to take direct responsibility for the experience of values through action. Arrangements of institutions may be flexible enough to allow people to experience values, but institutions cannot produce values if these values are experiences that are inherent in active ethical patterns of action. The challenge of institutions, therefore, is the potential for taking direct responsibility for the experience of values in action.

---

2.   *Other institutions exclude human beings from values.* The second dimension of any worldview is the classification of people. Some people are classified as like us; others are classified as not like us. Those who are not like us are often excluded from participating in the shared values that are held in common by any Us. People

who fall into the primary classifications of otherness in modern societies, criminality and insanity, are removed from society by means of institutions of exclusion. These images of deviance, abnormality, and otherness reinforce shared cultural norms in modern social relations. The criminal and the insane are the Them by which Us is defined, sustained, and reinforced. The regimen of confinement within which these others are excluded also reinforces cultural values of discipline, order, and rationality, which are important ethical ideals in the modern worldview. Finally, confinement does not simply serve the goal of exclusion, but is infused with explicit institutional goals of rehabilitation, indoctrination, and training that would transform these others into legitimate members of human society. These institutions of exclusion represent the culturally defined limits of legitimate human identity in the modern worldview. On this side of their walls, human beings can participate in the shared ethical values of the modern worldview.

———

3.   *Shared values represent the ethos of a worldview.* The anthropologist Robert Redfield

suggested that "the ethos of a people is its organized conceptions of the Ought."[64] The ethics of social relations in any community is committed to the proposition that things *ought* to be good. When shared images of the good are organized in institutionalized patterns of social interaction, they can be characterized as the ethos of a community. The ethos of modern, western, industrialized societies is closely aligned with institutions that organize the human experience of values. These institutions orient some people toward values and exclude other people from values. They create a structured pattern for the experience of values in the modern world.

One element in that pattern is the pervasive influence of technology in the modern ethos. A technological ethos, as an organized conception of how things ought to be done, permeates the modern world. Modern social ethics cannot be fully appreciated without seriously considering the role of technology in the shaping of the modern worldview. A technological spirit pervades both the institutions of orientation and exclusion that shape the experience of ethical values in modern social relations.

CHAPTER

TEN

TECHNOLOGY

In the modern worldview, ethics tends to be divorced from the traditional ritual practices that provided a sense of structure, pattern, and harmony for action. Ethics is no longer grounded in ritual. The agenda for ethics in the modern world is set by new technological abilities to control the natural environment. A vision of the good society is not based on personal virtues cultivated through religious worship, prayer, and meditation; to a large extent, such a vision is based on the technological power to control, manipulate, and dominate nature. In traditional western societies, the development of moral virtue (*arete*) once represented the definition of the good life. In modern, western, industrial societies, however, the ideal of virtue has been replaced by technical competence (*techne*). "The good society and the vision of the good is," as Lionell Rubinoff has observed, "whatever happens to result from technology and science. It is not, in Plato's language, *arete* that governs *techne* but *techne* that determines *arete*."[1] The explosion of technology in the modern world has presented human beings with new ethical challenges. We will examine the impact of technology on the religious ethics of social relations.

At the basis of the challenge posed by technology is the relation between ethical values and action in the world. Action can be viewed as a way of communicating values. Different types of action communicate different personal and social values. Ritual represents meaningful action, work represents useful action, and leisure represents pleasurable action. These three modes of action in the world communicate qualitatively different experiences of the values in human activity. Therefore, we must first examine the values that are embodied in these three modes of action.

Second, technology has had a greater impact on the modern world than merely changing human patterns of work and leisure. A set of basic technological values has suddenly invaded the worldviews of modern, western, industrial societies. These technological values are abstract, rational, and mechanical, and they have had a profound effect on the ethics of social relations in the modern world. We need to clarify this technological ethos before exploring a third issue: the relation among religion, technology, and the natural environment.

Religious ethics has supported a variety of attitudes toward nature. These attitudes have shaped patterns of social action in relation to the natural environment. We will look at the ways in which religious ethics has both supported and resisted the expansion of technological control over nature. Behind all of these issues is the question of how action embodies inherent values in the ethics of social relations.

Three Modes of Action

Every culture supports a general idea of what it means to act in the world. The dominant concept of action in western societies, influenced by classical Greek philosophy, is *praxis*. Practical action, according to Aristotle, involves selecting appropriate means to achieve specific goals. Praxis is goal oriented. Actions are means to designated ends, and actions can be evaluated in terms of their effectiveness in achieving those ends. In eastern religious traditions, specifically in Hinduism, Buddhism, and Jainism, the central concept of action is *karma*. Karmic action does not distinguish between means and ends. The quality of an action is inherent in the act itself. It is sufficient to perform each action as a duty (*dharma*), without concern for the consequences, results, or fruits of action. Although both terms—*praxis* and *karma*—literally mean "action," they represent different attitudes toward the value of action.

Action is a medium of communication. Human beings do not simply act in order to achieve what they need, want, or desire. They act in order to realize certain values that are inherent in action, and to communicate those values within a social context. If action in a social world can be understood as a medium of communication, it

appears that there are three basic values that are represented by human action: (1) the value of meaning, (2) the value of usefulness, and (3) the value of pleasure. These values are inherent in action. They are internal goods that are experienced, realized, and communicated through human activity. The value of meaningful action is experienced in ritual; the value of useful action is experienced in work; and the value of pleasurable action is experienced in leisure. Ritual, work, and leisure are the three modes of action in the world.

Ritual

Ritual is action that communicates the meaning of the universe that human beings inhabit. It is a method for realizing the value of meaning. What is it about ritual that makes it meaningful? First, it is action that refers to myth. Ritual re-enacts mythic models of action. In referring to the creative acts of gods, founders, or ancestors, ritual places the participant in direct contact with the meaning and power associated with those acts. Ritual creates a meaningful context within which that creative power is experienced. Second, ritual is action that creates a perfect, ideal, controlled pattern of action. As we have seen, ritual eliminates the contingencies, variables, and accidents of ordinary action in the world and creates a perfect pattern of action. The meaning of ritual rules may lie in their ability to demonstrate that human beings can, in fact, conform their behavior to rules. Ritual is evidence that human beings can invest their actions with meaning.

The ritualized perfection of such meaningful patterns of action may spill over into the ordinary human activities of work and leisure. Ritual patterns of action may be superimposed on the everyday, ordinary activities of life in the world. In this sense, work and leisure may also assume the meaningful quality of ritual. Although the primary values of work and leisure are usefulness and pleasure, systems of religious ethics may ritualize these activities and superimpose the value of meaning upon these ordinary modes of human action. The ethics of social relations, in religious ethics, tends to transfer a pattern of ritualized perfection to the ordinary activities of work and leisure.

Work

Work is action that demonstrates the useful, productive, and creative involvement of human energy. Work is a means of realizing the value of utility, a way of acting usefully, or simply useful action. Work, as pure utility, has undergone a profound reconceptualization in the modern world. The Industrial Revolution is usually considered the major turning point in the history of work. But even before the massive industrialization of western societies, utility, as the goal of productive action, had gained prominence in the scheme of values. Utility was becoming a self-justifying end for action. The utopia imagined by Francis Bacon in *New Atlantis* (1627) was a society based on a scientific institute devoted to making useful commodities. Technological innovations that would reduce labor and multiply production held the greatest value. By 1780, innovations such as the steam engine, pumps to drain mines, and cheap transportation had succeeded in mechanizing the work of utility.

This mechanization of work was accompanied by a new quantification of the value of work. Human labor came to be measured in monetary terms. The motive for work became economic exchange. In wage labor, human beings work for a salary—to satisfy needs and gratify appetites—or for personal gain—to acquire the most money for the least amount of effort. But beyond this immediate compensation for labor, the question arises: Why work? Do human beings work to live? Or do they live to work? When the value of work is simply utility, human beings seem to be caught in a cycle of working so that they can survive and surviving so that they can work. Religious traditions tend to superimpose a set of religious values upon the processes of working, laboring, making, and creating. These values supplement the basic value of usefulness that is inherent in work. They invest work with a sense of meaningfulness that gives work a ritual-like character.

Work as Vocation   The most powerful religious motive for work in western, industrial societies was the concept of work as vocation. *Vocation* means a calling; it is the idea that human beings are called to do productive work as a religious vocation. This notion can be traced back to the Protestant Reformation, and particularly to the tradition of theological reflection identified with John Calvin. Calvinist theology subscribes to a doctrine of double predestination: Some are predestined to salvation, and others are predestined to damnation. People can do nothing to influence their salvation. No works in the world can merit the kingdom of heaven. Salvation is simply the result of the inscrutable will of God. Even though actions cannot produce salvation, productive, useful, and disciplined work may count as evidence that one is among the elect. Useful work, therefore, became an end in itself. A disciplined devotion to useful action in the world was interpreted as significant proof that a person was among the chosen of God.

This Protestant work ethic was referred to by the sociologist Max Weber as *inner-worldly asceticism.* By working at a vocation or a calling, a person denies the undisciplined pleasures of the flesh without withdrawing from the social world. The monastic ideal—"to work is to pray"—is transferred to all kinds of work in the world. The ritual value of prayer is superimposed upon work. As the Church of Scotland Hymnal put it:

> *Work shall be prayer, if all be wrought*
> *As Thou wouldst have it done,*
> *And prayer, by Thee inspired and taught,*
> *Itself with work be one.*[2]

In the Protestant work ethic there was no place for the traditional Catholic ritual cycle of sin and atonement. Even with the ritual acts of the tradition one was not able to achieve salvation. Salvation was viewed as a free, unmerited gift of God. But the presence of this gift in the lives of individuals could be demonstrated by the evidence of useful work in the world. The Protestant work ethic suggested a ritual basis for work: Work became a symbolic action (vocation) with reference to the sacred (for example, evidence of election).[3] Work could be useful, as well as meaningful.

Work as Meditation   Work may also be viewed as a form of meditation. Although Hindu thought tends to see work in a particular

occupation as a religious obligation necessary for the fulfillment of a person's *varnadharma,* work is also seen as providing opportunities for devotion. Work can be a type of devotional activity. In the *Bhagavad Gītā,* Kṛṣṇa exhorts his devotees to perform all their daily activities with single-minded attention on his divine form. Work becomes a form of devotional meditation. Zen Buddhism also suggests that work can become a form of meditation. Zen (and Chan) Buddhist legends tell of monks who experienced the sudden illumination of enlightenment while stirring cake batter, mending shoes, or engaged in other mundane activities. Zen cultivates ways of acting in any human endeavor as if it were a form of meditation.[4] The notions of work as vocation and work as meditation are attempts to infuse labor with meaning beyond the sheer utility of working to survive; they superimpose a ritual pattern of meaning upon work.

Leisure

Leisure is action devoted to pleasure. Three definitions of leisure are involved in the ethics of action. First, leisure may be considered a detached attitude, state of mind, or condition of the soul, which may be called "contemplative time." Second, leisure may be regarded as a period of time that remains after the demands of work, which may be called "surplus time." Third, leisure may be defined as any activity devoted to enjoyment, self-expression, or play, which may be called "pleasurable time." We need to consider these three definitions of leisure in more detail in order to analyze the ethics of pleasurable action in human social relations.

Contemplative Time   The classical definition of leisure is the contemplative life. The *vita contemplativa* is an alternative to the active life of work. This contemplative time is not just freedom from the demands of labor, but a special condition of the soul. "Leisure refers to a state of being," as Sebastian de Grazia has noted, "a condition of man, which few desire and fewer achieve."[5] Leisure is not simply "free time" left over from the work schedule. Contemplative time is a quality of experience that no time budget could measure. In this type of leisure, human beings are free to engage in arts that cultivate, refine, and awaken the soul: the visual arts, music, and philosophy. In this ideal of leisure, as de Grazia has suggested, "one senses a different element, an ethical note, a hint that spare time when misused is not leisure."[6] Leisure is not empty time, but time that is devoted to the contemplative cultivation of the soul.

The philosopher Josef Pieper, in his *Leisure: The Basis of Culture,* sees leisure as the contemplative celebration and affirmation of life. Pieper also would define leisure as "a mental and spiritual attitude—it is not simply the result of external factors. . . . It is, in the first place, an attitude of mind, a condition of the soul."[7] This attitude cultivated in contemplative leisure is understood to be an important dimension of the total health, balance, and harmony of human life. Contemplative time is essential to maintaining an inner ecology of the spirit. Just as the ecosystem of the planet needs uncultivated forests to replenish the supply of oxygen in the atmosphere, the human being needs free spaces of contemplation, study, and reflection to revitalize the soul. Leisure provides the opportunity for this contemplative time.

Surplus Time

The most common definition of leisure in the modern world, however, is surplus time. Leisure tends to be defined as whatever time happens to be left over after the requirements of work and subsistence have been met. Thorstein Veblen introduced this definition of leisure in his book, *The Theory of the Leisure Class* (1899): Leisure is "non-productive consumption of time."[8] This leftover time is one of the major ethical challenges of the modern world. It is what Robert MacIver has called "the great emptiness."[9] Leisure is an empty space in the work cycle that people often are not certain how to fill. This empty time may be put to useful social ends of rehabilitation, skill development, and social participation. In this sense, leisure is justified only because it increases a person's usefulness at work.

This empty, surplus time is also used as a compensation for the dissatisfactions of modern work. Surplus time is used, as Harold Wilensky has noted, to "develop patterns of creative, challenging leisure to compensate for an inevitable spread in dehumanized labor."[10] Surplus time may be filled with activities of human interest that compensate for dehumanizing work. But, this nonproductive consumption of time often tends to be used for the consumption of commodities. Hannah Arendt has suggested that the free time of human working animals tends to be spent in the frenzied consumption of food, possessions, and entertainments. "The spare time of the *animal laborans,*" she observed, "is never spent in anything but consumption, and the more time left to him, the greedier and more craving his appetites."[11] Surplus time, or what Aristotle would have seen as the freedom from the necessity of labor, does not specify what purposes this freedom might serve. Leisure, in this sense, is simply empty time.

Pleasurable Time

The final definition of leisure is pleasurable time. Leisure may be viewed as an end in itself for the experience of pleasure, self-expression, or self-fulfillment. In this sense, leisure is a playful self-expression through action. The historian Johan Huizenga, in *Homo Ludens,* has taken play seriously as an activity that transports human beings "out of the ordinary."[12] Play creates a temporary, transcendent reality, in which the ordinary rules of daily life are suspended, action does not have to be useful, productive, or meaningful, and human beings can play for the sake of playing. Huizenga has suggested that play is the basis of civilization. Out of the pleasure of self-expression and social interaction demonstrated in play, human societies take form. "Civilization is, in its earliest phases, played. It does not come *from* play, like a baby detaching itself from the womb: it arises in and as play and never leaves it."[13] In this sense, leisure as pleasurable time is the basis of human culture.

In preindustrial societies, work and leisure are sometimes divided into two spheres. The Baluchi of Western Pakistan, for example, divide time between a sphere of duty or obligation and a sphere of what they call "one's own will." This latter time is said to be devoted to the exercise of one's personal energy, imagination, and ingenuity. This is creative time for the play of one's own imagination and will.[14] More often, however, these two modes of action—work and leisure—are interwoven in experience. As one anthropologist has observed, "I do not believe that any Bushman could tell us—or would be interested in telling us—which part of his activity was work and which part was play."[15] Work and play must be interwoven in any kind of work that shows care. The self-expression of play and the creation of useful values are combined in work as craftsmanship.[16] It is possible to imagine pleasurable work, in which a person could invest care, enthusiasm, and love, that would have the quality of leisure. Leisure, as pleasurable time, holds the potential for infusing the very experience of work.

Religion and Leisure
Traditionally, religion and leisure have been closely related. The Sabbath day of rest has been an important part of the ritual calendar in both Judaism and Christianity. The Sabbath is a free time to refrain

from work and to imitate God's primordial rest from the work of creation. The Emperor Constantine decreed Sunday as a public day of rest throughout the Roman Empire in 321.[17] In addition, a variety of harvest and spring festivals of religious origin have been celebrated in traditional religions. In Medieval Europe, one out of every three days was some kind of holy day: saints days, feast days, or fast days. Such celebrations set certain times apart from ordinary life. They were sacred times devoted to both ritual and leisure. Josef Pieper has suggested that ritual transformations of ordinary time are the origin and essence of leisure.

> *In celebrating, in holding festivals upon occasion, man experiences the world in an aspect other than the everyday one. The festival is the origin of leisure and the inward and ever-present meaning of leisure. . . . If real leisure is deprived of the support of genuine feast-days and holy days, work itself becomes inhuman.*[18]

Ritual celebrations of leisure transcend the ordinary cycles of work, and their ritualized perfection enriches the ordinary experience of useful, productive activity in the world.

A number of significant analogies can be drawn between religion and leisure. First, religion and leisure are both dedicated to personal well-being and spiritual renewal. As Robert Lee has noted, "Leisure is the occasion for the development of broader and deeper perspectives and for renewing the body, mind and spirit."[19] Leisure, therefore, transforms the ordinary experience of time to produce a sense of regeneration in much the same way as ritual.

Second, religion and leisure both involve the whole person. In a world where human actions are segmented into many different role performances, religious and leisure activities are two areas in which human beings feel most integrated as persons. Leisure, as Gordon Dahl has suggested, "is man's synthesizing factor in a 'component' civilization."[20] Leisure, like religion, has the potential to totally involve all the faculties of the human person in an integrated whole.

Third, religion and leisure both involve ritualized actions that transcend ordinary experience. Leisure pursuits, particularly sports, assume the proportions of heroic myth and ritual drama in the modern worldview. M. R. Cohen has suggested that the sport of baseball in the United States embodies the religious value of transcending ordinary human experience.

> *The essence of religious experience, so we are told is the "redemption from the limitations of our petty individual lives and the mystic unity with a larger life of which we are a part." And is this not precisely what the baseball devotee or fanatic, if you please, expresses when he watches the team representing his city battling with another? . . . Careful students of Greek civilization do not hesitate to speak of the religious value of Greek drama . . . baseball purifies all our emotions, cultivating hope and courage when we are behind, resignation when we are beaten, fairness for the other team when we are ahead, charity for the umpire, and above all the zest for combat and conquest.[21]*

True baseball devotees would probably agree that the baseball diamond, complex rules, and rhythms of play are the closest that humanity has come to achieving ritualized perfection in action. Another common leisure activity, tourism, might be compared to rituals of pilgrimage. Tourist attractions become like holy shrines, and tourists derive a sense of sacred power by simply being present at such a sacred site.[22]

Although religion and leisure have much in common, the Protestant world attempted to separate them. The puritan strain within Protestant thought opposed all forms of recreation that could not be translated into the values of work and worship. Puritan Calvinists, imbued with the

work ethic, tried to place religious restrictions on leisure activities such as drinking, gambling, fairs, and other idle pursuits. They attempted to control all leisure time because they saw the nonproductive waste of time as a grave sin.[23] The result of this separation of religion and leisure, however, was to place them in competition with each other for people's interest, attention, and enthusiasm. Religion itself has almost become a leisure pursuit; it is something private and personal that people do when they are off work. As work becomes increasingly routine and repetitive, individuals look to leisure for excitement and novelty. Because religious practices require repetition in prayer, worship, and ritual, they have become less attractive as a leisure activity in the modern world.[24] Pressures have been exerted on religion to be more innovative, novel, and entertaining in order to compete with other leisure activities in the modern time budget. In modern, western, industrialized societies work has become increasingly repetitive, mechanical, and dehumanized, leisure has assumed the qualities of religious ritual, and religion has become a leisure-time pursuit.

Ritual, work, and leisure are the three modes of action in the world. They embody the values of meaning, utility, and pleasure in human activity. In the human experience of action, however, any activity could potentially involve all three modes: Any action could simultaneously be meaningful, useful, and pleasurable. Anything less, in fact, might be the definition of boredom. One of the Seven Deadly Sins in the Christian Middle Ages was the sin of sloth. *Sloth* was a unique combination of laziness and boredom. The primary symptom of sloth was diminished energy in human action. Sloth disempowered the human soul. Perhaps the antidote to slothfulness is human action that is simultaneously invested with a sense of meaning, usefulness, and pleasure. The integration of these three modes is the central challenge to the ethics of action in human social relations.

The Technological Ethos

Technology is a mode of action devoted solely to utility. It is an extension of the value of work through the implements of rationalized, effective action. The historian Charles Singer, in *A History of Technology,* defined technology simply as "how things are commonly done or made."[25] Plato and Aristotle used the term *techne* for the arts of making things for human use. This included the collection of techniques, tools, and machines that extend human control over the environment. Tools are developed in order to serve the human desire for more efficient, productive, and useful action. But soon, human actions become adapted to the tools. Technology begins to enforce its inherent demands on human actions and the values that are experienced through action. This is the beginning of a technological ethos.

Techniques and Values

Karl Marx analyzed human history as the development of productive techniques. Human beings have certain basic needs for eating and drinking, habitation, clothing, and so on. The first historical act, according to Marx, was the "production of the means to satisfy these needs."[26] For Marx, the development of tools to satisfy basic needs was the first characteristically human act in history. He accepted Benjamin Franklin's definition of human beings: "Man is a tool-making animal."[27] As the technological tools of hunting, farming, building, and making began to satisfy the basic needs of survival, new needs, wants, and desires were generated by the tools themselves. Tech-

niques began to take on a life of their own. These new demands for ever increasing efficiency, productivity, and usefulness in human tools began to dominate the field of human action. New tools were produced to satisfy new desires that were generated by old techniques. The new desire for technical efficiency, for its own sake, culminated in the development of machines. As Marx suggested, inhuman forces bound human beings to the machine and made the essence of humanity mechanical. The machine set the standard for efficiency in work, and in order to live up to this standard of efficiency, human beings were made slaves to the machine.

With the Industrial Revolution, the domain of the machine was extended over the entire network of social relations. Mechanized techniques of production became universal. Industrial efficiency promoted a universally integrated and standardized system of methods for production. With this universalization of the machinery of production, techniques were integrated into a set of practices, values, and power relations that defines the technological ethos. Jacques Ellul, in his influential book *The Technological Society,* has described the change that occurred as western societies entered a technological age. According to Ellul, technology became "the totality of methods rationally arrived at and having absolute efficiency . . . in *every* field of human activity."[28] Technical efficiency became the dominant ethical standard for measuring human action, as western, industrialized societies underwent a profound change in human values. Technology set new terms for the ethical evaluation of action in human social relations.

In the system of values represented by technology, techne replaced ritual worship and ethical virtues as the normative basis for human action. The sociologist Bryan Wilson has noted how the ideals of technical efficiency, productivity, and utility displaced traditional ethical approaches to action in modern social relations. "One implication of this development," Wilson observed, "is that increasingly we come to look for technical solutions to our problems rather than rely on the maintenance of particular types of moral attitudes." [29] The expansion of technological innovation has not only outrun ethical reflection, but the ideal of technical solutions to all problems has set the terms within which such ethical reflection tends to be conducted. Rather than adapting technology to ethical patterns of action, the modern ethical orientation tends to adapt itself to the values of technology.

The anthropologist Robert Redfield has been even more emphatic regarding the dehumanizing effect of technology on the ethics of social relations. Personal ethics, which have traditionally cultivated human virtues of love, hope, and courage in the interest of some vision of the good life, are dominated by a technological social ethics whose only goal is efficiency. "The bonds that co-ordinate the activities of men in the technical order," Redfield observed, "do not rest on a conviction as to the good life. . . . The technical order is the order that results from mutual usefulness, from deliberate coercion. . . . In the technical order men are bound by things, or are themselves things." [30] This technological ethos dominates modern, western, industrialized societies. Technology is infused with a systematic network of values that condition ethical patterns of action within western societies. Technology is not simply the techniques, arts, skills, or methods of making; it is a disposition toward technological values that has pervaded the modern worldview.

Technological Values

Technological values affect all aspects of human life and action in the modern world. These values are not simply embodied in the institutions of work and labor, in the factories, bureaucracies, and organizations of modern societies. They dominate all areas of action, conduct, and behavior in the ethics of modern social relations.

Abstract Values   Technological values are abstract. The abstract, mathematical sciences provide the vocabulary for the technological ethos. Everything can be quantified; everything can be translated into mathematical terms. Calculation, precision, and regulation determine the quantitative values that are imposed on the rhythms of life. The historian John Nef has suggested that quantitative values were used to link scientific knowledge and material progress as early as the sixteenth century. The traditional Julian calendar that had been in operation since the year 325 lost 11 minutes and 42 seconds every year, which was not efficient enough for the new value of precision in the measurement of time. That calendar was replaced, therefore, by the more accurate Gregorian calendar in 1583 so that time could be measured exactly. [31] This emphasis on exact measurement was part of a larger attempt to quantify all human relations, with statistical precision and accuracy, in the interests of greater efficiency. Mathematic precision has supplied the terms for the abstract values of technology.

The process of abstraction has extended to all social relations. Technological norms tend to be abstract and impersonal; they measure the value of human beings in terms of abstract standards of efficiency, productivity, and usefulness.

The abstraction of values is not only the result of the fact that usefulness can be quantified; in addition, standards of human use-value can be generalized so that everyone's worth can be measured on the same value scale. Values are standardized. The traditional values of human worth were virtues demonstrated in particular settings of interpersonal relations within a family, clan, tribe, guild, or class. But technological values are general, abstract, and universal principles of efficiency. They are divorced from any specific context of human interaction. Technological virtues do not grow out of the unique character of particular situations, relationships, or conditions of human experience, but are universally imposed on all experience. As the sociologist Robert Nisbet put it, "the same society which made possible mass society made possible mass norms."[32] Mass norms are symptomatic of the abstraction, generalization, and quantification of values in the technological ethos.

Rational Values

The rational organization of behavior is based on uniform standards of efficiency. Rationality in human conduct, in this sense, is "the attempt to find the most efficient means for certain given ends."[33] Rational organization factors out any considerations of feelings, dispositions, or sentiment as inefficient. Other dimensions of human experience are sacrificed in the interest of rational efficiency. Technological values are, therefore, based on the rational adjustment of means to ends. The factory, the assembly line, interchangeable parts—these are all rational developments for more efficient industrial production. These rational values have also been applied to the organization and administration of situations that were once regarded as areas of individual decision making. Such rationalization has had a profound effect on social ethics in modern societies.

The rational administration of human beings—through detailed rules governing actions and decisions, bureaucracies with many levels of authority, and standardized policies and procedures—has changed the ethical role of the individual. Decisions are made according to the technological demands for a rational organization of human and natural resources. Bureaucracies arrive at decisions by following standardized policies and procedures. The responsibility for those decisions is diffused through the organizational structures of government, corporations, and bureaucracies. As Robert Presthis had pointed out, this diffusion means "that 'everyone' (i.e. no one) is responsible. . . . The probabilities that the organization may act unjustly are increased by the weakening of individual responsibility. Only the 'system' is responsible."[34] Like a machine, a rationalized system of administration makes decisions in the interest of greater efficiency. Since everyone is merely a part of the larger machine, no one is individually responsible for the direction in which the machine is going. This systematic rationalization of modern institutions directly reflects the rational values of efficient management of human conduct in the technological ethos.

Mechanical Values

Technological values are mechanical. The values of technology are the values of the machine. A good machine is valued because it is systematic and automatic. Systematic values emphasize order and conformity. In the technological ethos, individuals are valued as parts of a larger systematic order, like interchangeable machine parts, and they function for the benefit of the larger system. Automatic values emphasize the predictable, repeatable performance of actions within designated roles. When human beings are automatic, they can do the same thing over and over again, without any consideration about how they feel about doing it. These mechanical values are essential for the efficient operation of the technological world, but the development of personal virtues is sacrificed for the sake of efficient mechanical control over behavior. The mechanical individual has only a use-value and, therefore, may be manipulated, coerced, and shaped into a social role that contributes to the overall efficiency of the social order. This pervasive mechanization of human social relations has had such extensive social effects that it has, in the words of Karl Marx, "destroyed as far as possible ideology, religion, morality, etc., and where it could not do this, made them into a palpable lie."[35] Technological values have replaced traditional patterns of ethical action as the ultimate standard for evaluating human conduct in the technological ethos.

The power of these technological values, if it has not destroyed religious ethics, has certainly disrupted the traditional patterns of ethical norms, rules, and values that constituted ethical experience in the history of religions. The technological ethos embodies a power in the modern world in which, as Claude Alphonso Alvares has observed, "major clusters of social, economic and psychological commitments are eroded or broken down and people made available for new patterns of socialization and behavior."[36] This disruption of traditional social patterns has not only occurred in modern, western societies; it is taking place wherever modern technology is being introduced in the world.

Technology is not neutral. When technology is imported into a traditional society, it carries with it the values of the technological ethos. Technology adapts attitudes and behavior to the abstract, rational, and mechanical demands of the technological ethos. Robert Nisbet has described the inherent power of technology to transform human social relations into a "great, impersonal system within which human beings congregated not as members of a moral community but as so many abstract units of energy and production, rationally organized for specific, mechanical purposes."[37] These abstract, rational, and mechanical values empower the technological ethos to rearrange human social relations.

Technopower

Technopower is the power to mold human conduct in the interests of technological efficiency. This power cannot be held by one person, or one group, or one institution; it is a network of power relations diffused throughout the whole society. In the technological ethos, this power acts as an invisible force, like gravity, to which everyone's behavior must be adjusted. Four modes of technopower pervade the modern worldview.

Modes of Technopower   The first mode of technopower is the sheer power of technological possibility. In technopower the first criterion for evaluating any action is: "Is it possible? Is it within the power of modern science and technology?" Since the possibility of dominating nature through more efficient means of technology is a self-justifying end in the technological ethos, ethical questions regarding whether a particular technological innovation is good, or even desirable, are secondary issues. Technology has a self-generating power to realize its own inherent possibilities. A given technology will tend to expand until it reaches its own inherent limits. The independent power of technological possibility resists any control, direction, or limitation by independent ethical review. In this sense, technopower has a life of its own. Its power of possibility determines the agenda for any ethical reflection on the value of technology in human social relations.

Second, technopower is the power of expertise. The power of technology is diffused throughout society in a network of specialized social roles. The rational organization of society demands that each person fit into an interlocking system that makes up the larger social machinery. No one person could possibly master all the knowledge and skills that are required to support the technological order. "Technological man," as Edward Ballard has observed, "is the specialist *par excellence;* he has thoroughly identified himself with his role and feels it his highest privilege to contribute to the advance of progress."[38] The technocratic power of the expert—the scientist, technician, consultant, or social engineer—is located in the hierarchy of specialized roles in a technological society.

The third mode of technopower is the power of exclusion. Technopower systematically excludes all alternative value systems with the exception of rational efficiency. In the interest of efficiency, the technological order excludes all people who are not making a useful contribution to sustaining that order. The prison and the asylum, as institutions of exclusion, are necessary to maintain the uniform power of technological order throughout the social system. But this power of exclusion also leaves out a whole range of human values, commitments, and feelings that do not necessarily contribute to the effectiveness of technological production. Exclusive rationality, which plays a central role in science, technology, and the bureaucratization of social life, is not necessarily desirable or even reasonable. "Despite the increase in the rational ordering of life in modern times," as William Barrett remarked, "men have not become the least bit more reasonable in the human sense of the word."[39]

Finally, technopower is the power of reinforcement. This power establishes its control over human behavior through the manipulation of positive and negative reinforcement. Certain patterns of behavior are positively reinforced through wages, benefits, and promotions; other patterns of behavior are discouraged through fines, punishments, and confinement. These reinforcements support efficient, regulated, and disciplined behavior, but they leave little room for independent moral agency and responsibility. Under technopower, the cultivation of private virtues is replaced by public controls. As the sociologist Bryan Wilson has noted, "it is always easier to develop new techniques than to return to the long drawn out type of moral education of the past."[40] The manipulation of behavior through public patterns of positive and negative reinforcement is perceived as a more efficient way of achieving conformity to the normative pattern of action in a technological society. This emphasis on the disciplinary management of behavior tends to ignore the cultivation of moral responsibility and moral virtues, which was the concern of traditional patterns of religious ethics.

Ethical Responses to Technopower

Some people wish to reject the world of technology and return to the traditional life styles and social relations of preindustrial societies. Many people find technocratic social relations to be dehumanizing, and there is nostalgia for simpler, and perhaps more humane, social interactions. One ethical response to the power of technology, therefore, is to develop alternative life styles in the modern world. People have experimented with returning to small-scale, agricultural, communal life styles, in which techniques of subsistence may serve human values and relationships. Such alternative, relatively self-sufficient communities are ethical statements against the technological order that dominates the modern world. But even if modern human beings could somehow unlearn the technological advances of recent centuries, such romantic longings for a preindustrial past often forget that such a life could be, as the philosopher Thomas Hobbes put it, "nasty, brutish and short." Most people in a technological society require ethical resources to allow them to respond to a technological order from which they are not willing to escape into a preindustrial past.

The other extreme in ethical responses to

technopower is found in those who accept technology with great enthusiasm as the pinnacle of human achievement. Technological enthusiasts embrace technopower as the high point in human evolution. One enthusiast for modern technopower, Victor Ferkiss, has declared: "Technological man will be in control of his own development within a context of a meaningful philosophy of the role of technology in human evolution."[41] Through technology, human beings have assumed a transcendent control over their own destiny. But what kind of philosophy would make this control meaningful? Would it be a Social Darwinism that views those people who are able to exploit the planet's resources, and subjugate other people to their domination, as most fit to survive, flourish, and prosper? Or would it be a kind of technological messianism, like the philosophy of Teilhard de Chardin, which imagines technology's expanding power as representing a transformation of human consciousness to a higher level?[42] These optimistic visions of technopower ignore the mechanical, dehumanizing effects that seem to be inherent in technology. As ethical responses to technology, they support the expansion of technopower under the guise of a philosophy of human progress.

Postindustrial Values

Some signs indicate that we are entering a postindustrial age. The sociologist Daniel Bell has described a number of important socioeconomic changes occurring in western societies.[43] Bell has documented a shift from a goods-producing economy to a service economy, the increase in white collar and professional occupations over the industrial labor force, and the expansion of the nonprofit sector of the economy. These social changes are accompanied by changes in values.

Postindustrial values may allow more creative responses to the challenges of technology. These values reflect potential ethical responses to technopower in a postindustrial world.

The Power of Choosing

In response to the power of technological possibility, human beings have the resources to make choices about what is desirable in their own lives. All the small, detailed choices we make regarding food, shelter, clothing, occupations, and life styles contribute to an overall sense of the quality of life. We make daily choices about where we will invest our care, concern, and commitment in order to enhance the quality of experience for ourselves and those around us. The power to choose is also the power to take responsibility for these choices. In the ethics of social relations, human beings may recognize that simply because technology holds the possibility of splitting atoms, building weapons, and exploiting natural resources, the power of possibility alone does not make it desirable. Daniel Bell has noted that "the source of our predicament is not the 'imperatives' of technology but a lack of decision mechanisms for choosing the kinds of technology and social support patterns we want."[44] Such decisions reflect the power of choosing as an ethical response to technology.

The Power of Knowing

In response to the power of technocratic experts, with their exclusive claims to specialized knowledge, people in the postindustrial age are beginning to recognize that knowledge does not necessarily imply the wisdom to make responsible choices. Daniel Bell has suggested that postindustrial values display a dislike for materialism and for purely technical solutions to modern challenges; these new values show an interest in ideas, information, and communication.[45] The power of knowing lies in a willingness to be open to the widest possible field of information. This power of knowing is not the exclusive property of experts. It is a human potential that each person can cultivate. The awakening of this power of knowing is one ethical response to the exclusive power of technical expertise in the postindustrial age.

The Power of Expanding

In response to the power of exclusion, which excludes all human values except rational efficiency, there is the power to expand our sense of what it is to be human. Human beings do not have to be simply a use-value; their worth does not need to be measured exclusively by their usefulness to an industrial system of production. The sociologist Edward Shils felt that it was necessary to affirm that "every human being simply by virtue of his humanity is an essence of unquestionable, indiscriminable value with the fullest right to the realization of what is essentially in him."[46] This concern for self-realization, human rights, and the quality of life expands the field of human values beyond the narrow confines of utility. The power of exclusion in the technological order dehumanizes people who are not considered useful. But the power of expansion broadens the definition of human values in order to recognize that nothing human is alien to Us.

The Power of Acting

In response to the power of reinforcement, which coerces people to re-act to the manipulation of monetary and disciplinary controls, the power of acting resides in personal response-abilities. When human beings are regulated by mechanical controls, they are not responsible for their actions. The power of acting lies in taking that responsibility. Technopower has violated Kant's ethical imperative by regarding human beings simply as useful means to be manipulated toward designated goals. But human beings have the power of acting in ways that are meaningful and pleasurable, as well as useful; the integration of these three values in the power of acting restrains the tendency of technopower to reduce human beings to the value of their usefulness in the machinery of production.

The machine technology of the industrial age is gradually being replaced by an information technology in the postindustrial age.[47] In an information technology, human beings may not appear as cogs in the machinery of production, but as beings who are able to expand their imaginations, to know a wide range of information, and to choose among alternatives. The power of acting may be the highest form of communication. Our actions communicate to ourselves and others our deepest commitments to meaning, utility, and pleasure. The power of acting is not simply to be useful; its power lies in the human ability to infuse activity with meaning and enjoyment. This integration of human values in the power of acting is the major ethical challenge in forming a positive response to technology in modern social relations.

Religion, Technology, and the Environment

We have seen how human beings in the technological ethos are regarded as valuable only if they are useful. Technology also strives to transform nature for utilitarian purposes. In the technological ethos, nature, too, is regarded as primarily a use-value. Currents within religious ethics have both supported the technological exploitation of nature and, in recent years, provided resources for alternative ethical responses to the natural environment. Environmental ethics suggests that human social relations operate within the larger context of nature.

Western Environmental Ethics

Western religious ethics, in supporting the technological development, control, and domination of nature, has embraced the ethical values of utilitarian individualism: People are to be useful and things are to be used. The value of the natural environment is only realized when it can be transformed to human use. The utilitarian value of nature implies a unique relationship between human beings and their environment; this relationship has been supported by a set of values that have characterized basic ethical dispositions toward nature in western societies. The values of dominion, exploitation, consumption, private property, and scientific innovation have supported the expansion of technological control over the natural environment.

The Value of Dominion   In the myth of the Garden of Eden in the Hebrew Bible, Adam is given dominion over the earth by Yahweh. Man is to be lord and ruler over the natural world and all its creatures. He is placed at the center of the garden, but he is not part of it. To the western imagination, this suggested that human beings are independent of the natural environment, in superior isolation from nature, and dominating natural resources to meet their needs. The mythic image of human dominion led to a contempt of the world, a *contemptus mundi,* in western religious thought. Christian religious beliefs in particular called for a rejection of the earth as the ultimate dwelling place for human beings. They are in the world, but not of it. This resulted in a basic indifference toward nature: Whatever happens to the natural environment is of no ultimate significance.[48]

The myth of dominion, however, has often been understood as demanding a more active conquest of the natural environment. Nature must be subjugated to human control. It has no spiritual status of its own. From the dominant Christian perspective, to see nature as animated with spirit, or even with intrinsic value, is an act of idolatry. As the historian Lynn White has pointed out, "For nearly two millenia Christian missionaries have been chopping down sacred groves, which are idolatrous because they assume spirit in nature."[49] Christians have demonstrated their dominion over nature by conquering, dominating, and shaping it to their needs. Thus, Christian religious beliefs have supported the expansion of the technological exploitation of nature's resources.

The Value of Exploitation   In regarding it as something without any intrinsic value, the dominant environmental ethics of the western tradition has sought to make nature valuable by exploiting its resources. Nature only has value when it is exploited in the service of human needs. The natural world, therefore, must be molded and shaped in the interests of utility. Western sacred space has characteristically been architectural. The sacred is not felt to animate the natural environment of rivers, trees, animals, and mountains. A sacred order is carved out of the wilderness and imposed upon the landscape in the architectural forms of buildings, churches, temples, and monuments. It is not considered proper for the natural environment to be

worshiped or merely enjoyed; it must ultimately be put to some practical use. The exploitation of nature takes something that is believed to be intrinsically useless and makes it a thing of human value.

The Value of Consumption

Western environmental ethics has assumed that human beings have the right to consume as much of the world's resources as practically possible. Unrestrained consumption has been assumed as a human right and privilege. Human beings are valued as almost infinite consumers of natural resources. The United States, for example, consumes over half of the world's resources. In the value of consumption, there is a sense that the worth of a people can be measured by their capacity to consume. The power to dominate and exploit natural resources, which may be regarded as the common heritage of all humanity, has conferred a comparatively high standard of living upon a small proportion of the planet's population. The assumption often made is that this standard of living can continue to rise, with its increasing consumption of the world's wealth, without concern for the eventual depletion of nonrenewable natural resources.

The Value of Private Property

The philosopher John Locke maintained that each individual has the fundamental right to own property and to dispose of it as that individual sees fit. This notion of the sanctity of property rights was almost enshrined in the American Declaration of Independence. An early draft of the declaration listed the inalienable, God-given rights of persons as life, liberty, and the pursuit of property. Private ownership, whether on the part of individuals or multinational corporations, tends to be viewed as a sacred right in modern, western, industrial societies. Other societies, such as Native American communities,

have no concept of the individual, private ownership of land. The earth was regarded as a common environment for the support of all living things, and not a commodity to be bought and sold for profit. The private ownership of property, and the right of owners to use it as they desire, has made it difficult to achieve a consensus on the best ways to use land in the interests of all the earth's inhabitants, future generations, and the planet itself.

The Value of Scientific Innovation

The unrestrained exploitation of the earth's resources has been supported by a tremendous confidence in scientific ingenuity to solve any environmental problems that might arise. If at present we do not have effective techniques for safely disposing nuclear waste, we can continue to produce waste, confident that science will find a way. When an American president was recently asked how an antiballistic missile system in space could be 100 percent effective, he responded: "That's for the scientists to figure out." This places tremendous trust in the ability of scientific experts to manipulate the natural environment as if the earth was a scientific laboratory. However, the expansion of technology, and the very scientific innovations that have made this expansion possible, have created serious disruptions of the natural environment. The values of dominion, exploitation, consumption, private property, and scientific innovation have all contributed to the creation of a set of environmental problems in the modern world.

Purity and Danger

Industrial expansion has created serious dangers for the ecosystem of the planet. Modern human beings have been convinced that the natural environment can be freely exploited and converted to energy for human use. But, according to Newton's second law of thermodynamics, every increase in energy in one part of a system results in an overall decrease of energy in the system as a whole. This is the law of entropy.[50] As primary fuel sources shifted from wood to coal to oil and natural gas, the total available energy in the ecosystem of the planet has been gradually depleted. New awareness of this physical law of entropy has encouraged the search for renewable sources of energy, like solar and wind power; and a recognition that human beings need to live within the limits imposed by a careful conservation of resources. On the ethical level is a growing awareness that more is not necessarily better for the fate of the earth. The technological exploitation of natural resources has generated the need for a new sense of ethical responsibility in relation to the natural environment.

Increased technological productivity has also resulted in more environmental pollution. The United States alone emits close to 200 million tons of pollution into the air every year. Pollution from automobiles, factories, and industrial waste threatens the life-support system of air, water, and soil that makes any life on earth possible. The earth is a unique environment in which an intricate network of interrelated natural conditions support life. The earth is a living system.[51] Evidence is mounting that suggests that the disruption of one element in the life chain has an effect on all other links in the ecosystem of the planet.

Human industry has endeavored to dominate the environment, but it has had a number of unexpected consequences. The total temperature of the earth has been gradually increasing through the concentrated release of energy caused by industrial production, automobiles, and other sources of heat. Some scientists have estimated that a 10 percent increase in the earth's temperature will cause melting of the polar ice caps and make much of the present land areas uninhabitable. Fluorocarbons from spray cans are believed to have a damaging effect on the ozone layer of the earth's atmosphere, which filters out harmful ultraviolet rays from the sun. Nuclear radiation, and the production of radioactive waste materials, have increased the overall radioactivity of the planet and have provided potential dangers to health and well-being. These environmental dangers are just a few of the unexpected consequences of the technological exploitation of the environment. Whether these dangers are real, exaggerated, or imagined, they have played an important role in reshaping a sense of ethical responsibility toward the natural environment.

The ethical imagination is often motivated by a powerful desire for purity in relation to its environment. Perhaps the deepest level of the human ethical imagination is reflected in the desire for purity and the fear of defilement. These desires are also strong forces in environmental ethics. One reason that the automobile, for example, was initially such an attractive technological innovation was that it promised to be a cleaner mode of transportation than traditional horse-drawn vehicles. The automobile seemed to be the answer to the problem of "horse-pollution" that plagued the streets of cities, towns, and villages. Eventually, the automobile has turned out to be more dangerously polluting than even good old-fashioned horse manure. But its initial acceptance was supported by a desire for purity.

The other side of the desire for purity is the fear of defilement. Deeply ingrained in humanity's ritual and ethical imagination is the fear of contagion from contact with polluting objects. One aspect of the heightened perception of danger in environmental pollution is certainly a trace of this ancient fear of defilement. Many people feel victimized, dehumanized, and defiled by the vast industrial technologies of the modern world. These are powerful forces that are beyond human control. The horrors of industrial pollution take on an almost mythic proportion in the popular imagination.[52] Pollution represents dangerous, contaminating, and defiling forces that threaten to disrupt the human and natural order of the world.

At the same time, however, many people feel the need to affirm a greater sense of solidarity with the planet. This is not simply the fear of pollution, but an impulse to assume greater responsibility for human actions that affect the natural order. It is a desire to maintain the natural purity of the earth. The purity, order, and harmony of nature are affirmed as values in their own right. This affirmation of natural values is essentially an aesthetic sense that the design, rhythms, and forces of nature have an intrinsic beauty that should not be disrupted through human intervention. Religious ethics in the western tradition have supported the disruption, domination, and exploitation of the natural order. Recently, however, people have turned to alternative traditions of religious ethics to draw resources for an environmental ethics that would allow human beings to fulfill their potential in harmony with the natural environment.

The Environmental Ethics of the Tao and St. Francis

Images from eastern religious traditions, which bring the harmony between humanity and nature into focus, have been attractive in recent environmental ethics. The ancient Chinese symbol of the Tao, with its deep commitment to a harmonious balance between the forces of nature, has been invoked by the historian and philosopher of religion Huston Smith to represent a new ecological consciousness in the western world. "To designate this complete divine ecology," Smith observed, "the Chinese used the word Tao."[53] The order, symmetry, and harmony of the Tao suggest a view of the natural world in which all its diverse forces are interrelated. The natural and human worlds are woven together in this complex unity. As the Taoist sage Chuang-tzu said, "Heaven and Earth and I are one."[54] The Way of the Tao is a path of harmony with the sacred natural environment. It is a unified relationship of mutual interdependence.

The harmony of the Tao is based upon the rhythms of nature that alternate between creative expansion (*yang*) and passive contraction (*yin*). To act in harmony with this alternating rhythm demonstrates natural wisdom. The Taoists describe the possibility of an effortless, balanced, and harmonious action. This style of being in the world does not simply impose human projects upon the natural environment, but it listens to the unspoken voice of nature. In this sense, it is described as non-doing (*wu-wei*). But the ideal of the Tao is not a passive inactivity. That would simpy be the yin without the yang. Taoist texts encourage a balance between contemplation and action: "Now *yin*, now *yang:* that is the Tao."[55] This sensitivity to the rhythms of nature, responsive to the powers and the limits of the natural environment, has provided resources for a religious ethics of the environment that presents an alternative to the western preoccupation with the domination of nature.

Some have suggested that there are already resources for a new ecological awareness within western religious traditions. The historian Lynn White has nominated St. Francis of Assisi as the patron saint of ecologists. According to legend, Francis preached sermons to the birds and the wolves and sang hymns of praise to nature that expressed a common bond between humans and the natural environment. Francis sang to Brother Sun and Sister Moon. The creation was not held in contempt, but was felt to be animated with the glory of its creator. The creation was not an alien wilderness to be dominated, but a common family in which the brotherhood and sisterhood of all creatures were affirmed. Francis tried to replace the myth of dominion with a poetic vision of the world based on the sacred bonds of love that link all living things.

White has suggested that the solution to environmental problems does not lie in more science and technology, but in precisely such a revolutionary spiritual vision of the relation between humanity and nature.

> *Both our present science and our present technology are so tinctured with orthodox Christian arrogance toward nature that no solution for our ecologic crisis can be expected from them alone. Since the roots of our trouble are so largely religious, the remedy must also be essentially religious, whether we call it that or not. We must rethink and refeel our nature and destiny.*[56]

This rethinking and refeeling calls for a new spiritual ecology that would revolutionize the technological ethos. The remedy would require a deeper commitment to discovering, or rediscovering, powerful images of the relation between human beings and the world around them that would hold a compelling power for thought, feeling, and action. This would be, as Lynn White has noted, a fundamentally religious enterprise in environmental ethics.

Nature is not a constant in human experience. It has been shaped and reshaped in the history of the human imagination. The technological ethos has been the dominant force in molding the modern imagination of nature, as well as in transforming the natural environment itself. In the most immediate human experience, nature is already shaped by cultural images: desires and fears, projects and dreams, creativity and destructiveness. The challenge of environmental ethics is to channel that creativity and limit the destructiveness in order to build a context for action that is at once more human and more natural.

Patterns of Technology

The technological ethos so pervades the modern worldview that it sets the agenda for ethics in the modern world. Technological innovations in science, industry, and social engineering have developed at such a rapid pace that the ethical imagination has struggled to keep up with the new challenges posed by technology in human social relations. Technology determines the normative pattern of action—techne determines how things ought to be done—in areas of personal and social action that were once governed by ritual, ethics, and the cultivation of moral virtues. Traditional systems of religious ethics were grounded in ritual; modern ethics is grounded in the ritualized perfection promised by the technological manipulation of the environment. Ritual and technology are both attempts to factor out the accidents, contingencies, and uncontrollable forces of ordinary life in order to create a perfectly controlled environment for human action. Technological control establishes an ideal pattern of action within which modern religious ethics struggles to define itself. Chapter 10 has drawn a number of conclusions regarding the challenges of technology in the ethics of social relations.

1.   *The three modes of action—ritual, work, and leisure—potentially can be integrated in any human activity.* Human action can be interpreted as a communication network that invests

activity with meaning, usefulness, and pleasure. Ritual communicates meaningful action, work communicates useful action, and leisure communicates pleasurable action. Religious ethics has traditionally found ways to superimpose meaning on the sheer utility of work. Work as vocation, prayer, meditation, service, and so on is regarded as both useful and meaningful within a larger religious context. The superimposition of religious meaning upon human work has been a way of transcending what might be experienced as the meaningless cycle of working to live and living to work. But the values of leisure may also be infused in work. Work that is invested with enthusiasm, care, and craftsmanship may also assume the pleasurable qualities associated with leisure. A pattern of action that integrates meaning, utility, and pleasure fulfills the experiential potential of human action.

———

2.   *The technological ethos supports the value of utility in action to the exclusion of all other values.* Technology serves the value of efficiency in useful, productive work. This technological value of efficiency is supported by abstract standards of measurement, rational organization of behavior, and the mechanized industrialization of work. These factors contribute to the overarching cultural value of technical efficiency in action. The technological ethos pervades the modern worldview. Technology may have made human life more efficient, but, in the process, it has shaped human identity, action, and experience to its own demands. "The great cultural fallacy of industrialization," as the cultural anthropologist Edward Sapir noted, "is that in harnessing machines to our uses it has not known how to avoid the harnessing of the majority of mankind to its machines."[57] The technological ethos upholds a significant reversal in the relation between human beings and machines. Machines designed to extend human power acquire

an inherent technological power of their own, which ultimately extends over human action.

The power of the technological ethos has gained a tremendous degree of control in the modern world. It is not a power that is wielded by one person, or group of persons, even though it is identified with specific political, social, and economic interests in modern social relations. Rather, the power of the technological ethos pervades the entire network of social relations, and everyone is enmeshed in its inherent demands for technical efficiency in action. This techno-power is reinforced by the power of possibility, which allows technological innovations to develop according to their own internal logic; by the power of expertise, which reserves the relevant technological knowledge for specialized, scientific experts; by the power of exclusion, which sets aside all other considerations of human values with the exception of utility; and by the power of reinforcement, which disciplines, manipulates, and controls human behavior through a system of rewards and punishments. This pervasive power of the technological ethos is a profound ethical challenge in modern social relations. Religious ethics may provide important resources for recovering a sense of the human potential for choosing, knowing, expanding, and acting in response to the technological ethos of the modern worldview.

———

3.   *Religious ethics supports certain attitudes toward the relation between human technology and the natural environment.* Two dominant metaphors are available to the ethical imagination in its confrontation with nature: nature as machine and nature as organism. Each metaphor implies a different attitude toward the natural environment. Mechanical nature may be controlled, manipulated, and adjusted to human purposes. A long tradition of western religious ethics has supported this kind of human dominion over

nature. But to treat nature as a living organism is to assume that nature has its own independent vitality, rhythms, and forces that simply cannot be reduced to human ends. Recent environmental ethics has attempted to uncover ethical resources in both western and eastern religious traditions for a more responsible human relationship with the natural environment that would preserve the internal balance of nature as a living organism. Perhaps the metaphors of machine and organism can be integrated in an environmental ethics that acknowledges the necessity of transforming nature to human use, but also respects the inherent meaning and potential enjoyment of nature as an ecological organism in its own right. The technological ethos has isolated the value of utility in the exploitation of human and natural resources. The challenge of technology in the modern world lies in the potential for integrating utility with meaning and pleasure in patterns of ethical action within human social relations.

CHAPTER

ELEVEN

ECONOMICS

Only recently in western societies have human beings become "economic animals."[1] The economy of modern, western, industrialized societies, in which self-regulating markets determine value through a pricing system based only on supply and demand, is unprecedented in the history of human societies. No previous society was ever controlled by markets. Gain made on exchange never before played such an important role as a social motive for action. The institution of markets has been fairly common in human social relations since the Stone Age, but its role was always incidental to the overall economic life of the community. In the modern world, however, economic life is governed by a set of market values. These purely economic values and motives provide the basic context within which ethical issues of goods, exchange, and scarcity arise in the modern world.

The economist Adam Smith, in *The Wealth of Nations* (1776), defined the marketplace as the arena in which human beings express their "propensity to barter, truck and exchange one thing for another."[2] He assumed that this propensity, motivated by the human desire for profit, gain, and economic advantage through exchange, was the controlling factor in all human activities. Modern economic theory is based on this assumption that the desire to maximize profit and to minimize loss is a universal human motive for action in the world. In this sense, human beings are perceived as essentially economic animals.

This exclusively economic definition of human desires, motives, and values, however, ignores the fact that human economies are embedded in a deeper network of social relations. In traditional societies, economic motives spring from the context of social life. The ethical conduct of economic exchange is grounded in social patterns of custom, law, and religion. Economic activity is part of a larger social environment of shared meanings, motives, and desires; it is what the French sociologist Marcel Mauss called a "total social fact," which is simultaneously economic, social, ethical, and religious.[3] It may be hard to imagine a society in which economic life is not motivated by a desire for profit at the expense of others, where people do not labor for wages, where business is not conducted on the principle of the least effort for the greatest gain, and where there are no separate institutions based on purely economic motives. Yet, this is what students of economic anthropology discover when examining the production and distribution of goods in traditional societies. We will consider how economic activity is grounded in the ethics of social relations.

Powerful ethical values are at work in economic action. First, ethical values infuse the acquisition, possession, and use of goods. Goods are not simply useful for consumption, but they are also meaningful within a network of social relations. Goods communicate the order of the social world, a person's place in that world, and a system of shared values that are represented by the goods that people possess, consume, or display. We will begin with a consideration of the symbolic significance that human beings invest in the world of goods.

Economic exchanges are embedded in ethical patterns of social action and interaction. The history of economics reveals three basic patterns of economic exchange: reciprocity, redistribution, and market exchange. Reciprocity is a balanced pattern of exchange, redistribution is a centralized pattern of exchange, and the market economy establishes a competitive pattern of exchange. Each type of economic activity is grounded in a different arrangement of social relations, and these social arrangements reveal the contrasting ethical values that are invested in processes of economic exchange. Finally, the central challenge in economic ethics is the problem of scarcity. We will consider the variety of religious and ethical responses to the challenge of scarcity, lack, and deprivation in the economic ethics of human social relations.

The World of Goods

Why do people want goods? Why do people want to acquire, possess, and consume things? Economists assume that people want goods for three reasons. The first reason is material welfare. Human beings want to acquire those things that are necessary to satisfy the basic physical needs of food, shelter, and clothing. The second reason is psychic welfare. The acquisition of goods can bring various psychological benefits. People may want goods in order to feel a sense of security, peace of mind, status, enjoyment, and so on. Finally, the third reason why people want goods is competitive display. Thorstein Veblen coined the term *conspicuous consumption* to capture the sense in which human beings acquire things in order to compete with each other for social prestige. The public acquisition, display, and consumption of goods communicates the consumer's status in a world of consumers. This last motive for acquiring goods suggests that people do not want things simply for their utility. Things, objects, and artifacts convey something about the person who possesses them. Goods are part of a larger system of social communication.

Goods as a Communication System

Besides the fact that commodities are good for eating, clothing, and shelter, goods also provide a network of information about a person's identity, social standing, and the social world he or she inhabits. Goods are a communication system for shared values within a society. They are not simply good to use, but they are also good to think with. People want goods, not only because they are useful, but also because they form a system of symbolic communication within human social relations.

The Order of the World of Goods

Goods communicate the structure, pattern, and order of the social world. Objects carry social meanings. They give a visible, tangible, and relatively stable form to the social categories of a community. Goods serve as a system of fixed public meaning, a network of nonverbal symbolism, that makes social relations possible. "A social life," as the sociologist of religion Emile Durkheim insisted, "in all its aspects and in every period of its history, is made possible only by a vast symbolism."[4] Goods form the raw materials for social life. The acquisition, possession, and exchange of commodities provide a material basis for social relations. But goods also organize a system of symbolic meanings that provide a sense of the meaningful order of the social world.

The goods that human beings acquire, exchange, and consume are units within a social code; they are units of meaning and value within the symbolic order of any society. Every product is a symbol. It embodies a particular meaning, significance, or value within social relations that,

as Karl Marx observed, "converts every product into a social hieroglyphic."[5] The meaning and value attributed to different goods are part of a larger order of meaning and value in any worldview. Goods do not simply satisfy material needs; they communicate the basic order of meaning and value in the social world in which human beings live.

Personal Place in the World of Goods

Goods communicate something of the identity of the person who acquires, consumes, or exchanges them in the social world. The products that are available in a society form the symbolic vocabulary from which people make statements about who they are in that social world. Out of the material stuff that is available to work with, people create visible, tangible, and material images of themselves. The foods we eat, the clothes we wear, the houses we live in—everything we possess—contribute in subtle, and detailed, ways to communicate our personal place in the world.

Everything has intricate symbolic associations. A ring, for example, may have a value that cannot be expressed in purely economic terms. It may symbolize a certain social status, a personal history, and a variety of feelings, memories, and associations. All objects weave a rich texture of associations. Out of these symbolic associations, human beings communicate in a detailed, tangible, and concrete way the precise quality of their involvement in the world. A person's place in the social world corresponds to the person's place in the world of goods.

Shared Values in the World of Goods

The public meaning of objects grows out of a shared network of symbolic associations. The symbolic vocabulary of goods reflects shared values regarding the significance of different possessions. The possession of some types of goods may symbolically separate one class of people from those who do not possess these things. The symbolic vocabulary of goods reinforces inequalities of social status, but may also allow people to share a common identity through sharing goods. Human beings identify with each other by sharing in a common participation in the world of goods. A system of shared values takes three basic forms: marking, naming, and proving. Each of these activities demonstrates shared values through the communication medium provided by goods.

First, human beings use goods to visibly, tangibly, and publicly mark values. Goods are used to inscribe values on the world. Symbolic marking makes use of goods to indicate the value of certain events and the value of different classes of people. Goods are used to mark events of importance: feasts, birthdays, and celebrations. On such occasions, goods may be given, exchanged, or consumed. The value of such goods does not lie in their consumption, but in their ability to signify an important event within the social world. Goods may also define different types of people by the characteristic objects that are associated with certain social classes, geographic areas, ethnic groups, genders, and occupations. Goods tangibly mark out a classification system of different types of people within a society.

Second, goods provide a shared system of communication through the common names that are given to things. The anthropologist Mary Douglas has observed that "enjoyment of physical consumption is only part of the service yielded by goods; the other part is the enjoyment of sharing names."[6] Consumer's learn a sophisticated vocabulary of brand names, designer names, manufacturer's names, endorsement names, and so on. These names create a shared communication system within which people make judgments about the relative value of different goods. The familiarity with such names allows for a sense of shared values. This knowledge represents a tremendous investment of time, attention, and energy spent acquiring the information necessary to share in the detailed knowledge of the names of things.

Finally, goods are used to validate the shared values within a society. The proof of the proverbial pudding is in the eating; physical consumption allows people to experience for themselves whether or not a particular cultural value is really valuable. It is a way of testing, proving, and demonstrating that one object is better than another. The consumption of goods provides this opportunity for testing whether a shared system of public values should be trusted in the world of goods. The use of goods, therefore, is not simply motivated by utility. Goods provide the tangible symbols that demonstrate a person's particular involvement, participation, and investment in a world of shared meanings and values.

Money

Money is not simply one type of good among many. It is a relatively independent system of value that may be imposed upon the world of goods. A symbolic system of monetary value may be used to classify the value of goods. "Money is a system of symbols," as the economist Karl Polanyi observed, "similar to language, writing, or weights and measures."[7] Money was first developed in ancient Mesopotamia, during the third millennium B.C., for use in keeping temple records, carrying out public works projects, allowing for a division of labor, and facilitating borrowing and lending.[8] In the market economies of modern, western, industrialized societies, money has become the dominant symbolic system for the measurement of value.

Money is used in three ways. First, it serves as payment. In a situation of obligation, or indebtedness, handing over certain socially designated objects is invested with the symbolic power of voiding the obligation. Second, money serves as a standard of measurement. It provides a way of measuring the value of different goods on a common scale. This quantitative standard of measurement is useful in bartering—to equalize two sides of an exchange—and in budgeting—to add up and balance the values of different things. Finally, money serves as a means of indirect exchange. Money may be acquired for future exchange in a transfer of goods that is unrelated to the initial exchange. The three uses of money demonstrate the common role that this symbolic medium of payment, measurement, and exchange plays in an economic system.

The power of money has stretched far beyond its simple uses. Shakespeare called money "the visible god."[9] It has assumed an almost sacred power to determine values in human social relations. Money has become the dominant symbol system in the modern world. Its economic measurement of value has transformed, and often neutralized, other ways of measuring worth. Karl Marx insisted that "the divine power of money" has succeeded in "overturning and confounding all human and natural qualities."[10] Money has become the primary symbol of both power and alienation in the modern world. The possession of money is a profound cultural symbol of transcendence, but the lack of money is an equally powerful symbol of alienation, frustration, and oppression.

Money has different symbolic significance in different cultures. Traditional societies tended to be locative money cultures. Money was used as a symbolic medium of exchange to maintain an equilibrium in society through an equal balance in the exchange of wealth. In locative money cultures, as the historian of religion Jonathan Z. Smith has observed, "exchange, the acquisition of foodstuffs or other wealth, is ultimately a means of keeping one's place."[11] Money was used to maintain this sense of place in the social order through balanced economic exchanges among members of the same social group.

Modern societies, however, can be described as open money cultures. Money is a means for climbing the ladder of social status, class, or place. It is a symbol of social mobility. Money symbolizes a certain freedom to transcend social limits. As J. Z. Smith has noted: "In an expansive, open culture money becomes an important means of expressing transcendence of place."[12] The symbolic system represented by money, therefore, may be used to maintain or transcend place depending on the nature of the social order in which it operates.

Wealth

The transcendent power of money in the modern world has evoked a variety of responses in religious ethics. The way Christian social ethics dealt with the monetary economy of America in the nineteenth century suggests two different ethical responses to wealth. The first ethical response emerged in the Gospel of Wealth. Here the unrestrained acquisition of money was viewed as a basic Christian virtue and a symbolic demonstration of moral worth. The expansion of personal wealth was seen as an intrinsically Christian moral calling. The theologian D. S. Gregory wrote in the 1880s, in his *Christian Ethics,* that "by the proper use of wealth man may greatly elevate and extend his moral work. . . . The Moral Governor has placed the power of acquisitiveness in man for a good and noble purpose."[13] That noble purpose included the stewardship of the earth's resources, the authority to discipline less fortunate people to be productive workers, and the moral privilege to enjoy the fruits of their labors. The accumulation of treasures on earth was not seen as a symbol of sinful greed, but as a sign of morality. "In the long run," as Bishop Lawrence of Massachusetts declared, "it is only to the man of morality that wealth comes. . . . Godliness is in league with riches."[14] The Gospel of Wealth proclaimed that the possession of the transcendent power of money demonstrated moral virtue.

A different response to the expanding monetary economy in American society appeared in the nineteenth century Social Gospel. This movement within American Christianity sought to change those social practices and institutions that led to extreme poverty, poor living conditions, undernourishment, and disease among the industrial working class. The Social Gospel insisted that "men are obliged to act directly upon the social order and work for its reconstruction, as part of their religious responsibility to their fellow men."[15] Wealth was not perceived as a demonstration of moral virtue, but rather as the result of immoral social conditions that created such vast inequalities in the distribution of wealth in society. Wealth did not appear as a sign of moral transcendence, but as a power that alienated the poor, disinherited, and underprivileged people in modern, industrial social relations.

Traces of these two responses to the symbolic power of money are still present in religious social ethics today. Some still perceive money as a symbol of transcendence. The Baptist minister and founder of the Moral Majority, Jerry Falwell, has insisted that the Bible supports free enterprise, competition in the marketplace, and effective business practices. Falwell has affirmed an ethics of wealth in his book *Listen America:*

> *The free-enterprise system is clearly outlined in the Book of Proverbs in the Bible. Jesus Christ made it clear that the work ethic was a part of His plan for man. Ownership of property is biblical. Competition in business is biblical. Ambitious and successful business management is clearly outlined as part of God's plan for His people.*[16]

From Falwell's perspective, Christianity is seen to be consistent with the accumulation of wealth and power. On the other hand, some still see money as a symbol of alienation. Various movements have emerged under the title of Liberation Theology to insist that Christian social ethics address the institutionalized poverty in Latin America, Africa, and elsewhere, which has created suffering, disease, and death for the poor. Liberation theology refers to the economic ethics of the early Christian community—as described in the Book of Acts when Christians "held all things in common"—to suggest that Christian social ethics demands an equitable distribution of resources, opportunities, and wealth.[17]

Charity

Many religious traditions seek to resolve the dilemma of economic inequity through the ideal of charity. In acts of charity goods are again valuable not just for their utility, consumption, or monetary value. By giving goods away a person can make a symbolic statement about the level of his or her commitment to the ideals of the religious tradition. In traditional Hindu social ethics this is expressed in the ethical ideal of *danadharma*— the duty of giving. Danadharma is the ongoing religious obligation to give money, food, or clothing to the poor, the homeless, beggars, and monks. According to the karmic law of cause and effect, good will result for the gift freely given. As the sociologist Marcel Mauss described the process of danadharma, "the thing given brings return in this life and in the other."[18] Buddhism also holds danadharma as an important ethical obligation. To give charity is to demonstrate the highest virtue in the Buddhist life: the virtue of compassion. Another incentive for lay Buddhists, who seek to gain merit in this life that will be of benefit in a future life, is that charitable gifts to monks are believed to be repaid with spiritual merit. The act of *dana* will be rewarded by a reciprocal return of spiritual value.

Western religious traditions have also placed value upon acts of charity. In Judaism, the giving of charity (*tzdakah*) is regarded as a very important ethical duty. The third of the five basic ritual practices of Islam is charity (*zakat*). Giving alms to the poor is seen as a basic ethical duty to the community, just as giving worship through prayer is a ritual duty to Allah. The Christian New Testament elevates the ethical virtue of charity to a special status. In one passage, Jesus informs his followers that admittance to the kingdom of heaven will be based on their charity to fellow human beings in need. (Mt. 25:31–46) Acts of charity in these traditions are seen as an ethical means of redistributing wealth to the poor. They symbolize ethical responsibility for the distribution of wealth through the society as a whole.

The ideals of charity in religious ethics represent attitudes toward the ethical value of economic exchange that differ from the attitudes that pervade modern market economies. In Hinduism and Buddhism, the ideal of dana is supported by a pattern of equivalent, or balanced, exchange of material goods for spiritual merit. This is an example of economic exchange based on reciprocity. The ideal of charity in Judaism, Christianity, and Islam is motivated by the desire for a more equitable distribution of material goods according to need. This is an example of economic exchange based on redistribution. Both reciprocity and redistribution are creative responses to inequities in goods, possessions, and wealth. They are the basic patterns of economic exchange in traditional societies. As traditional strategies for exchanging goods, reciprocity and redistribution conflict with the competitive values of modern, market-based economies. The differences among these three systems of economic exchange reveal how exchange functions as a total social fact within the world of goods.

Exchange

Economics is necessarily involved in ethical patterns of action in human societies. Economic anthropology has shown that the complex activities concerned with the production, distribution, exchange, and consumption of goods and services are grounded in social relations. This is particularly evident in tribal, primitive, or peasant economies where economic practices are "embedded in the social matrix."[19] In each society, the accepted practices of exchanging goods and services represent a particular quality of social interaction. The motive behind economic activity, as George Homans has suggested, is the quality of these "interactions between persons in an exchange of goods, material and non-material."[20] The interactions are conditioned by social, religious, and ethical norms that limit the impulse to maximize profit, gain, acquisition, utility, and so on. Purely economic motives are always embedded in a pattern of social interactions. And the ethical obligations governing these interactions make economic exchange a total social fact.

We have become so accustomed to thinking of economic activity as unrestrained competition for advantage in the marketplace—buying and selling goods, services, and labor in the interests of profit—that it is hard to imagine other motives at work in economic exchange. But, as the anthropologists Firth and Yamey have noted, "it is possible to conceive of an economic system in which the items of productivity . . . are status tokens and symbolic ties."[21] Economic exchange is a symbolic system that represents the ties of kinship, the relative status of people in society, and ethical ideals of human interaction in the ways that goods and services are distributed. Economic exchange is also symbolic exchange. Exchange is not simply a useful activity; it is also a meaningful symbolic system that represents the most deeply held ethical values within social relations.

There are three basic patterns of economic exchange. The first is *reciprocity,* which is a balanced exchange of goods or services. It is an exchange based on cooperation between equal partners for the advantage of both. Reciprocity is an equal exchange: neither one up nor one down, neither more nor less. The second pattern of economic exchange is *redistribution,* which is a rhythmic exchange where goods flow into the possession of a centralized authority—a chief, a Big Man, or a rulership—and then are redistributed, according to social convention. Goods are usually redistributed through feasts, festivals, or gift-giving ceremonies in such a way as to define and reinforce the hierarchy of status within the network of social relations. The third pattern of economic exchange is *market exchange,* which is the competitive style of economic activity that dominates modern, western, industrial societies. Market exchange is not grounded in the traditional ethical norms, obligations, and ties of the previous systems of exchange, but is determined solely by economic activity within free-floating markets. The major principles of market exchange are supply and demand and the profit motive. In market exchange people buy and sell goods, services, and labor in an open marketplace where supply and demand set the value. People are motivated by the competitive impulse for gain through exchange. However, we must recognize that all of these systems of exchange are total social facts (even market exchange) where social, ethical, and religious norms influence the economic process of exchange.

Reciprocity

In subsistence societies, in which people produce just enough goods to satisfy the basic needs for survival, cooperation is essential in both the natural and social environments. Cooperation takes the form of kinship obligations for the mutual support of all family members. This cooperation is extended among kinship groups through social mechanisms for distributing goods and thereby maintaining a pattern of interactions within a larger social network. This reciprocal cooperation is necessary for survival. In the exchange of goods and services, as the anthropologist Bronislaw Malinowski observed, human beings are not "activated by pure economic motives of enlightened self-interest."[22] Exchange takes the form of reciprocal gifts that are intended to be to the advantage of everyone involved. These reciprocal exchanges of goods and services, however, are not simply an economic activity: They are events that are simultaneously social and economic, religious and magical, utilitarian and sentimental, legal, moral, and customary.

First, reciprocity is regarded as an ethical act. The norm of reciprocity involves a commitment to a quality of human relations. Here, as the anthropologist Radcliffe-Brown noted, "the purpose of exchange is primarily a moral one; to bring about a friendly feeling between the two persons who participate."[23] Exchange is a symbolic activity that reinforces the recognized ethical responsibilities between two people for their mutual support. The ethical norm of reciprocity defines a basic pattern of justice in social relations. The rule of reciprocity, as Alvin Gouldner has suggested, is that "people should help those who help them; and should not injure those who help them."[24] Reciprocal exchange is an ethical commitment to mutual advantage in economic relations.

Second, reciprocity involves basic ethical judgments. Those people who are included in a system of reciprocal exchange are classified as good, but those who are excluded are classified as evil. Reciprocal exchanges make implicit ethical statements about the moral value of trading partners. The anthropologist Claude Lévi-Strauss has explored the ways in which patterns of economic exchange become ways of classifying people.

> *The primitives know only two ways of classifying strangers; strangers are either "good" or "bad."* . . . *A "good" group is that to which, without hesitating, one grants hospitality, the one for which one deprives oneself of most precious goods; while the "bad" group is that from which one expects and to which one inflicts, at the first opportunity, suffering and death. With the latter one fights; with the former one exchanges goods.* [25]

To enter into a reciprocal exchange is to make an ethical judgment that one's partner is good and worthy of support. To deny economic exchange to someone is part of a larger pattern of social exclusion, antagonism, and conflict. These ethical judgments are embodied in patterns of economic exchange.

Third, reciprocity may be regarded as a social obligation with ethical consequences. Giving a gift places the recipient under obligation to return either material or nonmaterial values in exchange. In order to complete the balanced exchange, the receiver is obligated to reciprocate with something of equal or greater value. As Marcel Mauss noted, this return may take the form of "courtesies, entertainments, rituals, military assistance, women, children, dances, feasts and fairs." [26] But, however the recipient responds, these relations of mutual obligation are perceived as values in and of themselves. They represent the values of human friendship, community, and support as symbolized through the activity of exchange. In this way, the pattern of

reciprocal exchange is a social obligation that reinforces the ties that bind the community together.

We can illustrate the ways in which reciprocity operates as a total social fact through selected examples of economic exchange in subsistence societies. Reciprocity is the most common form of exchange in hunting and gathering societies, animal-herding (or pastoralist) societies, and small-scale agricultural communities. In these examples, as the economic anthropologists Barry Hindess and Paul Hurst have noted, reciprocity is "generated and sustained by . . . ritual and ceremony, and by social practices of reciprocal acknowledgement of relationship." [27] Religious, social, and economic forces combine to form a total pattern of ethical action in reciprocal exchange.

Hunting and Gathering Societies

Economic anthropologists have analyzed the relation between religion and economic activities in hunting and gathering societies. One example of a religio-economic pattern of reciprocal exchange is found among a group of Australian aborigines. The world of these aborigines is ordered by a classification system that divides everything into different sections. In this organizing system, all the elements of nature fall into one of four classifications. People are also divided among these four groups, and each group has its own specific rights and obligations. One group, the *Palt'arri* section, performs rituals that allow a person to have a baby or to breed kangaroos. The Palt'arri have the responsibility for performing these rites because they are identified with the division of the world that includes sperm. The *Karimarra* section performs rituals for rainmaking because they belong to the division of the world that includes thunder and the sun. The Australian aborigines believe that the maintenance of the world depends on the ongoing cooperation among each of the sections in performing the necessary rituals.

The same cooperation and mutual support is carried out in the exchange of goods and services. The shared responsibilities among sections, which are defined by their ritual practices, determine the pattern of economic exchange. There is a formal analogy between ritual cooperation and cooperation in the distribution of goods and services. As Maurice Godelier has described this arrangement, ritual cooperation "is thus formally identical to the generalized and reciprocal cooperation which exists between sections within the relations of production."[28] The pattern of economic exchange imitates the reciprocal cooperation among sections that is carried on in their ritual practices. Economic reciprocity supports the social world, as ritual cooperation is felt to sustain the natural order.

Another example of how ritual practices can determine economic relations is found in the reciprocal pattern of exchange among the !Kung Bushmen of the Kalahari. In the naming rituals of the community, each child is named after a relative and is thereby introduced into the network of mutual economic support formed by that relative's kinship allegiances. But in addition to this, anyone who shares that same name is considered to be part of the same kinship system, for purposes of material aid and support. Since there are relatively few names—46 male names and 41 female names in the Nyal Nyal region—the individual can draw upon a wide range of economic support from all the people who share the same name.

The naming ritual, and the economic interdependence of all people who have the same name, is supported by the !Kung belief in two gods: a great god and a lesser god who was named for the great god. Because these gods share the same name, they are felt to have a common sacred essence. To share a name is to share a common identity. For the !Kung, this is true in both the divine world and the human world. All people who share the same name are responsible for their mutual economic support as if they shared a common identity. "Thus through this system of social relations," as Jeremy Keenan has observed, "all !Kung can expect the same kind of reciprocity from virtually all members of the 'collectivity' as they would expect from their own kinsmen."[29] The !Kung's religious beliefs in the sacred power of names reinforces a system of reciprocal economic exchange for mutual support of all members of society.

Pastoralist Societies

Societies that base their subsistence on raising livestock may also develop forms of economic exchange based on reciprocity. The raising of cattle, and the distribution of cattle among members of the society, have important religious associations among the herders of the Nile. Pierre Bonte has asked, "Why do these economic practices take a religious form? These herdsmen are certainly engaged in production, but why do they consider it part of their religious practice?"[30] The answer lies in the fact that these societies are held together by ritual practices that involve the ritual slaughter, consumption, and circulation of cattle. Livestock performs a dual symbolic function: It creates a ritual relationship between human beings and God through rituals of sacrifice, and it establishes and sustains social relations through the gifts, loans, and exchanges of cattle.

The Jie tribe, a group of Nilotic pastoralists, unite the members of the community through ritual practices that involve cattle. Ritual sacrifices regulate the consumption of meat. These practices determine the times, places, and order for the ritual eating of cattle. The community members believe that they share a common relationship with God by performing rituals with cattle that they all hold in common. Thus, the proper ethical relationship between human beings and cattle is circulation. The ritual requirements for the common possession of cattle encourages reciprocal exchanges through giving, loaning, and trading livestock.[31]

Among the Nuer pastoralists, as the anthropologist E. E. Evans-Pritchard observed, cows are not simply a symbol of wealth: "They are the means by which men can enter into communication with God."[32] Through the ritual sacrifice of cattle, the Nuer communicate with God, and through the reciprocal exchange of cattle, they communicate with each other. The reciprocal exchange of livestock maintains a certain social and ethical equilibrium within these pastoralist groups.

Small-Scale Agricultural Societies

Reciprocity may also be the normative pattern of economic exchange in the social life of small agricultural villages. The sociologist Stanley Tambiah has described how the ethics of reciprocity operates in the economic life of a Buddhist village in Thailand. "Reciprocity is a conspicuous social norm in the village," Tambiah has observed, "It is expressed in the mutual aid in economic tasks in which the notion of equivalence in giving and receiving is explicit."[33] This general pattern of reciprocity in economic exchange supports the social life of the village. It is also demonstrated in periodic religious gift-giving ceremonies devoted to the support of the local Buddhist monks. The villagers believe that their donations to the monks will be reciprocated by spiritual merit.

The sociologist Melford Spiro has also shown that reciprocity is the center of economic life in the Buddhist villages of Burma. Any surplus from agriculture, and the production of goods, is spent almost entirely on religion: alms for the monks, decorations for the temples, and elaborate religious celebrations. Saving economic surplus for the purpose of investment is discouraged. Resistance to saving and investment is not simply a factor of small surpluses, limited opportunities, and political instability. These Buddhists live within a worldview that encourages people to gain spiritual merit by giving away any surplus goods. Perhaps this could be described as a form of spiritual investment: material gifts for spiritual merit.

These Burmese Buddhists derive social benefits from giving, such as prestige in the community and pleasure at the festivals. But to understand the function of reciprocity in Burmese Buddhist villages we must consider the specifically religious motives for this kind of economic behavior. "Given *their* behavioral environment," Melford Spiro concluded, "religious spending is more efficacious for the satisfaction of material desires than economic savings."[34] The Buddhist ideal of charity (*dana*) allows the Burmese villagers to satisfy their material desires for security, prestige, and pleasure through religious rituals of reciprocity. In this sense, reciprocity weaves together religious, social, and economic functions in a total pattern of exchange.

Redistribution

Redistribution is another pattern of economic exchange that tends to be based on ritualized social relations. But in patterns of redistribution the relations are unequal. In a system of exchange based on redistribution, as the economic anthropologist Harold Schneider has noted, "decisions about production and distribution are made in terms of obligations (which has the effect of achieving the persistence of society) and not in terms of profit."[35] The distribution of goods is determined by some centralized leadership authority in the community. Food, produce, and supplies go into a central storage area, and then are given out to people according to their standing in society or according to their needs. This redistribution may be simple—lasting only for the duration of a hunt or for the length of a growing season—or it may be complex—involving a permanent network of kinship and marriage relationships or social hierarchies of status, prestige, and power. These patterns of redistribution are certainly economic transactions. However, they are guided by social, religious, and ethical customs, duties, and obligations.

In the island societies of Melanesia, for example, the distribution of goods and services is supervised by tribal leaders who are called "Big Men."[36] The Big Men are in a position of religious and social power within these societies because they have managed to inherit, or put together, a network of alliances, mutual support, and dependence among a number of families and clan groups. The Big Men, however, are not themselves wealthy; they do not possess or display great riches. But these impoverished entrepreneurs have the social authority to determine how the produce of the whole community will be distributed to its various members. This authority is based on social standing, not on any quantitative measurement of material wealth.

In many tribal societies wealth is not measured in financial terms. The Ngaju Dyak of Borneo, for example, classify each person into one of three groups: the wealthy, the poor, and the slaves. The wealthy are those people who possess the ritual objects necessary for religious worship. The poor are poor by definition because they do not possess these ritual objects. However, the poor may in fact possess greater material wealth than the so-called wealthy.[37] In redistribution, the exchange of goods and services is regulated by a network of social obligations based on status, class, and prestige.

The Potlatch

One example of the ritual redistribution of goods that has received considerable attention from anthropologists is the ritual of potlatch practiced by Native American Indian tribes in the Pacific Northwest. *Potlatch* comes from a word in the Chinook language meaning "to give."[38] It was a ritual distribution of goods that marked many different religious and social events of the tribal groups. Gift-giving ceremonies would be held to commemorate marriage, death, building a house, initiating a young person, naming an heir, or the annual winter ceremonial. As Irving Goldman has noted, these were "ritual occasions in their own right, at which properties were distributed."[39] The potlatch was a ritualized form of economic redistribution.

A typical potlatching ritual began with invitations from the host to specially selected individuals or groups. When they arrived, the host would entertain the guests with a display of family emblems, dances, and songs. The host family would tell of its hereditary authority and invoke the memory of its ancestors in order to claim social prestige and power over local economic resources. The ritual culminated in a distribution of goods to the guests. Gifts would be given out according to the social rank of the guests. Those with higher rank would be given the finest quality of food, clothing, canoes, and copper coins. Sometimes the host would ceremoniously destroy large quantities of goods to demonstrate his wealth. The end of the ceremony was celebrated with a communal feast.

A number of reasons have been suggested to explain the potlatch as a form of economic behavior among the Pacific Northwest Indians. Attention has been focused primarily on the practices of the Kwakiutl tribes. One explanation sees the potlatch as a ritual means for reinforcing the social prestige of the chiefs among the various Kwakiutl tribes. By competing with each other in giving (or destroying) extravagant gifts, the chiefs demonstrate their wealth and power. Ruth Benedict maintained that the potlatch was motivated by a drive for prestige: "The object of all Kwakiutl enterprises was to show oneself superior to one's rivals."[40] Benedict felt that the whole system of economic exchange among the Pacific Northwest Indians was based on this obsession. The ethical obligation of gift-giving obliged the recipient of a gift at a potlatch to return something of equal or greater value. This led to competition among chiefs to put as many people as possible under their obligation with more and more extravagant gifts.

Other interpreters of the potlatch have emphasized its economic function in the redistribution of goods. Marvin Harris has insisted that "the potlatch is a competitive feast, a nearly universal mechanism for assuring the production and distribution of wealth among peoples who have not yet fully acquired a ruling class."[41] The surplus of fish, game, berries, and roots would be given out at the potlatch to those in need. According to Stuart Piddocke, the ritual was a way of "promoting exchanges of food from those groups enjoying a temporary surplus to those groups suffering a temporary deficit."[42] Those hosts who had surplus goods to give away could establish or reinforce their social prestige by giving these things away during the potlatch ceremony; but they could also facilitate a more efficient redistribution of wealth. Some have even suggested that the potlatch was a primitive system of finance, where gifts are in effect loans that were expected to be repaid with reciprocal gifts at very high interest.[43]

In any case, the potlatch was an important mechanism for the redistribution of goods, produce, and wealth throughout these societies. These economic activities, however, were based in very specific religious practices: They cannot be separated from the celebration of specific myths that stand at the heart of the ritual of exchange. The host would invoke the power and authority of sacred ancestors, whose names were taken by the host and his family, in order to assert their sacred authority over economic resources. According to their myths, these sacred ancestors laid down the customs of the community, instructed people how to dance, dress, paint themselves and wear masks, and initiated the first acts of giving. The ancestors were felt to be a godlike source of valued treasures and powers. "When a chief is proclaiming his powers," as Irving Gold-

man has observed, "it is said they are 'going back to the beginnings.'"[44] This redistribution of goods in the potlatch, therefore, is a total social fact: It has the economic function of circulating goods through the community; the social function of reinforcing the rank, standing, and prestige of certain members of society; and it has the religious function of invoking, celebrating, and appropriating the supernatural power of the ancestors.[45]

Ancient Economies

Redistribution is also the dominant mode of economic exchange in traditional societies with clearly defined social hierarchies. In ancient Egypt and Mesopotamia large palace and temple complexes dominated the economy. Most land was owned and administered by a royal and priestly bureaucracy. Strict political and religious control regulated the distribution of goods. Trade was managed by a single state administration that supervised the economic, military, political, and religious life of society. Ordinary people did not dispose of products on their own; produce was appropriated by the state to be redistributed. These ancient economies were controlled by social hierarchies that rationed out wealth according to a person's social standing. In fact, the economic exchange practiced in the societies of the ancient Near East could probably best be described as a form of rationing.[46]

A rigid social hierarchy also dominated the economy of ancient India. Economic activity was determined by caste relations, and the whole process of production and distribution was supervised by a centralized bureaucratic administration. As in the ancient Near East, the upper classes of priests and military rulers coordinated their efforts to control the redistribution of goods and services throughout the whole society. Some conflict existed between the priestly and military classes over which groups should have the supreme authority in the distribution of wealth. The *Laws of Manu,* or *Dharmaśastra,* was produced around the year 200 B.C. as a priestly document on ethics. In economic questions it emphasizes the importance of piety (*dharma*) over wealth (*artha*). Another text, the *Arthaśastra,* produced about the same time, provides ethical advice to military rulers on the acquisition and distribution of wealth. This work, which was written by Kautiliya, minister to the Emperor Chandragupta, justifies the power of wealth and goes so far as to place artha above dharma in the hierarchy of ethical goals. The text states that material wealth is the basis for "spiritual good and sensual pleasures."[47] Its primary concern was the proper administration of society so that the military rulers could supervise the production and distribution of goods.

These systems of economic redistribution in the ancient hereditary kingships of Egypt, Mesopotamia, and India have sometimes been referred to as the Asiatic mode of production. Maurice Godelier has described the character of this economic system:

> *The very essence of the Asiatic mode of production is the combined existence of primitive, land-holding communities, still partially organized on the basis of kinship, and of a state power which expresses the real or imaginary unity of these communities, controls the use of essential economic resources and directly appropriates part of the labor and product of the communities which it dominates.*[48]

The unity of these state powers in Egypt, Mesopotamia, and India was ensured through powerful priesthoods, elaborate temple complexes, and regular cycles of religious celebration. Religious, political, and economic dimensions were intertwined in the distribution of goods and services.

Although most patterns of redistribution reinforce the differences among the social standings of people and groups, there are some economic ethics that see redistribution as a way of achieving an equality of wealth and social status. The early Christian community transferred a religious ethics, in which every person was considered equal in the sight of God, into the economic sphere. We have already noted that the Book of Acts suggests that goods were held in common. In support of this, an active commitment to charity was a mechanism by which goods might be redistributed according to need. An economic ethics devoted to the redistribution of resources based on need is also found in those economic philosophies that can be traced back to the thought of Karl Marx. Marx maintained that goods should be distributed from each according to their abilities, to each according to their needs. Marxism, in its various forms, has claimed that the private ownership of property results in basic inequalities between two social classes: owners and workers. The utopian hope of a Marxist economic ethics is that these inequalities, and the class differences in which they are embedded, will be overcome by the elimination of private property. In Marxist economic ethics, the exchange of goods through a redistribution of the means of their production would equalize wealth and ensure the equality of persons within society.[49] Modern welfare states also embody this ideal of redistributing goods throughout society in response to individual need.

Market Exchange

Reciprocity and redistribution are patterns of economic exchange that are grounded in the norms and obligations of social ethics. But, market exchange is ethically neutral. In the competitive exchange of goods and services in a free market, value is determined almost exclusively by supply and demand. Pricing mechanisms in an open market set values, and, in theory, these markets are unregulated by any social controls. This excludes the influence of social, religious, and ethical controls on the distribution of goods. Evans-Pritchard has pointed to "the replacement of moral transactions of primitive societies with rational, mechanical economic systems."[50] With market exchange, human beings are economic animals in a world where value is set by price, and actions are motivated by the competitive desire to maximize profit. In self-regulating systems of market exchange, private vice is translated into public virtue: Economic selfishness, acquisitiveness, and even greed—with each person trying to maximize profit by buying low and selling high—are seen as public virtue that will ensure the most efficient distribution of goods and services. This is the spirit of capitalism.[51]

The Spirit of Capitalism

Although market exchange is largely independent of ethical controls, it became the dominant economic system in western societies under the influence of a very specific ethical environment. Max Weber argued in *The Protestant Ethic and the Spirit of Capitalism* that certain developments in Christian ethics following the Protestant Reformation provided a fertile field in which attitudes, dispositions, and habits conducive to capitalism could grow. These influences were to a great extent the result of the Protestant work ethic. We have already seen how the ethical demand that people make productive use of their time in useful vocations provided an important religious justification for work in much of Protestant thought. Hard work in a calling was an ethical end in itself. The first principle of this Protestant ethic was self-discipline; the second principle was self-denial. The material benefits of hard work were not to be enjoyed. Any wealth that accumulated through this disciplined effort was not to be spent on hedonistic pleasures or religious celebrations; wealth was also to be put to work. Profits were to be invested in enterprise.

The discipline and self-denial of what Max Weber called inner-worldly asceticism were values in themselves. But, the more profit that one accumulated, the more opportunity to demonstrate self-denial. There was a religious motive to accumulate, reinvest, and expand profits through rational calculation, continuous production, and long-range investment. No limits were imposed upon acquisition. The profit motive violated traditional ethical values of reciprocity and redistribution in the exchange of goods. As Weber put it, "The Spirit of Capitalism violates traditional values."[52] Everything (and everyone) was to be exploited for profit. Individuals found themselves in a competitive battle to maximize profits through exchange.

Protestantism provided a driving force behind the emergence of capitalism. Through its economic ethic of discipline and denial, it set a mood that was consistent with the rationalized way of life embodied in capitalism. Weber did not say that Protestantism, and particularly its Calvinist strand, caused the development of capitalism; but it was part of a larger configuration of forces that supported its development.

Some attempts have been made to explain why capitalism did not develop in other cultural settings. The limiting factors on its emergence seem to be primarily the influence of traditional religious worldviews. Asian religions did not encourage the development of capitalism for two reasons. First, there was a tendency toward a sanctification of the traditional social order. In Confucian and Hindu thought the social order was decreed by the heavens or instituted by the gods, and social standing was something ascribed to a person by birth. This social order did not allow for acquiring social status through the accumulation of wealth, which is an important part of the profit motive in capitalism. And, second, there was a tendency to cultivate mystical disciplines, what Max Weber called other-worldly asceticism, that would lead to escape from the world. The passive nonaction of Taoism, the extinction of desire of Buddhism, and the Hindu renunciate's quest for *moksha* are obviously not harmonious with the competitive demands of a market economy.[53]

Nevertheless, there has been a historical momentum to extend the spirit of capitalism to territories that had once been governed by these religious limits on unrestrained economic activity. Some would see economic growth as a universal ethical imperative to be imposed on the whole world. In *The Achieving Society* (1961), a book dedicated to accelerating economic growth on a global scale, David McClelland set forth a number of priorities for the expansion of capitalist achievements in the world. It is interesting to note how many of his recommendations for the introduction of market exchange into traditional societies are not explicitly economic. His recommendations call for a basic shift in a society's worldview: "increasing other-directedness and market morality," "decreasing father dominance," "reorganizing fantasy life," and "Protestant conversion."[54] Market values require an ethical reorientation when they are introduced into traditional societies.

Market Values and Reciprocal Values

The introduction of market values has had a disruptive effect on traditional societies. The Yir Yoront aborigines of the Cape York Peninsula in Australia had a small-scale subsistence economy; it was built around the production of stone axes, which were made by the older men of the community and used by the women. When missionaries arrived in Australia they began to pay the Yir Yoront with steel axes in exchange for work or trade. The steel axes were not given to the elders, but were distributed indiscriminately to everyone in payment for labor. This destroyed the economic base of their social structure, and, unable to recover, they were effectively demolished as a society.[55] By introducing the rational market values of exchange, the missionaries dis-

rupted the traditional ties of obligation that had held that society together.

Another example of the economic disruption of tribal societies may be found in the myth that is told in different versions in New Guinea and Melanesia about the coconut girl Hainuwele.[56] In one version of the story, nine families emerged from bananas on Mount Nunusaku and ventured off to the island of West Ceram. There one of the men, Ameta, planted a coconut and it grew into a tall tree. From one of the blossoms of that tree a girl, Hainuwele, was born. She had one amazing ability: She excreted valuable objects that made Ameta very rich. A festival was held in the village. It was the custom for the women to sit at the center of the group and hand out betel nuts; but Hainuwele danced in the circle and excreted porcelain dishes, metal knives, copper boxes, golden earrings, and gongs. At the end of the festival the people rose up and killed her. They buried her and danced on her grave. And, as the story concludes, out of her body sprouted yams that would serve as the community's main source of food.

In order to appreciate this story, we have to see it in the context of the traditional pattern of economic exchange: reciprocity. Festivals were designed to maintain an equivalence of wealth among the members of the community; any surplus in goods would be consumed so that no one would have more or less. Skill in acquiring goods was not valued, nor was thrift in saving a surplus of goods; but there was a central religious, ethical, and social value in maintaining social equality through the reciprocal exchange of goods. As Sam Gill has described it, "When European goods and money were introduced into this situation they precipitated a crisis of a fundamental sort because they challenged the very worth of human life for the native peoples."[57] The natives could not achieve reciprocity or equivalence with manufactured European goods. Notice what kinds of goods Hainuwele produces: porcelain, silver, and gold objects manufactured from a strange and unnatural source. This version of the myth was probably formulated during a period between 1902 and 1910 when Dutch colonialists, traders, and missionaries dominated the islands and imposed taxes on the village communities to be paid in cash or its equivalent in labor. The myth responds to the threat of market values through a symbolic cannibalism; the natives kill the source of those values and eat it. The myth of Hainuwele may well represent a creative response to an ethical situation of economic conflict: the collision of reciprocal and market values.

Scarcity

When human desires for goods exceed their supply, the result is scarcity. In economic theory the scarcity of resources and goods is one measure of their value. It is assumed that the basic mechanisms of economic activity spring from a competition over scarce resources. The presence of scarcity is seen as a precondition of constraining and rationing social institutions and laws that monitor the use of resources. Scarcity, as Hobbes observed in *Leviathan,* generates laws to control competition over limited resources, and it inspires the development of technological innovations to utilize resources and satisfy desires.[58] We tend to assume that scarcity is the central fact of economic life. We also have great confidence in the ability of law to restrain the violent competition over goods and the ability of technology to eventually satisfy all our needs, wants, and desires.

But the experience of scarcity is not universal; it is not the same experience in every cultural environment. One kind of scarcity is based on the need for subsistence. Scarcity occurs where there is a lack of the vital material resources for survival; when there is not enough food, inadequate shelter, and insufficient raw materials to satisfy the basic demands of living. We will call this *natural scarcity.* Then, there is an experience of scarcity based on the desire for goods. There may be plenty of material support for survival, but desires constantly outrun these simple survival needs. An experience of scarcity may result from escalating desires for the acquisition, possession, and consumption of goods. It is not a question of survival, but an unlimited, expanding desire for things. We will call this *symbolic scarcity.* These two dimensions of scarcity have important consequences for economic ethics.

Natural Scarcity

The natural scarcity of goods is a constant challenge of subsistence level societies. They are often dependent upon unstable food supplies: draught, famine, and lack of resources create constant dangers to survival. The hand-to-mouth existence of most of the social groups in the world looks like extreme poverty from the perspective of the affluent societies of the industrialized West. And yet, in many subsistence societies, the problem of natural scarcity is not a technological problem to be solved by more efficient means of production; it is an ethical problem to be met with a certain attitude, temperament, or disposition. Such attitudes form an ethical response to scarcity.

The Jesuit missionary Father Jacob Baegert spent 17 years with the Native American Indians of Southern California during the mid-eighteenth century. He discovered these Indians living with natural scarcity. They barely found enough resources to survive, and yet they responded to this situation with a unique moral resolve. According to Baegert:

> *Though the Californians seem to possess nothing, they have, nevertheless, all that they want, for they covet nothing beyond the productions of their poor, ill-favored country, and these are always within their reach.* [59]

Their ethical response to natural scarcity is to place limits on desire; as long as their basic needs can be met within their natural environment, they do not desire more. As Father Baegert continues: "It is no wonder then, that they always exhibit a joyful temper, and constantly indulge in merriment and laughter, showing thus their contentment, which after all, is the real source of happiness." [60] He sees these natives as far happier than the civilized inhabitants of Europe, whose unrestrained desires lead to unhappiness, dissatisfaction, and an experience of scarcity. The Indians, although living in extreme poverty, are not motivated by unrestrained desires for the possessions of goods, and, therefore, they do not experience scarcity. The problem of scarcity results from possessive desire. Father Baegert observed: "The Californians do not know the meaning of *meum* (mine) and *tuum* (yours), those two ideas which, according to St. Gregory, fill the days of our existence with bitterness and unaccountable evils." [61]

Symbolic Scarcity

The existence of the Southern Californians described by Father Baegert is an example of natural scarcity, the lack of abundant material resources; nevertheless, it does not seem to have resulted in a condition of symbolic scarcity based on unfulfilled desires. Unlimited desire results in symbolic scarcity. It is an experience of lack in relation to experienced desires. If those desires are great enough, it is possible to feel a sense of lack in the midst of abundant riches. By the seventeenth century, unlimited desire had become rationally and morally acceptable as a motive for behavior. The expanding desire for goods became acceptable. As the political economist C. B. Macpherson has noted, "when this assumption is made, the real task of man becomes the overcoming of scarcity in relation to infinite desire." [62]

The acceptance of infinite desire as a motive for the acquisition, possession, and consumption of goods was fueled by the tremendous influx of wealth into European economies by the conquests in the new world. The European nations entered into tremendous competition for the gold and silver, precious jewels, natural resources, and human labor of the conquered countries. Behind this competition was an unlimited desire for acquisition. The administration of Christopher Columbus, on the island of Hispaniola, provides a striking contrast to the moral limits on desire among Father Baegert's California Indians. When Columbus first arrived on the island that is presently Haiti and the Dominican Republic, he found the native Arawaks to be gentle and friendly. He reported back to Spain that the natives showed "as much lovingness as though they would give their hearts . . . they remained so much our friends that it was a marvel." But Columbus soon decided his newfound friends were a use-value that could be exploited. In 1495, Columbus sent 500 of the Arawaks to Spain as slaves. Only 300 survived the voyage, and the rest died soon afterward from European diseases for which they had no immunities.

Seeing that the native population could not be practically exploited as slaves, Columbus put them to work to realize his unlimited desire for the acquisition of gold. He required each Arawak over the age of 13 to bring to his fort a bowl filled with gold dust. When the natives brought in the required quota of gold, they would be given a copper token stamped with the month, to be worn on a chain around the neck. Those who were caught without tokens would be killed by having their hands cut off. But the quotas for gold were impossible to fulfill. There were no gold fields on the island, and the Indians were forced to work all day at the streams, trying to wash out small amounts of gold dust. Those Arawaks who tried to flee were hunted down and killed. Many killed themselves in despair with cassava poison. Within two years the Arawak population, which had been estimated as high as 500,000, was cut in half. By 1515 only 10,000 Arawaks survived; 25 years later the entire race had ceased to exist.[63] The island's natural scarcity of gold had been transformed into a symbolic scarcity based on the unlimited desire for wealth on the part of Columbus and his associates. This sense of scarcity had devastating consequences in the genocide of the native population.

When desire is infinite there is, by definition, no end to scarcity. Desires for the acquisition, possession, and consumption of goods will multiply as fast as technological advances can meet them. As Macpherson has insisted, "No increase in productivity, however great, will end scarcity while people continue to see themselves as infinite consumers."[64] Symbolic scarcity is the result of a dominant self-image in systems of market exchange: Human beings are consumers motivated by unlimited desire. As long as there is unlimited desire, there will always be the experience of scarcity.

Ethical Responses to Scarcity

Malthusian Ethics

The eighteenth century economic philosopher Thomas Malthus insisted that scarcity was built into the human struggle with nature. In his influential book, *An Essay on the Principle of Population as it Affects the Future Improvement of Society* (1798), he maintained that "the power of population is infinitely greater than the power of the earth to produce subsistence for man."[65] There will always be a scarcity of natural resources, and as population increases the competition for those scarce resources will become more intense. Population increases at a far greater rate than the subsistence needed to support it. Population multiplies in a geometrical ratio. It took all of human history up to the year 1850 to reach a population of one billion; now the population adds another billion to its total in less than 15 years. It is estimated that if the present growth rate continues, in 600 years there will be one person for every square yard of land on the earth's surface.[66] According to Malthus, nature provides a limit on population growth through the scarcity of food resources.

In the face of scarcity, those who have food are not responsible for the survival of those who do not. Malthus recommended the elimination of parish and public relief for the poor. He was convinced that the poor were irresponsibly overpopulating the planet. A man who has a family he cannot support will be punished by the divine laws of nature. As Malthus declared:

> To the punishment therefore of nature he should be left—the punishment of want. . . . He should be taught to know that the laws of nature, which are the laws of God, had doomed him and his family to suffer for disobeying their repeated admonitions; that he had no claim of right on society for the smallest portion of food, beyond that which his labor would fairly purchase; and that if he and his family were saved from feeling the natural consequences of his imprudence he would owe it to the pity of some kind benefactor, to whom, therefore, he ought to be bound by the strongest ties of gratitude.[67]

Such compassion, of course, is an important ingredient in many systems of religious ethics. Through charity, sharing, or gift-giving, a sense of responsibility for the survival of all members of society is affirmed. But Malthus accepts no such responsibility. He proposes a pragmatic solution for natural scarcity: Allow food shortages to eliminate people and thereby reduce the growth in population that increases those same shortages of food.

Lifeboat Ethics

A similar approach to scarcity is suggested in what Garrett Harden has called the ethics of a lifeboat.[68] We can imagine the rich nations of the world in lifeboats on the sea of life. The poor, underprivileged, and starving masses are swimming around in the water clamoring to be let in to share the "goodies." To keep letting poor people into the wealthy lifeboat would eventually diminish the quality of life for the rich. In a sense, the poor nations deserve to be where they are because they are allowing their population to double at a rate much faster than the rich and they are not working to produce enough food to support themselves. The ethics of the lifeboat requires that the rich not intervene, but let the poor drown. As Harden has maintained, "Every life saved this year in a poor country diminishes the quality of life for subsequent generations."[69] If you feel guilty about not sharing the wealth with those less fortunate, the solution is simple: Get out of the lifeboat and give your place to someone else. Such a self-sacrifice might be a gesture on behalf of justice, but it will not change the basic situation of the lifeboat, which is to preserve a certain quality of living for those on board.

One problem in this analysis is its failure to recognize that the privileged position of the rich nations was largely produced out of a long history of exploitation of the resources, land, and labor of what are now called the poor nations. Self-sufficient subsistence economies all over the globe were systematically drawn into an international market economy during the period of European expansion and colonialism. Land, which had been used for food, grazing, and subsistence needs, was appropriated to grow one or two crops for export, such as tobacco, tea, or cotton. This mono-culture agriculture destroyed any possibility of independent subsistence. In addition, any industrial development that did occur was tightly controlled by the financial interests of urban centers in Europe and America.[70]

These factors, among others, shaped an international market economy in which the rich nations get richer at the expense of the poor. The United States, with 6 percent of the world's population, consumes 50 percent of the planet's raw materials; a baby born in the United States will use about 50 times as much raw materials during its lifetime as a baby born in India. The planet's resources may be considered the common inheritance of humanity; and, if one group claims a disproportionate right to their use, then perhaps this right is also accompanied by greater responsibilities for sharing the benefits.

Spaceship Earth

Another image that has entered into ethical discussions of scarcity in recent years is spaceship earth.[71] The planet is not made up of a series of isolated lifeboats, but is viewed as a single system. Kenneth Boulding invoked this image when he said,

> we have to visualize the earth as a small, rather crowded spaceship, destination unknown, in which man has to find a slender thread of a way of life in the midst of a continually repeatable cycle of material transformations.[72]

There can be no external inputs or outputs in a spaceship; all the necessary ingredients for survival—food, water, and energy—must circulate through the self-contained system. To survive, the passengers must be concerned with the conservation of their resources. This means conscious limits on the growth of population, as well as limits on the desire for the unlimited acquisition, possession, and consumption of material things. Boulding envisions a world in which "human life will be lived in a comfortable and need-satisfying environment, in which everyone will have enough to eat, agreeable surroundings, and a rich variety of experience."[73]

Buddhist Economics

This holistic vision of planetary economics is similar to what E. F. Schumacher has called Buddhist economics. The choice of Buddhism is, in a sense, arbitrary, because Christianity, Judaism, and Islam, or any of the other eastern religious traditions, could be drawn on for ethical resources to respond to the challenge of western materialism. All would insist on "the hollowness and fundamental unsatisfactoriness of a life devoted primarily to the pursuit of material ends, to the neglect of the spiritual."[74] They all provide standards for human action in the economic sphere that seek to transcend the profit motive of market exchange. According to Schumacher,

> *To the extent that economic thinking is based on the market, it takes the sacredness out of life, because there can be nothing sacred in something that has a price.*[75]

When economic thinking pervades a whole society, even basic values such as beauty, health, purity, and friendship can survive only if they can be proved to be economic. The market becomes the measure of all values.

In market terms, the quality of life is measured by total annual consumption. It is assumed that someone who consumes more is better off than someone who consumes less. And someone who consumes less must necessarily be suffering the pains of scarcity. But Schumacher proposes his Buddhist economics as a creative response to this dominant market mentality.

> *A Buddhist economist would consider this approach excessively irrational: since consumption is merely a means to human well-being, the aim should be to obtain the maximum of well-being with the minimum of consumption.*[76]

The Buddhist analysis reverses the logic of scarcity: We do not desire things because they are scarce, but we experience a sense of lack because we have uncontrolled desires. We cannot eliminate symbolic scarcity, this perception of lack, by satisfying our desires for consumption. As soon as we satisfy one desire, new desires multiply. The Buddhist economic ethic addresses desire. It strives for a balance between the denial of material things and the lust for material things. As Schumacher notes, "It is not wealth that stands in the way of liberation, but the attachment to wealth; not the enjoyment of pleasurable things but the craving for them."[77] Buddhist ethics calls for a reevaluation of consumption. It is not an end in itself, but a means toward a sense of well-being. The commitment to new images of human well-being is the greatest challenge to economic ethics. A sense of spiritual abundance may be an important resource for overcoming material scarcity, as well as addressing the human experience of symbolic scarcity.

Patterns of Economics

Economic patterns of action in human social relations identify, distribute, and exchange material values. But in these economic activities, human interactions are patterned in ways that necessarily involve basic ethical values. Economic action is a total social fact: Economic exchanges are interwoven with a network of social, political, and religious values in any society. In this sense, economics forms the basis of social relations; as Aristotle noted, "without exchange there could be no association."[78] But the social associations, interactions, and relations in which economics is embedded give human meaning and value to the purely material exchange of goods, commodities, and services. An interpretation of economic ethics should recognize the ways in which patterns of exchange shape social relations and should recognize that social relations give meaning, significance, and value to patterns of exchange. Chapter 11 has drawn a number of conclusions regarding the challenges posed by economics in the ethics of social relations.

------

1.   *Goods are a communication system that facilitate social interaction.* Objects, commodities, and artifacts are the visible and tangible outlines of a worldview. These goods are assigned a particular significance within a larger symbolic vocabulary in the world of goods. Goods are not simply good to use, consume, or exchange. They carry shared symbolic meanings that give order to the world of goods, identify a person's place in the social world, and provide a common vocabulary for human values in relation to nonhuman objects. The collection, consumption, and exchange of goods reinforces a shared system of values in social relations.

Religious traditions may support specific attitudes toward the accumulation of goods. Wealth may be identified with moral righteousness. The acquisition of economic power may be seen as evidence of moral virtue. On the other hand, the unequal distribution of wealth may be viewed as an ethical imbalance in human social relations. The accumulation of wealth may be perceived as a symptom of immoral social inequalities in the distribution of economic power. The economic ethics of many religious traditions invokes the ideal of charity to redress such economic imbalances in the distribution of wealth. The redistribution of wealth through charity is perceived within many systems of religious ethics as a way of transforming the purely material exchange of goods into a pattern of action that affirms certain religious and ethical values in human social relations. The ethical ideal of charity, however, may reinforce economic inequalities with religious legitimation. The first governor of the Puritan Massachusetts Bay Colony, John Winthrop, suggested this possibility when he declared that God made some people poor in order that the wealthy could develop the ethical virtue of magnanimity through giving charity.[79] Such an economic ethics would read the statement of Jesus—"The poor will always be with you" (Mk. 14.7)—as a description of how things should be, rather than as an indictment against social systems based on vast inequalities in the distribution of wealth. The ideal of charity does not necessarily address the distribution of wealth that is inevitably enforced by a particular system of economic exchange.

------

2.   *Patterns of economic exchange embody ethical values in social relations.* Traditional economies were based on patterns of exchange that can be characterized as reciprocity and redistribution. Reciprocity is a balanced exchange for the purpose of mutual support. Reciprocal economic exchange affirms the bonds of mutual recognition that are necessary for the survival of a subsistence level economy. The purpose of exchange is not economic gain, profit, or advantage at the expense of others. Reciprocity enacts an ethics of social solidarity in economic exchange. Redistribution is a pattern of rhythmic economic exchange. Goods flow into a central storage and then flow out to be distributed by specific social criteria of need, merit, or status in the community. Economic transactions are embedded in a pattern of social relations. Goods are redistributed according to social, religious, and ethical arrangements that give shape to a network of social relations. Reciprocity and redistribution are economic ethics that support the exchange of goods, commodities, and services in traditional societies.

The economic arrangements of modern, western, industrial societies are characterized by market exchange. A market economy is based on competitive exchange. Transactions are made for the purpose of competitive gain, and human beings are motivated by purely economic values of material advantage through exchange. In this sense, market exchange can be described as ethically neutral. Economic activity is divorced from the pattern of social, religious, and ethical patterns of action in which traditional economies were embedded. Human beings become economic animals. They become individuals, in the modern sense, as individual units in a purely economic system of production and consumption. Their value may be reduced to purely economic terms.

This ethical neutrality of market exchange, however, does not mean that the market economy is not supported by certain ethical and religious values. The affinity between Protestant Christianity and the market economy, as Max Weber suggested, is more than simply accidental.

Although the details of his thesis have been contested, in an important sense the Protestant work ethic, the ethics of vocation, and the ethical dispositions of inner-worldly asceticism have supported the expansion of the market economy.

Other religious traditions have not been so supportive. When David McClelland suggested that Protestant conversion was one of the necessary social changes that would support the introduction of market exchange into traditional societies, he indicated the extent to which the competitive values of a market economy may be supported by specific patterns of social, religious, and ethical values. The global economic history of recent centuries chronicles the disruption of traditional societies, based on economic ethics of reciprocity and redistribution, by the introduction of the competitive values of market exchange by western, industrialized, international powers. The incorporation of these traditional societies into international markets has made it difficult for the societies to sustain reciprocal patterns of economic ethics. The disruption of the economic basis of these traditional societies has had a devastating effect on their social, religious, and ethical patterns of action.

———

3.   *Economic scarcity may be the result of infinite desires that cannot be met in the world of goods.* Natural scarcities are a fact of life in any economy. Human and natural resources may, in fact, be scarce. But economic ethics is concerned primarily with what could be called symbolic scarcity, which is an experience of scarcity, lack, or deprivation in relation to desire. Things are not desired because they are scarce; they are experienced as scarce because they are desired. Modern economic theory tends to assume that things are valuable because they are scarce. The modern, western logic of desire has encouraged people to overcome scarcity by working to satisfy their desires. Scarcity may be overcome by producing the things that people need, want, and

desire. A problem arises, however, when human beings become motivated by infinite desire. The satisfaction of one desire gives rise to more desires, and human beings become subject to continuously escalating desires for goods, commodities, and services. This is symbolic scarcity: the inevitable experience of scarcity that arises when human beings are motivated by infinite desire.

Eastern religious approaches to desire, as suggested by the Buddhist logic of desire, have encouraged people to overcome scarcity by eliminating their desires. The experience of scarcity is removed not when human beings satisfy their desires—because this only gives rise to new desires and a new sense of lack—but when human beings eliminate desire. An alternative to an economic ethics of infinite desire, therefore,

would address the problem of desire itself. In this sense, Buddhist economics simply suggests a pattern of economic action that attempts to harmonize desires within an ethical order. Religious traditions often symbolize sin as misdirected desire; such an economic ethics proposes the possibility that human desires might be directed through moral choices, moral virtues, and moral responsibility. Economic activity would not be motivated by unrestrained desires for personal gain, acquisition, and gratification, but by an ordered harmony of desire within patterns of economic action that support the mutual survival of human beings. This commitment to mutual recognition, support, and survival is one of the most important challenges addressed by the religious ethics of social relations.

CHAPTER

TWELVE

SURVIVAL

War may be a natural expression of biological instincts and drives toward aggression in the human species. Natural impulses of anger, hostility, and territoriality are expressed through acts of violence. These are all qualities that humans share with animals. Aggression is a kind of innate survival mechanism, an instinct for self-preservation, that allows animals to defend themselves from threats to their existence.[1] But, on the other hand, human violence shows evidence of being a learned behavior. In the case of human aggression, violence cannot be simply reduced to an instinct. The many expressions of human violence are always conditioned by social conventions that give shape to aggressive behavior.[2] In human societies violence has a social function: It is a strategy for creating or destroying forms of social order. Religious traditions have taken a leading role in directing the powers of violence.

We will look at the ritual and ethical patterns within which human violence has been directed.

The violence within a society is controlled through institutions of law. The more developed a legal system becomes, the more society takes responsibility for the discovery, control, and punishment of violent acts. In most tribal societies the only recourse to an act of violence is revenge. Each family group may have the responsibility for personally carrying out judgment and retribution upon the person who committed the offense. But in legal systems, the responsibility for revenge becomes depersonalized and diffused. The society assumes the responsibility for protecting individuals from violence. In cases where they cannot be protected, the society is responsible for exacting retribution. In a state controlled legal system, individuals are removed from the cycle of revenge motivated by acts of violence, and the state assumes responsibility for their protection.

The other side of a state legal apparatus is a state military apparatus. While the one protects the individual *from* violence, the other sacrifices the individual *to* violence in the interests of the state. In war the state affirms its supreme power over the individuals within its own borders. War is not simply a trial by combat to settle disputes between states; it is the moment when the state makes its most powerful demands upon its people for their commitment, allegiance, and supreme sacrifice. Times of war test a community's deepest religious and ethical commitments.

The modern age has witnessed the advent of total war. Traditional military ethics, which identifies legitimate causes, objectives, and conduct in war, pale before the technological magnitude of death and destruction in modern warfare. Gil Eliot, in his gripping philosophical analysis of modern war, *The Twentieth Century Book of the Dead,* examines the total death machine that has been responsible for 110 million man-made deaths in the twentieth century.[3] He documents the magnitude of death for both combatants and civilians through the military technology of the modern world on a scale unimaginable in an earlier age. Even before the nuclear era, modern states had produced efficient machinery of death. But now, with the advent of nuclear weapons that threaten the extinction of the entire species, it becomes almost impossible to identify the human goals and values that might be served by such destruction. At this point, nuclear destruction ceases to be war as war was traditionally conceived: It is simply annihilation without hope of renewal, destruction of order without the possibility of new creation. We must first examine the ritual and ethical obligations of war in the history of religions before turning to ethical responses to the challenges of the nuclear age.

Religious War

The conduct of war in religious ethics is wrapped in a tradition's most fundamental myths representing the meaning and purpose of life. In some myths, warfare appears as a basic form of ritualized play. War may be seen as the play of the gods, or the play of the cosmos, or the playful celebration of humanity in ritual combat. War may be seen as a way of maintaining the order of the cosmos and a way of protecting the human world from being overwhelmed by chaos. But the involvement of participants is generally in the playful spirit of a ritual celebration. War assumes the aspect of a ceremony where the virtues of duty, honor, and courage are displayed on the battlefield. Other myths present warfare as a form of work. In these religious traditions, a transcendent god works his will through human events. The participants in warfare see themselves as employed in the service of this great work. Although there may be elements of work and play interwoven in every ritual of human warfare, some traditions—such as those of India, China, and Japan—emphasize the ceremonial participation in battle, while others—such as the religions of ancient Israel, Christianity, and Islam—emphasize the utilitarian goals of advancing the interests of religion through armed conflict.[4]

Sacred War

Sometime in the third millennium before the common era, a vast number of people migrated from Siberia into regions that stretch from what is today Ireland to India. They shared common linguistic roots, similar patterns of social organization, and religious mythologies that glorified the warrior. These people are referred to as Indo-Europeans. Traces of their warrior myths have survived in the mythologies of the Teutonic, Greco-Roman and Indo-Aryan legends, epics, and sacred texts. The Teutonic myths of battles tell of the warrior-god Wodin, who resides in the heaven of Valhalla. But this heavenly realm is not an abode of peace and repose; it is a place of eternal strife, where fierce warriors drink mead, feast on sacrificial meat, and gird themselves for battle. The Greco-Roman myths begin with the cosmic battle between the Olympian gods, led by the thunder-god Zeus, against the Titans. A living warrior mythology is preserved in the poetic medium of Homer's *Iliad* and *Odyssey;* it is a mythology of endless battles, in heaven and on earth, where heroic virtues are revered. The ancient myths of the Indo-Aryans, collected in the *Rg Veda,* also represent a warrior mythology. Praises are sung to the divine warrior Indra, who, fortified by the intoxicating soma-drink and the lightning bolt, is invincible in battle. In all these myths, the cosmic forces of the universe are in constant conflict, and the warrior is an active force that creates order out of the chaos of battle.[5]

Ancient India   In the earliest records of the religions of India, the warrior emerges as a special class. The *kṣatriya* has his own unique ethical obligation: the conquest of territories (*dharma dig-vijaya*). The military class is responsible for protecting the people, conquering other regions, and exacting tribute from the conquered. In the *Laws of Manu* this is the "blameless, primeval law for warriors."[6] A warrior ethics is embodied in the Indian epic, the *Mahabharata,* which tells of a great battle between two sides, the Kuru and the Pandu, of the same extended warrior family. In a vivid narrative, the text exalts the military virtues of the warrior and declares that death in battle is the greatest redemptive glory that a kṣatriya could achieve. One passage from the *Mahabharata* states:

> *Death on a bed of repose . . . is sinful for a* kṣatriya *. . . surrounded by kinsmen and slaughtering his foes in battle, a* kṣatriya *should die at the edge of keen weapons.*[7]

The religious ethics of all other social classes demands *ahimsa:* They are required to observe strict harmlessness toward all living creatures. Most people are required to practice nonviolence. But the warrior's duty (*dharma*) is to kill and be killed in battle.

Still, there are ethical standards for the conduct of warriors in battle that place restraints upon the free exercise of violence. The warrior must demonstrate ethical behavior in battle. He is instructed never to attack someone who is sleeping, naked, or without arms and armor; the kṣatriya must not harm someone who is watching without taking part in the battle, fighting with another foe, seriously wounded, afflicted with sorrow, or running away from the battle. "In all these cases," the *Laws of Manu* insists, "let him remember the duty of honorable warriors."[8]

Honorable war was not only demonstrated through these limitations on violence; it was evident in the style of conduct with which warriors participated in battle. War was a ritual ceremony with special costumes, decorative weapons, stylized exchanges, magical formulas, and rules of fairness. All these limited the harm inflicted on an enemy. Ideally these battles were large, loud, and colorful, but with relatively little loss of life.

Within the larger text of the *Mahabharata* is a section that recounts a dialogue between one of the warriors and his chariot driver. This is the *Bhagavad Gītā*. The warrior Arjuna is troubled by the sight of so many of his kinsmen arrayed for battle against each other and declares to his charioteer that he will not fight. The charioteer, Kṛṣṇa, turns out to be the *avatar* (manifestation) of the god Viṣṇu. Kṛṣṇa rebukes the warrior and tells him to take up his weapons and fight. It is his dharma as a kṣatriya. But Kṛṣṇa goes on to inform Arjuna that behind the appearances of death and destruction in battle is the play (*lila*) of God. The battlefield is a playful illusion (*maya*) spun out by the creative power of Viṣṇu. Arjuna is exhorted to look through the illusion to the pure essence of his eternal Self, the *Atman,* which transcends the field of action. Kṛṣṇa declares that the warrior "is not slain . . . when the body is slain . . . swords cut him not."[9] The warrior is urged to act as if he were attacking and killing the enemy in battle. But he must know, as Kṛṣṇa informs Arjuna, "by Myself they have already been slain long ago."[10] The warrior is merely an instrument in the divine play of life and death. In the Hindu tradition the battlefield of the *Mahabharata* is often interpreted as an extended metaphor for the conflicts of life. It symbolizes a religious conviction that beyond all conflicts resides the supreme Self. But it also supports a military ethics that imagines that war may give the appearance of death, but in reality no one kills and no one dies.

The ritual character of warfare in ancient India is best illustrated through the horse sacrifice (*aśva-medha*).[11] In this elaborate ceremony a horse would be selected by a king and dedicated to the Vedic god Varuna, the representative of the order of the heavens. The horse would be consecrated as a symbol of that sacred order extended over the world. The king who conducted the ritual would thereby make claims to being a world ruler (*chakravartan*). With prayers, hymns, and sacrifices the stallion of Varuna was set free to wander through the countryside for one year. It was accompanied by 100 mares and a contingent of soldiers. Wherever the horse wandered during that year, the inhabitants of those regions were given the choice of recognizing the authority of the king by paying tribute or contesting his authority by going into battle. Local rulers were not deposed. The *Laws of Manu* specifies that permanent political control over conquered people is not the object of war.[12] But payment of tribute and homage was a way of acknowledging the chakravartan as the sustainer of the sacred moral order on earth. At the end of the year, the horse would be killed and the queen would engage in ritual intercourse with its corpse. This symbolized the life-giving power of the world ruler, and it symbolized the rebirth of order in the world.

Numerous cases of the *aśva-medha* have been recorded from the time of the Gupta dynasty in the fourth century of the common era up to the Muslim conquests in India during the thirteenth century. Rulers even competed with each other for the honor of being consecrated as chakravartan. It is difficult to say how closely they adhered to the ethical standards of ceremonial warfare; but independent evidence is offered by the Chinese traveler Hiuen Tsiang (around 700 A.D.) that the Indian warriors warned their enemies before entering into battle, refrained from killing fugitives, and, rather than killing an enemy king, sought to embarrass him by dressing him in women's clothing.[13] Ritual warfare seems to have been an elaborate ceremony for gaining honor and creating a sense of moral order in the world.

Ancient China

In Chinese religion a sense of cosmic order also provided a model for the conduct of war. The Way of Heaven (*T'ien Tao*) represents cosmic order over the forces of chaos. This order is affirmed on earth through ritual. It is important to remember that the Confucian concept of *li* presents religious ritual as the proper pattern for all human conduct. As the philosopher Herbert Fingarette has observed, "Human life in its entirety finally appears as one vast spontaneous and Holy rite."[14] Human beings are united, and human life is ordered, through the exact performance of ritual actions that cultivate reverence, attentiveness, care, and devotion in action. The goal is a sense of beauty and harmony in human society.

War was also perceived as a ritual that preserved this sense of harmony. One of the Confucian Classics asserts that there are two rituals that affirm the sacred order of the state: sacrifice and war.

> *The Great Affairs of the state are sacrifice and war. At sacrifices (in the ancestral temple), the officers receive the roasted flesh; in war they receive that offered at the altar of the land: these are the great ceremonies in worshipping the Spirits.*[15]

This statement from the Confucian tradition is certainly not the only example of the religious identification of war with sacrifice. One of the most powerful and persistent religious legitimations of death in battle is the symbolism of redemptive sacrifice. The individual who dies in war is a sacrificial offering; that death is a sacrifice given to sustain the life of the community.

Confucian military ethics imagines the battlefield as a testing place for *li*. The ethical virtues of dignity, sincerity, tranquility, and compassion are all tested in times of war. The Chinese texts record the custom of ceremonial gift-giving exchanges before battle, the prescribed courtesies extended to opponents, and the appropriate condolences to be offered by the victors to those defeated in battle.

There were rules regarding the proper warning of attack. The warrior was instructed not to attack anyone who was unarmed and to refrain from attacking anyone who was considered to be of greater moral virtue. In Chinese military ethics, there was to be a minimum of violence. Even to cause an opponent disgrace was considered a violent act. The ancient military text of Sun Tzu (about 400–320 B.C.), which was used as a training manual for the Chinese army until 1912, specified that "the best-won victory is that obtained without the shedding of blood . . . to subdue the enemy without fighting is the acme of skill. . . . He who achieves victory without bloodshed is the talented commander."[16]

Some evidence suggests that bloodless battles were a common form of ceremonial warfare in ancient China. During a 20-year period in which 40 battles were fought, the *Summer and Autumn Annals* (770–464 B.C.) record only two casualties: a nobleman who was accidently killed by his own men and a king who was injured in a duel for which his opponent apologized.[17] Certainly there was death in battle; but the point of war was not to amass large body counts. War was a ceremonial drama to test the virtues of ritual and ethical propriety and to reaffirm the moral order of the world.

Traditional Japan

Japanese military ethics are conditioned by two factors: the identification of religion—particularly the Shinto tradition—with the state, and a mystical spirituality and meditative discipline cultivated with the introduction of Zen (Chinese Ch'an) Buddhism into Japan in the twelfth century. The *shogun,* or warlord, and his loyal warriors practiced a code of military ethics that came to be called *Bushido.* The samurai warriors adopted a military vocation as a spiritual discipline. Through military training, martial arts, and meditation, the warrior ethics of Bushido became a way of life.

One summary of this traditional Japanese military ethics is found in the seventeenth century manual, *Hagakure Bushido.* This text reviews the ethical values of the samurai code. In

Bushido, the samurai is dedicated to three basic values: loyalty to superiors, renunciation of reason, and acceptance of death. First, the warrior is instructed to dedicate his life, and ultimately his death, in absolute devotion to the service of his warlord. The samurai declares: "Our duty is to guard the interest of our lord. . . . This is the backbone of our faith, unchanging and eternally true." The samurai must act in ways that bring honor and avoid disgrace in pursuing the interests of his warlord.

Second, the warrior practices martial arts that are designed to develop innate human powers that transcend reason. The warrior is exhorted to give up reason in order to tap these more vital powers. "When you are on the field of battle," the samurai is instructed, "close your mind to reasoning; for once you begin to reason, you are lost. Reasoning robs you of that force with which alone you can carve your goal." The warrior's discipline becomes a type of meditation that achieves a state of "no-mind," which may be regarded as similar to the experience beyond ordinary reason that is cultivated in Zen Buddhism.

Finally, the warrior must accept death. The samurai is dedicated to making the final sacrifice on behalf of his warlord. This acceptance of death becomes the ultimate truth of Bushido: "When all things in life are false, there is only one thing true, death." [18] This warrior ethics in traditional Japan strives to achieve a transcendent orientation toward death in the service of the Bushido code.

The ritual forms in which the Bushido ethics took shape involved decorative costumes, elaborate ceremonies, and sacred weapons. The samurai long-sword, or *daito,* evoked feelings of awe and reverence. It was perceived as a numinous weapon. As the warrior Inazo Nitobe described the sacred sword,

> *Its cold blade, collecting on its surface the moment it is drawn the vapours of the atmosphere; its immaculate texture, flashing light of bluish hue, its matchless edge, upon which histories and possibilities ties hang; the curve of its back, uniting exquisite grace with utmost strength—all these thrill us with mixed feelings of power and beauty, awe and terror.* [19]

This is the language of religious devotion. The weapon is imbued with all the attributes of a transcendent divine power. The military ethics of Bushido provided an avenue of transcendence in which the world was experienced as a sacred drama of life and death. The warrior experienced himself at the center of that sacred drama.

Holy War

The sacred warfare of India, China, and Japan was seen as a ritual technique for maintaining the order of the cosmos; but, the holy war of ancient Israel, Christianity, and Islam had a different purpose. These religious traditions assumed that a transcendent almighty god worked his will upon human events in the world. This was a wrathful, jealous god of battles, who chose a select group of humans to represent his will on earth. War was not ritual play; it was the serious struggle to work out God's will in history.

The concept of *justice* was essential to the holy war. The wrath of God represents a just judgment against the sinfulness of the world. His armies become instruments of that justice endeavoring to bring retribution upon the wicked. The holy war polarizes humanity into forces of good and forces of evil. Those who have taken upon themselves the mantle of God's justice assume the responsibility of doing battle against evil. The soldiers of God reaffirm their own ethical purity by exterminating those others who are nonbelievers, sinners, or heretics. Holy war becomes a mechanism for imposing the pattern of God's justice upon the world.

The ritual drama of sacred war is replaced by the serious work of holy war. The implements in war are valued, not for their ceremonial splendor, but for their effectiveness in eliminating the enemy. Costumes, weapons, and strategies are measured by their efficiency. The extent of sin against God by disobedient nonbelievers is imagined to be infinite, and so measures taken to suppress the sinful must also be unlimited. Ritual restraints against violence tend to be dismissed in holy wars. The retribution of God's judgment must be as total as possible. Total war, with unrestrained violence, death, and destruction upon the enemy, is a common feature of the holy wars in the religions of ancient Israel, Islam, and Christianity.

Ancient Israel

The Hebrew Bible narrates the liberation of the people of Israel from their captivity in Egypt and their triumphant entry into the land that God had promised them. They are led out of Egypt by the prophet Moses; but they enter the promised land under the leadership of the warrior Joshua. Because the holy land of Canaan was already occupied, holy wars were waged against the native inhabitants to conquer these peoples who were perceived as the enemies of God. The 12 tribes of Israel went into battle with the war cry: "Arise, Yahweh, and let thy enemies be scattered." (Deut. 20.1–12; Num. 10.1–9) The holy war is motivated by the powerful symbols of promise and covenant; this land had been promised by God to the ancient patriarchs of the people of Israel, and this nation had entered into a special covenant with God to conquer it.

Preparations for battle began with a ceremonial gathering of the 12 tribes. The warriors were reviewed and chosen for their fitness for battle. As they approached an enemy city, its inhabitants were first given a choice: either surrender to the forces of Yahweh, and become tributaries to the Israelites, or prepare to fight.

If the decision was made to fight, the priests of Yahweh would perform rituals to divine the will of God. And, at the propitious time, the soldiers would enter into battle with their war cry. The spoils of war would be divided between the victorious soldiers and the Israelite community, with a portion reserved for Yahweh and the priests. These spoils included conquered peoples who were to be enslaved, sold, or taken as concubines. After the battle, rituals of purification were performed for the warriors in order to admit them back into the normal life of the community. (Num. 31:19–34)

The conduct of war tended to be unrestrained violence in the service of Yahweh. War was perceived as an absolute retribution brought upon the enemies of God, and the violence of that judgment led to total destruction. The most extreme example of total war in ancient Israel was the practice of *herem*. *Herem* was a sacrificial ban, or anathema, placed upon an enemy city, which marked that place and all its inhabitants for total destruction. The Israelites assumed that all villages, towns, and cities in the promised land already belonged to Yahweh. If they resisted His rule, they were to be given as a sacrificial offering to God. *Herem* comes from a word meaning "to separate." It means to take a thing out, consecrate it, and sacrifice it to God. When the herem was pronounced on a place, it was to be totally destroyed; every man, woman, and child was to be killed. "As regards the towns of those people which Yahweh your God gives you as your inheritance, you must spare not the life of any living thing. . . . Thou shalt utterly destroy them." (Deut. 20.15–18) The Bible gives evidence of over 20 such cities that were given as sacrifice to Yahweh in holy war.[20]

Islam

Islam is a religious tradition that was spread by the sword. The prophet Muhammad began with a small group of followers in Medina, and within 12 years, had led the military conquest of the entire Arabian peninsula. His successors continued to fight the holy war of religion. The term *jihad* means "struggle." It refers to the constant endeavor to spread the true religion of Islam over the world by struggling against the errors of polytheism. But jihad also means the holy war by which Muslims force unbelievers to surrender to the will of Allah. War as jihad is a means of extending the realm of Muslim influence.

The Qu'ran states that it is the duty of the community to "fight those who believe not in God . . . until they pay the tribute out of hand and have been humbled."[21] The opponents of Allah were divided into two kinds: (1) unbelievers who were to surrender to Allah or be destroyed; and (2) the "people of the book," the *dhimmi,* who were protected Jews and Christians who could continue in their religions, but must submit to Muslim political rule. Eventually the world was divided into two opposing realms: *dar al-harb* (the abode of war) and *dar al-Islam* (the abode of Islam). Jihad was the constant military struggle to bring the whole world under the dominion of Allah.

Muhammad, and later the Caliphs, assumed the authority to initiate war as representatives of Allah. Battle would begin with a warning; as the Qu'ran states, "We never punish a people until We have first sent to them a Messenger to warn them."[22] The enemy is warned to convert to Islam or die. After a three-day grace period, if the enemy has not surrendered, the warriors rush into battle with the battle cry (*takbir*): "*Allah hu akbar,* Allah is great." It is a call to battle and a call to prayer, as the jihad is understood to be a form of religious devotion to Allah.

As in the wars of ancient Israel, the enemy is subjected to the total vengeance of God. Captured combatants are killed, enslaved, or ransomed, women are married or enslaved, and children are taken into slavery. The spoils of war, including all movable goods, are divided, with four fifths going to the soldiers and one fifth going to Allah and the Caliph.[23] In jihad, total war

is a strategy for spreading the true religion; it demands total obedience to God or death. No limits were placed on the weapons, tactics, or violence in war. Any means that were regarded as necessary to cleanse the world of unbelievers could be used. Death could be total. "When you meet the unbelievers (in battle), smite their necks, then, when you have made wide slaughter among them, tie fast the bonds."[24] The Qu'ran insists upon the ethical obligation of Muslims to rid the world of polytheism; in jihad this means ridding the world of unbelief by exterminating the unbelievers: "Slay the idolaters wherever you find them."[25]

War is the testing ground of Islam. It is the supreme test of the Muslim's willingness to surrender to the will of Allah. In battle, the Muslim warrior is instructed to focus his devotion upon Allah. "When ye are face to face with the enemy, stand ye fast and concentrate on Allah so that you succeed."[26] But the outcome of battle is already determined by the all-powerful will of God. It is Allah who acts in human events. The Qu'ran instructs the warriors of Allah: "When you were aiming arrows it was not you who aimed, it was Allah who aimed. It was not you who slew them it was Allah who slew them."[27] The only option that human beings have in the field of action is to surrender to the will of Allah and let Allah act. The justice of God will bring about the destruction of His enemies, and His armies in holy war will be instruments of that justice.

Christianity   The ethics of the early Christian communities required pacifism. The highest ethical virtue was an unconditional self-sacrificing love that turned the other cheek and returned good for evil. The ethic of *agape* was seen as inconsistent with military violence, and the story of Jesus commanding Peter to put away his sword was often interpreted as an illustration of nonviolence. The second century theologian Tertullian saw any Christian involvement in military service as an idolatrous involvement in the world when Christians should be directing their efforts toward achieving the other-worldly kingdom of heaven.

All of this changed when Christianity became the religion of the Roman Empire under Constantine in the fourth century. The first Christian emperor rose to power by defeating his enemies under the sign of the cross, and his emblem—*In Hoc Signo Vinco* (Under This Sign I Conquer)—represented the beginning of a union between religious and political power. Throughout the middle ages, the tenuous balance between religious and political power was symbolized in the image of the two swords—wielded by Pope and emperor—that cooperated to rule Christendom.

Another important factor in the development of a Christian military ethos was the conversion of the barbarian tribes, who had been imbued with the Teutonic warrior mythology, to Christianity. The Frankish warriors, who converted to Christianity under King Clovis in 496, became defenders of the Christian faith. They performed the mass before battle and carried relics of saints into the fight.[28]

By the eleventh century warriors were ordained as knights by the Church, and the Church assumed control over the order of knights. Beginning with Gregory VII, the Popes claimed to be world rulers with authority over heaven and earth. The soldiers of Christ—*militia Christi*—received special dispensations for the remission of sins for participating in the Pope's battles. In the following century Pope Urban II called for a *bellum peregrini,* a pilgrim's war, against the Islamic Saracens to capture the sacred center of Jerusalem. The crusades were an extended holy war sponsored by the Church. The mystic, theologian, and church leader Bernard of Clairvaux preached on behalf of the holy war. In his *De laude novae militae,* he declared that killing in holy war was not a sin; it was *malecide,* the killing

of evil. The soldiers of Christ fight for the glory of God. These holy warriors "can fight the Lord's battles in all safety. For whether they kill the enemy or die themselves, they need fear nothing. To die for Christ and to kill enemies, there is no crime in that, only glory."[29] Holy war was total war. Urban II called upon the soldiers of Christ to attack the Saracens and "exterminate that vile race."

Accounts of the battles recorded the brutality of total war. Raymond du Aguilers described Saracens who were beheaded, shot with arrows, and thrown from towers; they were tortured for days and then burned. He describes the piles of heads, hands, and feet in the streets with horses wading up to their bridles in blood. He concludes: "It was a just and wonderful judgment of God."[30] The magnitude of God's justice in holy war called for the total destruction of the enemy.

The Catholic church did try to restrain the violence of war within Christian Europe. A number of church councils laid down conditions for the *Treuga Dei* (Truce of God), which would forbid battle on Thursdays—in memory of the Last Supper; Fridays—in memory of the crucifixion; Saturdays—in memory of the burial of Christ; and Sundays—in memory of the resurrection.[31] Medieval arms control agreements banned the use of the crossbow. As the Lateran Council of 1139 ruled: "The deadly art, hated of God, of crossbow-men and archers against Christians and Catholics is prohibited on pain of anathema."[32] In addition, the fifteenth century manual of military conduct, *The Tree of Battles,* sought to restrain acts of violence only to armed combatants.[33] All of these limits on violence in war applied only to battles between Christians; such restraints were suspended when doing battle against unbelievers or heretics. In these cases, total violence was thought to be warranted to rid the world of evil.

Protestant ethics, from the beginning of the sixteenth century, tended to free secular states from such religious controls on warfare. Luther's doctrine of the "separation of kingdoms" reserved the religious sphere to matters of private faith; the public administration of the affairs of state used sinful power to punish sin. Luther claimed that "the emperor's sword has nothing to do with faith; it belongs to physical worldly things."[34] This tended to free the rulers of states from religious limits on the use of violence; nevertheless, Luther saw that even this state of affairs had been instituted by God. "The hand that wields the sword and kills with it is not man's hand but God's; and it is not man, but God, who hangs, tortures, beheads, kills and fights."[35] Christians must submit to the worldly rulers who have been allowed to reign by God, and they may not revolt against rulers they feel are unjust. The test of this principle came in the Peasant Wars (1524–25), when Luther supported the German princes in their brutal suppression of the revolt, leaving over 100,000 dead.

The religious wars of the seventeenth century assumed an intensity never before experienced in European warfare. The extent of the violence, death, and destruction was unprecedented. These were perceived as holy wars between Protestants and Catholics for religious supremacy. The Protestant Henry Bullinger declared that "the magistrate is compelled to make war upon men . . . whom the very judgment of the Lord condemneth and biddeth to kill without pity or mercy."[36] On the other side, the Catholic Bishop William Cardinal Allen could claim that "there is no war in the world so just or honorable . . . as that which is waged for Religion."[37]

By the time the Thirty Years War was ended by the Peace of Westphalia (1648) the population of Germany was less than one third what it had been when the wars started. The agreement reached settled on the formula *eius regio, cuius religio:* Whoever ruled a territory would determine the religion that would be practiced within its borders. This transferred the effective power over religion to the rulers of the European states. A dramatic change in the relation between religion and politics had occurred over this period. As the historian of religious warfare James Aho has observed, "In the Middle Ages every calling including that of the knight could be viewed as a liturgical ministry of the Corpus Christianum," but "after the wars of the Reformation, all men including the clergy could see themselves as functionaries of the state."[38] The role of religion in modern warfare has primarily been the efforts of national churches to legitimize the interests of the state. The Church plays the role of *pastor,* ministering to the private faith of individuals while the state determines public affairs. Or the Church plays the role of *chaplain,* justifying the actions of the state with hymns of praise and prayers for victory. But rarely does the Church assume the role of *prophet,* condemning the injustices of the state in the name of a higher moral order. This prophetic voice is found in the just war tradition in the history of religious ethics.

Just War Theory

The ethical theory of the just war, which has been developed by theologians, canon lawyers, and international agreements, has had a long history in western religious thought. It can be traced back to Augustine's attempt in the fourth century to wrestle with the question: "When is a Christian justified in participating in war?" The just war theory tries to set forth the conditions under which war may be permitted and to place ethical limits on the conduct of war once it has been engaged. The first conditions, the *jus ad bellum,* indicate the proper criteria for going to war. The second conditions, the *jus in bello,* specify the proper criteria for conducting war. The holy war was considered just simply because it was waged in the interests of religion by God's self-ordained representatives on earth. But the just war must be measured against independent standards of justice with regard to its causes and its conduct.

Justice in Declaring War

Just war theorists have agreed that a state is justified in going to war if the cause is just, if the war is initiated by a proper authority, and if the ultimate intention is to restore peace.

Just Cause

Justice is a concept in natural law that insists upon a basic fairness. The Roman philosopher Cicero defined *justice* as the protection of fairness in human relations. War might be a legitimate recourse in cases where the standards of fairness in the relations between states had been violated. A state was justified in going to war to restore the balance of justice. But Augustine, in developing a just war theory within the Christian tradition, insisted that justice must be based on love. Any attempt to achieve justice in the relation between states must be motivated by *caritas.*[39] This implied, for Augustine, that Christian participation in war must be entered into reluctantly, conscious that both sides of any dispute live in a sinful, imperfect world; war can be entered into only if it gives expression to the ethical commandment of love for neighbors. This would include wars for the protection of the innocent, for the redress of wrongs; but this does not include wars for self-defense, because a Christian should be willing to suffer.

Most of the causes of war in the modern world are ideological. War may be waged to defend such ideas as civilization, freedom, national destiny, the American way of life, free enterprise, or the historical necessity of world communism. These causes take on the character of holy wars. The world is symbolically divided into absolute powers of good and evil. But where the holy war justified preemptive wars to eliminate evil from the face of the earth, the just war theory tends to accept only defensive wars as legitimate means for restoring the balance of justice in the world.

Proper Authority

Augustine understood the state to be a provisional means for keeping peace and restraining sin. The state was regarded as a legitimate temporal power that would ultimately be judged by the higher power and authority of God. Within its own sphere, the state has the authority to wage war, but only if that war is declared by its duly constituted sovereign ruler. This implies that duly constituted rulers have the right to be right in calling their states to war. Just war theory recognizes that a state is the organized exercise of violence over a territory; the sovereign of any state is invested with the proper authority to martial that violence against other states.

This issue of proper authority calls into question the justice of revolutionary wars in overthrowing a regime that may be perceived as unjust. Theologians from Augustine to Luther instructed Christians to simply submit to unjust rulers and await the kingdom of heaven. John Calvin and other reformed theologians did recognize the right of minor rulers to take action against the rule of oppressive sovereigns. But for the most part, revolutions were not recognized as just wars. Only recently have just war theorists tried to defend the claims of revolutionary groups to wage war. Criteria such as control over a substantial territory or the accumulation of a mass following have been proposed to identify the conditions under which a revolutionary movement might be regarded as having the proper authority to wage war within just war theory.[40]

Modern nationalism seems to be based on the assumption that any ruler is justified with the proper authority to wage war. Individuals have increasingly disputed this ultimate authority invested in the leadership of the nation-state. There is a long tradition of objections by individuals to the authority of states to involve their citizens in war. A conscientious objector may raise ethical objections to a particular war or may adopt a pacifism that rules out participation in all wars.[41] Although there has certainly been support for this option of individual conscience in the Christian tradition, there has also been considerable resistance. Archbishop Groeber, for example, rejected pacifism as an option for German Catholics because he regarded Hitler as the duly constituted authority over the German nation. Pope Pius XII rejected conscientious objection at the time of the formation of NATO (North Atlantic Treaty Organization).[42] These examples simply illustrate the possibility that individual conscience may be sacrificed to the authority of the sovereign state in just war theory. This emphasis on the proper authority for declaring war may diminish the importance of individual conscience, and self-determination, in deciding when a war has been justly declared.

Peaceful Intention

The just war is not regarded as a total war; its intention must be to restore and maintain peace. The objective of the just war is not the elimination of the enemy, but peaceful coexistence. Therefore, according to just war theory, entering into war must be a course of last resort. Nonviolent alternatives, such as diplomatic negotiations and economic boycotts and sanctions, must first be exhausted.

What are the criteria for determining that a nation has exhausted all other resorts? Two sets of priorities come into play in international conflicts: humanitarian necessities and military necessities.[43] The humanitarian priorities are values, virtues, and purposes that make life worth living. Many of these values may in fact be shared by the participants in a conflict. The military priorities are defined by the inviolability of national sovereignty and the struggle for power. Here, conflicting states may have mutually exclusive interests. The just war theory requires that humanitarian values have priority over military necessity. Only in an environment where human values can no longer be sustained should a state resort to war, and not simply out of an interest in military superiority. Just war theory requires that a peaceful intention in warfare should be demonstrated by placing limitations on the destruction of human values through military violence. This insistence on peaceful intention in just war theory raises questions regarding the proper conduct of war.

Justice in Conducting War

Just war theory has proposed two principal standards for the conduct of war: proportionality and discrimination. The first principle insists that a greater proportion of good than evil must result from the conduct of war; the second principle tries to ensure that military violence will be used discriminately in order to protect noncombatants. These standards define the conditions that must be met for the conduct of a war to be considered just in just war theory.

Proportionality

A just war is considered to be one in which more good than evil results from the conflict. The conduct of war should guarantee the "minimum unnecessary destruction of values."[44] This involves a certain amount of calculation of the projected gains and losses in the exercise of armed violence. Proportionality is concerned with the consequences of war. This has given rise to efforts to limit the use of weapons that would create suffering, death, and destruction out of proportion to the gains that could be expected from their use. The Hague Declarations of 1899 and 1907, for example, prohibited the following weapons: projectiles discharged from the air, the use of asphyxiating gases, contact mines, and expanding bullets.

The attempts to decrease the proportion of violence in relation to military gains in warfare have also resulted in some curious calculations about more or less humane ways of killing people. For example, expanding bullets were considered so inhumane that a doctor of the Berlin Military Medical Society, in 1885, celebrated the development of a high-speed nonexpanding bullet by declaring, "I welcome the new bullet with great joy and believe that if it were generally adopted by international consent, all humanity would have cause to rejoice."[45] And Hiram Maxim praised the invention of the machine gun, with its nonexpanding bullets, as "the greatest life-saving instrument ever invented."[46] Proportional calculation acquires an almost surreal quality when extreme acts of military violence, such as the saturation bombing of Dresden and the atomic destruction of Hiroshima, are justified as prudent acts designed to bring about a greater good in proportion to the hundreds of thousands of deaths these actions entailed.

The principle of proportionality in just war theory involves a distinction between unleashing destructive violence and using military force for political ends. It implies that a moral distinction exists between unrestrained violence and the responsible use of force to achieve political objectives in a just cause. But the use of that force can only be justified if the benefits it brings outweigh the destruction it causes. This raises difficult questions about the relative values of human life, property, and ideals. What is the calculus that could measure human pain and suffering in relation to political objectives in the just war?

Discrimination

The principle of discrimination in just war theory insists that only armed combatants should be subject to the violence of war. It demands the safety of civilian populations. Where the principle of proportionality is a matter of consequential calculations, protecting noncombatants from violence in war is perceived as an unconditional ethical obligation. Augustine, for example, who saw the protection of innocents from unjust attack as the only acceptable cause for war, extended the protection of innocent noncombatants to the conduct of war. Both were seen as extensions of the Christian duty to express love in action.[47] At the beginning of the modern era, the just war theorist Franciscus de Victoria repeated Augustine's definition of justice in the cause and conduct of war. He stated that "the basis of a just war is a wrong done. . . . But wrong is not done by an innocent person (that is, a noncombatant). Therefore war may not be employed against him."[48] Victoria listed children, women, priests, monks, foreigners, guests, "harmless agricultural folk, and also . . . the rest of the peaceable civilian population," as noncombatants. They were to be immune from the violence of war. Victoria did introduce a new note by suggesting that it may be permissible to kill noncombatants in a just war if they were killed as an indirect effect of an attack on a military target. The use of cannon, for example, in a siege against a city would inevitably kill civilians. Victoria suggested that this might be permitted as long as it was not the intention of the military strategy, but an unavoidable by-product.[49]

The discrimination between armed combatants and innocent civilians has been blurred in the modern world of total war. The effects of the machinery of war tend to affect everyone. It becomes difficult to argue that the death of innocent civilians in an attack on a military target, such as a harbor, power station, or arsenal, is simply an unintentional by-product of military strategy. The death of civilians is directly caused by such actions. The principle of discrimination is not often evident in modern warfare. Military violence tends to be directed toward entire populations. As one just war theorist, Thomas Murray, has observed:

In World War I a major strategic instrument was the naval blockade by which it was hoped to starve out both population and industry; in World War II a combination of blockade and strategic bombing was used; in World War III the strategy will call for striking industry and population directly, without the slow intermediate step of starvation. I submit that the strategy is immoral. It was immoral in previous decades, and it is immorality gone beserk today.[50]

Murray and others have tried to apply the principles of the just war to the situation of the nuclear age. Some feel that the standards for conducting war justly are still applicable in an era of nuclear weapons. But it may be that a theory that justifies war in certain cases already justifies too much. Religious ethics faces unprecedented challenges to human survival in the nuclear age.

Ethics in the Nuclear Age

Before the first assembly of the World Council of Churches in 1948, the planning committee for the conference wrote that "man's triumph in the release of atomic energy threatens his destruction. Unless man's whole outlook is changed, our civilization will perish."[51] The nuclear age has not simply created new political problems; it has raised religious and ethical challenges of ultimate significance to human survival. The threat of nuclear destruction has called for creative ethical responses. For the most part, nations with nuclear capabilities continue to think of nuclear weapons within the older, conventional patterns of military strategy. Conventional weapons were used to defend and promote the political interests of sovereign nation-states. Nuclear weapons may simply be incorporated into conventional military strategy. Military strategists have identified four levels of nuclear deployment in which these weapons might be used to protect, defend, or promote national interests: (1) battlefield missions, which would release tactical nuclear weapons at enemy forces advancing across borders; (2) theater missions, which would direct nuclear weapons not only at invading troops, but also at targets inside the enemy country; (3) strategic counter-force missions, which would aim long-range nuclear missiles at military targets within the enemy's territory; and (4) strategic counter-city missions, which would direct nuclear missiles at enemy cities and civilian populations.

These four strategies for deploying nuclear weapons represent a gradual increase in the intensity of nuclear destruction. But, many strategists are convinced that it is unrealistic to expect that the use of nuclear weapons would remain limited. Any use could quickly escalate to an all out exchange of weapons that would be targeted against enemy cities resulting in tremendous devastation of civilian populations. Recourse to nuclear weapons in battlefield missions would in all likelihood escalate to counter-city exchanges of nuclear weapons. This prospect of total war is responsible for the nuclear super-powers' tenuous balance of mutual terror, in which the awesome potential of devastation protects their political interests.

Albert Einstein once suggested that the nuclear age has changed everything except our ways of thinking.[52] The weapons that the nuclear age has produced continue to be regarded within traditional patterns of political interests and military strategy. But, because many people have felt that traditional mythologies of war are inadequate to accommodate the prospect of nuclear destruction, new mythic images have been taking shape in the nuclear age. We will consider the powerful role that nuclear weapons play in the popular imagination, before reviewing some of the ethical responses that have been proposed for human responsibility in the nuclear age. A first step in rethinking the myths of war, the ethics of military action, and the challenges to human survival in the nuclear age may be to examine the projections that have been made regarding the potential consequences of the use of nuclear weapons.

Projected Effects of Nuclear Weapons

To think about the magnitude of destruction that would be brought about by nuclear weapons is to try to imagine the unimaginable. We have the images of devastation at Hiroshima and Nagasaki, but the weapons used there cannot compare to the power of nuclear weapons currently in the arsenals of the United States and the Soviet Union. Nevertheless, some attempts have been made to estimate the effect of nuclear weapons. These can be separated into the primary effects of a nuclear explosion and the secondary effects of subsequent destruction to the human and natural environments that would be expected to result.

Primary Effects   The initial explosion of a nuclear bomb would produce the following effects:

1. *Initial Nuclear Radiation.* The superstellar blast from nuclear fusion and fission would produce an immediate pressure millions of times greater than the normal atmospheric pressure. High-energy electromagnetic radiation, gamma rays, would stream out into the environment. A medium-sized bomb of 1 megaton that exploded in the air above a human population would instantly kill all unprotected human beings in an area of about 6 square miles.

2. *Electromagnetic Pulse.* The gamma radiation would set up a shock wave that would effectively knock out all electrical equipment over a wide area by sending a powerful surge of voltage through various conductors, such as antennas, overhead power lines, pipes, and railroad tracks. A Defense Department study in 1977 estimated that a single large nuclear blast detonated 125 miles over Omaha, Nebraska, would generate a pulse strong enough to damage electrical circuits throughout the entire continental United States and parts of Canada and Mexico.

3. *Thermal Pulse.* At the center of the explosion a wave of blinding light and intense heat would form a fireball. A 1-megaton thermal pulse would last 10 seconds and produce second degree burns within a radius of 280 square miles; a larger 20-megaton weapon would produce a thermal pulse lasting 20 seconds and second degree burns on people within a radius of 2460 square miles.

4. *Blast Wave.* As the fireball expands it sends out a shock wave in all directions. The force

of this wave from a 1-megaton air burst would flatten or severely damage all buildings within a 4½-mile radius; the 20-megaton air blast would destroy all buildings in a radius of 12 miles.

5.   *Local Fallout.* As the fireball burns, it rises and condenses water from the atmosphere to form the mushroom cloud. If the bomb is a ground blast, or the fireball touches the ground, it will produce a tremendous crater and tons of debris will be sucked up into the air. As this debris returns to earth, mostly in the form of fire ash, it is highly radioactive. The Office of Technological Assessment estimates that a 1-megaton blast would lethally contaminate an area of over 1000 square miles with radioactive fallout.

Secondary Effects

After the initial shock of the explosion, it is expected that mass fires would break out, which would probably kill more people than the original thermal pulses and blast waves. But even if people survived all this, other effects would follow that would devastate human life.

1.   *Breakdown of Medical Support Systems.* Medical services would be unable to respond adequately to the extent of human suffering. The Office of Technological Assessment concluded in 1977 that "even if only one city is attacked, and the remaining resources of the nation are available to help, medical facilities would be inadequate to care for the injured."[53] This would condemn countless numbers of people to lingering death without medical attention.

2.   *Breakdown of Cultural Support Systems.* Nuclear attack would disrupt the intricate network of life-support systems in modern urban environments. It would break off supply chains of food, water, fuel, and basic necessities. It would seriously cripple communication links with the rest of the world. Economies would immediately be reduced to subsistence levels, without the skills or resources to effectively respond.

3.   *Breakdown of Environmental Support Systems.* The devastation to the earth's ecological balance would be hard to underestimate. A U.S. Government report projected that 10,000 megatons of nuclear explosions, which would be sufficient to entirely destroy the United States, would reduce the ozone layer in the atmosphere of this hemisphere by 70 percent. It would also produce enough radiation to kill most mammals and birds. Only insects, and especially cockroaches, are resistant to radiation. It is possible that they might inherit the earth.

Jonathan Schell, in his book *The Fate of the Earth,* has catalogued the unimaginable extent of the destruction that could be expected from nuclear war.

> *Bearing in mind that the possible consequences of the detonations of thousands of megatons of nuclear explosives include the blinding of insects, birds, and beasts all over the world; the extinction of many ocean species, among them some at the base of the food chain; the temporary or permanent alteration of the climate of the globe, with the outside chance of "dramatic" and "major" alteration in the structure of the atmosphere; the pollution of the whole ecosphere with oxides of nitrogen; the incapacitation in ten minutes of unprotected people who go out into the sunlight; the blinding of people who go out into the sunlight; a significant decrease in photosynthesis in plants around the world; the scalding and killing of many crops; the increase in rates of cancer and mutation around the world, but especially in targeted zones, and the attendant risks of global epidemics; the possible poisoning of all vertebrates by sharply increased levels of Vitamin D in their skin as a result of increased ultraviolet light; and the outright slaughter*

on all targeted continents of most human beings and other living things by the initial nuclear radiation, the fireballs, the thermal pulses, the blast waves, the mass fires, and the fallout from the explosions, and, considering that these consequences will all interact with one another in unguessable ways and, furthermore, are in all likelihood an incomplete list, which will be added to as our knowledge of the earth increases, one must conclude that a full-scale nuclear holocaust could lead to the extinction of mankind. [54]

This catalogue of catastrophe presents a worst-case situation. But it places in stark relief the unprecedented challenge to human survival posed by nuclear weapons. For the first time in human history, it becomes conceivable that an individual's death may coincide with the death of all human beings. Nuclear weapons threaten not simply the survival of individuals, communities, or nations, but the entire human species. The magnitude of this threat to survival has generated new responses of ethical imagination in the nuclear age.

Myths of the Nuclear Age

New myths have emerged in the modern world in an attempt to accommodate the reality of nuclear weapons. Like all myths, they give a sacred aura to human experience, and they evoke powerful symbols of life and death. Three basic myths have come to dominate religious and ethical responses to the prospect of nuclear destruction.

Nuclearism The psychologist Robert Lifton has defined *nuclearism* as the "passionate embrace of nuclear weapons as a solution to death anxiety and a way of restoring a lost sense of immortality." [55] We can stop worrying and worship the bomb. Nuclear weapons may represent the ultimate defeat of death. By bringing life and death into the realm of human control, a new transcendent power seems to be within human grasp. The adherents of the myth of nuclearism are convinced that by assuming control over the survival of the species they have transcended the mystery of death. Robert Oppenheimer described his response to the awesome power of the first atomic test: "At that moment . . . there flashed into my mind a passage from the Bhagavad-Gita, the sacred book of the Hindus: 'I am become Death, the Shatterer of Worlds.'" [56] Nuclearism is the belief that humans have gained the ultimate power of death through access to nuclear weapons.

Another observer of that first atomic test used religious imagery of a new birth. He said, "On that moment hung eternity. Time stood still. Space contracted to a pinpoint. It was as though the earth had opened and the skies had split. One felt as if he had been privileged to witness the Birth of the World." [57] The explosion was a new creative "big bang" to usher in a new world; these religious images of death and birth signified that human beings had taken control over the ultimate power of life and death.

Of course, there were other responses to the first test. One scientist was reported as saying, "Now we're all sons of bitches." But others felt the exhilaration of this new release of power. President Harry Truman exclaimed after the bombing of Hiroshima: "This is the greatest thing in human history." A new sacred power had been unleashed in the course of human events.

The science writer William Lawrence praised the bomb as the second coming of Prometheus. As Prometheus stole fire from the gods to give to men, so the bomb has taken power from the gods and placed it in the hands of human beings. As Lawrence watched the test of America's first airborne hydrogen bomb in the North Pacific during May of 1956, he invoked the images of nu-clearism: "This great irridescent cloud and its mushroom top, I found myself thinking as I watched, is actually a protective umbrella that will forever shield mankind . . . any sizable war has become impossible; for no aggressor could now start a war without the certainty of absolute and swift annihilation."[58] The bomb is mankind's savior, a protective umbrella from war, that would serve as a powerful deterrent against any aggression. Nuclearists often point to the benefits of the uneasy truce between East and West that has prevented the outbreak of war between them since World War II. But, in that time there have been over 130 wars, in many different regions of the world, which have left as many as 20 million people dead. The nuclear savior has not pre-vented these wars.

Nuclearism manifests a mythic inclination to deify the tools of destruction and to dehumanize the enemy. The political scientist George Kennan has pointed to "the peculiarly American tendency to what I would call dehumanization of any major national opponent: the tendency that is to form a species of devil image of that opponent, to de-prive him in our imaginations of all human at-tributes and to see him as totally evil and devoted to nothing but our destruction."[59] The myth of nuclearism requires an absolutely evil enemy in order to justify a nation's purposes in preparing for its total destruction. Nuclearism has the char-acteristics of holy war. A nuclear nation moti-vated by such a myth would be preparing for malecide. Eliminating a dehumanized enemy would be regarded as removing evil from the world and reinforcing the purity of that nation's purpose.

Heroic Survivors   In many examples
of modern science fiction literature, the plots re-volve around characters who survive a nuclear holocaust and struggle heroically to rebuild a new world.[60] In many cases we imagine that they will be able to create a better future after surviv-ing the wreckage of the past. There are variations on this theme. George Orwell's *1984* paints a bleak vision of a future where a few heroic survi-vors struggle to preserve human values in the oppressive political structures that resulted from the nuclear wars. Others, such as Walter Miller's *A Canticle for Liebowitz,* imagine a return to pre-industrial life without memory of the tech-nological past that had brought about its own destruction. Heroic survivors pass through the trials of the nuclear initiation to create a new life. Nuclear war appears as a kind of purification; out of the ashes of destruction a new world will be born. The hope for survival in this new world is reflected in the remark of a U.S. senator, who said, "If there had to be a new Adam and Eve I want them to be American."

Government policies and projects of civil defense are based on the assumption that some will be able to survive a nuclear war. The fallout shelters, with their preparations for food, water, and sedatives for a family of four, are monuments to the myth of heroic survivors. But the optimism in these expectations of rebuilding the world may be misplaced. "The factors that make rapid recovery from a small-scale disaster possible . . . will almost certainly be absent following a nu-clear attack. . . . Even the simplest requirements of survival will become major tasks."[61]

Even if it were possible to survive and go on with the business of living, what kind of a world would it be? Evidence from survivors of Hiro-shima and Nagasaki indicate that survivors felt as if they were themselves dead, walking through a world of the dead. As Lifton has put it: "The im-portant question is not 'Would there be survi-vors?' or 'Would the survivors envy the dead?' but rather 'Would the survivors themselves feel *as if* dead?'"[62] Any heroic survivors would cer-tainly have to do their rebuilding under the reign of death.

A special form of the myth of heroic survi-vors is found in the assumption held by some

Fundamentalist Christians that a nuclear holocaust would fit with biblical imagery of a final cosmic battle between the forces of good and evil. They believe that Christians will be the heroic survivors of this nuclear Armageddon. A best-selling book of the 1970s was Hal Lindsey's *The Late Great Planet Earth.*[63] In this book, and in his *Countdown to Armageddon,* Lindsey has tried to correlate biblical imagery with current historical events to suggest that the nuclear destruction of the world is imminent. The heroic survivors will be the true Christians who will be raptured up into the air to be with Jesus, wait out a period of tribulation, and then return as soldiers in Christ's army to defeat the forces of evil.

The Fundamentalist Jerry Falwell has also given some support to this mythic expectation of a nuclear Armageddon. He has predicted a nuclear war between the Soviet Union and the United States that will fulfill biblical prophecy by being centered on Israel. God is expected to miraculously intervene, bringing victory for the United States and Israel, who are regarded as the divine representatives of the forces of good.[64] In the meantime, Falwell has recommended that the United States continue to build up the strength of its nuclear arsenal to be prepared for this holy war. This type of millennial thinking is certainly not new in American history. But some Protestant Fundamentalists have incorporated the imagery of nuclear destruction into the eschatological myth of the end of the world in order to claim that only true Christians will be the heroic survivors of nuclear war.

Absolute Annihilation

Perhaps the most pervasive myth of the nuclear age evokes the imagery of the absolute annihilation of the human species. Robert Lifton has observed that "we feel nagged if not threatened by a new wave of millennial imagery—of killing, dying, and destroying on a scale so great as to end the human narrative."[65] In this myth there will be no heroic survivors, no hope of rebuilding the world, no life. It is a myth of ultimate and absolute emptiness. This is what the historian of religion Ira Chernus has called the myth of the "big whoosh." "The key image in this myth," according to Chernus, "is the mushroom cloud—an image which is burned into our mind's eye as the most characteristic emblem of total and instantaneous extinction. In one awful moment, in one big 'whoosh,' everything is destroyed."[66]

For most people the mushroom cloud does not represent William Lawrence's protective umbrella spread over the earth to save the world from war; it is the symbol of sudden, impersonal, and absolute death. Part of the symbolic power of the myth is the expectation of a quick, painless death: It will all be over before anyone even knows what has happened. But this hope for a quick, painless death is belied by the projections of lingering suffering, illness, and death over a period of hours, days, or weeks. Nevertheless, the catastrophe of nuclear destruction represents the absolute termination of all human plans and projects, all hopes and dreams, all values, in one explosive conclusion to the human drama.

The psychological consequences of this imagery of imminent annihilation are far-reaching. They may be described as a tendency toward the numbing of awareness, a pervasive death anxiety, and a sense of the insignificance of human life. The psychologist Robert Lifton has defined numbing as the "capacity to move beyond the perception of threat and to constitute a psychic world (even momentarily) independent of that threat."[67] Avoidance is a common strategy in the face of the prospect of nuclear annihilation. Many people find ways to not think about the unthinkable. To paraphrase T. S. Eliot, human beings cannot stand too much reality. The first psychological consequence of the myth of annihilation, therefore, may be a psychological avoidance of confronting the dangers to human survival posed by nuclear weapons.

A second consequence of this imagery of annihilation is a pervasive, shapeless death anxiety. Lifton has called this "the anxiety deriving from the sense that all forms of human associations are perhaps pointless because subject to sudden irrational ends."[68] Recent studies of men, women, and children living under the shadow of the bomb have revealed how extensive this anxiety can be. This sense of anxiety may permeate human relationships and affect major life plans, decisions, and goals.

Finally, the myth of absolute annihilation calls into question the very meaning of human life. It challenges the ultimate significance of the human species given the possibility that it could be so suddenly terminated. Again, as Lifton has observed, "the ultimate threat posed by nuclear weapons is not only death but meaninglessness: an unknown death by an unimaginable weapon."[69] The apparent meaninglessness of such a death seems to deny the significance of human life. And a life that is lived with such an extreme sense of the insignificance of all human actions may already, in effect, be annihilated. Nuclearism is a myth that dehumanizes the enemy, but the possibility of nuclear annihilation holds the prospect of dehumanizing all human beings.

Ethical Responses to Nuclear War

Ethical responses to the challenges of the nuclear age are attempts to recover a sense of the significance of human life and actions in the face of this prospect of total annihilation. Four basic ethical strategies can be identified.[70] Although they may have much in common, and at times overlap, they each represent a different ethical analysis of the challenge to human survival in the nuclear age.

Pacifism   There is a long tradition of pacifism, renouncing any use of violence to promote political goals, within the Christian tradition. The nuclear age has strengthened this commitment for many people and created a special variety of nuclear pacifists. As one representative of this position has suggested, "the central question for Christian citizens in this instance is whether the use and possession of nuclear weapons is consistent with our Christian commitment."[71] The traditional peace churches—The Church of the Bretheren, the Mennonites, and the Society of Friends (Quakers)—have renounced all militarism, condemned nuclear weapons, and called for an end to their research and production.[72] These traditional pacifists have also been supported in recent years by mainstream Protestant and Catholic statements against nuclear weapons. The United Church of Christ issued a resolution opposed to the nuclear arms race. It stated: "The nuclear arms race is first and foremost a false religion. It is, to be sure, also bad politics, bad economics, bad science, and bad war . . . however, to confront its vital nerve, the church must come to understand it theologically."[73] This resolution represented a theological commitment to resist the myth of nuclearism and support the disarmament of the nuclear arsenals that nuclearism worships.

The National Conference of Catholic Bishops pastoral letter of 1983 was the most significant American Catholic statement against nuclear weapons. The bishops reaffirmed the "pacifist option" that recognizes the individual's right of conscientious objection to all warfare or selective objection to particular wars. The letter insisted on gradual, bilateral disarmament of nuclear arsenals as the top priority in international relations. It accepted the theory of deterrence, not as an end in itself, but only on the condition that it lead eventually to negotiated disarmament of nuclear weapons.[74]

Pacifism has often been identified with unilateral disarmament. The real question raised by pacifists is not "Are you willing to die in a nuclear attack?" but "Are you willing to kill?" Nuclear pacifists have maintained that they would rather die than be responsible for the killing of millions of innocent people in a nuclear war. They have called for unconditional disarmament as an ethical imperative. Some have seen this willingness to die, rather than to kill, as a direct extension of their Christian faith. Archbishop Raymond Hunthausen, for example, has called for unilateral disarmament as "one meaning of the cross."[75] And the Catholic monk Thomas Merton reminded Christians that their religion teaches the willingness to suffer rather than to inflict pain on another human being."[76] This commitment has been extended to the use of nuclear weapons. Other nuclear pacifists have called for unilateral disarmament as a sign of good faith. Nuclear pacifists in the United States, for example, have recommended that the nation should reduce its nuclear arsenal, with its redundant power of overkill, in order to lessen tensions in the global arena. It is hoped that the Soviet Union would respond by also reducing its stockpile of weapons. If the Soviets did not reciprocate, this would convince world opinion of their intentions for war.

Just War Theory

Attempts have been made to revive the traditional standards for a just war and to apply them to the use of nuclear weapons. The Christian ethicist Paul Ramsey has suggested that the use of tactical nuclear weapons as a strategy of defense against foreign aggressors may be regarded as a moral, rational, and just use of military power. Ramsey has claimed that just war theory would allow for the use of tactical weapons only against forces that crossed recognized borders. "This is certainly a clear case of 'just conduct' in a first resort to nuclear weapons. It is counter-force warfare surrounded by the additional limitation of the aggressor-defender distinction."[77] Although tactical counter-force

uses of nuclear weapons may be permitted, in Ramsey's view, the strategic use of weapons against civilian populations could never be justified, because it would immediately violate the two provisions of just war theory: proportionality and noncombatant immunity from attack.

Other just war theorists, however, have not seen the ethical line as so clearly drawn between tactical and strategic uses of nuclear weapons. James T. Johnson, for example, has maintained that "an alternative should be found to tactical nuclear weapons intended for use against land forces. Use of such weapons, besides risking escalation to a general nuclear exchange, would cause immediate and long-term damage to noncombatants that is hard or impossible to justify."[78]

Just war theory in the nuclear age has tended to follow Paul Ramsey in requiring the absolute immunity of noncombatants from direct intentional harm. Some theorists have argued that if the intent is to destroy enemy forces and military targets, and not to kill civilians, then the principle of discrimination in the just conduct of war may be upheld. It has been estimated, however, that counter-city targeting in a nuclear war would result in the deaths of 215 million civilians, while counter-force targeting would reduce that number to 25 million. But if 25 million deaths are regarded as acceptable losses, than the principles of both discrimination and proportionality appear to be strained in order to justify nuclear war as just war. Nevertheless, Paul Ramsey has argued that the selective use of nuclear weapons may be permitted within the theory of the just war. "Counter-force nuclear war," he has maintained, "is the upper limit of rational, politically purposeful military action."[79] It can be justified by the principle of discrimination because weapons are not intentionally directed at civilian populations.

One problem with a military strategy that relies on the deployment of nuclear weapons aimed at the enemy's military targets is that such counter-force strategy may make the actual use of nuclear weapons more likely. Such a strategy could actually contribute to instability. Knowing that the other side has the capability of disarming a nation's weapons may put that nation on a hair-trigger alert, where miscalculation, accident, or anxiety might cause a first strike in order to anticipate the other side's disarming attack on its weapon systems. In this situation, a nuclear nation might feel compelled to use its weapons before they are destroyed.[80] A nuclear strategy of counter-force targeting, designed to be more consistent with the just war theory of discriminating between military targets and noncombatants, might actually lead to a more unstable and precarious military situation among nuclear powers.

The historian Michael Walzer has observed that "nuclear wars explode the theory of the just war. They are the first of mankind's technological innovations that are simply not encompassable within the familiar moral world."[81] The likelihood that any nuclear war would violate the just war principles of proportionality and discrimination is not the only reason for this difficulty in encompassing nuclear war in traditional ethical theory. A nuclear war would probably violate both principles: It is likely that more destruction than good would result and that innocent noncombatants would be killed. But the prospect of nuclear war seems to confound the theory of just war for a more subtle reason. The very attempt to think of nuclear war in just war terms—as a limited use of force to serve the military and political ends of conventional wars—may make the exchange of nuclear weapons, and the resulting destruction of human lives, more likely. These considerations have led many just war theorists to conclude that the magnitude of violence in nuclear war is too great to be justified in terms of the traditional standards of justice in declaring and conducting conventional wars.

Paul Ramsey's response to those who argue that just war theory is irrelevant in the nuclear age is that the use of nuclear weapons may be justified if they are in the service of a higher good. Just wars may be regarded as just because they work to preserve basic human values. But there are higher values, Ramsey has claimed, than merely survival. What the world needs is not simply peace, but a just peace. "Liberty and justice," Ramsey has maintained, "can only be preserved by forces which today can be used only at risk of vastly destructive nuclear war."[82] In this sense, just war theory has suggested standards of justice in declaring and conducting wars that may be able to accommodate nuclear war. But even if nuclear war cannot be justified by the criteria of just war theory, many have argued that the *threat* of nuclear war can serve the interests of justice. This raises questions about the role of nuclear weapons as a deterrent to war.

Deterrence

A third ethical response to the challenge of survival in the nuclear age rests on the potential of nuclear weapons to deter their actual use. The principle of deterrence has been used to justify maintaining a nuclear arsenal in the interest of preventing other nuclear nations from using their weapons. From this perspective, the use of nuclear weapons may never be regarded as just, but the threat of their use may be seen as a sufficiently powerful force to preserve peace and justice. Deterrence assumes that both sides recognize that they would be destroyed in a nuclear exchange, so neither side would be mad enough to start a nuclear war. Ironically, this has been called the doctrine of Mutual Assured Destruction (MAD). It is an ethical strategy based on the assumption that the principal function of an armed force is to prevent war. Possession of nuclear weapons makes clear to any potential aggressor that a nation has sufficient force to cause unacceptable damages in the event that an aggressor should resort to nuclear weapons. The maintenance of nuclear arsenals, therefore, has been ethically justified in terms of their ability to deter the actual use of nuclear weapons.

As an ethical response to the existence of nuclear weapons, deterrence necessarily involves a calculated bluff. A nation may assume that it is immoral to use nuclear weapons but that it is moral to have them as long as they are simply a deterrent threat for maintaining peace. The proponents of deterrence have claimed that the intention is to provide a sufficient threat to discourage any other nation from using nuclear weapons and thereby maintain the delicate balance of peace in international relations. If the use of these weapons is regarded as immoral, however, it would appear that a nuclear nation would be obligated not to use them even if it is attacked. For the threat to be effective, however, a nation's enemies must be uncertain as to whether it is bluffing or not. A nuclear nation must declare its willingness to use nuclear weapons in case of an attack. In order for deterrence to work, a nation must convince its enemies that there is at least a strong possibility that it will resort to using its nuclear weapons. This results in an apparent split between private ethical commitments and public political postures. A nation may be convinced that it has no intentions of using nuclear weapons, but in public it must create the appearance that it is willing to resort to nuclear war in certain extreme situations. The theory of deterrence, therefore, may involve a type of nuclear schizophrenia as a nation tries to balance its ethical commitments with this public declaration of willingness to bring about mass death if provoked.

The theory of deterrence does not explicitly require military superiority in order for a nation to present a credible nuclear threat. A deterrent nuclear force would not need to be strong enough to conquer other nations, but simply strong enough to ensure that any aggressor would sustain unacceptable damages if it initiated a nuclear war. The political scientist Theodore Draper has noted that if deterrence is truly the policy of a nuclear nation, then "nuclear weapons over and above what is necessary to have a devastating effect on the other side is no more than an exercise in redundancy."[83] From this perspective, the goal of a nuclear nation should be deter-

rence, not competition; enough, not more. It has been estimated that the United States and the Soviet Union possess nuclear arsenals sufficient to destroy each other seven times over. This has inspired George Kennan's proposal for an immediate reduction of the nuclear arsenals of both nations by 50 percent.[84] Each side would still have a sufficient deterrent force to threaten total destruction of the other, but the lower levels of nuclear weaponry might begin a move toward a more stable balance of power. Such a reduction would be in keeping with the expressed goals of a nuclear strategy based on deterrence.

If deterrence were the reason for maintaining nuclear arsenals, however, such reductions would probably already have taken place. Nuclear weapons have also been tied to the interests of sovereign states that perceive themselves in direct competition with each other over a range of social, economic, and political issues. Nuclear weapons have simply been introduced into this system of political competition between nation-states. Political realists have maintained that "war is an inherent element in a system of sovereign states which lacks any supreme and acknowledged arbiter."[85] Nuclear weapons have become a new part in that old system. But the devastating force of these weapons, even as a deterrent, may result in disruption of the conventional military relations between states. It has been said that a nuclear policeman, for example, who is armed only with an atomic bomb, could not prevent someone from breaking into a house, unless the policeman was willing to destroy the whole neighborhood. To promote its own interests, a nuclear nation may be willing to put the interests of all humanity at risk. At the very least, according to the theory of deterrence, a nuclear nation must create a credible international perception that it is willing to resort to such destruction. But the magnitude of this threat in military strategy may make conventional use of military force more problematic, due to the potential for any conflict escalating to a nuclear confrontation. For deterrence to be effective as an ethical response to nuclear weapons it has to be based, not simply on competitive threats, but on a mutual recognition among nations that they have a common interest in preventing their use. This would require a shared ethical commitment to avoiding the destruction, and ensuring the survival, of humanity in the nuclear age.

Survival

One attempt to work toward such a common perspective on the dangers to human survival in the nuclear age has been proposed by Jonathan Schell in his book, *The Fate of the Earth*. Schell has accepted the notion that nuclear war could never be classified as a just war, but he has also suggested that it cannot even be regarded as war. The initiation of a nuclear exchange cannot be regarded as a strategic use of military force in the interest of pursuing a nation's political goals. Rather, it should be seen as naked violence, unrestrained and absolute in its destruction. With the introduction of nuclear weapons, Schell has claimed, "it became impossible for violence to be fashioned into war, or to achieve what war used to achieve. Violence can no longer break down the opposition of the adversary; it can no longer produce a victory and defeat; it can no longer attain its ends. It can no longer be war."[86] Schell has suggested that the threat of violence in the nuclear age can be compared to a group of people sitting in a dark room around a huge bomb. Each person holds a string that could detonate the device and destroy everyone. What personal interests could possibly justify destroying everyone? Each lives with the hope that the others will not pull their string. And yet they all live with that fear. This is not an image of war, but an ordeal of terror with the prospect of unlimited violence. It does not seem to fit the conventional concept of war as the use of force for the advancement of political objectives.

The single most important ethical imperative in such a situation would be to prevent this destruction. Schell has insisted that the preservation of any human values depends upon the survival of the human species. Without survival, no other values could be pursued. "There are no ethics apart from service to the human community," Schell has maintained, "therefore no ethical commandments that can justify the extinction of humanity."[87]

Some Christian ethicists, such as Paul Ramsey, have held that mere survival is not the highest value in the ethics of human social relations. There may be situations worse than death, even the death of the species. The ethical values of freedom, dignity, and justice may be regarded as more important than mere survival. Systems of religious ethics that include some belief in human immortality, resurrection, or survival after death may in fact support this idea that the continuation of the human species is not an issue that is of ultimate concern. But Jonathan Schell has suggested that in the nuclear age survival has been elevated to a new status. It has become the condition upon which all other values are based. This commitment to the survival of the human species may be regarded as consistent with the ethics of the unconditional love of others in the Christian tradition. Schell has suggested that in the ethical teachings of Jesus, "religious faith that is divorced from love of human beings is empty and dangerous."

> He said, "If thou bring thy gift to the altar, and there rememberest that thy brother hath aught against thee; leave there thy gift before the altar, and go thy way; first be reconciled to thy brother, and then come offer thy gift." We who have planned out the deaths of hundreds of millions of our brothers plainly have a great deal of work to do before we return to the altar. Clearly, the corpse of mankind would be the least acceptable of all conceivable offerings on the altar of this God.[88]

This ethical commitment to the survival of the human species may provide a common ground for religious ethics and humanistic ethics. Resources within religious ethics may be drawn upon to support the human value of survival and to respond creatively to the challenge of the nuclear age.

Jonathan Schell has tried to locate the central problem of the nuclear age in the prevailing system of national sovereignty into which nuclear weapons have been introduced. Nuclear weapons have not been instruments of deterrence to protect humanity from war. Rather, they have been deployed to protect and promote national interests. Nuclear weapons have been incorporated into the conventional military forces, and military logic, which regard violence as the legitimate means of reinforcing and extending the interests of national groups. Schell has insisted that it will not be possible to dismantle the arsenals of nuclear weapons that threaten the entire planet without a dramatic change in the international competition for power among national states. Even if all existing nuclear weapons were destroyed, humanity could not dis-invent the scientific technology that developed them. Human beings could not forget that knowledge. If the same system of competitive nation-states prevailed, these weapons would most likely be developed again. Scientific technology developed them, but political decisions have deployed them. Particularly in the arena of political decisions nuclear weapons have changed everything except ways of thinking.

To contemplate such changes in political power, organization, and decision making, however, is to think in terms of revolutionizing the politics of the earth. Schell has suggested that precisely such a new political order may be necessary in international relations in order to guarantee the survival of the human species.

The task we face is to find a means of political action that will permit human beings to pursue any end for the rest of time. We are asked to replace the mechanism by which political decisions, whatever they may be, are reached. In sum, the task is nothing less than to reinvent politics: to reinvent the world.[89]

With this exhortation to reinvent the world, we have suddenly entered the realm of religious myth. The challenge to recreate the political order of the planet takes on the mythic proportions of a new creation, a new ordering of the human world. But perhaps in examining ethical responses to the nuclear age, we have never left the realm of myth. The mythic images of nuclearism, heroic survivors, and absolute annihilation lie in the background of any ethical response to the preservation of human values in the nuclear age. An ethical response based on the concept of deterrence, for example, may be supported by the mythic images of nuclearism. The bomb may be imagined as a protective umbrella that will preserve human values from the destruction of war. A response from the perspective of just war theory, which would allow for the limited use of nuclear weapons in the interests of justice, may be supported by the myth of heroic survivors. Jonathan Schell seems to have fashioned his ethical response to the nuclear age in the face of the mythic image of absolute annihilation. He has been accused of being utopian in his plea for a new world. Theodore Draper has suggested that "if we have to 'reinvent the world' to control nuclear war, the chances of saving the human race must be somewhere near the vanishing point."[90] But the world has been changed with the advent of the nuclear age, and it requires all the resources of imaginative vision and creative commitment to respond to that change.

Patterns of Survival

Ethical patterns of action in the history of religions have been committed to the preservation of values. It is easy to forget, however, the important role that violence has played in defending, protecting, and extending particular systems of ethical values. Violence seems to be endemic to human social relations. Legal violence, and the threat of violence, are employed to maintain the internal order of a community; and military violence, and the threat of violence, are used to establish a community in relation to other communities. These exercises of violence in human social relations may be enveloped in a network of ethical and religious values that are felt to be so important that they must be preserved by force. The religious ethics of violence within any given society may give legal and military force an aura of sacred meaning and value. That sacred meaning and value of violence may be shared by a community, or it may serve the special interests of its ruling class; but, in either case, it reinforces, supports, and preserves a particular configuration of ethical values. Chapter 12 has drawn a number of conclusions regarding the ethical significance of military violence in religious ethics.

––––––

1.   *Communities have attempted to preserve, reinforce, and expand basic values in human social relations through religious wars.* Warfare has often been legitimized in religious traditions as a means of reaffirming basic religious and ethical values. An exercise of military power may perform more than the social function of reinforcing a community's borders. War may support specific religious goals that are felt to be vital to the life of a community. There is an important distinction between sacred wars and holy wars. The sacred wars of traditional India, China, and Japan were

perceived as ritual strategies for maintaining the order of the cosmos. War was a type of ritual play for the affirmation of sacred order and heroic virtues. The holy wars of traditional Judaism, Christianity, and Islam, however, were perceived as attempts to do the work of a transcendent God on earth. They were conceived as mortal contests between absolute forces of good and evil. Goodness was felt to work its will upon the world by exterminating evil, which was manifested in the form of nonbelievers, sinners, and heretics. Both of these forms of religious warfare have been conducted in the interests of certain ethical values, but the holy war has been engaged in expanding the realm of divine goodness on earth by destroying all those who are seen to be aligned with the forces of evil.

––––––

2.   *Just war theory strives to restrain the declaration and the conduct of war in order to preserve human values.* The ethical theory of just war is the product of centuries of religious reflection on military violence within the Christian tradition. Just war theory makes a compromise with the necessity of war by trying to place certain restraints on the destruction of human lives and values that inevitably result from warfare.

Just war theory analyzes two aspects of war: justice in declaring war and justice in conducting war. The first aspect tries to specify the legitimate ethical conditions within which a war might be declared. The theory requires that war be declared only by a duly constituted authority, for a just cause, and in the interest of restoring peace. The theory of *jus ad bellum* allows for the ethical legitimacy of defensive wars that are declared to redress certain wrongs that have been perpetrated by aggressors. But the theory leaves a certain degree of ambiguity regarding the definition of proper authority, the range of causes that might be regarded as just, and the status of revolutionary wars that might be declared to redress grievances, persecution, or oppression.

The second aspect of just war theory attempts to restrain the destruction caused by military violence in the conduct of war. The theory of *jus in bello* proposes the criteria of proportionality and discrimination as ethical standards intended to restrain the destruction caused by war. In these terms, justice in the conduct of war requires that more good than evil result from the use of military force and that noncombatants be protected from the effects of violence. Just war theory has been an attempt within one system of religious ethics to devise standards for the ethical evaluation of war.

_____

3.   *Nuclear war threatens the survival of the human species and, therefore, may be regarded as a threat to the preservation of any values.* The prospect of nuclear war is difficult to accommodate into traditional theories of the just war. This is not simply because it would seem to violate the principles of proportionality and discrimination in the conduct of war, but also because nuclear war is no longer war in any recognizable sense. War has traditionally been the use of military force for the preservation or extension of certain perceived values. But nuclear war promises to unleash a potentially total violence that, in destroying the human species, would destroy the basis for any human values.

Religious responses to the prospect of nuclear annihilation have argued that there are greater values than the mere survival of the human species. Some religious ethicists might be willing to pay the price of the extinction of the human species to preserve certain religious and political values. Particularly when those values are tied to hope of an after-life, a system of reli-

gious ethics might find some way of accommodating the elimination of the human species within a larger design of sacred values. But within the limited scope of the human life cycle and human social relations, it is difficult to see how such an ultimate sacrifice would serve the preservation of human values.

The ethics of human social relations is engaged in the definition, production, exchange, and preservation of basic human values. In the modern world, a complex, differentiated network of specialized institutions define and orient human beings toward values. Technology largely determines the conditions for the production of values by narrowing the scope of human values to efficiency in the production of useful commodities. A market economy encourages the competitive exchange of values with little concern for the traditional social, religious, and ethical values that could be affirmed through patterns of exchange. In very broad outline, these institutional, technological, and economic forces establish the conditions of possibility for ethical action in modern social relations. These forces place definite restraints on human action. But they also provide challenges to which the ethical imagination may respond by drawing upon the resources of traditional religious ethics, or by improvising new patterns of action that might affirm a sense of harmony, integrity, and mutual recognition in human social relations.

The challenge of global conflict, and the prospect of nuclear annihilation, are precisely such tests for the ethical imagination. They suggest for many people a new ethical obligation that requires that the survival of the human species be recognized as the precondition for the preservation of any ethical values. This may not be merely survival, but a survival that reaffirms a commitment to imagining, clarifying, and responding to ethical values in human social relations.

EPILOGUE

This book has not solved any ethical problems, proposed any solutions to ethical dilemmas, or offered any guidance for ethical decision making. If this were a book in normative religious ethics, it would be a complete failure. Fortunately, this book was never intended to solve problems, propose solutions, or offer guidance. The primary intention throughout has been to provide access to the variety of ethical patterns of action by describing, analyzing, and interpreting that variety. This has been an exercise in ethical imagination: to imagine the patterns and processes, challenges and dilemmas, persistence and change in religious ethics within the history of religions. Perhaps this attempt to imagine the conditions of possibility for ethical action will have unexpected consequences in awakening our ability to respond more creatively to actual ethical challenges. The resources of imagination may play an important role in creating new arenas of ethical action in which human beings are able to live more fully with themselves and with each other. But this would be an unintended benefit of the work of interpretive religious ethics.

Religious ethics has been divided into three basic areas: ethical experience, ethical rules, and ethical values. In a sense, this division is arbitrary. Ethical experience is necessarily related to norms, rules, and values; ethical rules support certain kinds of experience and reinforce certain values; and ethical values are embodied in rules and realized in human experience. These three areas are inevitably interwoven in any ethical system. For the purposes of analysis, however, it has been useful to separate them. In this way, ethical experience can be analyzed as a dynamic tension between dissonance and harmony in relation to ethical norms; ethical rules can be analyzed as standards that define what counts as right conduct within an ethical system; and ethical values can be analyzed as organized conceptions of whatever may be regarded as good within human social relations. In describing, analyzing, and interpreting religious ethics, this book has made certain other basic assumptions that it might be useful to briefly review.

Interpretive Religious Ethics

An interpretive approach to religious ethics is consistent with the cross-cultural and interdisciplinary techniques, methods, and categories that have been developed in the history of religions. This approach begins with a description of religious phenomena that is made possible by a certain detachment—setting aside personal prejudices and value judgments—and an attitude of empathic appreciation of the variety of religious beliefs, practices, and experiences. This purely descriptive enterprise has been perceived as inadequate by those who insist that ethics is necessarily the science of making normative judgments and putting those judgments into practice. The mathematician Henri Poincaré once said that descriptive ethics "can be no more a substitute for morality than a treatise on the physiology of digestion can be a substitute for a good dinner."[1] Aristotle probably intended something similar when he said that merely having a theoretical knowledge of the good is like reading a textbook on medicine in order to be healthy. For Aristotle, and normative ethics in general, one knows the good by doing the good. Normative ethics requires a kind of practical wisdom in action.

The work of interpretive religious ethics, however, is neither normative nor simply descriptive. It does not pursue the normative project of deciding what in fact *is* fitting, right, or good in human action; but, on the other hand, it does not merely record, collect, and catalogue the actual ethical beliefs and practices of living ethical communities. Interpretive religious ethics may begin with such descriptions, but it necessarily seeks to interpret the patterns and processes that give shape to ethical experience, rules, and values in the history of religions. In this sense, interpretive religious ethics is not a substitute for morality, but perhaps an important supplement to our understanding and appreciation of how ethical beliefs, actions, and experiences operate in a variety of religious contexts.

Two basic obstacles may intervene to block an interpretive understanding of religious ethics: The first is intolerant value judgments; the second is reductive explanations. Certainly intolerance, prejudice, and unexamined value judgments make the interpretation of otherness more difficult. From the perspective of modern, west-

ern human beings, a certain degree of prejudice is already evident when others are regarded as primitive or exotic. So-called primitive societies tend to be associated with immoral customs and practices in the popular imagination. A recent collection of American popular folk beliefs has suggested that Americans believe "that there is no human custom—no matter how disgusting, unnatural, or immoral—that anthropologists have not found to be the norm among members of remote tribes."[2] Perhaps the accounts of abortion practices, euthanasia, and revenge suicide, to select a few at random, that have been described in this book serve to reinforce this belief. But these practices have not been interpreted as disgusting, unnatural, or immoral, but as illustrations of the rich variety of ethical practices that are available for interpretation. If we wanted to label anything as disgusting, we might first want to look at the ethical instructions of Erasmus and La Salle on the discipline of bodily functions, spitting, nose blowing, and sleeping in the western tradition. In any event, such value judgments do not assist our understanding of these ethical norms, but serve as obstacles to any appreciation of their meaning and function within their context.

A certain degree of prejudice may also be inherent in western perceptions of religious beliefs, practices, and experiences that are regarded as exotic. Since the nineteenth century, this term has generally been applied to the religious traditions of the East. Eastern religious traditions may appear exotic, strange, and foreign to the western imagination. The British Lord Macaulay demonstrated the kind of intolerant disdain that a westerner might hold for the exotic cultures of the East when he declared in 1835 that "I have never found one amongst the orientalists who could deny that a single shelf of a good European library was worth the whole native literatures of India and Arabia." These exotic native literatures, Macaulay was convinced, are filled with "absurd history, a metaphysics, a physics, a theology . . . which are of less value than the paper on which they are printed was while it was blank."[3] Fortunately for our understanding of religion, Macaulay's attitude was not shared by F. Max Müller, who has often been referred to as the father of comparative religions. Müller's maxim—"He who knows one, knows none"—suggests that an interpretive understanding of religion can only begin by studying, appreciating, and taking seriously the religions of others. This interpretive survey of religious ethics has tried to be consistent with that commitment by drawing on a wide range of cross-cultural materials in analyzing ethical experience, rules, and values. But in the brief compass of this book, it has only been possible to make a preliminary mapping of the territory. Much remains to be explored.

A second obstacle to the interpretation of religious ethics is the attempt to formulate reductive explanations. An explanation is different than an interpretation. To explain a phenomenon is to try to identify the necessary and sufficient causes that account for its emergence as a phenomenon. An explanation of religion necessarily reduces the rich array of religious phenomena to one or more causal factors: Religion becomes an epi-

phenomena of class interests, social solidarity, infantile neurosis, wish fulfillment, or the drive toward individuation. In each case, religion is reduced to social or psychological forces that are invoked to account for its very existence.

An interpretation of religion, however, takes the phenomenon of religion as a given. It is simply present as a dimension of human experience. Religion is not regarded as a problem that requires an explanation, but as a symbolic constellation of meaning, significance, and value to be interpreted. An interpretation works to expand our understanding of the frame of reference, or the different frames of reference, within which a religious phenomenon may derive its significance. In this regard, social and psychological modes of analysis may be drawn upon, not as explanations, but as complements to an interdisciplinary interpretation of the multidimensional phenomenon of religion. These same considerations apply to the interpretive study of religious ethics. This book has not attempted to explain the causes of religious ethics, but to interpret the patterns and processes that appear to be inherent in ethical action.

Patterns and Processes

Ethical experience appears to be inevitably organized in a characteristic pattern within the history of religions. That experience is patterned in terms of an aesthetic tension between dissonance and harmony in relation to sacred obligations that are felt to be binding on ordinary behavior. This aesthetic play of dissonance and harmony is the pattern of ethical experience in the history of religions. But that pattern is also a process. Human beings respond in a variety of ways to obligation, and the process of responding to obligation suggests that ethical patterns

of action necessarily involve a variety of dynamic modes of engagement with a sense of obligation. Moral responses, disciplined responses, antinomian responses, and improvisational responses all suggest the dynamic process that is inherent in ethical patterns of action.

Ethical rules of the human life cycle also suggest a certain pattern that shapes personal development within an ethical system. Those rules pattern behavior during the liminal transitions of the life cycle when personal identity may be most in question. But that pattern is also a process. There may be a different process by which rules are enacted in habitual customs, coercive laws, or moral choices. Again, these different types of rules imply a qualitatively different experiential engagement with the religious rules that pattern ordinary behavior during the course of the human life cycle.

Finally, ethical values in human social relations appear in patterns. The most tangible, concrete, and visible outline of the pattern of values in any society is revealed in its social institutions. The network of social institutions embodies a pattern of values—a sense of the sacred, historical continuity, vitality, knowledge, order, security, well-being, and so on—that may orient human beings toward ethical values in the social world they inhabit. But that pattern is also a process.

Values are not only defined within a network of social relations; they are also produced, exchanged, and preserved in an ongoing process of negotiating a collective sense of values. In all these cases, ethical patterns of action in religious ethics are also dynamic processes of engagement with sacred norms that govern ordinary behavior, conduct, and action. That engagement is often felt to be ambiguous, contradictory, and even counterproductive; sometimes, however, it is experienced as a transcendental harmony when actions and desires come into alignment with an ethical pattern of action that is regarded as infused with sacred meaning and power. This is the dynamic potential within both personal and social ethics in the history of religions.

Personal and Social Ethics

It has been useful to distinguish between the ethics of personal development and the ethics of social interaction. One is concerned with proper personal conduct in response to the challenges, dilemmas, and uncertainties of the human life cycle; the other is concerned with patterns of social interaction that define, produce, exchange, and preserve human values. Again, this distinction between personal and social ethics is somewhat arbitrary. Persons are always social persons, and societies are networks comprised of persons and interpersonal relations. The personal ethics of the life cycle, therefore, is necessarily enmeshed in social patterns that support traditional customs, provide a range of moral choices, and enforce specific legal injunctions and prohibitions that discipline personal behavior. Likewise, social ethics necessarily entails the personal involvement of individuals in the ongoing work of negotiating an experience of value in relation to social institutions, technology, economic ex-

change, and the particular pattern of systemic legal and military violence in which the self finds itself.

One important theme that has emerged in this survey of personal and social ethics is the role of violence in ethical patterns of action. Many of the ethical challenges of the human life cycle and social relations involve some variety of inherent violence. Ethical responses in these situations may use violence, avoid violence, or allow violence to continue, but in each case it is necessary to acknowledge the presence of violence in religious ethics.

Violence may assume a variety of forms. First, religious ethics may provide ways of coming to terms with the violence inherent in causing death. The ethical issues of abortion, infanticide, euthanasia, suicide, and war each involve the violence of causing death. Suicide, and euthanasia in many cases, are issues of self-inflicted violence; but abortion, infanticide, and war are issues of violence against others. Self-violence tends to occur when people feel that their lives are not worth living. But violence against others tends to be supported by social classifications which dehumanize the target of violence. Abortion tends to be allowed when the fetus is not classified as a human being; it is not perceived as causing a human death. Infanticide also tends to be allowed within social classifications that do not regard the infant, or certain infants, as fully legitimate human beings. But it is important to remember that the violence of war is also supported by the dehumanization of others. Religious and ethical attempts to justify war in the history of religions, particularly those wars that take on the characteristics of holy wars, require a dehumanized enemy in order to support the military exercise of violence against others. In all these cases, the violence of causing death tends to be supported by an ethical imagination that classifies the target of violence as nonhuman.

Second, religious ethics may extend this violence of dehumanization through the subclassification of certain persons within a network of social relations. The subclassification of women within many traditional patterns of religious ethics may be regarded as a systemic violence against women. The ethics of obedience to which women have been subjected in these traditions may be an inherent structural violence that limits, restricts, and confines women to social roles defined by men. But the violence of subclassification is also found in a variety of social hierarchies, rituals of exclusion, and unequal distributions of wealth that may be supported by any given system of religious ethics. A network of social, political, or economic relations that systematically subclassifies certain persons on the basis of race, ethnicity, occupation, gender, and so on demonstrates an inherent structural violence against these classes of persons. Religion has often been invoked to validate such subclassifications, and when this occurs, religion is necessarily implicated in a pattern of structural violence.

Finally, religious ethics may resort to the violence of coercion in order to enforce a certain pattern of ethical action. When moral rules become legal rules, they necessarily assume a certain degree of violence. They become involved in a system of legal enforcement that attempts to mold human behavior through force, punishment, and the threat of reprisals in this life or another. The discipline of the body, the punishment of nonconventional sexuality, the threat of exclusion, and many other areas of religious ethics enmesh persons within a coercive regimen that is supported by violence. Religious ethics, therefore, is inevitably involved in a number of different employments of violence to enforce patterns of action.

Personal and social ethics within religious traditions, however, may also develop resources for avoiding, minimizing, or deflecting the violence of social relations. The familiar Golden Rule, which appears in one variation or another in many different religious traditions, is an ethical strategy for human relations that refuses to dehumanize others. Doing to others what you would want them to do to you necessarily involves an active acknowledgment of mutual humanity in human interactions. It is an attempt to avoid the violence in human social relations that results from subclassifying or dehumanizing others. Perhaps the most rigorous strategy of nonviolence is the ideal of *ahimsa* in Jainism, and in other religions of India, which strives for a perfect harmlessness, not only in social relations, but in every action that might have an impact on the surrounding world. In a sense, the practice of ahimsa not only refuses to dehumanize other persons, but it even "humanizes" other species of living beings by treating them with the same ethical regard that is felt to be appropriate to all life. These ethical strategies for resisting violence in personal and social ethics do not attempt to meet violence with violence. These embody ethical aspirations for breaking the dehumanizing cycle of violence in personal and social relations.

Religion has been invoked to support, sustain, and legitimize cycles of violence, and it has been drawn upon to break through the network of violence in human relations. Religion has served political repression, and it has supported political liberation. Religion is perhaps the worst and the best in human experience: It represents the most constraining, limiting, and divisive force in personal development and social relations, yet, at the same time, it represents the aspirations of the human imagination to transcend those constraints, limits, and divisions that permeate human experience with violence. Since religious ethics is necessarily integrated into this ambiguous character of religion, ethical norms, rules, and values are also implicated in supporting and transcending cycles of violence.

The ethical dimension of religion is the cutting edge of religious practice in the ordinary situations and circumstances of human actions and interactions. Ethics is that point at which religion becomes practical and its practical consequences are most directly felt. The practical consequences of religion may be experienced in the tension between dissonance and harmony, the conflict between expectations and behavior, and the incongruity of ideals and actual experience. But religious ethics also holds the potential for an ongoing creative engagement with the most basic conditions of possibility for being human. The comparative study of religious ethics suggests that human beings are most fully human when they are engaged in imagining their personal and social actions in terms of ethical patterns of action.

NOTES

INTRODUCTION

1.   T. S. Eliot, *Four Quartets* (New York: Harcourt, Brace and World, 1971): 59.

2.   Jonathan Z. Smith, *Imagining Religion* (Chicago: University of Chicago Press, 1982): xi.

3.   Wilfred Cantwell Smith, *The Meaning and End of Religion* (New York: New American Library, Mentor, 1962).

4.   Paul Tillich, *Theology of Culture* (New York: Oxford University Press, 1959): 7–8; and *Christianity and the Encounter of the World Religions* (New York: Columbia University Press, 1963): 4; see Robert D. Baird, *Category Formation in the History of Religions* (Mouton: The Hague, 1971): 18*ff.*

5.   Edward Burnett Tylor, *Primitive Culture,* 2 vols. (London: John Murray, 1920): I: 424*ff.*

6.   Melford Spiro, "Religion: Problems of Definition and Explanation," in: Michael Banton (ed.), *Anthropological Approaches to the Study of Religion* (London: Tavistock, 1966): 96.

7.   Rudolf Otto, *The Idea of the Holy* (tr.) John W. Harley (London: Oxford University Press, 1950).

8.   This approach to the descriptive analysis of religion is suggested by the work of Joachim Wach, *Sociology of Religion* (Chicago: University of Chicago Press, 1944): 17–34; and Ninian Smart, *Worldviews: Crosscultural Explorations of Human Beliefs* (New York: Charles Scribner's, 1983).

9.   See the articles on myth collected in Alan Dundees (ed.), *Sacred Narrative: Readings in the Theory of Myth* (Berkeley: University of California Press, 1984); also see

G. S. Kirk, *Myth: Its Meaning and Function in Ancient and Other Cultures* (Berkeley: University of California Press, 1970); and Mircea Eliade, *Myth and Reality* (New York: Harper and Row, 1963).

10.   See the survey of religious beliefs in Mircea Eliade, *A History of Religious Ideas,* 3 vols. (tr.) Willard R. Trask (Chicago: University of Chicago Press, 1978); for an exemplary analysis of one set of religious doctrines, see Ninian Smart, *Doctrine and Argument in Indian Philosophy* (New York: Humanities Press, 1964).

11.   On ritual, see Ronald L. Grimes, *Beginnings in Ritual Studies* (Lunham, MD: University Press of America, 1982); Arnold van Gennep, *Rites of Passage* (tr.) Monika B. Vizedom and Gabrielle L. Cafee (Chicago: University of Chicago Press, 1976); and Victor Turner, *The Ritual Pocess: Structure and Anti-structure* (Ithaca, NY: Cornell University Press, 1969).

12.   See James F. Smurl, *Religious Ethics: A Systems Approach* (Englewood Cliffs, NJ: Prentice-Hall, 1972).

13.   For a classic study of religious experience, see William James, *Varieties of Religious Experience* (New York: Modern Library, 1929); for more recent discussions, see Stephan Katz (ed.), *Mysticism and Philosophical Analysis* (New York: Oxford University Press, 1978).

14.   For introductions to the sociology of religion, see Peter L. Berger, *The Sacred Canopy: Elements of a Sociological Theory of Religion* (Garden City, NY: Doubleday, 1967); J. Milton Yinger, *The Scientific Study of Religion* (New York: Macmillan, 1970); and Bryan R. Wilson, *Religion in Sociological Perspective* (Oxford and New York: Oxford University Press, 1982).

15.   Bronislaw Malinowski, *The Foundations of Faith and Morals* (London: Oxford University Press, 1936): 25–26.

16. In Franz Boas (ed.), *General Anthropology* (Washington, D.C.: D. C. Heath and Co., 1944): 633; see Ronald M. Green, "Religion and Morality in the African Traditional Setting," *Journal of Religion in Africa* 14 (1983): 1–23.

17. Cornelius Loew, *Myth, Sacred History and Philosophy: The Pre-Christian Religious Heritage of the West* (New York: Harcourt, Brace and World, 1967): 13.

18. On Hindu ethics, see Georg Bühler (tr.), *The Laws of Manu* (Mystic, CT: Lawrence Verry, 1965); J. A. Dubois, *Hindu Manners, Customs and Ceremonies* (London: Oxford University Press, 1972); Roderick Hindery, *Comparative Ethics in Buddhist and Hindu Traditions* (India: South Asia Books, 1979); P. V. Kane, *History of the Dharmasastra* (Poona: Bhandarkar Oriental Research Institute, 1946); John McKenzie, *Hindu Ethics: A Historical and Critical Essay* (London: Oxford University Press, 1922); I. C. Sharma, *Ethical Philosophies of India* (New York: Harper and Row, 1970).

19. On Buddhist ethics, see Arthur C. Danto, *Mysticism and Morality* (New York: Basic Books, 1972); K. N. Jayatilleke, *Ethics in a Buddhist Perspective* (Ceylon: Buddhist Publishing Society, 1972); Winston L. King, *In the Hope of Nibbana: An Essay on Theravada Buddhist Ethics* (La Salle, IL: Open Court, 1964); H. Saddhatissa, *Buddhist Ethics* (New York: George Braziller, 1970); S. Tachibana, *The Ethics of Buddhism* (Oxford: Oxford University Press, 1926).

20. On Jain ethics, see Dayanand Bhargava, *Jaina Ethics* (Delhi: Motilal Benarsidass, 1968); Padmanabh S. Jaini, *The Jaina Path of Purification* (Berkeley and Los Angeles: University of California Press, 1979).

21. On Confucian ethics, see Herbert Fingarette, *Confucius—the Secular as Sacred* (New York: Harper and Row, 1972); Donald J. Munro, *The Concept of Man in Early China* (Stanford: Stanford University Press, 1969); Arthur Waley (tr.), *The Analects of Confucius* (New York: Random House, 1938).

22. On Taoist ethics, see Max Kaltenmark, *Lao Tzu and Taoism* (tr.) Roger Greames (Stanford: Stanford University Press, 1969); P. Rawson and L. Legeza, *Tao: The Chinese Philosophy of Time and Change* (London: Thames and Hudson, 1979); Arthur Waley (tr.), *The Way and Its Power* (New York: Grove Press, 1958).

23. On Jewish ethics, see S. Ganzfried, *Code of Jewish Law: A Compilation of Jewish Laws and Customs* (New York: Hebrew Publishing, 1927); R. Travers Herford, *The Ethics of the Talmud: Sayings of the Fathers* (New York: Schocken Books, 1962); Moritz Lazarus, *The Ethics of Judaism* (tr.) Henrietta Szold (Philadelphia: The Jewish Publishing Society of America, 1900).

24. On Christian ethics, see Morton Scott Enslin, *The Ethics of Paul* (New York: Abingdon, 1957); J. L. Houlden, *Ethics and the New Testament* (New York and London: Oxford University Press, 1977); John Macquarrie (ed.), *A Dictionary of Christian Ethics* (London: SCM, 1977); Eric Osborn, *Ethical Patterns in Early Christian Thought* (Cambridge: Cambridge University Press, 1976); Amos Wilder, *Eschatology and Ethics in the Teachings of Jesus* (New York: Harper and Row, 1950).

25. On Islamic ethics, see Frederick S. Carney, "Some Aspects of Islamic Ethics," *The Journal of Religion* 63 (1983): 159–74; D. M. Donaldson, *Studies in Muslim Ethics* (London: S.P.C.K., 1953); Marshall Hodgson, *The Venture of Islam: Conscience and History in a World Civilization*, 3 vols. (Chicago: University of Chicago Press, 1974); George F. Hourani, *Islamic Rationalism: The Ethics of 'Abd al-Jabbār* (Oxford: Clarendon Press, 1971); Mohamed Ahmed Sherif *Ghazali's Theory of Virtue* (Albany: State University of New York Press, 1975).

26. Morris Singer, "The Golden Rule," in: Paul Edwards (ed.), *The Encyclopedia of Philosophy* (New York: Macmillan, 1967): III: 365–67; Lewis Browne, *The World's Great Scriptures* (New York: Macmillan, 1956): xv.

27. Bronislaw Malinowski, *Scientific Theory of Culture* (New York: Oxford University Press, 1960): 120.

28. Stephen Pepper, *The Source of Values* (Berkeley: University of California Press, 1958).

29. Emile Durkheim, *The Elementary Forms of the Religious Life* (tr.) Joseph Ward Swain (New York: Free Press, 1965): 55.

30. Rodney Needham (ed.), *Death and the Right Hand* (London: Cohen West, 1960): 22.

31. A. R. Radcliffe-Brown, "On the Comparative Method in Social Anthropology," *Journal of the Royal Anthropological Institute* 81 (1951): 15–22; in: R. H. Manners (ed.), *Method in Social Anthropology* (Chicago: University of Chicago Press, 1958): 165.

32. E. E. Evans-Pritchard, *The Comparative Method in Social Anthropology* (London: University of London, The Athlone Press, 1963): 16.

33. *Ibid.,* 17.

34. Raymond Firth, *Elements of Social Organization* (London: Watts, 1951): 18.

35. These four types of comparison have been adapted from Jonathan Z. Smith, "Adde Parvum Parvo Magnus Acervus Erit," in: *Map is Not Territory: Studies in the History of Religions* (Leiden: E. J. Brill, 1978): 240–64; see

Gopāla Śaraṇa, *The Method of Anthropological Comparisons: An Analysis of Comparative Methods in Social and Cultural Anthropology* (Tucson: University of Arizona Press, 1975).

36. Margaret T. Hodgen, *Early Anthropology in the Sixteenth and Seventeenth Centuries* (Philadelphia: University of Pennsylvania Press, 1964): 25.

37. *Herodotus* II.35–37; Aubrey de Sélincourt (tr.), *Herodotus* (Harmondsworth, Middlesex: Penguin, 1954): 115.

38. Edmund R. Leach, *Social Anthropology* (New York and Oxford: Oxford University Press, 1982): 41–42.

39. See David Little, "The Present State of the Comparative Study of Religious Ethics," *Journal of Religious Ethics* 2 (1974): 210–11.

40. See the useful history provided by Eric J. Sharpe, *Comparative Religions: A History* (New York: Harper and Row, 1975).

41. Cited in Michel Foucault, *The Order of Things: An Archaeology of the Human Sciences* (New York: Random House, 1970): xv.

42. Edward Westermarck, *The Origin and Development of the Moral Ideas* (London: Macmillan, 1924); and L. T. Hobhouse, *Morals in Evolution* (New York: Henry Holt, 1916).

43. Edmund R. Leach, *Rethinking Anthropology* (London: University of London, The Athlone Press, 1961): 2.

44. Bronislaw Malinowski, *Crime and Custom in Savage Society* (London: Routledge and Kegan Paul, 1926): 126.

45. Mircea Eliade, *Patterns in Comparative Religion* (tr.) Rosemary Sheed (New York: New American Library, 1958).

CHAPTER ONE

1. C. Jouco Bleeker and Geo W. Widengren (eds.), *Historia Religionum: Handbook for the History of Religions*, 2 vols. (Leiden: E. J. Brill, 1969): I:358.

2. Bronislaw Malinowski, *Magic, Science, and Religion* (New York: Doubleday, 1954): 108.

3. Emile Durkheim, *The Elementary Forms of the Religious Life* (New York: Free Press, 1965): 464; see Ernest

Wallwork, *Durkheim: Morality and Milieu* (Cambridge, MA: Harvard University Press, 1972).

4. Max Weber, *Sociology of Religion* Ephraim Fischoff (tr.) (Boston: Beacon Press, 1963): 35.

5. Mircea Eliade, *Myths, Dreams, and Mysteries* (New York: Harper and Row, 1960): 30.

6. Joachim Wach, *The Comparative Study of Religion* (New York: Columbia University Press, 1958): 113.

7. Mircea Eliade, *The Sacred and the Profane* (New York: Harper and Row, 1961): 14.

18. *Ibid.,* 129.

9. Mircea Eliade, *Patterns in Comparative Religion* (New York: Harper and Row, 1958): 194.

10. Tertullian, *De Baptismo,* 3; cited in Mircea Eliade, *Patterns in Comparative Religion,* 196; *Myths, Dreams, and Mysteries,* 135; *The Sacred and the Profane,* 129–36; and *Images and Symbols* (New York: Harper and Row, 1961): 151*ff.*

11. John Chrysostom, *Homilies in Johannem* 25.2; cited in Eliade, *The Sacred and the Profane,* 129.

12. Mircea Eliade, *No Souvenirs* (New York: Harper and Row, 1977): 72.

13. Mircea Eliade, *Cosmos and History* (New York: Harper and Row, 1959): 23.

14. Joachim Wach, *Understanding and Believing* (New York: Harper and Row, 1968): 33–34.

15. For a bibliography on the interpretation of sacrifice, see Richard D. Hecht, "Studies on Sacrifice, 1970–1980," *Religious Studies Review* 8 (1982): 253–59.

16. See Jonathan Z. Smith, "The Bare Facts of Ritual," in *Imagining Religion* (Chicago: University of Chicago Press, 1982): 53–65.

17. D. Zelenin, *Les Cultes des Idoles en Siberie* G. Welter (tr.) (Paris, 1952): 143; cited in J. Z. Smith, *Imagining Religion,* 59.

18. A. I. Hallowell, "Bear Ceremonialism in the Northern Hemisphere," *American Anthropologist* 28 (1926): 39; cited in J. Z. Smith, *Imagining Religion,* 61.

19. J. Z. Smith, *Imagining Religion,* 63.

20. Paul Wheatley, *The Pivot of the Four Quarters* (Edinburgh: Edinburgh University Press, 1971): 225.

21. E. A. Wallis Budge, *Osiris and the Egyptian Resurrection* (New York: G. P. Putnam's, 1911): 338–39; see

Budge, *The Book of the Dead* (New York: E. P. Dutton, 1938): 365–71.

22.   A. Leo Oppenheim, *Ancient Mesopotamia: Portrait of a Dead Civilization* (Chicago: University of Chicago Press, 1964): 176.

23.   T. J. Meek (tr.), "The Code of Hammurabi," in: J. B. Pritchard (ed.), *Ancient Near Eastern Texts* (Princeton: Princeton University Press, 1955): 138–67.

24.   Cited in Henri Frankfort et al., *Before Philosophy: The Intellectual Adventure of Ancient Man* (Baltimore: Penguin, 1949): 226.

25.   *Rig Veda* X.90; adapted from R.T.H. Griffith, *The Hymns of the Rigveda,* 2 vols. (Benares: E. J. Lazarus and Co., 1920–62).

26.   *Laws of Manu* 4.17; Georg Bühler (tr.) *The Laws of Manu;* in: F. Max Müller (ed.), *Sacred Books of the East* (Oxford: Oxford University Press, 1886): XXV:131.

27.   *Majjhima-nikāya* III.248–52; in: Lord Chalmers (tr.), *Further Dialogues of the Buddha* (London: Oxford University Press, 1927): II:296–99.

28.   James Legge (tr.) *Li Chi* (Secaucus, NJ: University Books, 1967): I:410.

29.   *Analects* XII.2; adapted from Arthur Waley (tr.) *The Analects of Confucius* (New York: Random House, 1938): 162.

30.   *Chung Yung* 1.4; cited in Wing-Tsit Chan (ed.), *A Source Book in Chinese Philosophy* (Princeton: Princeton University Press, 1963): 98; Alan L. Miller (tr.), *Religions of the World,* Niels C. Nielsen, Jr. (ed.) (New York: St. Martin's Press, 1983): 258.

31.   *Tao-te ching* 8; cited in Chan (ed.), *A Source Book in Chinese Philosophy,* 143.

32.   *Tao-te Ching* 63; cited in Chan (ed.), *A Source Book in Chinese Philosophy,* 169.

33.   *Tao-te ching* 19; cited in Chan (ed.), *A Source Book in Chinese Philosophy,* 149.

34.   *Tao-te ching* 3; cited in Chan (ed.), *A Source Book in Chinese Philosophy,* 141.

35.   See Mircea Eliade, *Yoga: Immortality and Freedom* Willard R. Trask (tr.) (New York and London: Routledge and Kegan Paul, 1958): 284–90; and Mircea Eliade, *The Two and the One* J. M. Cohen (tr.) (London: Harvill Press, 1965): 47–49.

36.   See Michael R. Saso, *Taoism and the Rite of Cosmic Renewal* (Pullman: Washington State University Press, 1972).

37.   See Helmer Ringren, *Ancient Israelite Religion* (Philadelphia: Fortress Press, 1975): 136–37.

38.   See Mary Douglas, *Purity and Danger: An Analysis of the Concepts of Pollution and Taboo* (London: Routledge and Kegan Paul, 1966): 41–57.

39.   See Abraham Heschel, *The Prophets* (New York: Harper and Row, 1962).

40.   John A. T. Robinson, *Honest to God* (Philadelphia: Westminster Press, 1963): 105.

41.   Bleeker and Widengren (eds.) *Historia Religionum,* I:153.

42.   Ludwig Wittgenstein, *Tractatus Logico-Philosophicus* D. F. Pears and B. F. McGuiness (tr.) (London and New York, 1961): 6.421.

43.   Hans Mol, *Identity and the Sacred: A Sketch for a New Social-Scientific Theory of Religion* (Oxford: Basil Blackwell, 1976): 10.

44.   Edmund R. Leach, *Social Anthropology* (New York and Oxford: Oxford University Press, 1982): 112.

45.   See Robert J. Lifton, *The Life of the Self* (New York: Simon & Schuster, 1976).

46.   Robert Redfield, *The Primitive World and Its Transformations* (Ithaca, NY: Cornell University Press, 1953): 51.

47.   Clifford Geertz, *The Interpretation of Cultures* (New York: Basic Books, 1973): 127.

48.   *Ibid.,* 136.

49.   Michael Gilsenan, *Recognizing Islam: Religion and Society in the Modern Arab World* (New York: Pantheon Books, 1982): 269–70.

CHAPTER TWO

1.   Henry Wilder Foote, *Thomas Jefferson: Champion of Religious Freedom, Advocate of Christian Morals* (Boston: Beacon Press, 1947): 52; see Dickinson W. Adams (ed.), *Jefferson's Extracts from the Gospels: The "Philosophy of Jesus" and "The Life and Morals of Jesus"* (Princeton: Princeton University Press, 1983).

2.   *Analects* II.4; adapted from Chan (ed.), *A Source Book in Chinese Philosophy,* 22.

3. *Papancasudani* 9.7–23; Edward Conze (tr.), *Buddhist Scriptures* (Harmondsworth, Middlesex: Penguin, 1959): 70.

4. *Ibid.,* 73.

5. *Tao-te ching* 18; in Chan (ed.), *A Source Book in Chinese Philosophy,* 148.

6. Gananath Obeyesekere, "Theodicy, Sin and Salvation in a Sociology of Buddhism," in: Edmund R. Leach (ed.), *Dialectic in Practical Religion* (Cambridge: Cambridge University Press, 1968): 19.

7. Edward Conze (ed.), *Buddhist Texts through the Ages* (Oxford: Oxford University Press, 1954): 222.

8. Norman Cohn, *The Pursuit of the Millenium* (New York: Harper and Row, 1961): 178.

9. A. L. Morton, *The World of the Ranters: Religious Radicalism in the English Revolution* (London: Beekman Publishers, 1970): 77.

10. Gershom Scholem, *The Messianic Idea in Judaism and Other Essays in Jewish Spirituality* (London: Schocken, 1970): 130.

11. In *Poetry LA* 6 (Spring/Summer, 1983): 6–7.

12. Obeyesekere, "Theodicy, Sin and Salvation in a Sociology of Buddhism," in: Leach (ed.), *Dialectic in Practical Religion,* 30.

13. See Paul Helm (ed.), *Divine Commands and Morality* (Oxford: Oxford University Press, 1981).

14. See Terence Irwin, *Plato's Moral Theory: The Early and Middle Dialogues* (Oxford: Clarendon, 1977).

15. Aristotle, *Ethics* (tr.) John Warrington (New York: E. P. Dutton, 1963); see Anthony Kenny, *The Aristotelian Ethics* (Oxford: Clarendon, 1978).

16. Immanuel Kant, *Fundamental Principles of the Metaphysic of Morals* (tr.) T. K. Abbott (Indianapolis: Bobbs-Merrill, 1949): 11.

17. *Ibid.,* 38.

18. *Ibid.,* 46; see Allen Wood, *Kant's Moral Religion* (Ithaca, NY: Cornell University Press, 1970); and Carl A. Raschke, *Moral Action, God and History in the Thought of Immanuel Kant* (Missoula, MT: Scholars Press, 1975).

19. John Stuart Mill, *Utilitarianism* (New York and London: E. P. Dutton, 1910): 30; see Jeremy Bentham *An Introduction to the Principles of Morals and Legislation* (ed.) J. H. Burns and H. L. Hart (New York: Humanities Press, 1970).

20. G. E. Moore, *Principia Ethica* (Cambridge: Cambridge University Press, 1959); see W. D. Ross, *The Right and the Good* (London: Oxford University Press, 1930).

21. C. L. Stevenson, *Ethics and Language* (New Haven: Yale University Press, 1945); see A. J. Ayer, *Language, Truth and Logic* (London: Gollancz, 1936).

22. Alisdair MacIntyre, *After Virtue: A Study in Moral Theory* (Notre Dame, IN: University of Notre Dame Press, 1981): 2.

23. *Ibid.,* vii.

24. See the articles on this question collected in Bryan R. Wilson (ed.), *Rationality* (Oxford: Basil Blackwell, 1970).

25. Ronald M. Green, *Religious Reason: The Rational and Moral Basis of Religious Belief* (New York: Oxford University Press, 1978): 108.

26. *Ibid.,* 121.

27. *Ibid.,* 53.

28. *Ibid.,* 73.

29. *Ibid.,* 110.

30. See Frederick Bird, "Paradigms and Parameters for the Comparative Study of Religious Ethics, *Journal of Religious Ethics* 9 (1981): 157–85.

31. David Little and Sumner Twiss, *Comparative Religious Ethics* (San Francisco: Harper and Row, 1978): 56, 96.

32. *Ibid.,* 29; 96.

33. *Ibid.,* 109.

34. Edmund S. Morgan, *The Puritan Dilemma: The Story of John Winthrop* (Boston: Little, Brown, 1958): 149.

35. Little and Twiss, *Comparative Religious Ethics,* 117–18.

36. *Ibid.,* 118.

37. Bird, "Paradigms and Parameters for the Comparative Study of Religious Ethics," 157.

CHAPTER THREE

1. Leon Festinger, *A Theory of Cognitive Dissonance* (Stanford: Stanford University Press, 1957); for case studies in cognitive dissonance, see Leon Festinger, Henry W.

Riecken, and Stanley Schachter, *When Prophecy Fails* (New York: Harper and Row, 1956); and John G. Gager, *Kingdom and Community: The Social World of Early Christianity* (Englewood Cliffs, NJ: Prentice-Hall, 1975): 37–49.

2.   *Confessions* 8.7; R. S. Pine-Coffin (tr.), *Saint Augustine: Confessions* (Harmondsworth, Middlesex: Penguin, 1961): 169.

3.   Ruth Benedict, *The Chrysanthemum and the Sword* (Boston: Houghton Mifflin, 1946): 222–23.

4.   *Ibid.;* for other discussions of the distinction between shame and guilt in religious ethics, see Margaret Mead, *Cooperation and Competition among Primitive Peoples* (New York: McGraw-Hill, 1937): 494; Clyde Kluckhohn and Dorthea Leighton, *The Navaho* (Cambridge: Harvard University Press, 1946): 106–7; and E. R. Dodds, *The Greeks and the Irrational* (Berkeley: University of California Press, 1951): 28–63; this distinction has been called into question by Gerhart Piers and Milton Singer, *Shame and Guilt: A Psychoanalytic and Cultural Study* (New York: Norton, 1972).

5.   *Analects* II.3; cited in Wing-tsit Chan (tr.), *A Source Book in Chinese Philosophy* (Princeton: Princeton University Press, 1963): 22.

6.   *Mencius* 6A.6; Wing-tsit Chan (tr.), *A Source Book in Chinese Philosophy,* 54.

7.   Plato, *Symposium* 216b; Michael Joyce (tr.), *The Collected Dialogues of Plato* (ed.) Edith Hamilton and Huntington Cairns (Princeton: Princeton University Press, 1961): 567.

8.   Cited in Paul Ricoeur, *The Symbolism of Evil* (tr.) Emerson Buchanan (Boston: Beacon Press, 1967): 25.

9.   *Ibid.,* 35.

10.   *Ibid.,* 40.

11.   Mary Douglas, *Purity and Danger: An Analysis of the Concepts of Pollution and Taboo* (London: Routledge and Kegan Paul, 1966).

12.   *Ibid.,* 3.

13.   Ricoeur, *The Symbolism of Evil,* 25.

14.   Cited in Douglas, *Purity and Danger,* 34.

15.   Sigmund Freud, *Civilization and Its Discontents* (tr.) James Strachey (New York: W. W. Norton, 1961): 81.

16.   Ricoeur, *The Symbolism of Evil,* 100–108.

17.   S.G.F. Brandon, *The Judgment of the Dead* (New York: Charles Scribner's, 1969).

18.   See Jal Dastur Cursetji Pavry, *The Zoroastrian Doctrine of a Future Life* (New York: AMS Press, 1965).

19.   W. Y. Evans-Wentz (ed.), *The Tibetan Book of the Dead* (London: Oxford University Press, 1960).

20.   Cited in Ninian Smart and Richard D. Hecht (eds.), *Sacred Texts of the World: A Universal Anthology* (London: Macmillan, 1982): 301–302.

21.   See Morton Bloomfield, *The Seven Deadly Sins: An Introduction to the History of a Religious Concept* (East Lansing, MI: Michigan State University Press, 1967).

22.   William James, *The Varieties of Religious Experience* (New York and London: Macmillan, 1961): 393.

23.   E. E. Evans-Pritchard, *Witchcraft, Oracles and Magic among the Azande* (Oxford: Oxford University Press, 1937); see Geertz, *The Interpretation of Cultures,* 172–73.

24.   Max Weber, "The Social Psychology of the World's Religions," in: H. Gerth and C. Mills (eds.), *From Max Weber* (New York: Oxford University Press, 1958): 274.

25.   James R. Averill, "Emotion and Anxiety: Sociocultural, Biological, and Psychological Determinants," in: Amelie O. Rorty (ed.), *Explaining Emotions* (Berkeley: University of California Press, 1980): 44–48.

CHAPTER FOUR

1.   H. D. Lasswell and A. Kaplan, *Power and Society* (New Haven, CT: Yale University Press, 1950): 49–50.

2.   R. M. Chisholm, "Contrary-to-Duty Imperatives and Deontic Logic," *Analysis* 24 (1963–64): 33–36.

3.   Donald A. Crosby, *Interpretive Theories of Religion* (The Hague: Mouton, 1981): 255.

4.   C. H. Buck, *Faiths, Fairs and Festivals of India* (New Delhi: Asian Publication Services, 1977): 86–87.

5.   I. M. Lewis, *Ecstatic Religion* (Harmondsworth, Middlesex: Penguin, 1971).

6.   R. A. Knox, *Enthusiasm* (Oxford: Oxford University Press, 1950).

7.   Manmatha Nath Dutt Shastri (tr.), *Agni Puranam: A Prose English Translation* (1903; rprt. Benares: Chowkhamba Sanskrit Series, 1967).

8.   Stanley J. Tambiah, "The Ideology of Merit and Social Correlates of Buddhism in a Thai Village," in: Edmund R. Leach (ed.), *Dialectic in Practical Religion* (Cambridge: Cambridge University Press, 1968): 69.

9.   *Qur'an* 25.64–76; A. J. Arberry (tr.), *The Koran Interpreted* (New York: Macmillan, 1955): II:62.

10.   *Mahavagga* 2.1; Henry Clarke Warren (tr.), *Buddhism in Translations* (New York: Atheneum, 1979): 405.

11.   *Ākāngāra Sūtra* 2.15.1; Hermann Jacobi (tr.), *Jaina Sutras,* in: F. Max Müller (ed.), *Sacred Books of the East* (Oxford: Oxford University Press, 1884): XXII: 202.

12.   Cited in Ninian Smart and Richard D. Hecht (eds.), *Sacred Texts of the World: A Universal Anthology* (London: Macmillan, 1982): 289.

13.   *Bhagavad Gītā* 2.47–48; Franklin Edgerton (tr.), *The Bhagavad Gītā* (Cambridge: Harvard University Press, 1944): 14.

14.   J. M. Rist, *Stoic Philosophy* (Cambridge: Cambridge University Press, 1969): 26.

15.   *Enneads* I.2.19; Elmer O'Brien (tr.), *The Essential Plotinus* (New York: New American Library, 1964): 113.

16.   Max Weber, *Sociology of Religion* (tr.) Ephraim Fischoff (Boston: Beacon Press, 1963): 166–69.

17.   *Bhagavad Gītā* 9.27–28; Kees W. Bolle (tr.), *The Bhagavad Gītā: A New Translation* (Berkeley: University of California Press, 1979): 109–11.

18.   John D. Sinclair (tr.), *Dante's Paradiso* (New York: Oxford University Press, 1939): 455.

19.   Martin Buber, "Symbolic and Sacramental Existence in Judaism," in: Joseph Campbell (ed.), *Spiritual Disciplines: Papers from the Eranos Yearbooks* (New York: Pantheon Books, 1960): 176–85.

20.   Paul Ramsey, *Deeds and Rules in Christian Ethics* (New York: Charles Scribner's, 1967): 7–8, 111–13, 224–25.

21.   William Frankena, *Ethics* (Englewood Cliffs, NJ: Prentice-Hall, 1973): 44–45.

22.   Carl Rogers, *On Becoming a Person* (New York: Houghton Mifflin, 1970).

CHAPTER FIVE

1.   Erik Erikson, *Identity and the Life Cycle* (New York: W. W. Norton, 1980): 57–67.

2.   W.H.R. Rivers, *The Todas* (London: Macmillan, 1906): 313–33.

3.   Arnold van Gennep, *Rites of Passage* (tr.) Monika B. Vizedom and Gabrielle L. Cafee (Chicago: University of Chicago Press, 1976): 53.

4.   E. E. Evans-Pritchard, *The Nuer* (Oxford: Oxford University Press, 1940): 84.

5.   Plato, *Republic* V.460–462; Paul Shorey (tr.), *The Collected Dialogues of Plato* (eds.) Edith Hamilton and Huntington Cairns (Princeton: Princeton University Press, 1961): 699–701.

6.   Aristotle, *Politics* 7.16; Benjamin Jowett (tr.), *Politica* (ed.) W. D. Ross (Oxford: Clarendon Press, 1921): 1335a–36b.

7.   Aristotle, *Politics* 1.6; Jowett (tr.), *Politica,* 1225.

8.   Cicero, *De legibus* 3.8.

9.   Seneca, *De ira* 1.15; L. D. Reynolds (ed.), *Senecae Dialogi* (Oxford: Clarendon Press, 1977): 53.

10.   Justin Martyr, *Apologia* I.27–29; Alexander Roberts and James Donaldson (eds.), *Ante-Nicene Fathers* (Grand Rapids, MI: William B. Eerdmans, 1981): I:172.

11.   Augustine, *De peccatorum meritus et remissione* 1.21.16; Marcus Dods (ed.), *The Works of Augustine* (Edinburgh: T & T Clark, 1908): IV:21–22.

12.   G. H. Pertz, *Monumenta Germaniae historica* (Hanover, 1863): III:413.

13.   John T. Noonan, *The Morality of Abortion: Legal and Historical Perspectives* (Cambridge, MA: Harvard University Press, 1970): xvii.

14.   Joseph F. Fletcher, "A Protestant Minister's View," in: Robert E. Hall (ed.), *Abortion in a Changing World* (New York: Columbia University Press, 1970): I:27–28.

15.   For detailed references to the motives for abortion in tribal societies that are summarized in the following pages, see George Devereux, *A Study of Abortion in Primitive Societies,* rev. ed. (New York: International University Press, 1976): 7–24.

16.   Seneca, *Ad Helviam* 16; Moses Hadas (tr.), *The Stoic Philosophy of Seneca* (New York: Doubleday, 1958): 129.

17.   Tertullian, *Apologeticus* 9; Alexander Souter (tr.), *Tertullian's Apology* (ed.) J.E.B. Mayor (Cambridge: Cambridge University Press, 1917): 33.

18.   Augustine, *Questiones in Exodum* 21.80; *Questiones Veteris et Novi Testamenti* 23; cited in Edward Westermarck, *The Origin and Development of the Moral Ideas,* 2 vols. (London: Macmillan, 1924): I:416.

19.   Fulgentius, *De Fide ad Petrum* 27; in: *Corpus Christianorum* (Turnhout: Typographi Brepolis, 1968): 91A: 728–29.

20.   Cited in Westermarck, *The Origin and Development of the Moral Ideas,* I:417.

21.   Meyer Cohen, "Statement on Abortion on Behalf of Orthodox Rabbis of the United States and Canada," (New York, 1971); cited in Arthur J. Dyck, "Religious Views," in: Robert M. Veatch (ed.), *Population Policy and Ethics: The American Experience* (New York: Irvington Publishers, 1977): 304.

22.   Israel R. Margolis, "A Reform Rabbi's View," in Robert E. Hall (ed.), *Abortion in a Changing World,* I:30–31.

23.   *Ibid.,* I:32.

24.   Joseph Donceel, "A Liberal Catholic's View," in: Robert E. Hall (ed.), *Abortion in a Changing World,* I:39–45.

25.   Daniel Callahan, *Abortion: Law, Choice and Morality* (New York: Macmillan, 1970).

26.   Dyck, "Religious Views," in: Veatch (ed.), *Population Policy and Ethics,* 299.

27.   *Ibid.,* 300.

28.   *Ibid.,* 299.

29.   Paul Ramsey, "Feticide/Infanticide Upon Request," *Religion in Life* 39 (1970): 170–86.

30.   *Ibid.,* 171.

31.   *Roe v. Wade,* 410 U.S. 113 (1973).

32.   Noonan, *The Morality of Abortion,* 17.

33.   Cited in Betty Sarvis and Hyman Rodman, *The Abortion Controversy* (New York and London: Columbia University Press, 1974): 68.

CHAPTER SIX

1.   Sigmund Freud, *General Introduction to Psychoanalysis* (New York: W. W. Norton, 1960): 295.

2.   A. W. Howitt, *The Native Tribes of South-East Australia* (London: Macmillan, 1904): 532.

3.   Carol P. MacCormack, "Sande: The Public Face of a Secret Society," in: Bennetta Jules-Rosette (ed.), *The New Religions of Africa* (Norwood, NJ: Ablex, 1979): 27–37.

4.   See Lillian Passmore Sanderson, *Against the Mutilation of Women* (London: Ithaca Press, 1981).

5.   Mary Douglas, *Purity and Danger* (London: Routledge and Kegan Paul, 1966): 116.

6.   Bruno Bettelheim, *Symbolic Wounds* (New York: Collier, 1962): 264.

7.   Philippe Ariès, *Centuries of Childhood: A Social History of Family Life* (New York: Random House, 1965): 411.

8.   *Ibid.,* 413.

9.   *Ibid.,* 375.

10.   Norbert Elias, *The Civilizing Process: The Development of Manners, Changes in the Code of Conduct and Feeling in Early Modern Times* (New York: Urizen Books, 1978): 140.

11.   *Ibid.,* 87–88.

12.   *Ibid.,* 89.

13.   *Ibid.,* 89.

14.   *Ibid.,* 95–96.

15.   *Ibid.,* 130.

16.   *Ibid.,* 130.

17.   *Ibid.,* 130.

18.   *Ibid.,* 130.

19.   *Ibid.,* 132.

20.   *Ibid.,* 133.

21.   *Ibid.,* 132.

22.   *Ibid.,* 144.

23.   *Ibid.,* 147.

24.   *Ibid.,* 153–54.

25. *Ibid.,* 155.

26. *Ibid.,* 155.

27. *Ibid.,* 161.

28. *Ibid.,* 161.

29. *Ibid.,* 162.

30. *Ibid.,* 162.

31. G. Stanley Hall, *Adolescence,* 2 vols. (New York: D. Appleton, 1919; 1904): see Dorothy Ross, *G. Stanley Hall: The Psychologist as Prophet* (Chicago and London: University of Chicago Press, 1972).

32. Erik Erikson, *Identity: Youth and Crisis* (New York: W. W. Norton, 1968): 159–60.

33. See Cushing Strout, *The New Heavens and the New Earth: Political Religion in America* (New York: Harper and Row, 1974): 345–46.

34. Robert Jay Lifton, "Protean Man," in: Donald R. Cutler (ed.), *The Religious Situation* (Boston: Beacon Press, 1969): 812–28.

35. Kenneth Kenniston, *Youth and Dissent: The Rise of a New Opposition* (New York: Harcourt Brace Jovanovich, 1971).

36. Erikson, *Identity: Youth and Crisis,* 128–29.

37. Kenniston, *Youth and Dissent,* 255–56; on the theory of moral development, see Lawrence Kohlberg, *The Philosophy of Moral Development: Essays in Moral Development* (New York: Harper and Row, 1981); and *The Psychology of Moral Development* (New York: Harper and Row, 1983).

38. *Analects* 8.7; Arthur Waley (tr.), *The Analects of Confucius* (New York: Random House, 1938): 134.

39. Ira M. Lapidus, "Adulthood in Islam: Religious Maturity and the Islamic Tradition," in: Erik Erikson (ed.), *Adulthood* (New York: W. W. Norton, 1978): 97.

40. *Mencius* 4B:12; Wing-tsit Chan (tr.), *A Source Book in Chinese Philosophy* (Princeton: Princeton University Press, 1963): 76.

41. *Confessions* 10.17; R. S. Pine-Coffin (tr.), *Saint Augustine: Confessions* (Harmondsworth, Middlesex: Penguin, 1961): 224.

CHAPTER SEVEN

1. Arnold van Gennep, *Rites of Passage* (tr.) Monika B. Vizedom and Gabrielle L. Cafee (Chicago: University of Chicago Press, 1976): 116.

2. W.H.R. Rivers, *The Todas* (London: Macmillan, 1906): 515–21.

3. See E. Neufeld, *Ancient Hebrew Marriage Laws* (New York: Longmans, Green, 1944): 23–55.

4. *Qur'an* 4.2; 4.129; A. J. Arberry (tr.), *The Koran Interpreted* (New York: Macmillan, 1955). I:100; I:119.

5. Mary Boyce, *The Zoroastrians* (London: Routledge and Kegan Paul, 1982): 97.

6. H. Hopkins, "Brother-Sister Marriage in Roman Egypt," *Comparative Studies in Society and History* 22 (1980): 303–54.

7. M. S. Adams and J. V. Neel, "Children of Incest," *Pediatrics* 40 (1967): 55–62.

8. Edward Westermarck, *The History of Human Marriage,* 3 vols. (London: Macmillan, 1921): II:162–239.

9. See Bernard I. Murstein, *Love, Sex and Marriage Through the Ages* (New York: Springer, 1974): 23.

10. Yehudi Cohen, *The Transition from Childhood to Adolescence: Cross-Cultural Studies of Initiation Ceremonies, Legal Systems, and Incest Taboos* (Chicago: Aldine, 1964): 15–16; also see Talcott Parsons, "The Incest Taboo in Relation to Social Structures," in: Rose Laub Coser (ed.), *The Family* (London: Macmillan, 1974): 48–70.

11. Claude Levi-Strauss, *The Elementary Structures of Kinship* (tr.) James Harle Bell, John Richard Sturmer, and Rodney Needham (Boston: Beacon Press, 1969).

12. Gaius, *Institutiones* 1.56; Francis de Zulueta (tr.), *The Institutes of Gaius* (Oxford: Clarendon Press, 1946): 19.

13. E. W. Hopkins, *Religions of India* (London, 1896): 294; and Monier Williams, *Buddhism* (London, 1890): 88.

14. Edward Westermarck, *The Origin and Development of the Moral Ideas* (London: Macmillan, 1924): II:399.

15. *Ibid.,* II:399.

16. *Laws of Manu* 3.1–62; Georg Bühler (tr.), *The Laws of Manu,* in: F. Max Müller (ed.), *Sacred Books of the East* (Oxford: Oxford University Press, 1886): XXV:74–87.

17.   *Mencius* 4A:26; Wing-tsit Chan (tr.), *A Source Book in Chinese Philosophy* (Princeton: Princeton University Press, 1963): 75; see Jan de Groot, *The Religious System of China,* 6 vols. (Tapei: Literature House, 1964): II:617.

18.   *Vendidad* 4.47; James Darmester (tr.), *The Zend Avesta,* in: F. Max Müller (ed.), *Sacred Books of the East* (Oxford: Oxford University Press, 1882): IV:46.

19.   Chaim N. Denburg (tr.), *Code of Hebrew Law: Even ha-Ezer* (Montreal: The Jurisprudence Press, 1955): Chapter 1.

20.   Ira Lapidus, "Adulthood in Islam," in: Erik Erikson (ed.), *Adulthood* (New York: W. W. Norton, 1978): 99.

21.   Tertullian, *Ad uxorum* 1.3; Alexander Roberts and James Donaldson (eds.), *Ante-Nicene Fathers* (Grand Rapids, MI: William B. Eerdmans, 1979): IV:40.

22.   Cited in Murstein, *Love, Sex and Marriage Through the Ages,* 115.

23.   *Ibid.,* 115.

24.   See Justin Martyr, *Apologia* I.29; Roberts and Donaldson (eds.), *Ante-Nicene Fathers,* I:172; and Clement, *Stromata* 2.23; William Wilson (tr.), *The Writings of Clement of Alexandria,* 2 vols. (Edinburgh: T & T Clark, 1867): II:78–83.

25.   *Laws of Manu* 9.79; Georg Bühler (tr.), *The Laws of Manu,* 341.

26.   See Murstein, *Love, Sex and Marriage Through the Ages,* 86–107.

27.   Josephus, *Antiquitates* 15.7.10; Ralph Marcus (tr.), *Jewish Antiquities* (Cambridge, MA: Harvard University Press, 1963): VIII:123.

28.   See M. Mielziner, *The Jewish Law of Marriage and Divorce in Ancient and Modern Times* (New York: Bloch, 1901); and Rabbi K. Kahana, *The Theory of Marriage in Jewish Law* (Leiden: E. J. Brill, 1966).

29.   See Ahmed Shukri, *Muhammedan Law of Marriage and Divorce* (New York: Columbia University Press, 1917; New York: AMS Press, 1966).

30.   Plato, *Republic* IV.431; V.455; Paul Shorey (tr.), *The Collected Dialogues of Plato* (eds.) Edith Hamilton and Huntington Cairns (Princeton: Princeton University Press, 1961): 673; 694.

31.   Tertullian, *De cultu foeminarum* 1.1; Roberts and Donaldson (eds.), *Ante-Nicene Fathers,* IV:14.

32.   Gregory of Tours, *Historia Francorum* 8.20; O. M.

Dalton (tr.), *The History of the Franks,* 2 vols. (Oxford: Clarendon Press, 1927): II:345.

33.   James M. Robinson (ed.), *The Nag Hammadi Library in English* (New York: Harper and Row, 1979): 130.

34.   Westermarck, *The Origin and Development of the Moral Ideas,* I:663.

35.   James Legge (tr.), *The Chinese Classics* (Oxford: Clarendon, 1895): I:103*ff.*

36.   *Laws of Manu* 5.148; Bühler (tr.), *The Laws of Manu,* 195.

37.   *Laws of Manu* 5.164; 9.30; Bühler (tr.), *The Laws of Manu,* 197; 332.

38.   Aristotle, *Oeconomia* 1.7; cited in Westermarck, *The Origin and Development of the Moral Ideas,* I:652.

39.   *Yasts* 22.18; 22.36; James Darmester (tr.), *The Zend Avesta,* in: F. Max Müller (ed.), *Sacred Books of the East* (Oxford: Oxford University Press, 1883): XXIII:318.

40.   Mary Daly, *The Church and the Second Sex* (Boston: Beacon Press, 1968).

41.   Mary Daly, *Gyn/Ecology: The Metaethics of Radical Feminism* (Boston: Beacon Press, 1978).

42.   Ivan Illich, *Gender* (New York: Pantheon Books, 1982).

43.   J. Gumilla, *El Orinosco illustrado,* 2 vols. (Madrid, 1745): II:274*ff.*

44.   Hanna Papanek and Gail Minault, *Separate Worlds: Studies of Purdah in South Asia* (Columbia, MI: South Asia Books, 1982).

45.   D. M. Feldman, *Birth Control in Jewish Law* (New York: New York University Press, 1968): 60–80.

46.   *Ibid.,* 103–105.

47.   *Ibid.,* 162.

48.   *Ibid.,* 169–73.

49.   *Ibid.,* 162.

50.   Pope Paul VI, *Humanae Vitae* (Boston: Daughters of St. Paul, 1968): 7–8.

51.   *Ibid.,* 10.

52.   C. F. Westoff and N. B. Ryder, "United States: The Papal Encyclical and Catholic Practices and Attitudes," *Studies in Family Planning* (February, 1970): 1–12.

53.   Daniel Callahan (ed.), *The Catholic Case for Contraception* (New York: Macmillan, 1969): 69.

54.   *Ibid.,* 70.

55.   Martin Luther, *The Estate of Marriage* (1522); in: Walther I. Brandt (tr. and ed.), *The Christian in Society,* 3 vols. (Philadelphia: Muhlenberg Press, 1962): II:45.

56.   Cited in Arthur J. Dyck, "Religious Views," in: Robert M. Veatch (ed.), *Population Policy and Ethics: The American Experience* (New York: Irvington Publishers, 1977): 294.

57.   *Ibid.,* 295.

58.   Reay Tannahill, *Sex in History* (New York: Stein and Day, 1980): 151–53; see Jean-Louis Flandrin, "Contraception, Marriage and Sexual Relations in the Christian West," in: Robert Forster and Orest Ranum (eds.), *Family and Society: Selections from the Annales* (Baltimore and London: Johns Hopkins Press, 1976): 23–47.

59.   Tannahill, *Sex in History,* 195–98; see Robert H. Van Gulik, *Sexual Life in Ancient China: A Preliminary Survey of Chinese Sex and Society from ca. 1500 B.C. to 1644 A.D.* (Leiden: E. J. Brill, 1961): 246–50.

60.   Athenagoras, *Legatio pro Christianis* 33; William R. Schoedel (tr.), *Athenagoras: Legatio and De Resurrectione* (Oxford: Clarendon Press, 1972): 81.

61.   D. S. Bailey, *Sexual Relations in Christian Thought* (New York: Harper, 1959): 133–34.

62.   G. T. Staunton (tr.), *Ta Tsing Leu Lee* (London, 1810): 404.

63.   *Laws of Manu* 3.164; Bühler (tr.), *The Laws of Manu,* 106.

64.   Thomas Aquinas, *Summa theologica* 2a–2ae 154.4; (New York: McGraw-Hill, 1968): 43:221.

65.   Staunton (tr.), *Ta Tsing Leu Lee,* 409.

66.   *Apastamba* II.10.27.8ff; Bühler (tr.), *The Sacred Laws of the Aryas,* in: F. Max Müller (ed.), *Sacred Books of the East* (Oxford: Oxford University Press, 1897): II:164–65.

67.   See Adolf Berger, *Encyclopedic Dictionary of Roman Law* (Philadelphia: American Philosophical Society, 1953): 352.

68.   Staunton (tr.), *Ta Tsing Leu Lee,* 570.

69.   *Laws of Manu* 11.175; Bühler (tr.), *The Laws of Manu,* 466.

70.   *Herodotus* I.135; Aubrey de Sélincourt (tr.), *Herodotus* (Harmondsworth, Middlesex: Penguin, 1954): 70.

71.   *Sad Dar* 9.2–3; E. W. West (tr.), *Pahlavi Texts,* in: F. Max Müller (ed.), *Sacred Books of the East* (Oxford: Oxford University Press, 1885): XXIV:267; see *Dina-i Mainog-i Khirad* 36.1ff; and *Vendidad* 8.26.

72.   See R. D. Bailey, *Homosexuality and the Western Christian Tradition* (London: Longmans, Green, 1955).

73.   E. H. Hare, "Masturbational Insanity: The History of an Idea," *Journal of Mental Science* 108 (1962): 1–25; and R. A. Spitz, "Authority and Masturbation," *Yearbook of Psychoanalysis* 9 (1953): 113–45.

74.   Cited in Alex Comfort, *The Anxiety Makers: Some Curious Preoccupations of the Medical Profession* (London: Panther Books, 1968): 84.

75.   Emma Drake, *What a Young Wife Ought to Know* (Philadelphia, 1901); cited in Comfort, *The Anxiety Makers,* 96.

76.   Sylvanus Stall, *What a Young Boy Ought to Know* (Philadelphia, 1897); cited in Comfort, *The Anxiety Makers,* 101.

77.   See Kenneth M. Ludmerer, *Genetics and American Society: A Historical Appraisal* (Baltimore and London: Johns Hopkins University Press, 1972).

78.   Francis Galton, "Hereditary Talent and Character," *Macmillan's Magazine* 12 (1865); cited in Ludmerer, *Genetics and American Society,* 10.

79.   H. J. Muller, *Man's Future Birthright* (New Hampshire: University of New Hampshire Press, 1958): 18.

80.   Paul Ramsey, *Fabricated Man: The Ethics of Genetic Control* (New Haven, CT and London: Yale University Press, 1970): 41.

CHAPTER EIGHT

1.   Jonathan Z. Smith, "Healing Cults," *The New Encyclopedia Britannica,* Macropaedia (Chicago: University of Chicago Press, 1977): VIII:685.

2.   Albert Camus, *The Myth of Sisyphus and Other Essays* (New York: Knopf, 1955): 11.

3.   Virgil J. Vogel, *American Indian Medicine* (Norman, OK: University of Oklahoma Press, 1970): 52–54.

4.   Otho T. Beall, Jr. and Richard H. Shryock, *Cotton Mather: First Significant Figure in American Medicine* (Baltimore: Johns Hopkins Press, 1954): 46.

5. John Wesley, *Primitive Physic: Or an Easy and Natural Method of Curing Most Diseases* (1791; rprt. London: The Epworth Press, 1960): 24.

6. Donald Sander, *Navaho Symbols of Healing* (New York: Harcourt Brace Jovanovich, 1979); Catherine Albanese, "The Poetics of Healing: Root Metaphors and Rituals in Nineteenth Century America," *Soundings* 63 (1980): 384–88.

7. Alfonso Ortiz, *The Tewa World: Space, Time, Being and Becoming in a Tewa Society* (Chicago: University of Chicago Press, 1969): 81–82; Albanese, "The Poetics of Healing," 388–90.

8. Robert E. Davies, "Medical Science Before Christ," in: John Crowlesworth (ed.), *Religion and Medicine* (London: The Epworth Press, 1962): 4.

9. See Morton Smith, *Jesus the Magician* (New York: Harper and Row, 1978).

10. Davies, "Medical Science Before Christ," in: Crowlesworth (ed.), *Religion and Medicine,* 12.

11. *Ibid.,* 12.

12. *Ibid.,* 12–13.

13. Stephen Powers, *Tribes of California* (Washington, 1877): 178.

14. L. H. Morgan, *League of the Iroquois* (Rochester, 1851): 171.

15. R. H. Codrington, *The Melanesians* (Oxford: Oxford University Press, 1891): 347.

16. L. Fison and A. W. Howitt, *Kamilaroi and Kurnai* (Melbourne, 1880): 175.

17. Robert F. Drinan, "Should There Be a Legal Right to Die?" in: Robert F. Weir (ed.), *Ethical Issues in Death and Dying* (New York: Columbia University Press, 1977): 299.

18. *Ibid.,* 300.

19. Joseph Fletcher, "The Patient's Right to Die," in: A. B. Downing (ed.), *Euthanasia and the Right to Death* (Los Angeles: Nash Publishing, 1969): 69.

20. *Ibid.,* 69.

21. Arthur J. Dyck, "An Alternative to the Ethic of Euthanasia," in: Weir (ed.), *Ethical Issues in Death and Dying,* 281–96.

22. *Ibid.,* 282.

23. Paul Ramsey, *The Patient as Person* (New Haven, CT: Yale University Press, 1970): 101–12.

24. Leo Alexander, "Medical Science Under Dictatorship," *New England Journal of Medicine* 241 (July 14, 1949): 9–47; cited in Dyck, "An Alternative to the Ethic of Euthanasia," in: Weir (ed.), *Ethical Issues in Death and Dying,* 292.

25. Robert Jay Lifton, *Broken Connection* (New York: Simon & Schuster, 1979): 13–23.

26. Antonin Artaud, *Artaud Anthology* (ed.) Jack Hirschman (San Francisco: Harper and Row, 1965): 56.

27. Jack Seward, *Hara Kiri: Japanese Ritual Suicide* (Tokyo: Charles Tuttle, 1968).

28. See Frederick Holck, *Death and Eastern Thought* (Nashville and New York: Abingdon, 1974): 32.

29. M.D.W. Jeffreys, "Samsonic Suicides: Or Suicides of Revenge among Africans," in: Anthony Giddens (ed.), *The Sociology of Suicide* (London: Frank Cass, 1971): 185–94.

30. Bronislaw Malinowski, "Baloma: The Spirits of the Dead in the Trobriand Islands," *Journal of the Royal Anthropological Institute* 46 (1916): 360.

31. T. E. Bowditch, *Mission to Ashantee* (London, 1819): 258–59.

32. R. H. Stone, *In Africa's Forest and Jungle* (London, 1900): 248.

33. James Pritchard (ed.), *Ancient Near Eastern Texts* (Princeton: Princeton University Press, 1950): 405*ff.*

34. Cited in Henry Romily Fedden, *Suicide: A Social and Historical Study* (London: Peter Davies, 1938): 81.

35. Seneca, *Epistulae* 70; E. Phillips Barker (tr.), *Seneca's Letters to Lucilius,* 2 vols. (Oxford: Clarendon Press, 1932): I: 238–45; see Paul W. Pretzel, "Philosophical and Ethical Considerations of Suicide Prevention," in: Weir (ed.), *Ethical Issues in Death and Dying,* 389.

36. Josephus, *The Jewish War* VII.7; H. St. J. Thackeray (tr.), *Josephus,* 9 vols. (Cambridge, MA: Harvard University Press, 1968): III: 601.

37. See Robert O. Crummey, *The Old Believers and the World of Anti-Christ; The Vyg Community and the Russian State 1694–1855* (Madison: University of Wisconsin Press, 1970).

38. Shiva Naipaul, *Journey to Nowhere: A New World Tragedy* (New York: Simon & Schuster, 1980): 58.

39. Cited in Edward Westermarck, *The Origin and Development of the Moral Ideas* (London: Macmillan, 1924): II: 242–43.

40. Norman Chevers, *A Manual of Medical Jurisprudence for India* (Calcutta, 1870): 664; see *Laws of Manu* 6.31; Georg Bühler (tr.), *The Laws of Manu,* 204.

41. Josephus, *The Jewish War* III.8; Thackeray (tr.), *Josephus,* III:679.

42. Augustine, *De civitate Dei* I.17–27; Marcus Dods (tr.), *The City of God* (New York: Random House, 1950): 22–32.

43. Thomas Aquinas, *Summa Theologica* 2a–2ae, 64.5 (New York: McGraw-Hill, 1968): 38:33.

44. Alisdair MacIntyre (ed.), *Hume's Ethical Writings* (Notre Dame, IN: University of Notre Dame Press, 1965): 301.

CHAPTER NINE

1. Robert Redfield, "The Primitive World View," *Proceedings of the American Philosophical Society* 94 (1952): 30–36; reprinted in Redfield, *Human Nature and the Study of Society: The Papers of Robert Redfield,* Volume 1 (Chicago: University of Chicago Press, 1963): 270.

2. *Ibid.,* 272.

3. Mircea Eliade, *A History of Religious Ideas,* 3 vols. (tr.) Willard R. Trask (Chicago: University of Chicago Press, 1978): I:3.

4. Redfield, *Human Nature and the Study of Society,* 273.

5. Robert Redfield, "Ethnic Relations: Primitive and Civilized," in: Jitsuichi Masuoka and Preston Valien (eds.), *Race Relations: Problems and Theory* (Chapel Hill: University of North Carolina Press, 1961); reprinted in Robert Redfield, *The Social Uses of the Social Sciences: The Papers of Robert Redfield,* Volume 2 (Chicago: University of Chicago Press, 1963): 163.

6. Georg Simmel, *The Sociology of Georg Simmel* (tr.) K. H. Wolff (New York: Free Press, 1950): 412.

7. Richard Hofstadter, *The Age of Reform* (New York: Vintage Books, 1960): 23.

8. Max Weber, *From Max Weber* (tr.) H. H. Gerth and C. W. Mills (London: Routledge and Kegan Paul, 1970): 261–62.

9. *Ibid.,* 228.

10. Max Weber, *The Protestant Ethic and the Spirit of Capitalism* (tr.) Talcott Parsons (New York: Charles Scribner's, 1958): 182.

11. David Martin, *The Breaking of the Image* (Oxford: Blackwell, 1980): 130.

12. Ernest Gellner, *Thought and Change* (London: Weidenfeld and Nicolson, 1964): 184–85.

13. Bronislaw Malinowski, *The Dynamics of Culture Change* (New Haven, CT: Yale University Press, 1945): 50.

14. Erving Goffman, *Asylums* (New York: Penguin, 1961): 15.

15. Bryan R. Wilson, *Religion in Sociological Perspective* (Oxford and New York: Oxford University Press, 1982): 44–45.

16. Bryan R. Wilson, *Religion in Secular Society: A Sociological Comment* (London: Watts, 1966): 10.

17. Charles Y. Glock, "Religion and the Integration of Society," *Review of Religious Research* (Fall, 1960): 59.

18. Robert J. Lifton, "Protean Man," in: Donald R. Cutler (ed.), *The Religious Situation* (Boston: Beacon Press, 1969): 812–28.

19. Robert Michaelsen, "Is the Public School Religious or Secular?," in: Elwyn A. Smith, *The Religion of the Republic* (Philadelphia: Fortress Press, 1971): 22–44.

20. *Ibid.,* 43.

21. *Ibid.,* 43–44.

22. Malcolm Muggeridge, *Jesus Rediscovered* (London: Collins, 1969): 52.

23. Ivan Illich, *Deschooling Society* (New York: Harper and Row, 1971).

24. Asa Briggs, *The Age of Improvement, 1783–1867* (London: Longmans, Green, 1959): 63.

25. E. P. Thompson, "Time, Work-Discipline and Industrial Capitalism," *Past and Present* 38 (1967): 90.

26. Hannah Arendt, *The Human Condition* (Chicago: University of Chicago Press, 1958): 146.

27. Robert Merton, *Social Theory and Social Structure* (New York: The Free Press, 1949): 552–61.

28. Cited in Y. H. Krikorian (ed.), *Naturalism and the Human Spirit* (New York: Columbia University Press, 1944): 45.

29. Baldwin Spencer and F. J. Gillen, *The Arunta,* 2 vols. (London: Macmillan, 1927): I:388.

30. Simone Weil, *The Need for Roots: Prelude to a Declaration of Duties for Mankind* (tr.) Arthur Wills (Boston: Beacon Press, 1952): 11.

31. J. D. Mabbot, *The State and the Citizen* (New York: Arrow Books, 1958): 166.

32. See Bronislaw Malinowski, *Crime and Custom in Savage Society* (London: Routledge and Kegan Paul, 1926).

33. Robert Redfield, "Primitive Law," in: Paul Bohannen (ed.), *Law and Warfare: Studies in the Anthropology of Conflict* (Garden City, NY: The Natural History Press, 1967): 4–5.

34. John Rawls, *A Theory of Justice* (Cambridge, MA: Harvard University Press, 1971): 60.

35. Robert Nozick, *Anarchy, State and Utopia* (New York: Basic Books, 1974): 153.

36. See Michel Foucault, *The Birth of the Clinic: An Archaeology of Medical Perception* (tr.) A. M. Sheridan Smith (New York: Random House, 1973).

37. J. Marion Sims, *The Story of My Life* (New York: Appleton, 1889): 116.

38. Editorial, "American vs. European Medical Science," *Medical Record* 4 (May 15, 1869): 113.

39. See Paul Starr, *The Social Transformation of American Medicine* (New York: Basic Books, 1982).

40. Jan van Baal, *Dema* (The Hague: Martinus Nijhoff, 1966): 695.

41. Napoleon A. Chagnon, "Yanomamo Social Organization and Warfare," in: Morton Fried, Marvin Harris, and Robert Murphy (eds.), *War* (Garden City, NY: The Natural History Press, 1967): 128.

42. See Louis Dumont, *Homo Hierarchicus: An Essay on the Caste System* (tr.) Mark Sainsbury (Chicago: University of Chicago Press, 1970).

43. See Thomas Virgil Peterson, *Ham and Japheth: The Mythic World of Whites in the Antebellum South* (Metuchen, NJ: Scarecrow Press, 1978).

44. *Codex Theodosius* XVI.1.2; J. Stevenson (ed.), *Creeds, Councils, and Controversies: Documents Illustrative of the History of the Church, AD 337–461* (London: SPCK, 1966): 160.

45. Dennis Prager and Joseph Telushkin, *Why the Jews?: The Reason for Antisemitism* (New York: Simon & Schuster, 1983): 17–18.

46. Kai T. Erikson, *Wayward Puritans* (New York: Wiley, 1966): 12.

47. Michel Foucault, *Madness and Civilization: A History of Insanity in the Age of Reason* (New York: Random House, 1965): 38–64.

48. Goffman, *Asylums,* 73.

49. *Ibid.,* 73.

50. Donald Cressy, "Achievement of an Unstated Organizational Goal: An Observation on Prisons," *Pacific Sociological Review* 1 (1958): 43.

51. Goffman, *Asylums,* 25.

52. Louis Chevalier, *Labouring Classes and Dangerous Classes in Paris During the First Half of the Nineteenth Century* (tr.) F. Jellink (Princeton: Princeton University Press, 1981): 3.

53. Geoffrey Parsons, *The Deviant Imagination: Psychiatry, Social Work and Social Change* (New York: Holmes and Merer Publishers, 1975): 161.

54. *Ibid.,* 164.

55. Robert A. Scott, "A Proposed Framework for Analyzing Deviance as a Property of Social Disorder," in: Robert A. Scott and Jack D. Douglas (eds.), *Theoretical Perspectives on Deviance* (New York: Basic Books, 1972): 29.

56. Michel Foucault, *Discipline and Punish* (tr.) Alan Sheridan (New York: Pantheon Books, 1978): 228.

57. Goffman, *Asylums,* 83.

58. Richard McCleery, *The Strange Journey* (Chapel Hill: University of North Carolina Extension Bulletin, 1953); cited in: Goffman, *Asylums,* 58.

59. Phyllis Chesler, *Women and Madness* (London: Allen Lane, 1974): 33.

60. Thomas Szasz, *The Manufacture of Madness: A Comparative Study of the Inquisition and the Mental Health Movement* (New York: Harper and Row, 1970): xxvii.

61. *Ibid.,* 58.

62. *Ibid.,* 19–20.

63. Herbert J. Muller, *Religion and Freedom in the Modern World* (New York: Harper and Row, 1963): 41.

64. Robert Redfield, *The Primitive World and Its Transformations* (Ithaca, NY: Cornell University Press, 1953): 85.

CHAPTER TEN

1. Lionell Rubinoff, *Tradition and Revolution* (Toronto: Macmillan, 1971): 19.

2. Cited in Ninian Smart, *Reasons and Faiths* (London: Routledge and Kegan Paul, 1958): 183.

3. Max Weber, *The Protestant Ethic and the Spirit of Capitalism* (tr.) Talcott Parsons (New York: Charles Scribner's, 1958): 117–18.

4. See Eugene Herrigel, *Zen and the Art of Archery* (tr.) R.F.C. Hull (New York: Pantheon Books, 1953).

5. Sebastian de Grazia, *Of Time, Work, and Leisure* (Garden City, NY: Doubleday, 1964): 5.

6. *Ibid.,* 13–14.

7. Josef Pieper, *Leisure: The Basis of Culture* (New York: Random House, 1963): 40.

8. Thorsten Veblen, *The Theory of the Leisure Class* (New York: New American Library, 1953): 46.

9. Robert MacIver, "The Great Emptiness," in: Eric Larrabee and Rolf Meyersohn (eds.), *Mass Leisure* (Glencoe: Free Press, 1958): 118–22.

10. Harold Wilensky, "Work, Careers and Social Integration," *International Social Science Journal* 4 (1960): 546.

11. Hannah Arendt, *The Human Condition* (Chicago: University of Chicago Press, 1958): 47–48.

12. Johan Huizenga, *Homo Ludens* (Boston: Beacon Press, 1955): 4.

13. *Ibid.,* 173.

14. Rosalie H. Wax, "Free Time in Other Cultures," in: Wilma Donahue, et al. (eds.), *Free Time: Challenge to Later Maturity* (Ann Arbor: University of Michigan Press, 1958): 4.

15. *Ibid.,* 4.

16. C. Wright Mills, *White Collar* (New York: Oxford University Press, 1956): 222.

17. Willy Rordorf, *Sunday* (London: SCM Press, 1968): 162.

18. Pieper, *Leisure: The Basis of Culture,* 45.

19. Robert Lee, *Religion and Leisure in America* (Nashville: Abingdon, 1964): 34.

20. Gordon J. Dahl, *Work, Play and Worship in a Leisure-Oriented Society* (Minneapolis: Augsburg, 1972): 74.

21. Morris R. Cohen, "Baseball as a National Religion," in: Louis Schneider (ed.), *Religion, Culture and Society* (New York: Wiley, 1964): 37.

22. See Dean MacCannell, *The Tourist: A New Theory of the Leisure Class* (New York: Schocken Books, 1976).

23. Weber, *Protestant Ethic and the Spirit of Capitalism,* 156–64; See Robert W. Malcolmson, *Popular Recreations in English Society, 1700–1850* (Cambridge: Cambridge University Press, 1973): 6.

24. Bryan R. Wilson, *Religion in Sociological Perspective* (Oxford and New York: Oxford University Press, 1982): 45.

25. Charles Singer, E. J. Holmyard, and A. R. Hall (eds.), *A History of Technology* (Oxford: Clarendon Press, 1954): I: vii.

26. Karl Marx and Friedrich Engels, *The German Ideology* (tr.) S. Rayzanskaya (New York: International Publishers, 1964): 39.

27. Karl Marx and Friedrich Engels, *Capital,* 3 vols. (New York: International Publishers, 1967): I: 179.

28. Jacques Ellul, *The Technological Society* (tr.) John Wilkinson (New York: Vintage Books, 1964): xxv.

29. Wilson, *Religion in Sociological Perspective,* 42.

30. Robert Redfield, *The Primitive World and its Transformations* (Ithaca, NY: Cornell University Press, 1953): ix; 21; 22.

31. See John V. Nef, *Cultural Foundations of Industrial Civilization* (Hamden, CT: Archon Books, 1974).

32. Robert Nisbet, "The Impact of Technology on Ethical Decision Making," in: *Tradition and Revolution* (New York: Random House, 1968): 196–97.

33. Max Weber, *Theory of Social and Economic Organization* (tr.) H. P. Henderson and Talcott Parsons (London: Hodge, 1947): 31*ff.*

34. Robert Presthis, *The Organizational Society* (New York: Knopf, 1962): 53–54.

35. Marx and Engels, *German Ideology,* 75–76.

36. Claude Alphonso Alvares, *Homo Faber: Tech-*

nology and Culture in India, China and the West, 1500–1972 (Bombay: Allied Publishers, 1972): 10.

37.   Nisbet, *Tradition and Revolution,* 195.

38.   Edward Goodwin Ballard, *Man and Technology: Toward a Measurement of Culture* (Pittsburgh: Duquesne University Press, 1978): 222.

39.   William Barrett, *Irrational Man* (New York: Doubleday, 1962): 270.

40.   Wilson, *Religion in Sociological Perspective,* 43.

41.   Victor C. Ferkiss, *Technological Man: The Myth and the Reality* (New York: Mentor, 1970): 202.

42.   See Teilhard de Chardin, *The Phenomenon of Man* (tr.) Bernard Wall (New York: Harper and Row, 1959); and *The Future of Man* (tr.) Norman Denny (New York: Harper and Row, 1965).

43.   Daniel Bell, *The Coming of the Post-Industrial Society* (New York: Basic Books, 1976).

44.   Daniel Bell, *The Winding Passage: Essays and Sociological Journeys, 1960–1980* (Cambridge, MA: ABT Books, 1980): 29.

45.   *Ibid.,* 150.

46.   Edward Shils, "Plenitude and Scarcity," *Encounter* (May, 1969): 44.

47.   Bell, *The Winding Passage,* 29.

48.   Clarence J. Glacken, *Traces on the Rhodian Shore* (Berkeley: University of California Press, 1967): 162.

49.   Lynn White, "The Historical Roots of Our Ecological Crisis," in: *Machina ex Deo* (Cambridge, MA: MIT Press, 1968): 90; reprinted in: Jacob Needleman, A. K. Bierman, and James A. Gould (eds.), *Religion for a New Generation,* 2nd ed. (New York: Macmillan, 1977): 238.

50.   See Jeremy Rifkin, *Entropy: A New World View* (Toronto: Bantam Books, 1980).

51.   William G. Pollard, "The Uniqueness of the Earth," in: Ian G. Barbour (ed.), *Earth Might Be Fair: Reflections on Ethics, Religion and Ecology* (Englewood Cliffs, NJ: Prentice-Hall, 1972): 82–99.

52.   See Mary Douglas and Aaron Wildavsky, *Risk and Culture: An Essay on the Selection of Technical and Environmental Dangers* (Berkeley: University of California Press, 1982).

53.   Huston Smith, "Tao Now," in: Barbour (ed.), *Earth Might Be Fair,* 73.

54.   *Ibid.,* 75.

55.   *Ibid.,* 79.

56.   White, "The Historical Roots of Our Ecologic Crisis," in: Needleman, et al., (eds.), *Religion for a New Generation,* 239.

57.   Edward Sapir, *Culture, Language, and Personality* (ed.) D. G. Mandelbaum (Berkeley: University of California Press, 1961): 92.

CHAPTER ELEVEN

1.   Marcel Mauss, *The Gift* (New York: Free Press, 1954): 126 (n.85); 73*ff.*

2.   Adam Smith, *An Inquiry into the Nature and the Causes of the Wealth of Nations* (ed.) Edwin Canaan (Chicago: University of Chicago Press, 1977).

3.   Mauss, *The Gift,* 3.

4.   Emile Durkheim, *The Elementary Forms of the Religious Life* (New York: Free Press, 1965): 264.

5.   Karl Marx, *Capital,* 3 vols. (New York: International Publishers, 1967): I:74.

6.   Mary Douglas and Baron Isherwood, *The World of Goods* (New York: Basic Books, 1979): 75.

7.   Karl Polanyi, *Primitive, Archaic and Modern Economies* (Garden City, NY: Doubleday, 1968): 175.

8.   Morris A. Copeland, "Concerning the Origin of a Money Economy," *The American Journal of Economics and Society* 33 (1974): 1–18.

9.   William Shakespeare, *Timon of Athens* IV.iii.387; G. B. Harrison (ed.), *Shakespeare: The Complete Works* (New York: Harcourt, Brace and World, 1968): 1342.

10.   Karl Marx, *Manuscripts of 1844* (New York: International Publishers, 1964): 168.

11.   Jonathan Z. Smith, *Map Is Not Territory: Studies in the History of Religions* (Leiden: E. J. Brill, 1978): 142.

12.   *Ibid.,* 141.

13.   Cited in Walter G. Muelder, *Religion and Economic Responsibility* (New York: Charles Scribner's, 1953): 70.

14.   *Ibid.,* 70.

15. Paul Carter, *The Decline and Revival of the Social Gospel: Social and Political Liberation in American Protestant Churches, 1920–1940* (Ithaca, NY: Cornell University Press, 1956): 5.

16. Jerry Falwell, *Listen America* (Garden City, NY: Doubleday, 1980): 13.

17. See, for example, Jose Miguez Bonino, *Christians and Marxists* (London: Hodder and Stoughton, 1976).

18. Mauss, *The Gift,* 54.

19. Raymond Firth and Basil S. Yamey, *Capital, Savings and Credit in Peasant Societies* (Chicago: Aldine Atherton, 1964): 31.

20. George Homans, "Social Behavior as Exchange," *American Journal of Sociology* 63 (1958): 597.

21. Firth and Yamey, *Capital, Savings and Credit in Peasant Societies,* 26.

22. Bronislaw Malinowski, *Argonauts of the Western Pacific* (New York: E. P. Dutton, 1961): 60.

23. A. R. Radcliffe-Brown, *A Natural Science of Society* (New York: Free Press, 1957): 132.

24. Alvin W. Gouldner, "The Norm of Reciprocity: A Preliminary Statement," *American Sociological Review* 25 (1960): 161–78.

25. Claude Lévi-Strauss, "Reciprocity: The Essence of Social Life," in: Rose Laub Coser (ed.), *The Family: Its Structures and Functions* (New York: St. Martin's Press, 1974): 9.

26. Mauss, *The Gift,* 3.

27. Barry Hindess and Paul Q. Hirst, *Pre-Capitalist Modes of Production* (London: Routledge and Kegan Paul, 1975): 64.

28. Maurice Godelier, "Modes of Production, Kinship and Demographic Structures," in: Marc Bloch (ed.), *Marxist Analysis and Social Anthropology* (London: Malaby Press, 1975): 11.

29. Jeremy Keenan, "The Concept of the Mode of Production in Hunter-Gatherer Societies," in: Joel S. Kahn and Joseph R. Llobera, *The Anthropology of Pre-Capitalist Societies* (London: Macmillan, 1981): 17–18.

30. Pierre Bonte, "Marxist Theory and Anthropological Analysis: The Study of Nomadic Pastoralist Societies," in: Kahn and Llobera, *The Anthropology of Pre-Capitalist Societies,* 33.

31. P. H. Gulliver, "The Age-Set Organization of the Jie Tribe," *Journal of the Royal Africa Institute* 83 (1953): 165.

32. E. E. Evans-Pritchard, *Nuer Religion* (Oxford: Clarendon Press, 1970): 271.

33. Stanley Tambiah, "The Ideology of Merit and the Social Correlates of Buddhism in a Thai Village," in: Edmund R. Leach (ed.), *Dialectic in Practical Religion* (Cambridge: Cambridge University Press, 1968): 117.

34. Melford Spiro, "Buddhism and Economic Action in Burma," *American Anthropologist* 68 (1966): 1165–66.

35. Harold K. Schneider, *Economic Man: The Anthropology of Economics* (New York: The Free Press, 1974): 7.

36. Mary Douglas, *Natural Symbols* (New York: Random House, 1970): 89–91; 156–57; 170–71; 179; see D. L. Oliver, *A Solomon Island Society: Kinship and Leadership among the Siuai of Bougainville* (London: Oxford University Press, 1957).

37. Hans Shärer, *Ngaju Religion: The Concept of God among a South Borneo People* (tr.) Rodney Needham (The Hague: Martinus Nijhoff, 1963): 44.

38. Irving Goldman, *The Mouth of Heaven* (New York: Wiley, 1975): 144; Philip Drucker and Robert F. Heizer, *To Make My Name Good* (Berkeley: University of California Press, 1967): 8.

39. Goldman, *The Mouth of Heaven,* 131.

40. Ruth Benedict, *Patterns of Culture* (New York: Mentor, 1946): 190.

41. Marvin Harris, *Cows, Pigs, Wars and Witches: The Riddles of Culture* (New York: Vintage Books, 1975): 116.

42. Stuart Piddocke, "The Potlatch System of the Southern Kwakiutl: A New Perspective," *Southwestern Journal of Anthropology* 21 (1965): 244.

43. Helen Codere, *Fighting with Property* (New York: J. J. Augustin, 1950: 80.

44. Goldman, *The Mouth of Heaven,* 146.

45. See Steven Vertovec, "Potlatching the Mythic Past: A Re-evaluation of the Traditional Northwest Coast American Indian Complex," *Religion* 13 (1983): 323–44.

46. M. I. Finley, *The Ancient Economy* (Berkeley: University of California Press, 1973): 28–29; see Mary Douglas, "Primitive Rationing," in: Raymond Firth (ed.), *Themes in Economic Anthropology* (London: Tavistock, 1967).

47. Thomas R. Trautmann, *Kautiliya and the Arthaśastra* (Leiden: E. J. Brill, 1976).

48. Cited in Anne M. Bailey, "The Revived Discussions of the Concept of the Asiatic Mode of Production," in: Kahn and Llobera, *The Anthropology of Pre-Capitalist Societies,* 96–97.

49. See Milton Fisk, *Ethics and Society: A Marxist Interpretation of Value* (Brighton, Sussex: The Harvester Press, 1980).

50. E. E. Evans-Pritchard, "Introduction," in: Mauss, *The Gift,* ix.

51. See Michael Novak, *The Spirit of Democratic Capitalism* (New York: Simon & Schuster, 1982).

52. Max Weber, *The Protestant Ethic and the Spirit of Capitalism* (tr.) Talcott Parsons (New York: Charles Scribner's, 1958): 72.

53. Robert N. Bellah, "Reflections on the Protestant Ethic Analogy in Asia," *Journal of Social Issues* 19 (1963): 52–60.

54. David C. McClelland, *The Achieving Society* (New York: Irvington Publishers, 1976).

55. Cited in Schneider, *Economic Man,* 218.

56. See Jonathan Z. Smith, "A Pearl of Great Price and a Cargo of Yams: A Study in Situational Incongruity," *History of Religions* 16 (1976): 1–19.

57. Sam Gill, *Beyond the "Primitive": The Religions of Non-literate Peoples* (Englewood Cliffs, NJ: Prentice-Hall, 1982): 60.

58. Thomas Hobbes, *Leviathan* (ed.) C. B. Macpherson (Harmondsworth, Middlesex: Penguin, 1968).

59. Cited in Carleton S. Coon, *A Reader in General Anthropology* (New York: Henry Holt, 1940): 78.

60. *Ibid.,* 78.

61. *Ibid.,* 77–78.

62. C. B. Macpherson, *Democratic Theory: Essays in Retrieval* (Oxford: Clarendon Press, 1973): 18.

63. Hans Konig, *Columbus: His Enterprise* (New York: Monthly Review Press, 1976): 53.

64. Macpherson, *Democratic Theory,* 62.

65. Thomas R. Malthus, *First Essay on Population* (London: Macmillan, 1926): 13.

66. See Anthony J. Coale, "The History of the Human Population," *Scientific American* (September, 1974): 40–51.

67. Thomas R. Malthus, *An Essay on Population,* 2 vols. (New York: E. P. Dutton, 1958): II: 202.

68. Garrett Harden, "Living in a Lifeboat," in: Jacob Needleman, A. K. Bierman, and James A. Gould (eds.), *Religion for a New Generation,* 2nd ed. (New York: Macmillan, 1977): 240–53.

69. *Ibid.,* 249.

70. See L. S. Stavrianos, *Global Rift: The Third World Comes of Age* (New York: William Morrow, 1981).

71. Kenneth E. Boulding, *The Meaning of the Twentieth Century* (New York: Harper and Row, 1964); also see William G. Pollard, *Man on a Spaceship* (Claremont, CA: Claremont Colleges, 1967).

72. Kenneth E. Boulding, "The Wisdom of Man and the Wisdom of God," *Human Values on the Spaceship Earth* (New York: National Council of the Churches of Christ, 1966): 6.

73. *Ibid.,* 6.

74. E. F. Schumacher, *Small is Beautiful: Economics as if People Mattered* (New York: Harper and Row, 1973).

75. *Ibid.,* 45.

76. *Ibid.,* 57.

77. *Ibid.,* 57.

78. Aristotle, *Ethics* (Harmondsworth, Middlesex: Penguin, 1954): 154.

79. Perry Miller and Thomas H. Johnson (eds.), *The Puritans: A Sourcebook of Their Writings,* 2 vols. (New York: Harper and Row, 1938): I: 195–96.

CHAPTER TWELVE

1. See Robert Ardrey, *The Territorial Imperative* (New York: Atheneum, 1966); and Konrad Lorenz, *On Aggression* (New York: Harcourt, 1966).

2. See Ashley Montagu (ed.), *Man and Aggression* (New York: Oxford University Press, 1968).

3. Gil Eliot, *The Twentieth Century Book of the Dead* (New York: Random House, 1972).

4. This distinction between play and work in religious warfare, as well as a useful survey of warfare in the history

of religions, is found in James A. Aho, *Religious Mythology and the Art of War: Comparative Religious Symbolisms of Military Violence* (Westport, CT: Greenwood Press, 1981).

5. See Georges Dumezil, *The Destiny of the Warrior* (tr.) Alf Hitebeitel (Chicago: University of Chicago Press, 1970).

6. *Laws of Manu* 7.98; 7.90–93; Georg Bühler (tr.), *The Laws of Manu,* in: F. Max Müller (ed.), *Sacred Books of the East* (Oxford: Oxford University Press, 1886): XXV: 232; 230–31.

7. *Santi-parva* 96; Pratap Chandra Roy (tr.), *Mahabharata,* Volume 12 (Calcutta: Datta Bose, 1919–1933).

8. *Laws of Manu* 7.93; Bühler (tr.), *The Laws of Manu,* 231.

9. *Bhagavad Gītā* 2.20;23; Franklin Edgerton (tr.), *The Bhagavad Gītā* (Cambridge, MA: Harvard University Press, 1972): 11.

10. *Bhagavad Gītā* 11.33; Franklin Edgerton (tr.), *The Bhagavad Gītā,* 58.

11. See Joseph Campbell, *The Masks of God* (New York: Viking Press, 1970): II:190–92.

12. *Laws of Manu* 7.201–3; Bühler (tr.), *The Laws of Manu,* 248–49.

13. Samuel Beal (tr.), *The Life of Hiuen Tsiang* (Westport, CT: Hyperion Press, 1973): 146–47.

14. Herbert Fingarette, *Confucius: The Secular as Sacred* (New York: Harper and Row, 1972): 17.

15. James Legge (tr.), *The Chinese Classics* (Oxford: Clarendon Press, 1895): V:382.

16. Sun Tzu, *Art of War* (tr.) Samuel Griffith (New York: Oxford University Press, 1963).

17. Roswell S. Britton, "Chinese Interstate Intercourse Before 700 BC," *American Journal of International Law* 24 (1935): 619.

18. Z. Tamotsu Iwado, "Hagakure Bushido," *Cultural Nippon* 7 (1937): 33–35; see Oscar Ratti and Adele Westbrook, *Secrets of the Sammurai: A Survey of Feudal Japan* (Tokyo: Charles Tuttle, 1973).

19. Inazo Nitobe, *Bushido: The Soul of Japan* (Rutland, VT: Charles Tuttle, 1969): 134.

20. Roland de Vaux, *Ancient Israel: Its Life and Institutions* (tr.) John McHugh (New York: McGraw-Hill, 1961): 260; see Rudolf Smend, *Yahweh War and Tribal Confederation* (tr.) Max G. Rogers (Nashville: Abingdon, 1970).

21. *Qur'an* 8.40; A. J. Arberry (tr.) *The Koran Interpreted* (New York: Macmillan, 1955): I:201; see *Qur'an* 9.29.

22. *Qur'an* 17.15; Hashim Amir-Ali (tr.), *The Message of the Qur'an Presented in Perspective* (Rutland, VT: Charles Tuttle, 1974): 309–10.

23. *Qur'an* 8.41; Arberry (tr.), *The Koran Interpreted,* I:201.

24. *Qur'an* 47.45; Arberry (tr.), *The Koran Interpreted,* II: 220.

25. *Qur'an* 9.5; Arberry (tr.), *The Koran Interpreted,* I:207.

26. *Qur'an* 8.45; Amir-Ali, *The Message of the Qur'an,* 575–76.

27. *Qur'an* 8.17; Amir-Ali, *The Message of the Qur'an,* 572.

28. See Walter Ullman, *A Short History of the Papacy in the Middle Ages* (New York: Harper and Row, 1972): 182–83; and Marc Bloch, *Feudal Society* (tr.) L. A. Manyon (Chicago: University of Chicago Press, 1970): II:312–14.

29. Cited in H.E.J. Cowdrey, "The Genesis of the Crusades: The Springs of Western Ideas of the Holy War," in: Thomas P. Murphy (ed.), *The Holy War* (Columbus: Ohio State University Press, 1976): 23–24.

30. Will Durant, *The Age of Faith* (New York: Simon & Schuster, 1950): 592.

31. H.E.J. Cowdrey, "The Peace and Truce of God in the Eleventh Century," *Past and Present* 46 (1970): 42–67.

32. A. T. Hatto, "Archery and Chivalry: A Noble Prejudice," *Modern Language Review* 35 (1940): 40–54.

33. See Honore Bonet, *The Tree of Battles* (tr.) G. W. Copland (Liverpool: Liverpool University Press, 1949).

34. Martin Luther, *Selected Political Writings* (ed.) J. M. Porter (Philadelphia: Fortress Press, 1974): 130.

35. *Ibid.,* 103.

36. Henry Bullinger, *The Decades: The First and Second Decade* (ed.) Thomas Harding (Cambridge: Cambridge University Press, 1849): 376.

37. William Cardinal Allen, *A True, Sincere and Modest Defense of English Catholiques that Suffer for Their Faith* (London: William Cecil, 1583): 103.

38. Aho, *Religious Mythology and the Art of War,* 210.

39. See Paul Ramsey, *War and the Christian Conscience* (Durham, NC: Duke University Press, 1961): 15–33.

40. Denise Bindschedler-Robert, "A Reconsideration of the Law of Armed Conflicts," in: *The Law of Armed Combats* (New York: Carnegie Endowment for International Peace, 1971): 51–52; and Michael Walzer, *Just and Unjust War: A Moral Argument with Historical Illustrations* (New York: Basic Books, 1977): 290.

41. See Lillian Schlissel (ed.), *Conscience in America: A Documentary History of Conscientious Objection in America* (New York: E. P. Dutton, 1968).

42. Donald A. Wells, "The 'Just War' Justifies Too Much," in: Jacob Needleman, A. K. Bierman, and James A. Gould (eds.), *Religion for a New Generation,* 2nd ed. (New York: Macmillan, 1977): 349.

43. Myres S. McDougal and Florentino P. Feliciano, *Law and Minimum World Public Order* (New Haven, CT: Yale University Press, 1961): 71–75.

44. *Ibid.,* 72.

45. I. S. Bloch, *The Future of War* (New York: Doubleday, 1902): 150.

46. Hiram Maxim, *Defenseless America* (New York: Hearst, 1915): 83.

47. Ramsey, *War and Christian Conscience,* 34–59.

48. Franciscus de Victoria, *De Indis et De Jure Belli Relectiones* (tr.) John Pauley Bate, *Classics of International Law* (Washington: Carnegie Institute, 1917); cited in: James T. Johnson, *Just War Tradition and the Restraint of War* (Princeton, NJ: Princeton University Press, 1981): 200.

49. *Ibid.,* 201.

50. Thomas E. Murray, *Nuclear Policy for War and Peace* (Cleveland and New York: The World Publishing Co., 1960): 68.

51. World Council of Churches, *Peace and Disarmament: Documents of the World Council of Churches and the Roman Catholic Church* (Geneva and Vatican City, 1982): 1.

52. See Otto Nathan and Heinz Norden, *Einstein on Peace* (New York: Schocken Books, 1968).

53. Office of Technological Assessment, *The Effects of Nuclear War* (Washington: Congress of the United States, 1979): 6.

54. Jonathan Schell, *The Fate of the Earth* (New York: Alfred Knopf, 1982): 93.

55. Robert Jay Lifton, *Broken Connection* (New York: Simon & Schuster, 1979): 360.

56. Cited in Robert Jay Lifton and Eric Olson, *Living and Dying* (New York: Praeger Publishers, 1974): 118.

57. *Ibid.,* 119.

58. William L. Lawrence, *Men and Atoms* (New York: Simon & Schuster, 1959): 197.

59. Cited in Bruce Kent, "A Christian Unilateralism from a Christian Background," in: Geoffrey Goodwin (ed.), *Ethics and Nuclear Deterrence* (New York: St. Martin's Press, 1982): 58.

60. Ira Chernus, "Mythologies of Nuclear War," *Journal of the American Academy of Religion* 50 (1982): 257.

61. Arthur Katz, *Economic and Social Consequences of a Nuclear Attack on the United States* (Washington: U.S. Senate Committee on Banking, Housing and Urban Affairs, 1979): vi.

62. Lifton and Olson, *Living and Dying,* 123.

63. Hal Lindsey, *The Late Great Planet Earth* (New York: Bantam, 1973); *Countdown to Armageddon* (New York: Bantam, 1981).

64. Jerry Falwell, *Listen America* (Garden City, NY: Doubleday, 1980): 112–13.

65. Lifton, *Broken Connection,* 3.

66. Chernus, "Mythologies of Nuclear War," 261.

67. Lifton, *Broken Connection,* 345.

68. Lifton and Olson, *Living and Dying,* 129.

69. *Ibid.,* 129.

70. These ethical positions in the nuclear age were suggested in Stanley M. Hauerwas, "Surviving Justly: An Ethical Analysis of Nuclear Disarmament," in: Jill Raitt (ed.), *Religious Conscience and Nuclear Warfare* (University of Missouri-Columbia, 1982): 1–20.

71. Edward Laarman, "Nuclear Deterrence and the Bluff," *The Reformed Journal* (June, 1982): 15; see David Martin, *Pacifism: A Historical and Sociological Study* (London: Routledge and Kegan Paul, 1965).

72. See John Donaghy (ed.) *To Proclaim Peace: Religious Communities Speak Out on the Arms Race* (Nyack, NY: Fellowship Publications, 1983); and Jim Wallis (ed.),

Waging Peace: A Handbook for the Struggle to Abolish Nuclear Weapons (New York: Harper and Row, 1982).

73. Donaghy, *To Proclaim Peace,* 31.

74. National Conference of Catholic Bishops, *The Challenge of Peace: God's Promise and Our Response* (United States Catholic Conference, 1983).

75. Cited in Arthur Jones, "Bishops Tell How Views on Nuclear Arms Formed," *National Catholic Reporter* 18 (1981): 6.

76. Thomas Merton, *Thomas Merton on Peace* (New York: McCall, 1971).

77. Paul Ramsey, *The Just War* (New York: Charles Scribner's, 1968): 236.

78. James T. Johnson, *Just War Tradition and the Restraint of War,* xxxv.

79. Ramsey, *The Just War,* 211–15.

80. See Robert C. Aldridge, *The Counterforce Syndrome* (Washington: Institute for Policy Studies, 1978).

81. Michael Walzer, *Just and Unjust Wars,* 282.

82. Ramsey, *War and Christian Conscience,* 193.

83. Theodore Draper, "How Not to Think About Nuclear War," *New York Review of Books* 29/12 (July 15, 1982): 40.

84. George F. Kennan, *The Nuclear Decision: Soviet-American Relations in the Atomic Age* (New York: Pantheon Books, 1976).

85. Michael Howard, *War and the Liberal Conscience* (New Brunswick, NJ: Rutgers University Press, 1978): 132.

86. Schell, *The Fate of the Earth,* 191.

87. *Ibid.,* 132.

88. *Ibid.,* 134.

89. *Ibid.,* 226.

90. Draper, "How Not to Think About Nuclear War," 38.

EPILOGUE

1. Cited in Nigel Calder, *Technopolis: Social Control of the Uses of Science* (New York: Simon & Schuster, 1969): 98.

2. Paul Dickson and Joseph C. Goulden, *There are Alligators in Our Sewers and Other American Credos* (New York: Delacorte Press, 1983): 68.

3. Cited in Claude Alphonso Alvares, *Homo Faber: Technology and Culture of India, China and the West, 1500–1972* (Bombay: Allied Publishers, 1979): 4.

INDEX

Acknowledgments

Norbert Elias, *The Civilizing Process* (American title: *The History of Manners*) (tr.) Edmund Jephcott (Oxford: Basil Blackwell, 1978; New York: Pantheon Books, Random House, 1978): selected quotations from pp. 87–162. Used by permission of the publishers.

Jonathan Schell, *The Fate of the Earth* (New York: Alfred A. Knopf, 1982): selected quotations from pp. 93, 132, 134, 191, 226. © 1982 by Jonathan Schell. Reprinted by permission of Alfred A. Knopf, Inc.

Charles Bukowski, "I Enter the City of San Pedro," *Poetry/LA* 6 (1983): 6–7.

Jonathan Z. Smith, *Imagining Religion: From Babylon to Jonestown* (Chicago: University of Chicago Press, 1982): selected quotations from pp. xi, 63, and paraphrase of argument in pp. 57–65. Used by permission.

Jonathan Z. Smith, *Map Is Not Territory: Studies in the History of Religions* (Leiden: E. J. Brill, 1978): selected quotations from pp. 141, 142, and paraphrase of argument in pp. 240–64. Used by permission.